Praise for *Assessing the Impact of Transitional Justice: Challenges for Empirical*

D0851397

"Assessing success is one of the most vexing issues for scholars of transitional justice. While 'coming to terms with the past' has become a modern political expectation for societies in transition, not enough is known about the actual impact of transitional justice exercises, whether they are effective at achieving their goals, or even whether they do more good than harm. The authors of this volume persuasively argue that before we can know what works, we must first figure out how to figure it out. Determining the most appropriate methodology for answering the question 'how do we know?' is the core lesson of this book. A good research design can test assumptions and make the abstract real and knowable; any study that achieves this should automatically move to the front of the transitional justice scholarship line. This book will certainly help this movement along."

—**Tristan Anne Borer**, PhD, Connecticut College

"This timely and important contribution to transitional justice research and policy offers original insights and raises key arguments that will jump start renewed debate of transitional justice mechanisms."

—**Anita Isaacs**, Benjamin R. Collins Professor of Social Science, Haverford College

"Amid the international interest in truth commissions and other post-conflict justice efforts, there have been many more assertions about what works and what doesn't work than sustained effort to build and revise meaningful assessments. This fascinating collection brings diverse methodological approaches to bear on transitional justice in diverse settings and should be of immediate interest to policy-makers, scholars, and local communities."

—**Martha Minow**, Jeremiah Smith Jr. Professor, Harvard Law School, and author of *Between Vengeance and Forgiveness: Facing History After Genocide and Mass Violence*

"Thirteen years following USIP's three volumes on Transitional Justice, editors Hugo van der Merwe, Victoria Baxter, and Audrey Chapman revisit the state of this interdisciplinary field, this time building on its theoretical and methodological developments since 1995. The result is a comprehensive assessment of the state of our knowledge about transitional justice mechanisms and how they contribute to peace, justice, and reconciliation. Methodologically, the collection of chapters spans a diverse cross section of fields from law and area studies to political science and psychology. But it offers more than just an update on the state of the discipline by providing researchers with tips and pointers on how to do systematic research on ways in which societies come to terms with pasts that are as atrocious as they are unique."

—**Monika A. Nalepa**, Rice University

"For too long, the 'transitional justice' field has been dominated by lawyers, who may master the mechanics of courts and truth commissions but who don't always know whether these really work to heal divided societies. Finally, with this path-breaking study, social science methodologies are being brought to bear upon such a vital topic, informing existing strategies and pointing the way to new ones."

—**William Schabas**, Irish Centre for Human Rights, National University of Ireland, Galway

"Thoroughly researched, full of fresh empirical and comparative analysis, this volume offers an indispensable resource for contemporary debates about policymaking in transitional justice."

—**Ruti Teitel**, Ernst Stefel Professor of Comparative Law, New York Law School, and author of *Transitional Justice*

"This book illustrates well the dilemmas that underlie the current state of research in the field of transitional justice. Given the groundswell of international support for truth commissions, trials, and other forms of transitional justice, researchers are faced with the unenviable task of confronting widespread assumptions about the effects of these mechanisms. The book's authors recognize clearly the challenges of collecting empirical data to substantiate or refute these assumptions while simultaneously translating their findings into policy-oriented recommendations that will influence local and international decision-makers. The focus on methodology and the need for comparative study is an important contribution to a nascent but burgeoning field."

—**Harvey M. Weinstein**, MD, MPH

Assessing the Impact of
Transitional Justice

Assessing the Impact of
Transitional Justice

Challenges for Empirical Research

edited by

HUGO VAN DER MERWE

VICTORIA BAXTER

AUDREY R. CHAPMAN

UNITED STATES INSTITUTE OF PEACE PRESS
Washington, D.C.

The views expressed in this book are those of the author alone. They do not necessarily reflect views of the United States Institute of Peace.

UNITED STATES INSTITUTE OF PEACE
1200 17th Street NW, Suite 200
Washington, DC 20036-3011
www.usip.org

© 2009 by the Endowment of the United States Institute of Peace.
All rights reserved.

First published 2009

To request permission to photocopy or reprint materials for course use, contact the Copyright Clearance Center at www.copyright.com. For print, electronic media, and all other subsidiary rights, e-mail: permissions@usip.org

Printed in the United States of America

The paper used in this publication meets the minimum requirements of American National Standards for Information Science—Permanence of Paper for Printed Library Materials, ANSI Z39.48-1984.

Library of Congress Cataloging-in-Publication Data

Assessing the impact of transitional justice : challenges for empirical research / editors, Hugo van der Merwe, Victoria Baxter, and Audrey R. Chapman.
    p. cm.
  Includes bibliographical references and index.
  ISBN 978-1-60127-036-8 (pbk. : alk. paper)
  1. Crimes against humanity. 2. Truth commissions. 3. Reparations for historical injustices. 4. Restorative justice. 5. Reconciliation—Political aspects. I. Van der Merwe, Hugo, 1965– II. Baxter, Victoria. III. Chapman, Audrey R.
  K5301.A976 2008
  345'.0235--dc22

2008016335

Contents

Tables

Foreword

It has become almost routine. After the shooting stops, or the dictator is deposed, there is the talk of reckoning. Often it starts earlier: during peace talks, or, in recent years, with indictments by an international criminal court. Once considered a rarity, international negotiators, aid agencies, human rights groups, and even governments now speak of the need for transitional justice as a key to the emergence of a new, more just as well as peaceful social order. The term transitional justice raises questions. Transition from what to what? Transition by whom? Transition as a set of legal arrangements or as a moral and social rebirth? Given these ambiguities, one could opt instead for the term post-conflict justice, but that term raises the question of whether any society is, or ever could be, post-conflict. Perhaps post-armed conflict is the best we can aspire to. For the purpose of this book, I'll define transitional justice as that set of practices, mechanisms, and concerns that are aimed at confronting and dealing with the legacies of past violations of human rights and humanitarian law.

Until the 1990s, transitional justice measures were rare. The Nuremberg and Tokyo tribunals, the subsequent trials of Nazis in zones under Allied occupation, reparations by Germany for the Holocaust, and the trials of the Greek colonels in the 1970s were the main examples. Argentina was a precursor of the modern era in many ways. In 1983 the incoming civilian government created an investigative truth commission to look into forced disappearances during the former military regime, and in 1985 the Argentine juntas were prosecuted for human rights–related crimes arising from their rule and later, reparations were provided for the victims. The following decades saw an explosion of truth commissions, aimed at documenting the crimes, telling the stories of survivors, and recommending measures to make the promise of "never again" a reality. Early commissions focused on uncovering violations that governments had tried to disguise or cover up. Later ones such as those of South Africa, Sierra Leone, and Peru added public hearings and ceremonies aimed at giving a public voice to those who had suffered.

Starting in the early 1990s, the legacy of Nuremberg was revived in the form of international criminal tribunals. The first such tribunal dealt with ongoing crimes in the former Yugoslavia and was based on a UN Security Council resolution. It was followed a year later by a similar tribunal to deal with the 1994 genocide in Rwanda. Over time, the tribunals became more able to find and arrest suspects, including heads of state and key military figures. Their jurisprudence began filling in the contours of international criminal law outlined in a series of post–World War II treaties and resolutions. The international tribunals were criticized, however, for a lack of connection to the population they were intended to succor and for the lack of support for local courts.

A number of responses were developed to correct the perceived shortcomings of the two Security Council tribunals. One was the creation in 1998 of a permanent, treaty-based International Criminal Court, which would act as a backstop, not a substitute, for national prosecutions. The other response was the creation a handful of hybrid courts, set up by agreement between the national government and the United Nations, that combined national and international law and that operated in Sierra Leone, East Timor, Kosovo, Cambodia, and eventually, Lebanon. In addition, national courts became more active, trying their own cases, and also, on occasion investigating crimes committed elsewhere pursuant to laws that allow for universal jurisdiction over certain particularly heinous international crimes. The most famous of these cases involved the 1998 arrest in the United Kingdom of former Chilean dictator Augusto Pinochet on a Spanish warrant.

Other transitional justice measures focused on reparations. Government-run administrative reparations programs provided at least some services and some money to survivors and the families of victims. Governments apologized for the harm, erected monuments and memorial parks, and vetted the security forces and the military based on their human rights records. By the turn of the twenty-first century, states as well as local communities had begun adapting and recreating modes of informal or traditional justice as a way of reintegrating ex-perpetrators into communities while recognizing the victims' demands for some accounting. In all, the panorama of transitional justice became more complex, more variegated, at the same time more diverse and more based on an internationally recognized set of bedrock anti-impunity principles. Not that impunity was vanquished during this period, far from it, but amnesty laws became more nuanced, and in cases where efforts to impose sheer amnesia prevailed, they were criticized by other governments, civil society, and intergovernmental institutions.

And yet there was a nagging question underneath this expanding architecture of transitional justice. Did it make a difference? Were survivors succored, did the formerly persecuted now feel themselves recognized and included, did these measures usher in an accessible and just rule of law, or, indeed, were any of the proclaimed goals of transitional justice measures actually achieved? Did truth commissions actually lead to "closure" or catharsis for victims or lead to a more unified understanding of the causes of conflict? Did reparations divide and disempower the beneficiaries or lead to improved economic outcomes? Did trials—national, international, or mixed—do more harm or good, and according to what measure?

Responses to these questions have become more urgent as the difficulties have multiplied. Seeking justice in the midst of ongoing conflict has again raised calls for a prioritization of peace over justice, as if the two could ever really be separated. A new emphasis on context and particularity has accompanied a critique of "toolkit" or "cookie-cutter" approaches.

Answers proved elusive, although theories abounded. In part, many of those most involved in transitional justice had neither the time, the resources, nor the academic training to conduct the kinds of rigorous social science research needed to answer the many questions raised. The confounding variables were many, and the long-term data sets that would allow for comparisons over time were few and far between. How then can one evaluate the considerable efforts of the last quarter century?

This book begins to provide some answers. The authors, all experts in various methodologies or parts of the world, have carried out surveys, organized focus groups, interviewed perpetrators, immersed themselves in local histories, and meditated on the value of comparative research. Through both the specifics of their studies and the lessons they teach about methodological problems and possibilities, we can begin to imagine what exploring "did it make a difference?" might look like. The answers are, of course, tentative and replete with difficulties, but they point to ways of moving forward.

And the answers, as they should, raise more questions about generalizations, particularities, time frames, purposes, and about our own roles as researchers and advocates. Are we too professionally invested in the very processes we are seeking to evaluate? Whose voices are we seeking out, and whose are we hearing when we ask the necessary questions? The chapters in this volume begin to speak to those issues in ways that challenge, inform, and even inspire. This volume reminds us of how far transitional justice as a field of study has come and how much more we need to learn.

Naomi Roht-Arriaza
San Francisco, October 2008

Introduction

Hugo van der Merwe, Victoria Baxter, and Audrey R. Chapman

At this writing, several nations throughout the world are confronting the challenge of how best to come to terms with a history of human rights violations and abuses of power. Many are attempting to bring into the public forum stories of individual and private suffering and to ponder how to provide redress to victims of unspeakable atrocities. Even given the will to take action, the path to these goals is anything but clear. For example, the trial of former Liberian president Charles Taylor raises the opportunity for a legal remedy to some of the abuses committed in the West African region's turbulent recent history. But views differ sharply on the adequacy and appropriateness of these interventions. Should there be some domestic form of accounting as well? What role might a truth commission play? Should some perpetrators receive amnesty in exchange for their testimony and information? What kinds of reparations are due the victims? What are the likely consequences of these measures? And how do these options best provide a foundation for a democratic future based on respect for fundamental human rights norms and the rule of law? Rather than responding to an emotive call for justice, policymakers need to look at the consequences for fragile, war-shattered nations and their many victims of human rights abuses. How can we most effectively address the needs for justice, truth, reconciliation, and healing? At this point, no one seems to have clear answers.

And yet, these are not new questions. During the final decades of the twentieth century, countries in virtually every region of the world experienced severe repression, systematic human rights abuses, or intense social and political conflict that deepened internal social divisions and, in some situations, provoked collective violence. In the opening years of the twenty-first century, political change is the order of the day in many of these deeply divided societies. Settlements, some internationally brokered, have at least temporarily suspended several of the most destructive civil conflicts. New forms of government, some elected and some appointed, have replaced a series of repressive and authoritarian regimes.

These new administrations face the multiple challenges of coming to terms with their violent past and rebuilding and healing their societies. Many analysts and advocates use the term "transitional justice" to refer to societal responses to severe repression, societal violence, and systematic human rights violations that seek to establish the truth about the past, determine accountability, and offer some form of redress, at least of a symbolic nature. Beyond these initiatives, there is also the need to find ways to overcome or at least manage the conflicts among contending groups, rebuild the institutional and social infrastructure, and promote a sense of shared commitment to the new political system. Many of the societies moving away from repressive political systems and dictatorial rule also have the goal of establishing more democratic forms of governance.

All these processes are more fragile and fraught with peril than the terminology implies. One analyst suggests that the "transitional" paradigm often applied to these states is misleading because it implies that countries moving away from a problematic past will necessarily make the transition toward democracy and stability, when in fact few actually do so (Carothers 2002). Similarly, some analysts refer to deeply divided societies as "post-conflict societies" (Bloomfield, Barnes, and Huyse 2003). But the political settlements that end such internal conflicts or bring about the resignation of repressive regimes are not necessarily stable and enduring. In many instances the problems that gave rise to the strife persist, and efforts to deal with the past can give rise to new tensions. Often so-called transitional justice processes provide little in the way of meaningful justice to victims and to groups persecuted or disadvantaged by predecessor regimes.

Transitional Justice Mechanisms

Increasing numbers of societies are attempting to deal with a legacy of collective violence and severe human rights violations by introducing transitional justice mechanisms. These can take a variety of forms, the most common being truth commissions. Priscilla Hayner (2001, 23), the author of the most authoritative comparative study of such bodies, notes, "In virtually every state that has recently emerged from authoritarian rule or civil war, and in many still suffering repression or violence but where there is hope for a transition soon, there has been interest in creating a truth commission—either proposed by officials of the state or by human rights activists or others in civil society."

The mechanisms used in different national contexts vary widely. While the insistence on addressing the past has become almost universal, the range of options remains vast, and the policy choices very complex. While truth commissions have become a popular model, even these vary dramatically in structure, composition, and goals. Some countries have opted for a mix of mechanisms, and formal state processes often operate alongside a range of informal transitional justice initiatives.

Policy choices confront international bodies, national governments, and even local communities and institutions as they seek to deal with the legacy of systematic abuses at all these levels. Transitional justice mechanisms can be either formal or informal, involving international agencies and formal legal structures codified in treaties and legislation or local bodies relying on voluntary processes and traditional values.

Transitional justice mechanisms are often tasked with a wide range of responsibilities and expectations, some explicit and others implicit. Typically, the mandates of formal mechanisms, particularly truth commissions, include establishing an authoritative record of the past in order to overcome communal and official denial of the atrocity, violence, or abuses and to get official and public acknowledgment. But transitional justice mechanisms are generally also expected to accomplish a wide range of other goals:

- restoring dignity to victims and promoting psychological healing; ending violence and human rights abuses and preventing them in the future;
- creating a "collective memory" or common history for a new future not determined by the past;
- forging the basis for a democratic political order that respects and protects human rights;
- identifying the architects of the past violence and excluding, shaming, and diminishing perpetrators for their offenses;
- legitimating and promoting the stability of the new regime;
- promoting reconciliation across social divisions;
- educating the population about the past; and
- recommending ways to deter future violations and atrocities.[1]

This list points to the great hopes pinned on transitional justice mechanisms, and yet it is questionable whether a single effort can manage all or even many of these responsibilities. What seems desirable or appropriate in theory may not be feasible in practice, since each of these tasks is a major undertaking. Moreover, several of these goals have differing requirements that may actually conflict with one another. Such is often the case when trying to balance truth finding with legitimating a new regime and promoting reconciliation. Efforts to reconstruct the past may be divisive in the short term. The examination of the legacy of past human rights violations and collective violence risks reopening deep wounds and may exacerbate societal divisions. In a deeply divided society, the process of truth seeking and the conclusions drawn can be contentious and leave actors holding a wide range of perspectives, including deep dissatisfaction with, and alienation from, the process.

---

1. For lists of tasks assigned to various truth commissions, see Parlevliet (1998, 149) and Minow (1998, 88).

The Importance of Research

As transitional justice mechanisms, particularly truth commissions, become a significant means for transitional societies to deal with past human rights abuses and establish a basis for more democratic political systems, it becomes vital that the effectiveness and impact of these mechanisms be studied and evaluated. Much of the present debate about truth commissions is based on popular conceptions (or misconceptions) of the benefits and drawbacks of different models and on romanticized notions of their achievements. Empirically based research can make a vital contribution to understanding what it means for a society to go through a transitional justice process, and it can help analyze the process's short- and long-term impact. Such research can serve as the basis for more informed policy decisions in the future.

Empirical research moves beyond mere descriptions to evaluate systematically what transitional justice mechanisms have achieved and to answer the questions of why some initiatives have been more successful than others in reaching their target groups. The important growing body of literature on truth commissions and other transitional mechanisms provides the basis for understanding how these initiatives are structured and operate, but more research must be conducted on their impact and effectiveness. To date, the literature on transitional justice mechanisms has considered such varied topics as the rationales for certain transitional justice policies, the relative strengths and weaknesses of truth commissions compared with tribunals and with the prosecution of perpetrators through national courts, and the transitional justice mechanisms' legal foundations. Researchers dealing with truth commissions have explored such topics as the commissions' mandates, compositions, methodologies and approaches to truth finding, resources, research capacity, amnesty procedures, and recommendations for reparations. Other work addresses the nature of the commissions' findings and recommendations.[2] These are all useful investigations, but they often tell us little about the even more significant issue of the transitional justice process's impact on various sectors of society.

Empirical research can begin to answer some of the questions of impact and provide the very necessary basis for evaluating the mechanisms. It can investigate the reactions of various groups and sectors of society to the transitional justice policy, preferably at a series of points in time. For example, when a country uses a truth commission, a series of questions can be asked about how different groups evaluate or perceive the process. To what extent do key groups—victims, survivors, perpetrators, architects of the violence,

---

2. See, for example, Kritz (1995).

beneficiaries, and bystanders—believe that a truth commission proceeded in an unbiased, fair, and objective manner? Do most people believe that the commission used appropriate methodologies and considered valid sources of evidence? To what extent, and by which individuals and groups, were the findings contested, and on what basis? These questions and their answers are key components in understanding the commission's impact. And similar questions can be posed to get at the impact, effectiveness, and validity of other mechanisms as well.

The toughest test of a specific transitional justice mechanism's efficacy is not only how well it engages with past human rights violations but also how effectively it builds institutions, policies, and practices that will enable the embryonic democracy to deal with emerging and potential patterns of social conflict and violence. Amid all the change taking place, the harsh reality is that frequently too much stays the same, including the structural underpinnings of violence, the experiences of marginalization and racial or ethnic exclusion, and popular attitudes toward "the other" in historically divided societies. Can a transitional justice mechanism help forge the basis for a democratic political order that respects and protects human rights? Can it help legitimate a new constitutional order based on democratic values?

Whatever the goals of the transitional justice mechanism, whatever its methodologies and processes, there is no way to assess its ability to restore dignity to victims and promote psychological healing except by studying the experiences and responses of former victims. And this is quite complicated, especially since it calls for very sensitive methodologies that do not harm (or further traumatize) those participating in the research. Moreover, victims are not a homogeneous group. The nature of the abuses they have suffered varies, and in many cases, the victim category includes relatives of those killed. In some circumstances, entire groups and communities of people were victimized under repressive regimes. In others, the primary victims were a smaller group of political dissidents. Even the term "victim" itself can be problematic, with individuals who have suffered human rights violations preferring to call themselves "survivors."

Empirical research on the impact of transitional justice mechanisms requires very different methodologies from the legal and philosophical analysis that has dominated the literature to date. Instead, researchers will need to use a range of social science methodologies. A multitude of potential research methodologies exists, including surveys, focus groups, interviews, oral histories, transcript analysis, community studies, institutional change studies, and policy impact analysis. The selection of the most appropriate methodology will depend on the context of the situation, the types of data available, and the specific needs and goals of the research design. Each of these approaches must be adapted to the requirements of the research and the conditions in the transitional society it is studying. In virtually all cases, researchers will have to identify and study significant subgroups, and often this complexity will require refining methodologies. In most situations, the best approach will be to use several complementary methodologies.

About This Volume

This volume explores the strengths and weaknesses of a wide range of approaches and methodologies that can be adopted for empirical research on transitional justice mechanisms. Rather than attempt to summarize or present findings of individual cases, the various authors discuss potential research approaches and methodologies. The goal is to encourage further systematic empirical research by giving an overview of research's useful-ness in developing this new field, to clarify key concepts, and to examine (using some practical examples) various methodologies that can be employed to assess transitional justice processes.

The impetus for this book emerged from a conference convened by the Centre for the Study of Violence and Reconciliation (CSVR) and the American Association for the Advancement of Science (AAAS) to discuss the latest developments in transitional justice research. The conference brought to-gether experts on transitional justice research and policy to discuss existing research and exchange ideas about how research methodology in this field can be further developed. The chapters in this book are based on papers presented at the conference and also incorporate feedback from other par-ticipants. Our hope is to address a broader audience of researchers interested in this exciting new field.

The conference, held in South Africa in 2002,[3] served as a kick start for a process of networking among transitional justice researchers and the starting point for a more formal collaborative process of information sharing and ca-pacity building within the field. The overall aim of the conference and of the activities of the networks that are emerging from it is to provide a platform to coordinate cooperative research efforts, build research capacity, and provide mutual support and assistance to researchers, policymakers, and activists. This volume is the first product of this project and will hopefully serve as a valuable resource to all researchers as they wrestle with their own research designs on transitional justice issues.

---

3.   The Transitional Justice Research Conference took place in Stellenbosch, South Africa, in November 2002 and was sponsored by the United States Institute for Peace, the European Union's Conference, Workshop and Cultural Initiative Fund, the Ford Foundation, and the South African Foundation for Human Rights.

Overview of Contents of the Volume

This book seeks to demonstrate the value of empirical research in developing the field of transitional justice. It explores the various important ways that research can help us understand what works, what doesn't, and how policy choices and strategies can be assessed. It is not, however, a simple how-to manual. Rather, it is an attempt to unpack the difficulties of doing this kind of research, examining both the conceptual and the practical challenges in conducting such studies.

The contributors to this volume reflect on the challenges faced in past studies—their own and those of others in the field—and make suggestions on how to address these challenges in the future. These suggestions include ideas on how research questions could be better formulated and on choosing appropriate methodologies or approaches for particular research questions, strategies to improve the quality of data, and considerations and approaches to dealing with ethical challenges, to name but a few. The book thus serves as a reflection on the experience of key researchers in the field as they confront how their research is used and how it affects the context in which new research is conducted.

The first section of the book addresses the broader question of the utility of transitional justice research: What role can it play in conceptual clarification, policy development, and practical intervention strategies?[4] Neil Kritz outlines several ways that empirical research can contribute to a greater understanding of what policy options are available both to transitional regimes and to donor countries. He points to several specific areas where more research would improve the current understanding of transitional justice policy. Complementing that chapter, David Backer provides a broad overview of comparative analyses covering a wide array of transitional justice mechanisms. Backer's chapter advocates international comparative analysis as a useful methodology for empirical research on transitional justice processes. He discusses key methodological design parameters—what to compare, when to compare, and how to compare—as well as the various hurdles complicating the task of analysis. Backer also makes suggestions for future research with this methodology.

The second section deals with the challenges of clarifying key concepts addressed by empirical studies. It seeks to clarify these questions: What is the goal of transitional justice? How do we define and make practical sense of terms such as "truth," "justice," and "reconciliation"? How can we define these terms in a way that allows us to measure their achievement? What indicators can conceivably be used to determine whether a mechanism has

---

4.   More information on this transitional justice research network is available at www. transitionaljustice.org.za.

been successful? What competing interpretations have been used, and how do we make sense of the overlapping and sometimes contradictory meanings attached to these terms?

Looking at practical experience and existing literature, this section deals with how empirical research can use key concepts effectively and outlines an agenda for future research. Establishing the truth about past human rights violations and patterns of violence is a central dimension of transitional justice processes. However, as Audrey Chapman's chapter on truth finding points out, truth recovery is a complex and ambiguous task affected by a wide range of factors, including conceptions of what constitutes social truth; the mandate, methodology, and resources of the body undertaking the truth finding; procedural decisions made by those working within a specific transitional justice mechanism; and social and political receptivity to the process. Hugo van der Merwe shows that in a transitional justice context, "justice" takes on a very specific, though somewhat narrow, meaning, focusing on abuses that were motivated by gaining or maintaining political control and effectively ignoring other economic or social abuses that generally occur in oppressive regimes. According to van der Merwe, the conceptual clarification of justice and its components requires further development, and he outlines specific conceptual and practical challenges along with suggestions for clarification and agenda setting. In the next chapter, Chapman discusses the conceptual and methodological ambiguities related to reconciliation and their implications for conducting research in transitional justice contexts. She argues that within a transitional justice framework, reconciliation takes on meanings and assumptions different from those typically applied to interpersonal or religious conceptions of reconciliation. Chapman characterizes reconciliation as a multidimensional, long-term process and suggests that social or political reconciliation on a national level is particularly relevant for transitional justice research.

The third section of the book provides specific examples of research methods. Each chapter presents an overview of a specific methodology and discusses that approach's relative utility in determining the impact of transitional justice mechanisms. Using research by the chapter author and others, each discussion explains conceptual and practical challenges inherent in those approaches and gives suggestions and guidance on how future studies might address the challenges.

The section begins with a discussion of public opinion research. James Gibson's chapter draws on the author's long history of conducting public opinion studies on justice, reconciliation, and perceptions of the South African Truth and Reconciliation Commission (TRC). He discusses in depth how to design measures for reconciliation, justice, and other key concepts and assesses the strengths and weaknesses of such measures.

This section presents two chapters of studies with key actors in a transitional justice context: victims/survivors and perpetrators. Jeffrey Sonis has researched the effects on survivors of human rights violations of submitting a statement to, or testifying before, the TRC in South Africa, and his chapter discusses the challenges of conducting research studies with survivors of human rights abuses. He shows how to determine the most important questions to address in evaluating the effects of truth commissions on survivors of human rights violations and discusses the most suitable research designs and methods for such studies. Sonis makes a further important contribution by outlining the ethical principles that must be followed in research with survivors. Leigh Payne's chapter is an excellent example of the methodological eclecticism that may be required to study the impact of a transitional justice mechanism. In her study of perpetrators' confessions, Payne uses a performative approach that goes beyond a content analysis of the confessional text to explore the functions of the confessional act in a society. In her approach, the interaction of the actor (the perpetrator), script (the confession), timing, stage (the transitional justice mechanism), and audiences produces political meaning and political action. The author describes her work using this approach and describes its potential applications and limitations for future research projects.

Janet Cherry uses her experience as a researcher with the South African TRC to flesh out many of the issues related to the documentation of truth in a transitional justice process. She discusses how the TRC struggled to find the balance between forensic and narrative truth, qualitative and quantitative research, the global and the local, and the factual and the explanatory. She argues that an eclectic and multimethodological approach may hold the most promise in determining what is "truth."

Brandon Hamber and Gráinne Kelly discuss the methodology used in their research project on how reconciliation is conceived and implemented, politically and at the grassroots, in different areas of Northern Ireland. Differences were found not just between competing sides of the political divide but at various other levels as well. The research reflects the difficulty of using specific definitions of a key term such as "reconciliation," which means very different things to different people even within the same country. The impact of interventions is thus judged from very different angles, making such judgments a complex task engaging funding agendas, ideologies, and local political perspectives.

In her chapter on community studies, Matilde González argues that the local level is a privileged vantage point for observing the dynamics of conflict and transition. Using her sociohistorical research study on the internal armed conflict in Guatemala from the perspective of the Maya-K'iche community, she discusses the methodological challenges in conducting long-term microlevel community studies. Such research provides insight into the impacts of different transitional justice policies by demonstrating the stark contrast between national-level rhetoric surrounding transitional justice policies and the entrenchment of authoritarian concepts and the exercise of power at the societal level.

The chapter on international comparative analysis gives an overview of the methodology, as well as an example derived from an actual study. Victor Espinoza Cuevas and María Luisa Ortiz Rojas's chapter describes the many choices researchers face when mounting a large international comparative study. Using their five-country study of the implementation of truth commission recommendations in four Latin American countries and South Africa, the authors discuss issues of selecting cases, locating respondents, and synthesizing the research findings into a manageable format.

Although this volume will not provide a definitive answer on how to assess the impacts of transitional justice mechanisms, it will offer insights into the methodological considerations crucial to designing studies of those mechanisms. Taking into account the number of countries around the world facing the decision to opt for one transitional justice policy over another, this is no trivial matter. With limited resources and mounting pressure to take action, newly elected leaders, donors, and civil society groups enter the fray armed with the best intentions but, too often, with a paucity of research findings from other contexts.

This book's chief contribution to the research on transitional justice mechanisms is to raise the methodological considerations that too often are underdeveloped or remain an implicit rather than explicit part of the research dialogue. By focusing on methodology, we hope to allow future researchers the means to mull over the approaches, constraints, and relative strengths and utility of several different research methods. As the various chapters illustrate, the challenges of doing research are a complex interface between the research questions being asked, the difficult context of transitional societies, and the selected methodologies. Each element presents its own challenges.

Exciting and eminently useful research now under way holds great promise for helping policymakers arrive at more informed decisions when deciding transitional justice policy. We hope that this book will stimulate further quality research in this field.

References

Bloomfield, David, Teresa Barnes, and Luc Huyse. 2003. *Reconciliation after Violent Conflict: A Handbook.* Stockholm: International Institute for Democracy and Electoral Assistance.

Carothers, Thomas. 2002. "The End of the Transition Paradigm." *Journal of Democracy* 13 (1): 5–21.

Hayner, Priscilla. 2001. *Unspeakable Truths: Confronting State Terror and Atrocity.* New York and London: Routledge.

Kritz, Neil, ed. 1995. *Transitional Justice: How Emerging Democracies Reckon with Former Regimes.* Vols. 1–3. Washington, D.C.: United States Institute of Peace Press.

Minow, Martha. 1998. *Between Vengeance and Forgiveness: Facing History after Genocide and Mass Violence.* Boston: Beacon.

Parlevliet, Michelle. 1998. "Considering the Truth, Dealing with a Legacy of Gross Human Rights Violations." *Netherlands Quarterly of Human Rights* 16 (2): 141–74.

1

Policy Implications of Empirical Research on Transitional Justice

Neil Kritz

Over the years, the United States Institute of Peace (USIP) has supported and encouraged original research on transitional justice issues, both with its grantees and with projects conducted by USIP staff. One conclusion emerging from this work is that there is a clear need for serious empirical research on the impacts of transitional justice mechanisms. Empirical research is only one piece of the picture—by itself, it will never figure out all the answers for transitional justice policy. But there are several ways in which empirical research could contribute to a greater understanding of what policy options are available to transitional regimes and donor countries alike.

There are four basic objectives of any transitional justice program. In ascending levels of difficulty—in both attainment and amenability to measurement through empirical research—the first is to determine the truth by establishing a record of human rights abuses. Truth provides validation for victims and is aimed at the instruction of future generations. The second objective is justice. The third is meaningful democratic reform, entrenchment of the rule of law within society, and building a society with institutions that ensure that the kinds of abuses being dealt with will not recur. The fourth objective is a durable peace with assurance that a return to violence is fairly unlikely. This is not to imply that truth and justice are easy to accomplish but that they are slightly easier than democratic reform and durable peace. Together, these four objectives are the standards by which all transitional justice policies should be evaluated.

Transitional Justice Policy Choices

One of the first temptations for policymakers is to transfer policies across contexts, but this urge should be carefully considered. It is a mistake to suggest that any thoughtful or comprehensive approach that works in one country can automatically become the model for other transitional states.

We need only consider a draft proposal for the Rwandan government for a compensation scheme after the genocide. What became clear upon a quick reading was that it was based largely on Chile's compensation program. The Chile National Commission on Truth and Reconciliation had an extremely comprehensive compensation approach that included a variety of benefits and was more generous than any comparable program. The problem, of course, is that Chile had a very narrowly defined class of eligible beneficiaries and a fairly healthy economy. In Rwanda, the exact opposite exists: a massive class of beneficiaries and a nonexistent economy. A reparation policy under those circumstances would be akin to loading another insult and frustration onto victims because compensation would be no more than an undeliverable promise. Similarly, the South African Truth and Reconciliation Commission (TRC) experience has skewed the views of many policymakers who need to figure out transitional justice programs that make sense. The South African experience is unique and anomalous, yet it remains the dominant model in the transitional justice field—a model that should be reconsidered.

The good news is that a paradigm shift has occurred both for transitional countries and for those donor countries contemplating providing technical or financial assistance. Both recognize that dealing with the past is necessary. This was not always the case, and it represents real progress for the field. That said, however, policymakers in both situations remain in a bit of a muddle. They have a vague sense that dealing with the past is appropriate, but a government's decision to pursue a particular mechanism often depends less on well-grounded and proven policy considerations than on whether the junior staff member writing the policy memo has some experience with the South African TRC or another transitional justice process. The population of those who worked in some capacity or other with the South African TRC is quite large. By one count, there are also over 2,500 current and former staffers and hundreds of law students who have worked with or for the International Tribunals for Yugoslavia and Rwanda. In addition to their sheer numbers, these individuals tend to be mobile and influential on transitional justice policy. Another influencing factor can be how policymakers believe that a particular transitional justice approach will be perceived by the International Criminal Court (ICC) and by their own governments.

The Role of Research in Policy Choices

Empirical research can inform policy choices in several ways. The four main objectives of transitional justice policies—truth, justice, rule of law, and durable peace—occur over the very long term. Things like democratic reform and the establishment of the rule of law, despite the insistence of some policymakers, cannot take root overnight. This has obvious ramifications for empirical research. The snapshots of some research are only that: little pieces of a very long process. But empirical research can play a very helpful role in moving beyond snapshots of transitional justice policy and seeking to understand more fully the impacts of different mechanisms on society. In this way, empirical research allows for the testing of many of the current assumptions guiding transitional justice policy. The section that follows outlines some of these assumptions with suggestions on how research can be used to test theories and give policymakers of transitional governments and donor countries a better understanding of the impacts of different transitional justice policy choices.

One clear need for empirical research in the field is to find ways of disaggregating the different contextual factors and different transitional justice components at play in any particular case. If a researcher is going to measure truth commission against truth commission, issues need to be more clearly unpacked. For example, both Argentina and Chile undertook truth commission programs and compensation schemes. Did the truth commission in Argentina, accompanied by trials, have a substantially different impact from the truth commission in Chile, with the absence of criminal accountability? Political scientists and others are doing useful work in developing typologies of transitions. Empirical research should build on these and determine whether certain types of transitional justice mechanisms are more appropriate than others in specific kinds of transitions, such as a transition away from civil war versus a transition away from a repressive regime, or a radical replacement of government by revolution versus a negotiated transition based on an agreement.

Researchers have an important role to play in capturing baseline attitudes at the very beginning of the transition, that is, *before* a transitional justice mechanism is chosen rather than after the fact. This will allow researchers to better evaluate the mechanism's actual impact on a variety of sectors, such as the military, policy, public opinion, and potential spoilers. One consideration is what could be referred to as the "Malamud-Goti strategic shift." Jaime Malamud-Goti (1996), the former Argentine solicitor general, was involved in the prosecutions in Argentina for crimes committed during that country's "Dirty War," which began in 1976. Thinking through the actual contributions that trials make to accountability, he went back and did additional research and decided that he had been wrong about the impact of trials. It is now his view that prosecuting a small number of people for abuses can simply make it easier for large sectors of society to carry on with a clean conscience. By ascribing guilt only to those who were prosecuted,

Argentine society did not have to do the introspection necessary to bring about deeper societal changes.

International tribunals present additional challenges for researchers, who must measure the impact of this type of mechanism against not only local country attitudes but regional attitudes as well. Are the attitudes and actions of participants in conflicts half a world away affected in any way by their perception of international justice as represented by the tribunals? For example, does their awareness of the tribunals influence them to commit to an international acceptance of human rights principles and an understanding of human rights conventions? Anecdotal evidence on these issues as they relate to impunity has certainly contributed to the debate that led to the establishment of the two tribunals—and to the creation of the ICC, for that matter. Therefore, measuring the impact of the tribunals in distant parts of the world will be important in assessing their effectiveness.

As for evaluating the credibility of courts, there has been too much bifurcation between transitional justice and the construction of the rule of law. Different people work on the two issues, both in academic settings and on the ground. There are those donor programs that focus on building the judiciary and reforming society and those that work on the transitional justice mechanisms, this despite the fact that after a conflict, it is often the very same small pool of talent that will be available, whether to organize the trials, serve on commissions, or perform any number of other functions. Researchers should look at the nexus between transitional justice issues and rule-of-law programs, considering in particular the issue of resource allocation. No matter which judicial approach is taken—whether international tribunals, hybrid international/local courts, or local criminal proceedings—the goal is to establish a local criminal justice system that is capable of dealing with abuses, particularly before they can get out of control again. It does not make sense to have such a rigid dichotomy between rule-of-law and transitional justice studies.

Research will be particularly important in determining the credibility of the judiciary in transitional countries and the level of institutional reform needed within the legal systems. Without serious reform to the criminal justice system, any trials, including transitional justice trials, would lack credibility. There needs to be research in both the short and medium term on the impacts of various kinds of trials because this debate is ongoing. For example, how can one determine the impact of international tribunals versus hybrid international/local courts, versus local criminal proceedings on the ability to establish local judicial capacity and independence? Research can also tease out the impact of international or national judicial interventions on the level of public confidence in the rule of law.

The impact of various mechanisms in bringing about institutional reform may ultimately be more important than other aspects of transitional justice. This is especially significant for policymakers who must be concerned with keeping a country from falling back into a situation of violence or mass atrocities. Indeed, policymakers often will try to figure out the policy that best promotes stability as a separate issue from what is "right" in broader terms.

For truth commissions, policy determinations are usually based not on research but on instinct—a sort of a "gut sense" of what effect a truth commission will have. The policy decisions for truth commissions have become almost routine—standard practice, in effect. A country has a transition and everyone immediately says, "We have to have a truth commission," without any clear understanding of why or of what such endeavors are about. Except for some good-quality preliminary work, there is a real dearth of serious empirical research on exactly what impact truth commissions actually have—on victims, on perpetrators, on society as a whole, or on the four objectives of transitional justice: truth, justice, rule of law, and peace.

Certainly, enough time has passed for researchers to go back to some of the countries that completed the earlier commissions, such as Argentina and Chile, and assess the long-term impacts of the truth commission process by looking at the attitudes and actions of victims, perpetrators, government institutions, and the many people in all those categories who chose not to participate in the truth commission processes. There has been an interesting evolution in policymakers' opinions. For example, the human rights community hailed the early truth commissions in Latin America as major advances in terms of serving the goal of accountability. By the mid- to late 1990s, this same group, flush with notable successes in criminal accountability and moving toward establishment of the ICC, came to view truth commissions fairly skeptically as being soft alternatives that perhaps were not that useful after all. There has been a recalibrating of perspectives, not only of those hard-nosed realpolitik-driven policy bureaucrats but also of leaders in the human rights community.

A major frustration with the overwhelming majority of truth commissions has been the enormous chasm between, on the one hand, the wonderful mandates to develop detailed recommendations, directed at all sectors, on major societal reforms that should be undertaken and, on the other, the virtual dismissal, or at least nonimplementation, of these recommendations by the governments that receive them. Researchers should conduct studies to determine whether there is a nexus between a new government's level of responsiveness to truth commission recommendations and the achievement of the objectives of truth, justice, reconciliation, and establishment of the rule of law. A possible policy prescription to come out of such research would be, for example, donors tying aid to the improved implementation of truth commission recommendations.

One lesson that has emerged from the research on truth commissions is the relationship of the mechanism to civil society. If the goal is simply to research and write the truth (or at least a reasonably accurate version of it), a commission can go about its work in splendid isolation. But as commissions have evolved, these bodies are tasked with more than just researching and documenting the facts. To be effective, a truth and reconciliation commission has to engage and confront all of society in a painful national dialogue, with serious soul-searching, and attempt to look at the ills within society that make abuses possible. One can point to any number of commissions that have recently done this. This process is extremely difficult to do without the active participation of a fairly robust civil society. Civil society produces a sense of public ownership in this process, so that this dialogue actually leads to something. Otherwise, a country has merely a nice history lesson, destined for the bookshelf.

Research on the connections between civil society and truth commissions could result in a policy prescription along the following lines: A truth and reconciliation commission should be established only where, at the end of the regime or at the end of the conflict dissipation, a robust civil society remains intact. Where such conditions do not exist, the commission's mandate should be narrowly focused on documenting the truth along the lines of some earlier commissions rather than on the broader reconciliation goals established more recently. In a context that lacks a civil society altogether, a more top-down approach may be appropriate. This was part of the rationale in Rwanda, for example, where, after the genocide, the assumption was that civil society was so devastated that a top-down process such as Gacaca would be appropriate. But these are assumptions that need to be tested by empirical research.

It has often been argued that because the capacity of the criminal justice system often needs to go through the lengthy process of being rebuilt, a truth commission may be a better short-term policy choice. A truth commission can be quickly and easily organized. A commission can create an official record and preserve evidence, essentially buying time until trials are possible at a later time. These assumptions will make a difference in terms of the direction various countries take as they deal with transitional justice issues. What kind of empirical analysis can be generated to either confirm or repudiate these assumptions?

Taking this a step further, there is much to support the view that truth and reconciliation commissions—those based on broader models, at least—do engage a society in a national dialogue. Such commissions may be effective in developing a consensus for societal change that, one can argue, is more important for promoting of peace after conflicts between ethnic and religious groups than after conflicts of an ideological nature. Democratization and economic development can be transformative; in a purely ideological conflict, members of a national group that was previously at war with itself can attribute the past abuses to the former regime. This can provide a rationale and momentum for the new government to reform institutions and ideologies and may help the society move forward. In contrast, a situation of ethnic or religious conflicts, where the groups remain living next to each other while maintaining their distinct identities, presents a different scenario. It may be easier for extremists to tie responsibility for past crimes and human rights violations to their ethnic or religious adversaries. As a consequence, a broad societal discussion model seems to be more appropriate. Again, this is an assumption that needs to be tested through research.

Empirical research is worthwhile in determining the impact of the presence or absence of a United Nations (UN) or other international mission during a transitional justice mechanism process. Ironically, with only a couple of exceptions—perhaps Guatemala and East Timor—it seems that wherever a UN mission was a player, the approach to transitional justice has been less focused on pursuing prosecutions than in countries where no UN mission was involved. In Bosnia, Kosovo, Haiti, Cambodia, or Afghanistan, there may be obvious reasons why international missions are more concerned about being able to work with all sides and not aiding any faction disproportionately. Empirical research is needed to determine the issues at play when international actors are involved in the transitional justice process.

Research will also be needed to understand the impacts of local justice initiatives based on custom or ritual that may be happening in place of or alongside formal transitional justice processes. Any assumptions on how these formal processes may relate and resonate with local traditions must be examined carefully. Further, research must look at the impact of these localized processes on victims and perpetrators and on achieving the four main objectives of transitional justice: truth, justice, rule of law, and durable peace. Some will argue that certain of the more customary approaches may positively affect some of the goals but not others. Do victims feel that they get more justice or less justice in customary local trials than in a formal process?

Noncriminal sanctions, such as purges, lustration, and public access to security files, are a crucial piece of transitional justice programs and have been featured, in one combination or another, in almost every transitional justice case, yet they continue to get short shrift in the research literature. Noncriminal sanctions do not accomplish much in terms of the truth function, though they do provide an element of justice. They are more important for the democratic reform element and arguably for the peacebuilding element. Research must evaluate how effective these efforts have been. One research project could involve following up on those who have been purged from the security forces or government, to see what their activity has been since that time. Some purges involved extensive due process, whereas others were clearly political. In Greece, for example, 100,000 civil servants were purged from government positions. Some of these decisions were based on explicit title, others on evidence in secret police files, and still others on material evidence. It is necessary to unpack the process for each of these policy decisions.

In other cases, noncriminal sanctions had a limited duration, with a cooling-off period to allow those holding key positions in society to move out. Those who were implicated in past abuses were not prosecuted, in order to allow society to re-create itself. From this process, is it possible to derive lessons about what time period is too long or too short? Is an appropriate time determined based on other factors in society? Is an ad hoc commission that purges senior members of the military (such as the approach taken in El Salvador) or trials that are more focused on a smaller number of individuals (such as occurred in Argentina) more effective in changing the attitudes and culture of security forces? How extensive do purges need to be to effect change in the culture of security forces? How far down the chain of command do these projects need to go? And what is the nexus between that question and the impact on society?

Empirical research is also needed to shed some light on the impacts of compensation schemes. Many times, compensation occurs because it is seen as the right thing to do rather than for its potential to further the four objectives of a transitional justice process. Does a long-term reparation program serve a function by reminding governments to avoid a recurrence of abuses?

For all transitional justice mechanisms, research needs to examine the impact on key societal institutions, such as the military, police, and media. How do the media characterize problems within society? Is this characterization different before and after the adoption of various transitional justice mechanisms? Did the transitional justice mechanisms make a difference in terms of religious rhetoric in conflicts where religious adversaries are at play? What is the impact on nonstate actors? Did transitional justice mechanisms affect rebel and former rebel forces differently from state forces and agencies?

Conclusion

This chapter has provided some ideas for how empirical research might aid policymakers and donor countries in determining an appropriate transitional justice policy. Although a choice of transitional justice instruments should not be a zero-sum decision, the reality for transitional societies is that available resources are limited. From the perspective of a prototypical anonymous policymaker, if a transitional justice mechanism simply pacifies society for a couple of years, long enough for other dynamics to take hold, that may be reason enough to use certain transitional justice mechanisms without focusing on all the explicit and direct linkages that researchers think are at play. For countries emerging from devastating civil wars or long-term corrupt and repressive regimes, both human and material resources are extremely limited. With the two international tribunals costing approximately $2 billion, we inevitably must ask, while looking at all the different goals of a transitional justice mechanism, how else that $2 billion dollars might have been spent, and with what impact, in the former Yugoslavia and in Rwanda and the Great Lakes region. Those are real issues that research has to inform.

There are limits to what can be learned through empirical research on transitional justice choices. Ultimately, understanding precisely how and why humankind commits grotesque atrocities against itself and how societies move away from mass abuses toward truth and justice, establishing democracy, the rule of law, and durable peace, is not an exact science and probably will never be. But original, well-chosen, and well-coordinated empirical research can chip away at the edges of the problem and make it possible for policymakers to make better and more informed decisions in the future.

References

Malamud-Goti, Jaime E. 1996. *Game without End: State Terror and the Politics of Justice*. Norman, Okla.: University of Oklahoma Press.

2

Cross-National Comparative Analysis

David Backer

At a July 2002 conference held in Mexico City, the Corporation for the Defense and Protection of the People, a Chilean non-governmental organization (NGO), launched the report from its comparative study of the truth commission processes in Argentina, Chile, El Salvador, Guatemala, and South Africa (Espinoza Cuevas, Ortiz Rojas, and Baeza 2002). During the three days of sessions, a number of participants questioned the logic of drawing on these and other past transitional justice undertakings in search of lessons for countries that are currently pursuing or considering measures of their own. Each country is unique, they argued, and therefore, any courses of action should emerge out of, and be tailored to, local conditions. By implication, looking elsewhere for guidance will result in importing frameworks and institutions that are likely to be ill suited and unsuccessful.

While the proponents of this line of reasoning remained in the minority at the conference, their skepticism about comparing various countries' experiences in the area of transitional justice is noteworthy for those engaged in related scholarly inquiry and policy advocacy, formulation, and evaluation. The claims have some merit: At a minimum, to prescribe the same approach for all countries undergoing regime change, without proper reflection on what is feasible and appropriate in a given setting, would clearly be misguided. Yet such caveats are not a reason to ignore the historical record entirely and start de novo. Rather, they underline the need for careful, intelligent data collection and appraisal, leveraging experiences regarding transitional justice around the world to generate insights about patterns of decision making and their consequences.

This chapter demonstrates the utility of cross-national comparative analysis as a methodology for empirical research on transitional justice processes, which is advocated to enhance awareness of the processes' origins, implementation, and impact. Such an approach is warranted for three major reasons: (1) the prevalence of political transitions from repressive rule, civil war, and genocidal violence over the past several decades; (2) the diversity of measures that have been adopted to address legacies of human rights violations in these settings; and (3) the value of understanding how domestic and international factors affect the selection of approaches and of evaluating the implications of these choices for subsequent paths of political and social development. Section 3 then discusses the key issues of research design: what to compare, when to compare, and how to compare. Section 4 considers the hurdles in applying comparative methods to the study of transitional justice processes; these hurdles, including differences among countries, data constraints, and the challenge of attributing causality, have limited the extent of cross-national analysis. Section 5 surveys the strengths and weaknesses of this literature. Section 6 concludes by offering several suggestions for comparative research that contributes to the development, interpretation, and assessment of transitional justice measures. To emphasize, the aim throughout is to reflect on the relevance and applications of the comparative method to research in this field rather than to summarize findings from existing cross-national studies.

Why Compare?

Any choice of analytical methodologies should reflect the empirical landscape and the substantive questions of interest. In both respects, transitional justice is a subject ripe for cross-national comparison. To begin with, there is an identifiable and sizable population of cases: countries that have experienced a change in political regime or other significant transformation in political circumstances—however provisional, temporary, or incomplete—that offers the prospect of a departure from prior conditions of repression, conflict, and violence. These countries exhibit a variety of approaches to transitional justice and varying trajectories of political and social development. Whether the outcomes can be attributed to the earlier decisions is vital for those who seek to comprehend why transitional paths differ, to establish best practice, and to offer reasonable advice on how to proceed in other settings.

Cases

Attaching these labels, however, can give a misleading impression of uniformity across the population of cases when, in reality, these countries exhibit a wide range of political legacies and subsequent experiences. The prior governments include single-party monopolies, bureaucratic-authoritarian rule, personalistic dictatorships, military juntas, totalitarian regimes, racial oligarchies, colonial administrations, and fundamentalist theocracies. In some "failed states" (e.g., Afghanistan, Liberia, Sierra Leone), a central power structure was lacking, and warlords dominated segments of territory amid an atmosphere of widespread anarchic violence. While serious violations of human rights are the norm across all cases, the scope and character of abuses depend on the tactics employed by those responsible. The authorities—especially the state security apparatus—are

Table 2.1 Political Transitions by Region, 1974–2008

Year	Europe	Americas	Africa	Asia	Middle East
1974	Greece Portugal				
1975	Spain				
1977			Burkina Faso	India	
1979			Ghana Nigeria Zimbabwe	Cambodia	
1982		Bolivia Honduras			
1983	Turkey	Argentina Grenada			
1984		Uruguay			
1985		Brazil			
1986			Sudan Uganda	Philippines Taiwan	
1987			Tunisia	South Korea	
1988				Pakistan	
1989	Bulgaria Czechoslovakia Poland Romania USSR Yugoslavia		Nigeria		Lebanon
1990	East Germany Hungary	Chile Nicaragua Peru	Cameroon Chad Comoros Gabon Namibia Sao Tome	Mongolia Nepal	
1991	Albania Belarus Croatia Georgia Latvia Lithuania Macedonia Russia Slovenia Ukraine	Haiti Panama Suriname	Benin Burkina Faso Cape Verde Central African 　Republic Ethiopia Niger Seychelles Togo Zambia	Kazakhstan Uzbekistan	
1992	Bosnia and 　Herzegovina Estonia	El Salvador	Congo- 　Brazzaville Ghana Kenya Madagascar Mali Mauritania Tanzania	Turkmenistan	

continued

Table 2.1 Political Transitions by Region, 1974–2008, *cont.*

Year	Europe	Americas	Africa	Asia	Middle East
1993	Czech Republic Slovakia	Paraguay	Burundi Eritrea Rwanda	Cambodia Kyrgyzstan	
1994		Haiti	Angola Malawi Mozambique Rwanda South Africa	Sri Lanka	
1996		Ecuador Guatemala	Gambia Sierra Leone		
1997	Moldova		Liberia	Tajikistan	
1998	UK (Northern Ireland)			Papua New Guinea	
1999			Algeria Guinea-Bissau Lesotho Morocco Niger Nigeria	Indonesia Timor-Leste	
2000	Yugoslavia (Serbia)	Mexico	Burundi Côte d'Ivoire Sierra Leone		Lebanon
2001		Peru	DRC	Fiji	
2002			Comoros Madagascar	Afghanistan	
2003	Georgia		Liberia		Iraq
2005	Ukraine			Kyrgyzstan	Lebanon
2007			Mauritania		
2008	Kosovo?		Central African Republic Uganda? Zimbabwe?	Nepal	Lebanon

often to blame, but nonstate actors (e.g., paramilitaries, rebel groups) are frequently implicated as well. Specific groups may be targeted on ideological, cultural, or other grounds. During civil wars and genocides as well as totalitarian eras, large segments of the population are implicated as victims or perpetrators (or both).

The transitions also differ in form. Certain governments can no longer be sustained and simply collapse. Others fall via coup, revolution, or external intervention. More often, those in power reach a point of stalemate, where they are able to resist ouster but cannot fully quell opposition, and opt to negotiate a handover of authority. Similarly, wars can exhaust themselves, end with a clear victor, or be resolved through a peace accord. Post-transition trajectories likewise vary considerably. Democracy has been consolidated in only a minority of the countries (Diamond 1997, 1999). A greater number have exhibited modest progress but remain as illiberal democracies (Zakaria 1997) or competitive authoritarian regimes (Levitsky and Way 2002), and instances of reversion to past practices (e.g., the reinstallation of one-party rule, the reignition of conflict) are relatively common (Diamond and Morlino 2005). Some countries actually experienced multiple transitions, separated by interludes of renewed problems that lasted anywhere from a few years to a decade or more.

Despite these evident disparities, the countries in table 2.1 have a key feature in common: the experience of initiating a transition that could in principle permit or induce increased scrutiny of past injustices. Such a shift in circumstances ordinarily creates a window of opportunity and accelerates demands to address human rights abuses and other offenses and forms of aggression that were observed during the previous era (and possibly in the aftermath of the transition). This issue is regularly raised in negotiations between the incumbents and opposition groups, with relevant resolutions spelled out in a peace agreement, a pact, or new constitutional provisions. Even without such formal dealings, the question of accountability typically enters public discourse, spurred by calls from victims and their families, civil society groups, and communities and assisted by networks of activists and international organizations. Events in one country can also have diffusion, demonstration, and spillover effects that influence the approaches of countries throughout the region and the world.

Given their common experience of facing the same basic issue of how to address past violations, these countries constitute a clear population of cases that is readily distinguished from established democracies and entrenched nondemocratic regimes. Although each country exhibits unique characteristics, the cases provide a serviceable set of proxies for answering important counterfactual questions—in particular, what might have happened if different measures were adopted in a given instance—as well as the best available evidence about the likely dynamics of future transition processes. No experimental laboratories are available where events of this type can be simulated.

The large population of cases, dispersed around the world over the past several decades, also shows that the phenomenon of regime change is not rare or confined to a particular region or short time period. In fact, transitions continue to take place, with the recent additions to the list including several infamous "hot spots" in Africa and various Arab/Muslim countries.

Of course, these events will hopefully become less frequent as more countries achieve and maintain conditions of peace, stability, and democracy. Such a desirable state of affairs is far from universal, however, and many countries that have undergone transitions are still at risk of reverting to past unjust practices. Thus, issues of transitional justice will likely remain prominent for the foreseeable future. A natural gauge for evaluating transitional justice measures is whether they have yielded political and social improvements or, instead, worsened conditions.

Approaches to Transitional Justice

The decision about how to deal with a legacy of repression, violence, and conflict has been formulated as a dilemma of whether to prosecute or pardon (Pion-Berlin 1993). In practice, the options are far more extensive, including (1) criminal prosecution by existing or ad hoc courts; (2) other formal sanctions, such as lustration, purges, and bannings of political parties; (3) reparations, which can be financial, material, or symbolic; (4) investigations conducted by truth commissions or independent inquiries; (5) institutional reform, including the establishment of formal human rights oversight (i.e, commission, ombudsman, public protector, special parliamentary committee), and the introduction, amendment, or restoration of a constitution; and (6) immunity through amnesties, pardons, and other limits on accountability and punishment. Appendix table A2.1 summarizes the implementation of these different approaches around the world since the mid-1970s[1]; similar measures have also been actively considered or proposed elsewhere.

This overview and the subsequent examination of the use of each approach reveals notable patterns and prompts questions about the origins, significance, and efficacy of these measures, which comparative research might seek to address.

As table 2.2 shows, the criminal prosecutions to date were most often conducted in domestic courts (sometimes in response to charges filed by private citizens). In recent years, the international community has assumed an increasing role, harking back to the post–World War II prosecutions related to German and Japanese war crimes. Two ad hoc UN tribunals have been operating since the mid-1990s, with reference to the former Yugoslavia and Rwanda. Within the past five years, several hybrid courts with both domestic and international aspects were established, including the Special Court for Sierra Leone (SCSL), the Special Panels for Serious Crimes in Timor-Leste,

---

1.   Among the further options—not covered here—are the assassination or exile of individuals implicated in violations; the use of traditional community-level conflict resolution mechanisms and reconciliation rituals or the creation of official national bodies dedicated to similar purposes; and disarmament, demobilization, and integration programs.

Table 2.2   Criminal Prosecutions Related to Political Transitions by Country

Country	Type of Court	Defendant(s)	Charges
Afghanistan	Foreign (Netherlands)	Various	War crimes; crimes against humanity
	Foreign (U.S.)	Various	War crimes; terrorism; conspiracy
Albania	Domestic	Top leaders	Various
Algeria	Domestic	Militia member	Massacre; assassination
	Foreign (France)	Militia members	Disappearances; extrajudicial killings
Argentina	Domestic	Junta leaders	"Dirty War"
	Foreign (France, Spain)	Military officers	Murders; disappearances
Benin	Domestic	Political officials	Corruption
Bolivia	Domestic	Top political officials	Various
Bulgaria	Domestic	Top leaders	Embezzlement
Cambodia	Domestic	Khmer Rouge leaders	Genocide
	Hybrid (ECCC)	Political officials	Genocide
Central African Rep.	Domestic	Ex-president Bokassa	Political massacres
	Domestic	Military officers	Extrajudicial killings
	International (ICC)	Jean-Pierre Bemba	War crimes; crimes against humanity
Chad	Foreign (Senegal)	Ex-president Habré	Torture
Chile	Domestic	Political officials	Murders; disappearances
	Foreign (Spain)	Political officials	Murders; disappearances
Congo-Brazzaville	Domestic	Members of police and military	Disappearances (acquitted)
Czechoslovakia	Domestic	Communist officials	Various
DRC	Domestic	Various	Various (some acquittals)
	Foreign (Netherlands)	Death squad leader	Torture
	International (ICC)	Rebel leaders	War crimes; crimes against humanity
Ecuador	Domestic	Political officials	Murders; disappearances
El Salvador	Domestic	Military officers	Murders; disappearances
Estonia	Domestic	Former Soviet officials	Crimes against humanity
Ethiopia	Domestic	Various	Various
Fiji	Domestic	People involved in 2000 coup	Treason

continued

Table 2.2   Criminal Prosecutions Related to Political Transitions by Country, *cont.*

Country	Type of Court	Defendant(s)	Charges
(East) Germany	Domestic	Various	Various
Greece	Domestic	Military police	Torture; treason
Grenada	Foreign (U.S.)	Top leaders	Murders
Guatemala	Domestic	Military officers	Murders; disappearances
Guinea-Bissau	Domestic	Ex-president Vieira	Arms trafficking (canceled)
	Domestic	Military leaders	Treason (acquittals)
Haiti	Domestic	Military officers	Murders
Honduras	Domestic	Army and police officers	Disappearances
	Foreign (Spain)	Military officers	Disappearances
India	Domestic	Leader, officials, and policemen	Torture; murders
Indonesia	Domestic	Military officers	Murders
Iraq	Domestic	Various	War crimes
	Foreign (Netherlands)	Dutch businessman	War crimes; genocide
Kenya	Domestic	Judges	Corruption
Latvia	Domestic	Former Soviet officials	Genocide
Liberia	Hybrid (SCSL)	Charles Taylor	Various
	Foreign (Netherlands)	Dutch businessman	War crimes; arms trafficking (conviction overturned on appeal)
	Foreign (U.S.)	Charles Taylor's son	Torture
Lithuania	Domestic	Political officials	Genocide; murders; detainee abuse
Madagascar	Domestic	Ex-president Ratsiraka	Embezzlement
	Domestic	Various	Murders; torture; corruption
Malawi	Domestic	Ex-president Banda and other top party officials	Extrajudicial killings (acquitted)
Mali	Domestic	Various	Murders; embezzlement
Mexico	Domestic	Members of security forces	Murders; disappearances
Niger	Domestic	Police and military officers	Murders (canceled)
Panama	Foreign (U.S.)	Ex-president Noriega	Drug trafficking

Country	Type of Court	Defendant(s)	Charges
Paraguay	Domestic	Political officials	Murders; disappearances
Peru	Domestic	Various	Murders; disappearances
Philippines	Foreign (U.S.)	Ex-president Marcos and wife	Racketeering (acquittals)
	Domestic	Imelda Marcos	Corruption
Poland	Domestic	Police generals	Murders of priests
Portugal	Domestic	Political officials	Murders
Romania	Domestic	Ex-leader Ceausescu; Politburo	Abuses during 1989 uprising
Rwanda	International (ICTR)	Various	Genocide; crimes against humanity; war crimes (some acquittals)
	Domestic	Various	Genocide
	Foreign (Belgium, Canada, Denmark, France, Switzerland)	Various	Genocide; crimes against humanity; war crimes
Sierra Leone	Hybrid (SCSL)	Various	War crimes; crimes against humanity
South Africa	Domestic	Former defense minister Malan and 15 codefendants	Political massacre (acquitted)
	Domestic	Eugene de Kock	Murders
	Domestic	Gideon Nieuwoudt	Murders
	Domestic	Wouter Basson	Various (charges dismissed)
South Korea	Domestic	Ex-presidents	Treason; mass murder
Spain	Domestic	Political officials	Various
Sri Lanka	Domestic	Members of security forces	Disappearances
Suriname	Foreign (Netherlands)	Ex-president Bouterse	Drug trafficking
	Domestic	Ex-president Bouterse and others	Murders; torture
Timor-Leste	Hybrid (Special Panels)	Militias	Murders
	Foreign (Indonesia)	Militia commander	Crimes against humanity
Uganda	Domestic	Various	Various
Uruguay	Domestic	Top political officials	Various (canceled)
	Domestic	Political officials	Murders; disappearances
(Former) Yugoslavia	International (ICTY)	Top leaders and soldiers	War crimes; genocide

continued

Table 2.2   Criminal Prosecutions Related to Political Transitions by Country, *cont.*

Country	Type of Court	Defendant(s)	Charges
	Domestic (Bosnia)	Various	Genocide; war crimes
	Domestic (Croatia)	Various	Genocide; war crimes
	Domestic (Serbia)	Various	Genocide; war crimes
	Foreign (Denmark, Germany, Switzerland)	Various	Genocide; war crimes

Note: This list excludes the recent indictments by the International Criminal Court of the president of Sudan and four top leaders of the Lord's Resistance Army in Uganda, as well as the opinions rendered by the Permanent People's Tribunal. Additional information on foreign prosecutions is drawn from Trial Watch (http://www.trial-ch.org).

and the Extraordinary Chambers in the Courts of Cambodia (ECCC). Also, the International Criminal Court (ICC) has recently indicted individuals in Central African Republic, Democratic Republic of the Congo (DRC), Sudan, and Uganda. Meanwhile, at least a dozen countries—concentrated in Europe, though the United States has also played an active role—have initiated prosecutions for violations committed elsewhere. The focus of these legal proceedings can vary from one (e.g., the former leader) or a few select individuals (e.g., military generals) to broader classes of perpetrators (e.g., members of the security forces). The charges range from specific violations to programmatic policies such as war crimes, crimes against humanity, and genocide. In addition to human rights violations, political and economic transgressions have attracted considerable attention.

In principle, prosecutions can have several overlapping purposes. The most obvious is to hold perpetrators of past abuses formally accountable. Any resulting punishment may also remove some of the worst offenders from public life and send a strong signal to those who may contemplate committing such acts in the future. In the absence of such ramifications, the concern is that a sense of impunity will prevail, thereby giving free rein to both political violence and criminal activity. Prosecutions can therefore serve important social functions even as they affirm the fundamental rights of the victims. The risk, of course, is that potential targets may resist and threaten to subvert the new government, as happened in Argentina and Uruguay. These considerations raise at least two sets of questions. One set concerns the extent to which the prosecutions' ostensible aims are realized: Does political violence abate or reignite? Is crime held in check? Do victims and the general public still feel vulnerable to abuses? Another set focuses on

Table 2.3 Other Post-Transition Sanctions by Country

Country	Type	Group/Class Targeted
Albania	Lustration Purge	Communist party Elected and public officials
Bulgaria	Lustration	Elected and public officials; military and security officers; select educators
Cambodia	Banning	Democratic Kampuchea Group
Czechoslovakia	Lustration Banning	Collaborators Communist party
El Salvador	Purge	Armed forces
Ethiopia	Lustration	Elected and public officials
Georgia	Banning	Communist party
(East) Germany	Purge	Civil service; judges; lawyers; academics
Greece	Purge	Military; national and local government officials; educators; top businessmen
Hungary	Lustration	Elected and public officials
Iraq	Purge	Ba'ath Party; military
Latvia	Lustration Banning	Suspected Russian sympathizers Pro-Communist organizations
Lithuania	Lustration/purge	KGB agents; collaborators
Macedonia	Lustration	Elected and public officials
Poland	Lustration	Elected and public officials
Portugal	Purge	Government officials; military commanders; union leaders
Russia	Banning	Communist party
South Korea	Purge	Military; police
Sri Lanka	Banning	Liberation Tigers of Tamil Eelam
Turkey	Lustration Banning	Pre-coup politicians Pre-coup political parties
Ukraine	Banning	Communist party
Yugoslavia (Serbia)	Lustration	Elected and public officials

whether these outcomes bear any relation to the form of prosecutions: Does it matter how many defendants—and of what status—are charged, tried, or convicted? Are foreign and international proceedings as effective as those carried out domestically?

As table 2.3 illustrates, transitional governments have also sought to remove individuals from current positions of authority or bar them from future participation in politics. In fact, a common strategy across Eastern Europe and the former Soviet Union is *lustration,* a cleansing or vetting process used to exclude various elites and functionaries based on their actual or presumed complicity in past abuses. Purges of the civil service, military, police, and other key segments of government and society, as well as bans on discredited political parties, are used to similar effect. One can draw parallels between these sorts of sanctions and criminal prosecutions, since both achieve a measure of accountability. Lustration, bans, and purges, however, are typically more sweeping in their application, with case-by-case reviews being the exception. A natural question is whether such crude approaches are effective substitutes for prosecutions. If blame is assigned generically to a group or class of individuals, there is uncertainty about who did what—and even whether all those targeted are guilty of violations. At the same time, the punishment is arguably less severe: Those who are subjected to these sanctions forfeit access to positions of authority (except by regime change), but they still retain their freedom. Yet the indiscriminate nature of the penalties, combined with the loss of livelihood, status, and influence, may still prompt widespread resentment among the affected individuals. So again, a major risk is the prospect of persistent political conflict.

Many countries have opted instead to conduct a truth commission after a transition, especially when there is a balance of power between incumbent and opposition forces, making criminal accountability appear infeasible. These investigative bodies vary in several notable respects (table 2.4). Once again, a key issue is sponsorship, which can affect the size and composition of the staff, as well as resources. Another crucial dimension is a commission's mandate: Some are charged with examining narrow time periods or types of violations, whereas others are authorized to consider the full scope of events that spanned decades. Most commissions eventually compile the information they collect into a report. Until recently, public identification of alleged perpetrators has been unusual; amnesties regularly present a constraint. The trend, however, is toward greater transparency of proceedings, via public hearings, broad media access, and release of information. Yet the insulation of perpetrators by amnesties can frustrate victims of past repression and violence, whose options range from advocating for harsher measures to engaging in retribution. An important issue, therefore, is the extent to which the features of these commissions either exacerbate or mitigate the sense of impunity and injustice.

In situations where the transitional government is apparently unwilling, incapable, or slow to take any formal steps, both nonstate actors and intergovernmental organizations have sometimes taken the initiative to conduct their own independent investigations. Table 2.5 summarizes a number of the more notable inquiries. Since these investigations resemble—yet lack the official sanction of—truth commissions, contrasting their impact is only natural. Of particular salience, do such independent efforts have any advantages or unique capabilities compared with governmental undertakings? Are independent investigations more or less efficacious than truth commissions in redressing the past and promoting constructive changes in politics

Table 2.4 Truth Commissions Following Political Transitions

Country	Tenure	Purview	Origins	Staff	Focus of Inquiry	Outcome	Repercussions for Perpetrators
India	1977	1975–77	Central government	Domestic	State of emergency	Report	None
Bolivia	1982–84	1967–82	President	Domestic	Disappearances	Disbanded	None
Argentina	1983–84	1976–83	President	Domestic	Disappearances; torture; detentions	Report	Trials
Uruguay	1985	1973–82	Parliament	Domestic	Disappearances	Report	No IDs
Philippines	1986–87	1972–86	President	Domestic	Various	Disbanded	None
Uganda	1986–95	1962–86	President	Domestic	Various	Report	None
Poland	1989–91	1945–91	Parliament	Domestic	Murders	Report	No IDs
Chile	1990–91	1973–90	President	Domestic	Disappearances	Report	None
Nepal	1990–91	1961–90	Prime Minister	Domestic	Torture; disappearances; extrajudicial executions	Report	None
Chad	1991–92	1982–90	President	Domestic	Various	Report	IDs
El Salvador	1992–93	1980–91	UN-brokered peace accord	Foreign	Various	Report	IDs
Germany	1992–94	1949–89	Parliament	Domestic	Various	Report	None
Taiwan	1992–2006	1947	Cabinet	Domestic	Murders	Report	IDs
Honduras	1993	1981–84	President	Domestic	Disappearances	Report	IDs
Ethiopia	1993–97	1974–91	President	Domestic	Various	Report	Trials
Sri Lanka (3 regional)	1994–97	1988–94	President	Domestic	Disappearances	Reports	None

continued

Table 2.4 Truth Commissions Following Political Transitions, *cont.*

Country	Tenure	Purview	Origins	Staff	Focus of Inquiry	Outcome	Repercussions for Perpetrators
Haiti	1995–96	1991–94	President	Domestic	Various	Report	IDs
South Africa	1995–98	1960–93	Parliament	Domestic	Various	Report	IDs; public hearings; limited amnesty
Ecuador	1996–97	1979–96	Ministry of Government and Police	Mixed	Various	Disbanded	None
Guatemala	1997–99	1960–94	UN-brokered peace accord	Mixed	Various	Report	None
Morocco	1998	1956–98	Royal decree	Domestic	Disappearances	Press release	No IDs; amnesty
Guinea-Bissau	1998–99	1994–98	Parliament	Domestic	Arms trafficking	Report	IDs
Sri Lanka	1998–2002	1988–94	President	Domestic	Disappearances	Reports	None
UK/Northern Ireland	1998–2005	1972	UK prime minister	Mixed	Bloody Sunday incident	Report	
Lithuania	1998–2007	1940–90	President	Mixed	Various	Reports	IDs
Estonia	1998–	1939–91	President	Mixed	Various	Reports	IDs
Burkina Faso	1999	1983–97	President	Domestic	Various	Report	None
Uzbekistan	1999	1800s–1992	President	Domestic	Various	Report	None
Indonesia	1999–2000	1999	Human Rights Commission	Domestic	Atrocities in Timor-Leste	Report	IDs
Nigeria	1999–2002	1966–99	President	Domestic	Various	Report	Public hearings
Lebanon	2000–01	1975-90	President	Domestic	Disappearances	Report	None

Country							
Lesotho	2000–01	1998	Parliament	Domestic	Election-related violence	Report	IDs
South Korea	2000–02	1961–90	President	Domestic	Deaths of activists	Report	
Uruguay	2000–03	1973–85	President	Domestic	Disappearances	Report	
Grenada	2000–03	1976–83	Prime Minister	Domestic	Murders	Report	
South Korea	2000–	1947–54	Parliament	Domestic	Political violence	Ongoing	
Grenada	2001–06	1976–91	Governor-General	Domestic	Various	Report	None
Mexico	2001	1970–82	Human Rights Commission	Domestic	Disappearances	Report	None
Lebanon	2001–02	1975–90	President	Domestic	Disappearances	No report	Public hearings
Panama	2001–02	1968–89	President	Domestic	Various	Report	
Peru	2001–03	1980–2000	President	Domestic	Various	Report	Public hearings
Yugoslavia	2001–03	1991–2001	President	Domestic	War crimes	Disbanded	None
Ghana	2002–04	1957–93	Government	Domestic	Various	Report	Public hearings
Sierra Leone	2002–04	1991–99	Peace accord	Mixed	Various	Report	Public hearings
Timor-Leste	2002–05	1974–99	UN-brokered peace accord	Mixed	Various	Report	Public hearings
Central African Rep.	2003	1960–2003	National conference	Domestic	Various	Recommendations	Some IDs
Bosnia and Herzegovina	2003–04	1995	Parliament	Domestic	Srebrenica massacre	Report	IDs
Algeria	2003–05	1992–2002	President	Domestic	Various	Report	None
Zambia	2003–05	1972–91	President	Domestic	Torture	Report	None
Paraguay	2004–	1954–2003	Parliament	Domestic	Various	Pending	

continued

Table 2.4 Truth Commissions Following Political Transitions, *cont.*

Country	Tenure	Purview	Origins	Staff	Focus of Inquiry	Outcome	Repercussions for Perpetrators
Chile	2004–05	1973–88	President	Domestic	Imprisonment; torture	Report	None
Lebanon/ Syria	2004–05	1975–90	Governments of Lebanon and Syria	Domestic	Disappearances	Report	None
Morocco	2004–05	1956–99	Royal decree	Domestic	Various	Report	None
DRC	2004–?	1965–2003	UN-brokered peace accord; president	Domestic	Various	Public education	None
Timor-Leste/ Indonesia	2004–08	1999	Presidents	Domestic	Violence in Timor-Leste	Report	IDs
Burundi	2005–	1960–2003	UN-brokered peace accord; government	Mixed	Ethnic violence	Yet to begin work	
Liberia	2005–	1979–2003	UN-brokered peace accord; parliament	Mixed	Various	Ongoing	
Ecuador	2007–	1984–88	President	Domestic	Various	Ongoing	

Note: This list excludes several sets of cases that are characterized elsewhere as, or share features of, truth commissions: (1) intergovernmental inquiries that have a narrow focus and operational mandate or are initiated without local approval or involvement (which are reported in table 2.5); (2) investigations conducted in Uganda (1974–75) and Zimbabwe (1985) while the government responsible for the violations remained in power; and (3) institutions set up in Australia and Canada (to examine the abuses against aboriginal peoples), in the United States (to examine the internment of Japanese-Americans during World War II), and in the U.S. city of Greensboro, North Carolina (to examine an episode of racially motivated violence), since these operated in established democracies. Also omitted are institutions established in several countries (e.g., Chile, Morocco, Northern Ireland, Rwanda, Uganda) with formal responsibility for matters regularly addressed by truth commissions (e.g., reconciliation, reparations, amnesty) but that are limited in scope and do not have truth seeking as a principal function.

and society? Do these outcomes differ depending on whether independent investigations complement or substitute for official measures?

Though not a prerequisite, both truth commissions and independent investigations have provided a basis for reparations programs. As table 2.6 shows, the actual form of compensation varies. Monetary payments are common, but governments have also restored property, jobs, and pensions as well as provided special health, education, and housing benefits and preferential access to other social services for victims and surviving family members (in some instances across multiple generations). In part, these differences reflect local circumstances of violence and the nature of deprivations. Moreover, transitional governments exercise ultimate discretion over the choice of compensation, certain types of which may be more feasible given the available resources. Victims of violations, or their immediate family members, have also pursued civil actions to recover damages in several notable cases, including those listed in table 2.7. The favorable judgments are generally rendered in foreign or regional courts, raising issues of enforceability that are essentially moot with respect to official reparations programs. In addition, with the exception of the class action suit concerning the Philippines, these judgments stand to benefit only the particular plaintiffs—typically a relatively small number of victims (though several of the cases adjudicated by the Inter-American Court of Human Rights were filed by communities or indigenous groups).

Regardless of the process involved, the basic intent of reparations is to offset victims' physical, emotional, and economic losses. Both material compensation and symbolic reparations (e.g., memorials, museums) can represent a form of accountability and acknowledgment. In addition, reparations may substitute in the event that alternative approaches (e.g., prosecutions) are considered infeasible. A standard predicament, given prevalent financial and political constraints, is whether such measures are a necessary aspect of any transitional justice agenda: Do victims feel shortchanged and disaffected otherwise? The more specific question is how the various different types of reparations affect victims' sentiments and life circumstances. For example, a possible concern is that financial payments could be perceived as "blood money." By contrast, the return of appropriated land and property may constitute a satisfactory means of making victims whole. Thus, comparative analysis can usefully explore the implications of the absence or presence of reparations, as well as differences in their source, content, and duration.

Table 2.8 shows that expansive amnesties, as well as pardons, reduced sentences, and constraints on prosecutions, often foreclose efforts to hold perpetrators accountable and make them face punishment. The typical mechanisms are an act by the new legislature, a decree by the new president, or a provision in a peace accord. In Argentina, Brazil, Chile, and Nicaragua, however, amnesty laws carried over from the previous regime. These statutes may even be up-

Table 2.5 Select Independent Investigations Following Transitions

Category/ Country Context	Tenure	Dates Covered	Sponsor	Focus	Outcome
Domestic					
Algeria	2003–04	1992–2004	Justice Commission for Algeria	Massacres	Report
Bolivia	1984–86	1965–82	Church and civic organizations; Universidad Mayor San Simón de la Paz	Abuses of power by General Meza	Trial resulting in conviction of General Meza
Brazil	1985	1964–84	Archdiocese of São Paulo	Various	Report
Northern Ireland	1994–98	1969–98	Cost of the Troubles Study	Violence and trauma	Reports
	1998–2002	1969–98	Ardoyne Commemoration Project	Killings in North Belfast	Report
Uruguay	1985	1973–82	Peace and Justice Service	Abuses by military	Report
Mixed					
Cambodia	1995–	1975–79	Consortium of local NGOs and foreign universities	Mass killings	Online archive
International					
Burundi	1995–96	1993	UN Security Council	Attempted coup; assassination of president; civil conflict	Report
Côte d'Ivoire	2004	2002–04	UN Security Council	Various	Report
Lebanon	2005–	2005	UN Security Council	Assassination of former prime minister and others	Investigation ongoing; special tribunal created
Rwanda	1993	1990–93	International NGOs	Various	Report
	1999	1994	United Nations	Genocide	Report
	1999–2000	1994	Organization of African Unity	Genocide	Report
Timor-Leste	1999–2000	1999	United Nations	Referendum-related violence	Report

Note: This list omits the regular monitoring and reporting activities by NGOs such as Amnesty International and Human Rights Watch, as well other investigative initiatives undertaken entirely before transitions, such as Memorial's documentation of state repression in the USSR (1987–89); the Committee of Churches' report on political violence in Paraguay (1990); and the Skweyiya and Motsuenyane Commissions (1992 and 1993, respectively)—"self-examinations," conducted by the African National Congress, of abuses committed in its detention camps outside South Africa.

Table 2.6 Reparation Measures by Country

Country	Types of Compensation or Restitution
Albania	Restoration of property or compensation for owners
Argentina	Payments, pensions, and exemption from military service for family members of disappeared
Brazil	Payments to families of 135 disappeared individuals (reparations commission); payments to victims of police repression, imprisonment, and torture (São Paulo State)
Bulgaria	Amnesty and payments to political victims and exiles; restoration of, or compensation for, nationalized land
Chile	Payments; pensions; student financial aid; medical care
Czechoslovakia	Payments to victims of political crimes; return of property confiscated from individuals and church
East Germany	Payments to former political prisoners; return of property expropriated between 1933 and 1945 and after 1949
Ghana	Payments to victims of past military regimes
Greece	Employment reinstatement; restoration of pensions
Haiti	Payments for housing, education, and legal and economic assistance to victims of violence and property damage under military regimes
Honduras	Payments to families of victims of Honduran military intelligence
Hungary	Payments to former political prisoners; compensation for seized property; vouchers; auction of seized property
Kenya	Payments by UK to families of victims of violence in response to Mau-Mau rebellion
Lithuania	Special pensions; restoration of or compensation for confiscated property
Malawi	Payments by National Compensation Tribunal to victims of Banda regime
Mauritania	Payments and pensions for some survivors and family members of victims of 1989–92 abuses
Morocco	Payments to former political prisoners and families of disappeared
Paraguay	Payments to former political prisoners
Philippines	Payments to victims of Marcos regime
Poland	Payments to former political prisoners; return of seized church property
Russia	Compensation, including payments, pensions, and other aid, and preferential access to government services for victims of political crimes
South Africa	Payments to victims of gross human rights abuses; land reform program that provides property to communities that were dispossessed
Sri Lanka	Payments to families of victims of disappearances
Taiwan	Payments to former political prisoners and families of victims of executions and disappearances
Uruguay	Employment reinstatement and restoration of pensions for fired civil servants
Zimbabwe	Payments and health and education benefits for war veterans, plus land redistribution program

Table 2.7 Select Civil Judgments Related to Repression and Civil Conflict

Category/ Country Context	Legal Venue	Violation(s)	Ordered Remedies				
			Compensation	Property Restitution	Administrative/ Legal Action	Information/ Investigation	Reforms
Domestic							
Bosnia and Herzegovina (hundreds of cases)	Human Rights Chamber of Bosnia and Herzegovina	Various	•	•	•	•	•
Foreign							
Bosnia and Herzegovina	U.S. court	Various	•				
Chile	U.S. court	Torture; murder	•				
El Salvador (3 cases)	U.S. court	Torture; murder	•				
Haiti (2 cases)	U.S. court	Various	•				
Honduras	U.S. court	Various	•				
Philippines	U.S. court	Various	•				
Timor-Leste	U.S. court	Torture	•				
Regional							
Argentina (5 cases)	Inter-American Court of Human Rights	Various	•				
Bolivia (1 case)	Inter-American Court of Human Rights	Disappearances	•		•	•	•
Chile (4 cases)	Inter-American Court of Human Rights	Various	•				
Ecuador (6 cases)	Inter-American Court of Human Rights	Various	•		•	•	•
El Salvador (2 cases)	Inter-American Court of Human Rights	Various	•		•	•	•

Country	Court	Type				
Honduras (5 cases)	Inter-American Court of Human Rights	Various		•	•	
Nicaragua (3 cases)	Inter-American Court of Human Rights	Various	•	•	•	•
Panama (1 case)	Inter-American Court of Human Rights	Job dismissals		•		
Paraguay (5 cases)	Inter-American Court of Human Rights	Various	•	•	•	
Peru (20 cases)	Inter-American Court of Human Rights	Various		•	•	•
Suriname (3 cases)	Inter-American Court of Human Rights	Murder		•		•

Note: Information on the judgments for the Human Rights Chamber of Bosnia and Herzegovina cases is drawn from Nowak (2006); for the U.S. cases (with exception of the Philippines), from the Center for Justice and Accountability; and for the Inter-American Court of Human Rights (IAHCR) cases, from Cassel (2006) and the IAHCR (2008).

held, as in Chile, under threat of violence from those who might otherwise be subject to prosecution. Similarly, pressure from the military in Argentina and Uruguay led to amnesties, pardons, and other formal constraints—introduced *after* regime change—that cut short or overturned criminal prosecutions.

Such measures have several potentially worrisome repercussions. Exempting perpetrators from punishment, despite their responsibility for past abuses, can tend to reinforce perceptions that select people are invulnerable. As a result, victims of past repression and violence may be unwilling to place their trust in government, thus undermining its credibility and authority. This response may also echo broader perceptions of political, social, and economic inequality amid a culture of apparent impunity. One possible manifestation is ongoing political turmoil: Past antagonists are permitted to remain active and to pose an inherent threat to the new government, even as victims seek retribution against perpetrators. Another downside is increasing crime, fueled by the apparent lack of constraints, as well as social and economic problems inherited from the previous era. Narrower, more restrictive, and conditional amnesty provisions (as in South Africa, for example) could conceivably mitigate these risks by ensuring greater levels of accountability and leaving open the prospect of prosecutions. An evident task of comparative research is to establish whether such conjectures concerning the implementation and design of amnesties are borne out in actual practice.

A further and almost universal approach to transitional justice is to adopt institutional arrangements that are nominally intended to provide means of deterring and remedying future violations. Many countries have entrusted formal human rights oversight to a commission, ombudsman, public protector, special parliamentary committee, or high court (Reif 2000; Cardenas 2001; Backer 2004). Some of these changes are incorporated into constitutional reforms, yielding new, amended, and restored texts. Such reform measures do not establish legal accountability for past violations; rather, they are prospective in application. An obvious empirical question is whether the institutions that are put in place successfully constrain political authority, provide modes of conflict mediation, and promote a culture of rights (Widner 2008).

In sum, countries exhibit marked differences in the selection and implementation of transitional justice measures. No country's approach is entirely unique; rather, sets of cases share various features. These commonalities suggest certain tendencies in how these processes unfold and what they are designed to achieve. Yet the variation still bears explaining: What opportunities, constraints, and other factors affect which options are contemplated and which are chosen from among these alternatives? Are some approaches feasible only under certain conditions? Who is involved in deliberations and decision making? And who participates in the process? The answers to these questions illuminate the baseline conditions under which

Table 2.8 Amnesties, Pardons, and Other Limits on Accountability

Country	Year(s)	Sponsor	Type	Comment
Spain	1977	Prime minister	Amnesty	Applies to politically motivated crimes committed before June 15, 1977
Chile	1979	Legislature	Amnesty	Passed by previous regime; applies only to 1973–78
Brazil	1979	Military regime	Amnesty	Declared by previous government; reaffirmed in 1985
Zimbabwe	1980	Legislature	Amnesty	Members of security forces and war veterans
	1988	Legislature	Amnesty	Political dissidents and violators of human rights since 1980
Turkey	1983	Former military government	Amnesty	Introduction of civilian government contingent on immunity for generals
Argentina	1983	Interim military government	Amnesty	Immunity for military and police; repealed in 1983
	1986	Legislature	Constraint on prosecution	Established deadline on indictments for violations during military regime ("full stop" law)
	1987	Legislature	Amnesty	Exempted low-level officers from prosecution ("due obedience" law)
	1989–90	President	Pardons	Applies to convicted military officers
Uruguay	1985	Legislature	Amnesty	Acts with political motives or in fulfillment of orders; retained by 1989 referendum
Guatemala	1986	Military regime	Amnesty	Declared by previous government
Namibia	1989	Administrator-general	Amnesty	Covers all native-born individuals living outside the country, as well as their families
	1990	Administrator-general	Amnesty	1989 amnesty extended to members of the South African and South-West African military and police who committed offenses in the performance of their duties

continued

Table 2.8. Amnesties, Pardons, and Other Limits on Accountability, *cont.*

Country	Year(s)	Sponsor	Type	Comment
Tunisia	1989	President	Amnesty	Led to release of thousands of imprisoned activists, including some convicted of plotting against previous president; also exempted some of previous president's closest associates from prosecution
Nicaragua	1990	Previous government	Amnesty	Passed by Sandinistas after surprise loss in 1990 election
São Tomé	1990	President	Amnesty	Applies to individuals involved in March 1988 coup attempt
El Salvador	1991	Negotiating parties	Amnesty	Part of negotiated accords
	1993	Legislature	Amnesty	Passed after publication of truth commission report
Honduras	1991	Legislature	Amnesty	Persons sentenced, prosecuted, or subjected to judicial investigation as of 1991 for political acts committed in opposition to the state
Lebanon	1991	Legislature	Amnesty	Applies to political crimes committed before the law's enactment; excludes crimes against diplomats
Philippines	1991	President	Amnesty	Immunity for security forces
Togo	1991	Government and opposition	Amnesty	Adopted in advance of national conference, primarily to permit return of exiles
Lithuania	1991	Government	Amnesty	Available to KGB agents who signed declaration of loyalty or resigned, as well as KGB collaborators who reported to the police
Cameroon	1992	Legislature	Amnesty	Applies to subversion, detention, and offenses of a political nature
Ghana	1992	Constitution	Amnesty	Includes provisions pertaining to those involved in past military coups and regimes
Mozambique	1992	Legislature	Amnesty	Applies to "crimes against the state"
South Africa	1992	Legislature	Amnesty	Exempted political officials, military, and police from prosecution; superseded by truth commission legislation (1995)

Country	Year(s)	Sponsor	Type	Comment
	1995	Legislature	Amnesty	Requires application that provides the "full truth" and proof of a political motive regarding specific gross violations; subject to public hearings, at which the victims or surviving family members had an opportunity to testify and express their views
	2008–	President	Pardons	Applies to politically motivated violations; requires application, which is then reviewed by ad hoc parliamentary committee to make recommendation
Central African Rep.	1993	President	Pardon	Ex-president Bokassa (sentence previously reduced to life imprisonment)
	2008	Negotiating parties	Amnesty	Excludes war crimes and crimes against humanity
Mali	1993	President	Reduced sentence	Death penalty changed to life imprisonment for ex-president Traore
	1999	President	Reduced sentence	Death penalty (separate conviction) changed to life imprisonment for ex-president Traore and wife
	2002	President	Pardon	Offered to ex-president Traore (refused)
Mauritania	1993	Legislature	Amnesty	Covers those responsible for killings, torture, and other violence in 1989–92
Cambodia	1994	Legislature	Amnesty	Requires end to membership in Khmer Rouge
Chad	1994	President	Amnesty	Applies to everyone except former president Habré
Haiti	1994	Negotiating parties	Amnesty	Part of negotiated accords
Panama	1994	President	Pardons	222 members of the military
	1994	President	Pardons	130 awaiting trial for corruption and other criminal charges
	1995	Legislature	Amnesty	Applies to crimes against individual freedom and politically motivated offenses
Peru	1995	Legislature	Amnesty	Applies to members of security forces; includes pardon for those already convicted

continued

Table 2.8. Amnesties, Pardons, and Other Limits on Accountability, *cont.*

Country	Year(s)	Sponsor	Type	Comment
(East) Germany	1995	Government	Pardons	Applies to individuals who spied on West Germany
Sierra Leone	1996	Negotiating parties	Amnesty	Exempted members of Revolutionary United Forces from legal action
	1999	Negotiating parties	Amnesty	Part of negotiated accords
Morocco	1998	Government	Amnesty	Applies to individuals involved in secret detentions, unfair trials, and torture
Algeria	1999	Legislature	Amnesty	Requires application
	2005	Legislature	Amnesty	Excludes collective massacres, rapes, and use of explosives in public places
Niger	1999	Constitution	Amnesty	Applies to individuals involved in 1996 and 1999 coups
Uganda	2000	Legislature	Amnesty	Applies to individuals involved in conflict since 1986, who must apply and demobilize
Guinea-Bissau	2002	President	Amnesty	Applies to soldiers involved in plotting 2001 coup
	2008	Legislature	Amnesty	Applies to coup leaders and political prisoners for crimes committed in 1980–2004
Macedonia	2002	Legislature	Amnesty	Applies to ethnic Albanian rebels; excludes crimes already indicted by ICTY
Côte d'Ivoire	2003	Negotiating parties	Amnesty	Applies to military personnel accused of threatening state security and to soldiers in exile
	2003	Legislature	Amnesty	Applies to acts of rebellion; excludes violations of international law
	2007	President	Amnesty	Applies to crimes against state security; excludes international and economic crimes
Madagascar	2004	President	Amnesty	Applies to individuals sentenced to less than three years, imprisonment for offenses during 2002 political crisis and not found guilty of torture, murder, or corruption

Country	Year(s)	Sponsor	Type	Comment
Burundi	2005	President/justice minister	Provisional immunity	Applies to individuals identified by the Commission on Political Prisoners who had been incarcerated in connection with 1993 presidential assassination and subsequent violence; those released are ultimately expected to appear before the truth commission
Liberia	2005	Legislature	Amnesty	Truth and Reconciliation Commission has discretion to grant amnesty to specific individuals; recommendations binding on the president
Kenya	2007	Legislature	Amnesty	Applies to acts of corruption committed before May 2003
DRC	2008	Legislature	Amnesty	Applies to anyone who has engaged in acts of war and rebellion in eastern provinces
Iraq	2008	Legislature	Amnesty	Intended especially for suspected insurgents in detention

Note: This list excludes pardons for former political prisoners that are implemented as a measure of symbolic reparation.

divergent types of processes have taken place. Moreover, they provide vital guidance concerning realistic and practical tactics for those seeking to devise future transitional justice endeavors.

A single-country case study can offer insight into how and why a particular tack was adopted in that setting, but only cross-national comparative analysis can establish whether these motivations and mechanics are typical or unusual. Situating cases in a comparative context also takes into account that transitional justice processes rarely occur in isolation. Many of these countries have benefited from being able to observe the experiences of other similarly situated countries, even incorporating relevant elements of past approaches into their own programs of transitional justice. The extent of this influence has accelerated, thanks to the spread of the Internet and the growth in transnational networks of NGOs and other advocates (e.g., regional and international bodies, professional consultants), who greatly enhance the circulation of information, ideas, and hands-on expertise.

Variation in Outcomes

A latent question is whether the specific features of transitional justice processes have any repercussions, that is, do different approaches—

distinguished by initial choices as well as subsequent implementation—yield different results? As suggested earlier, a fundamental issue is whether a country exhibits improvements in political and social conditions and remains on a path to consolidating these gains and maturing into a full-fledged democracy. In practice, the prospects of success are uncertain: Transitional settings are notoriously fragile, and trajectories of development vary widely over both the short and long term. Some new governments are quickly overthrown, fall into disarray, or adopt habits of their predecessors. Many others survive, even despite ongoing violence or unrest. Only a few enjoy sustained peace and stability. The important question is, are such outcomes a function of the decisions made about accountability?

Once again, a single case can supply a narrative example of a causal link—here, between the adoption of a particular approach and its eventual results in a given setting. Whether this apparent empirical relationship is characteristic of a general pattern can be rigorously evaluated only with evidence from multiple cases. Applied to the domain of transitional justice, such a comparative analysis could aim to establish the relative benefits and costs of different approaches or the circumstances under which these strategies might yield more or less favorable results. A cross-national perspective is critical to ensure sufficient variation in both the outcomes of interest and the potential explanatory factors, thus permitting more rigorous and comprehensive tests of theories about how these variables are associated.

Research Design

The notion of conducting cross-national analysis related to transitional justice processes raises three basic issues in research design: (1) what to compare, (2) when to compare, and (3) how to compare. These queries have no single correct response; rather, there is both room and a need for an assortment of studies, each defined by a specific set of research questions that entails appropriate techniques of data collection and analysis. Even with different emphases and techniques, this research can be complementary. The following sections discuss possible avenues of exploration, with an emphasis on the benefits of substantive, empirical, and methodological diversity.

What to Compare

The discussion thus far has identified two main analytical perspectives. One emphasizes cataloguing countries' approaches to transitional justice and comprehending why certain options are adopted. The other involves examining the concrete impact of these processes—a perspective that deserves further attention for several reasons. To begin with, the first perspective is already evident in most of the existing literature on transitional justice. This research has considerable value, especially from a historical and informational perspective, as well as for those interested in the dynamics of transitions. Yet most of these contributions leave significant questions unanswered: In essence, a great deal is known about the literal mechanics of transitional justice processes, but far less is understood about the resulting implications.

The greatest untapped potential, therefore, is in the area of evaluating consequences. This task presupposes an adequate foundation of knowledge about the reasons underlying the choice of approaches, since outcomes may be subject to selection effects. Such observations highlight the need for theoretical groundwork in advance of empirical research. Consider the proposition made earlier that transitional justice processes can affect trajectories of political development. Existing literature on this subject tends to stress macrolevel (e.g., regime stability) and systemic properties (e.g., democratic consolidation). Such a focus is understandable given the salience of these outcomes, but fraught with complications. In particular, establishing a causal relationship may be difficult: These variables, in addition to being notoriously hard to quantify, may be relatively unresponsive to differences in approaches to transitional justice. Instead, the impact might be observable on a smaller scale, where the influence of the process is potentially more proximate and tangible.

Hence, the question of what to compare entails identifying substantive variables of interest and selecting the units of analysis; table 2.9 lays out some of the available options. These decisions should ultimately be theory driven but are not necessarily mutually exclusive: A process could simultaneously affect any combination of individual outlooks, interpersonal relationships, local customs, social structures, political institutions, and aggregate conduct. Since each of these potential consequences is significant for a country that has embarked on a transition, an ecumenical research agenda is in order. Investigations of macrolevel outcomes are worthwhile, but they ought to be supplemented by research into microlevel effects, such as how individuals react to a process and reflect these experiences in their political mind-sets and activities and how communities address and comprehend these processes.

Studies with different perspectives can conceivably be integrated—in essence, multilevel analysis—to more carefully trace out causal relationships among factors (Bates et al. 1998). For example, a finding that truth commissions correlate with a reduced rate of political unrest might be bolstered by evidence that they are a catalyst in increasing the public's faith in the new

Table 2.9 Theoretical Impact of Transitional Justice Processes

Unit of Analysis	Possible Outcome Measures
Political system	Incidence of riots; consolidation
Society	Racial tolerance; democratic norms
Government	Regime survival; policy reform
Political institution	Adherence to rule of law
Community	Intergroup reconciliation; rights discourse
Elite actor	Pact formation; leadership turnover
Individual	Perceptions of justice

government's ability to protect individual rights and freedoms. Similarly, the adoption of formal safeguards via constitutional reforms may prove more efficacious only under conditions where selective prosecutions provide sufficient assurances to victims that past offenders are no longer in control of citizens' security. The research may also uncover contrasting tendencies, such as an amnesty that initially helps to forestall a backlash from authoritarian forces but later exacerbates discontent among victims' families and undermines confidence in the extent of change in society. Being able to itemize these specific outcomes, supported by concrete empirical data, affords a more subtle profile of a transitional justice process, which inevitably unfolds with contours that are hard to capture via a single monolithic evaluation of good or bad, successful or unsuccessful.

This discussion speaks to the broader applications of the comparative method, which are hardly confined to cross-national analysis. Instead, differences within a country can manifest among individuals, groups, regions, institutions, and eras. Research might therefore seek to identify relationships that are present at a subnational level or that evolve dynamically over time. A single-country study has the analytical advantage of holding constant at least some potentially influential explanatory factors, whereas cross-national research must take into account any observed variation on these dimensions. The trade-off is that the results of individual case studies are merely *suggestive* of patterns that the broader population of a country may or may not exhibit. Demonstrating that these case study findings have wider validity would require an accumulation of evidence, via replication in contexts where conditions differ.

When to Compare

Determining whether a transitional justice process has induced any changes depends fundamentally on establishing the state of affairs that prevailed before the process began. At times, the baseline is self-evident and data collection is not time sensitive. In many situations, however, empirical research should ideally be conducted before and after—and perhaps even at various points during—the process. Monitoring the immediate aftermath and tracking relevant indicators over time can also be quite illuminating, since the initial effects of a process may deviate considerably from the impact that becomes apparent over the longer term.

One area where a longitudinal approach can be especially beneficial is research on individual attitudes. What people feel after a process is concluded may simply be an artifact of how they have felt all along rather than a result of the process itself. Panel studies take this concern into account: Identical questions are administered to the same individuals on multiple occasions, thereby affording a more precise measurement of how their perspective has evolved. In the absence of such a design, one can perhaps reconstruct this time-dependent information—for example, through questions tied to specific moments or events—or seek to infer a rough baseline from other data. The drawback is that these techniques are rarely as reliable as repeated observations. Another option is a case-control study: A contrast between individuals with different types of exposures, with the theoretical assumption that any observed disparities in attitudes should be attributable to these distinctive experiences. The basic point of each of these techniques is the same: Since many of the relevant questions pertain to how and why things change—instead of just to simple correlations between factors—data collection and analysis should ideally reflect the dynamic aspects of transitional justice processes.

Unfortunately, longitudinal studies are rare, for many practical reasons. Whenever multiple waves of data collection are involved, cost and infrastructure are major hurdles. These problems are exacerbated by the unpredictability and short lead times of many transitions and the events that ensue. Without sufficient notice, it can be nearly impossible to conceptualize, fund, and implement a research project that captures the snapshot before a process is initiated, nor does it appear that governments are especially interested in devoting resources and energy to such a task. Even where a formal transitional justice process is undertaken complete with its own institutional infrastructure, the matter of self-evaluation is logically sidelined in favor of the more pressing business of fulfilling a prescribed mandate. In fact, the essentially one-shot nature of these processes—notwithstanding the ongoing elements of any transition—arguably acts as a disincentive to engage in extensive internal appraisals of whether they have yielded the intended results. To the extent that any failings cannot be readily addressed by revisiting the same terrain—for example, another truth commission, more trials—such evaluations may effectively be moot, unlike evaluations of ordinary policy measures or programs. As a result, the data required to undertake standard forms of longitudinal analysis are rarely available.

How to Compare

This discussion has already alluded to a number of methodological approaches that could be employed in cross-national studies of transitional justice processes. As always, the principal criterion in determining which comparative technique(s) to apply should be the nature of the research question, which effectively determines the requisite scale and scope of the analysis, the corresponding information requirements, and the types of insights the analysis might yield.

A defining feature of comparative research is the number of cases. "Small-N" studies usually involve no more than twenty and often just a few cases. The cases may be characterized by a few salient variables, as part of a classification scheme or to relate the cases to a general theoretical framework. For the most part, however, such studies tend to employ the qualitative ethnographic approach of "thick description" (Geertz 1973). Each case is therefore documented in considerable detail, because this level of specificity is both feasible—given the limited number of cases—and integral to the analysis. In the context of examining differences in transitional justice processes, the small-N comparative case study approach is suited to examining different institutions, sectors, or communities, whether across countries or within a single country. For example, one could contrast prosecutions undertaken by domestic authorities (e.g., Argentina) with those undertaken by international actors (e.g., the International Criminal Tribunal for the former Yugoslavia, or ICTY) and with those with both domestic and international involvement (e.g., Sierra Leone). The aim might be to evaluate the significance of these arrangements for perceptions of their legitimacy. The cases would be selected not only to reflect the institutional differences of interest but also to illustrate their impact in practice via meticulous examination of relevant historical processes.

"Large-N" studies, meanwhile, examine a minimum of several dozen cases—generally at least seventy, and, if necessary, many times that number (depending on the theoretical model and research design)—comprising either the full population or a sizable representative sample. Most of the comparisons rely on statistical analysis of quantitative data, which is necessary in order to sort through the variation among the cases. The decision of exactly how many cases to examine is at least partly driven by the desired statistical "power" of the analysis, that is, its sensitivity in detecting significant relationships among variables. The tendency is to gather considerable amounts of data—again, following a theoretical framework—though each case is not necessarily documented, analyzed, and presented in the same depth as it would be in a small-N study. The applications of such an approach to the study of transitional justice processes are apparent. As table 2.1 amply illustrates, since the 1970s political transitions have happened in dozens of countries, most of which implemented transitional justice measures that affected thousands of individuals, as well as communities and entire societies, with a stake in the handling of past violations. Each of these levels of analysis is, in principle, amenable to large-N comparative analysis. For example, one could examine how the nature of the transition influences the choice of strategies, how these decisions affect intergroup relations and political culture, and how different classes of victims, perpetrators, and ordinary citizens respond to the various features of the process.

The temporal dimension of politics can also influence the design of cross-national studies. In particular, different approaches may be appropriate depending on the stage in the timeline of transitional justice processes being examined. If, for example, the aim is to explore the negotiations on which mode(s) of transitional justice to adopt, formal models are especially suited for studying how actors with distinctive characteristics, preferences, and incentives choose among options. A standard division of labor is that the models are used to generate hypotheses about what patterns of behavior should be expected in practice, given an abstract, stylized rendering of a situation. These propositions are then tested via comparative case studies or large-N statistical analysis. Formal models can also be employed to analyze other important decisions made by actors who are central to transitional justice processes. Such decisions include when people complicit in violations will seek amnesty, which perpetrators the courts should attempt to prosecute, and what forms of reparations should be afforded to victims.

If the objective is to assess the effects of these decisions, a longitudinal research design is preferable. At the individual level, an optimal strategy is a panel survey that captures relevant information on the same set of respondents at multiple points in time. For higher levels of aggregation, the requisite resource is time-series data on various indicators of interest, capturing snapshots both before and after the implementation of relevant transitional justice measures. These data are traditionally quantitative in nature and therefore analyzed using statistical techniques. Since the choice of measures is not necessarily a random process, and the factors that affect these decisions could influence their effects as well, a two-stage analytical approach is likely required. One may again use qualitative material to frame or elucidate such quantitative analysis or may resort entirely to multiple case studies over time.

Whether or not repeated observation is feasible, surveys represent an effective means of cross-national comparison because they impose a strict, consistent protocol of questions and response sets. Experimental and quasi-experimental designs might be incorporated to assess the impact of exposures to particular "treatments," which in this setting could be different parameters of an actual or prospective transitional justice process. Where individuals lack direct personal experiences on which to base their evaluations, such approaches are necessary in gauging what their reactions would be or would have been if they were faced with specific sets of circumstances. Focus groups, participant observation, community studies, and open-ended, in-depth interviews can also be constructive, whether as independent sources of information or combined with closed-ended surveys. These methods of data collection permit the sort of descriptive depth that is characteristic of comparative case studies. In fact, the resulting data are commonly evaluated using qualitative techniques such as narrative and discourse analysis, which are also helpful in studying primary source material like media accounts, public debates, and campaign literature. At the same time, one can potentially extract quantitative measures from qualitative material—for example, by assigning codes to different themes and then counting how frequently each theme is mentioned—to bolster rich anecdotal accounts with summary evidence of patterns.

To reiterate, these various approaches can complement one another, and the choice among them is largely a function of the questions of interest and the data that are available or can be collected through primary empirical research. In addition, all the methodologies can be used both for cross-national investigations and for single-country comparisons across a given unit of analysis, such as individuals or communities.

Constraints and Solutions

Of the various concerns that can arise about conducting cross-national studies of transitional justice processes, the most prominent are the following: (1) the cases are too dissimilar to allow comparison; (2) the extent of knowledge of the cases varies, due to their number and complexity as well as to information constraints; and (3) identifying any independent effect of these processes is impossible given everything else that is taking place. While these are valid issues, they do not necessarily present insurmountable hurdles to rigorous, effective research.

The cases are too different.

The point of departure for this chapter was the contention that each transitional process has a distinctively "local" flavor and is therefore essentially unique, thus undermining any prospect of making useful comparisons of individual processes. Without a doubt, countries that face issues of transitional justice are politically, culturally, historically, and economically diverse. Moreover, there are manifest differences among the various modes of transitional justice, and no two transitional justice processes are identical in every respect. Does this variation preclude all efforts to generalize about, or develop comprehensive accounts of, the initiation and implementation of these processes and their impact? Not necessarily. The observable differences need not imply that the cases are altogether incomparable. Instead, a plausible assumption is that at least some similarities exist, that not all differences are ultimately consequential, and that the remaining distinctions could account for the distribution of outcomes across the population of cases.

In grappling with such matters, Adam Przeworski and Henry Teune's (1970) seminal work *The Logic of Comparative Social Inquiry* is particularly instructive. Echoing notions originally put forth by John Stuart Mill, Przeworski and Teune describe two primary techniques of comparative analysis. The first entails studying "most similar" cases—those that resemble each other with the exception of one specific aspect. By keeping constant all other attributes, this approach isolates the impact of the lone difference. Any divergent outcomes can then be attributed to this single factor. The second involves studying "most different" cases—those that are dissimilar but for a single common feature. If the cases exhibit equivalent outcomes, all other factors lack explanatory force. In practice, though, comparative case studies merely approximate one or the other of these archetypes. Large-N studies effectively occupy a middle ground in that they can accommodate diversity among a set of cases in both features and outcomes and potentially establish how these two sets of variables are associated.

The fundamental lesson to be applied here is that variation alone is not grounds for writing off cross-national analysis of transitional justice processes. Instead, the diverse composition of these cases may actually be desirable, since it may demonstrate that particular factors are consequential in multiple settings, or perhaps even of generic significance. Even among the clusters of countries that have employed exactly the same mode of transitional justice, there are certain prominent discrepancies to evaluate. Meanwhile, countries with ostensibly divergent approaches may nonetheless follow similar trajectories; the goal of the comparative analysis here could be to identify one or more key characteristics they have in common. Admittedly, such efforts to match or distinguish cases are complicated by the fact that countries typically exhibit amalgams of multiple modes of transitional justice. The consequences of these amalgams cannot be fully appreciated unless the sample of cases includes instances of each. Here again, the diversity of the cases is beneficial, since it enables the evaluation of these different approaches as well as other contextual factors.

Regardless of the number and variety of cases, the best analyses are always constructed around solid theoretical and conceptual frameworks. The starting point should be an explicit hypothesis—for example, "greater impunity results in a higher incidence of political violence." One must then identify appropriate variables, establish schemes for grading or categorizing the individual cases, and find common metrics that capture differences in the outcomes the cases exhibit. With individual-level studies, translation of terms also becomes a major issue, since different languages correspond only imperfectly and some concepts may be intelligible in one context but incomprehensible in another. For this reason, King et al. (2003) propose incorporating "anchoring vignettes" as a means of improving cross-cultural comparability.

While the hope of cross-national analysis is to identify clear patterns and universal relationships, the likelihood is that actual findings will not neatly fit all the cases. Some will deviate from expectations; a few may even be obvious outliers. These sorts of results do not undermine the value of the comparative method, especially in this context. Transitions are highly contingent events and, thus, difficult to model with complete precision. Nevertheless, there is a realistic prospect of developing insights about transitional justice processes that are generally consistent with the range of experiences across countries (or across other units of analysis).

Not enough is known about some of the cases, and there are too many cases to know them all well.

Especially when conducting cross-national research, one encounters numerous problems relating to the availability and quality of information. Certain transitional justice processes—Argentina, Chile, and South Africa in particular—are well documented in publications by governmental authorities, international bodies, and independent observers and analysts. Others remain obscure or are marginalized because they do not appear to fit the mold or were delayed, disrupted, or left incomplete.

This information asymmetry has repercussions for the conduct and interpretation of cross-national analyses on transitional justice processes. The most obvious effect is bias in favor of studying particular countries and regions. In the likely event that these cases are unrepresentative of the actual or potential population of transition processes, this self-perpetuating pattern constitutes a significant limitation, since the resulting findings do not necessarily have wide application. This issue is magnified given recent events in countries such as Afghanistan, Ghana, Iraq, Nigeria, and Timor-Leste, which exhibit characteristics that lack adequate parallels in, for example, Latin America (e.g., recent independence, ethnic heterogeneity, low standards of living, Islam). As a result, it makes sense to juxtapose these cases with other, more analogous but less mainstream cases from Africa or Asia. Failing this, the recent processes—some of which are better publicized and more easily documented—can conceivably become resources for future comparisons. Meanwhile, although the stock of information about the well-documented cases should provide a foundation for more extensive and in-depth scrutiny, the ease of locating details about these transitional justice processes—and the state of accumulated wisdom about them—may have the opposite effect, discouraging fresh empirical research and ongoing reevaluation. Thus, there is a risk of recycling standard arguments and existing conclusions and of compiling comparative studies that are superficial or insufficiently grounded.

These concerns can be mitigated by exercising greater care in study design, incorporating a wider set of cases, devoting increased resources to original data collection, and collaborating consistently with country specialists. Thankfully, new technologies and international scholarly and advocacy networks have helped reduce the gaps of awareness across countries and regions (and academic and professional disciplines). Nevertheless, there are still immense reservoirs of "local knowledge" that have not entered the broader public domain. Rather than accepting this circumstance as inevitable, comparative analyses must seek to bridge these divides, aggregate relevant empirical data, and reveal whatever similarities and differences are found.

Too much else is happening for a transitional justice process to have a real impact.

Another monumental issue is whether it is even reasonable to attribute effects to specific policies or institutional measures that are implemented during a wave of major political and social changes. This is not to say that transitional justice processes are trivial or meaningless. Rather, the challenge is that their impact can be difficult to ascertain or quantify, because it may be highly collinear with other factors, contingent on precise constellations of circumstances, modified by numerous intervening variables, and subject to complex interaction effects. These concerns are magnified because many formal processes are onetime events of relatively short duration—generally a few years at most. Reparations programs may extend over a longer time frame, as in Chile, and the prosecutions conducted by the ICTY and the International Criminal Tribunal for Rwanda (ICTR) are still ongoing a decade after they began; however, these are the exceptions. The quick bursts of activity on the transitional justice front could possibly cause an adjustment of attitudes, incentives, relationships, and practices, at least in the short term. Yet it is debatable whether such effects will be sustained over the longer term in the absence of other initiatives—for example, institutional transformation or wholesale changes in elites—that bring about lasting changes to the political landscape.

This speaks to the need for realistic conceptions of the outcomes that one expects to observe. Some effects are clearly more plausible than others, such as when there is a direct connection or exposure to the process itself. Consider as an example the public hearings of a truth commission. For individual victims, the experience of testifying is presumably a direct, tangible experience that would tend to influence their sentiments about their suffering, the perpetrator, and other matters. In theory, certain other participants and observers—especially those who commiserate or can identify with the victims—could also be deeply affected. The rest of the population, however, might register nothing more than a cursory, temporary reaction. Whether substantial changes in public opinion or social norms will ever be observed is therefore uncertain.

The fact that transitional justice processes can have varied and uneven results is not a justification for forgoing comparative research; rather, such considerations should be reflected in both theoretical frameworks and study designs. Particular effort should be devoted to establishing clear causal links among variables that are amenable to analysis. For instance, there is a reasonable prospect of identifying specific immediate effects that could presage broader, sustained changes, even if the latter cannot be directly measured.

Prior Research

Over the years, the transitional justice literature has been principally the province of legal scholars, human rights activists, and individuals who have served as judges, prosecutors, commissioners, or policymakers or in other related official capacities. Until recently, contributions from social scientists were relatively infrequent. The result has been an emphasis on the moral-philosophical and jurisprudential aspects of these processes, as well as on broad issues of institutional design and implementation. From this work, one can potentially extract analytical issues, lists of factors, classification schemes, typologies, and other building blocks that are relevant to cross-national comparisons. Yet the authors do not generally seek to conduct structured studies of particular hypotheses, based on primary empirical research. Instead, much of the published material adopts a theoretical or prescriptive orientation or else is largely descriptive in nature.

The more analytical inquiries tend to highlight the experiences of single countries, even if other cases are mentioned in passing or implicit as a backdrop to the discussion. These in-depth case studies are often revealing and represent a vital source of basic information on individual processes. Of note, some single-country studies even engage in comparisons at different levels of analysis, including individuals (Gibson and Gouws 1999, 2003; Gibson 2002; Sonis et al. 2002; David and Choi 2003; Backer 2004), communities (van der Merwe 1999; Backer 2004), and racial groups (Gibson and Gouws 1999, 2003; Gibson 2002, 2003, 2004a, 2004b). Again, however, such research does not necessarily afford a basis for detecting or validating general patterns that may be attributable to the different modes of transitional justice or to the ways in which these measures have been implemented. For this purpose, comparative data are best suited to offer clear, credible insights.

The roster of cross-national analyses of transitional justice processes has been rapidly expanding and shows clear signs of progressing beyond the theoretical and descriptive orientations of earlier literature on the subject. Appendix table A2.2 summarizes nearly seventy empirical studies that have compared countries' experiences during the past several decades. This inventory suggests a growing acceptance of the necessity of empirical research on transitional justice and the relevance of cross-national analysis to that agenda. The investigations range in scope from pairs of countries to the occasional large-N analysis; taken together, they cover a large majority of the relevant countries. Qualitative approaches, especially historical institutional analyses and other comparative case studies, predominate, but applications of quantitative methodologies have emerged in recent literature. The most popular subjects are the design and implementation of transitional justice measures, although some contributions seek to compare their impact on outcomes such as accountability, truth, justice, forgiveness, reconciliation, memory, norms, and democratic consolidation. The efforts to link the domain of transitional justice to broader political and social phenomena, including long-term paths of development, have also enriched the literature with explicit and sophisticated theoretical frameworks and with tests of corresponding hypotheses—elements clearly lacking in earlier writings. As a result, the many normative discussions of different options are now balanced by an evolving collection of insights drawn from rigorous assessment of actual experiences around the world.

The summary also reveals several shortcomings in this segment of the literature. First, many of the cross-national studies limit their attention to clusters of cases from a single region—Latin America and Eastern Europe are the most popular. Other than the analyses that address the ICTR and ICTY, the extent of cross-regional comparison is nearly always confined to including at most a few of the best-known examples (e.g., Argentina, Chile, El Salvador, Guatemala, South Africa, Timor-Leste), alongside the other cases. A regional sample does tend to ensure a greater level of homogeneity in political legacies, cultures, levels of development, and other circumstances and attributes. Since such similarities effectively control for factors that could exert an influence, this design improves analytical precision. Without a representative sample of cases, however, the trade-off is that the results cannot readily be generalized to countries in other regions.

Second, many of these same studies concentrate on a single mode of transitional justice; in particular, comparisons of truth commissions have emerged as a fashionable subject. The narrow focus may reflect the first limitation, since the regions exhibit some tendencies in the approaches that are most often favored—for example, lustration policies were prevalent in Eastern Europe. Yet this research effectively overlooks the composite nature of transitional justice processes, which means that many cases have at least one mode in common, even if they are not identical in all respects. Given these similarities as well as the shared circumstance of facing a fundamental issue of addressing past violations, there seem to be strong substantive and methodological justifications for extending cross-national analysis to encompass the full spectrum of modes of transitional justice. In particular, such systematic comparisons should provide a better gauge of the relative impact of different modes and combinations.

Third, few studies are devoted to examining the nature of microlevel engagement in, and responses to, these processes. Instead, there is more focus on (a) institutional design and implementation and the underlying policymaking process; (b) macrolevel properties such as regime stability and democratic consolidation; and, to a lesser extent, (c) cultural phenomena such as social discourses and national narratives. This imbalance is curious, if not ironic. After all, many of the debates on how to address the issue of accountability revolve around a fundamental tension between showing appropriate consideration for the victims who suffered and properly acknowledging the threat of resistance by perpetrators (along with a host of other practical and ethical issues). Primary research on the attitudes and behaviors of both categories of individuals should give some indication of how well particular modes or processes have reconciled these inherent tensions. To emphasize, the point is not to shift all efforts to individual-level research. Instead, there is room for research with different perspectives, and integrated multilevel analyses could prove especially illuminating. More studies should also compare how transitional justice plays out at the subnational level, especially across communities and administrative units, as well as between urban and rural areas.

Fourth, although detailed histories of transitional justice processes are quite abundant, longitudinal studies of their impact are rare. In fact, little of the cross-national analysis involves ongoing observation, repeated measures (such as the Reconciliation Barometer, devised by the Institute for Justice and Reconciliation to measure public sentiment on issues of racial tolerance in South Africa), or multiple waves of data collection. Rather, it generally reflects research conducted at a particular point in time—either while these processes are under way or within a few years after their completion—supplemented with some historical information. As a result, the literature offers at best an incomplete sense of the dynamic effects of different types of processes over both the short and long term. Greater emphasis on these dimensions would likely entail increased application of quantitative methods, to more accurately assess differences across countries in outcomes such as patterns of governance and the evolution of attitudes.

Conclusions and Recommendations

This chapter suggests several useful contributions from cross-national comparative analysis of transitional justice processes. The first is the compilation of richer and more precise accounts of the experiences in each country. By (re)examining cases in a comparative perspective, one can better appreciate the principal issues, political constraints, potential courses of action, expectations of various stakeholders, and significance of the decisions that were made. This deeper understanding has the related benefit of honing retrospective evaluations of the transitional justice measures employed in each setting. Whether particular efforts ought to be characterized as intelligent or misguided is most evident when one has a baseline of evaluation, namely, other countries that have tackled a similar situation.

Likewise, comparative analysis, across as well as within countries, affords an ideal means for assessing the impact of these processes at various levels of political society. Different strategies can have distinct effects. The wealth of empirical evidence from countries around the world supplies the data needed to investigate whether direct relationships exist in practice, as well as the extent to which these associations constitute general patterns that can be anticipated elsewhere in the future. Transitional justice processes also provide a revealing look at political dynamics in transitional settings. In theory, one can extrapolate from this domain and make reasonable inferences about key aspects of the political system, such as institutional capacity and the relationship between government and civil society.

All this information should help to enlighten best practice in the area of transitional justice. A natural by-product of comparing cases is an improved sense of how policies have evolved over time due to the diffusion of ideas, learning by example, the circulation of professionals, and the transmission of expertise. Tracking this progression is not merely a historical exercise; rather, part of the purpose can be to isolate improvements and mistakes and understand their genesis. Knowing more about the available strategies, their applications, key hurdles, and the potential successes and failings facilitates the selection and implementation of policies in future cases.

Despite a vast and ever-expanding literature, further bolstered by the 2007 launch of the *International Journal of Transitional Justice*, considerable scope remains for comparative research. Most often, the "most similar" systems approach prevails, and analysis is limited to several cases. Relatively few studies span different regions of the world or types of processes, much less examine a large sample of cases, if not the entire population of post-conflict transitions. A major hurdle to undertaking such broader, complex comparative studies has been insufficient information, especially if the goal is to conduct a systematic analysis, ensure adequate equivalency in the details and documentation pertaining to each case, or include less known cases. This problem is not for lack of effort. Over the past two decades, substantial energy has been devoted to documenting the steps undertaken in various countries and making associated primary materials more widely accessible. In this regard, the following merit special recognition:

- Hayner (1994, 2001), whose two works are widely cited as the best compilations on truth commissions;
- Kritz (1995) and the online archives of the United States Institute of Peace, which are significant collections that merge secondary literature with extensive primary source material;
- The American Association for the Advancement of Science, which has published online and translated versions of truth commission reports and other related material, in addition to developing and analyzing large-scale databases for numerous commissions;
- The UN Office for the Coordination of Humanitarian Affairs, which has posted profiles of fifty-nine transitional justice measures in forty-one countries;
- The Centre for the Study of Violence and Reconciliation, which has posted overviews of truth commissions and other transitional justice processes in fifty-two countries (http://www.justiceinperspective.org.za);
- Trial Watch, which is an online database of nearly six hundred war crimes prosecutions; and
- The International Center for Transitional Justice (ICTJ), which was founded in 2001 and quickly emerged as a prominent clearinghouse and policy adviser, capitalizing on its international staff's expertise and research capacity.

The collective efforts of these and other individuals and organizations have established a reasonably rich stock of knowledge. Yet, unlike many topics of comparative significance (e.g., political regimes, democratic transitions, conflict processes, human rights practices, minority groups), the field of transitional justice lacks an essential resource: a publicly accessible, reliable, consistent, comprehensive, and up-to-date inventory of measures employed around the world.

Thus an initial recommendation is to fill this gap by gathering, organizing, and distilling pertinent information into a database of country profiles, according to a standard protocol:

- A political chronology. Relevant details include the tenure of the previous regime; when the transition took place; and the timing of post-transition elections (initial and subsequent), institutional changes (constitutional reform, restructuring, and so on) and any reversion to authoritarian rule or reignition of armed conflict.
- The type of former regime. One possible classification scheme distinguishes among authoritarian regimes based on whether political authority is held by the military, a single party, a personalistic ruler, or a racial oligarchy (Huntington 1991).
- The form of transition. Huntington (1991) also differentiates transitions based on whether they occurred through external intervention, forcible replacement by an indigenous opposition, top-down transformation via reforms by the previous regime, or transplacement via a negotiated pact between the incumbents and the opposition.
- The program of transitional justice. As suggested earlier, it would be helpful to have a list of the approaches and their timeline of implementation, as well as other features such as the extent of public input, the source of personnel and financing, and the ultimate work product.

In addition to the material discussed above, the construction of these profiles could rely on a variety of primary sources (trial transcripts, truth commission reports, constitutions, legislation) and secondary sources (academic literature, political almanacs, media stories, NGO studies), which are plentiful and readily available for at least the majority of cases. These profiles could then be converted into a form suitable for analysis, perhaps after being merged with relevant information from existing comparative data sets.

As it happens, a team of researchers at the University of Wisconsin-Madison, under the direction of Leigh Payne (now of Oxford University), spent the past several years assembling the Transitional Justice Data Base. This project, which was launched after I submitted the initial manuscript of this book chapter in February 2004, relies significantly on a previous iteration of the information presented in the earlier tables and executes some of the suggestions I made immediately above. Around 2005, a team at the International Peace Research Institute's (PRIO) Center for the Study of Civil War, headed by Scott Gates, separately augmented the Uppsala-PRIO armed conflict data set with details on transitional justice measures.

Another significant shortcoming of the transitional justice literature has been insufficient cross-national analysis at the microlevel. The apparent preoccupation with institutional design and system-level effects has arguably resulted in too little concern for assessing the extent to which these processes affect people. The current wisdom on how different modes of transitional justice influence the attitudes and behaviors of individuals and communities is based primarily on rough assumptions and anecdotal evidence. This circumstance has at least two undesirable consequences. One is an excess of written material that is subjective and ideological: The authors advocate particular viewpoints and policies without ever justifying their stances based on sound empirical findings. Another is a lack of consensus, if not outright disagreement, about certain fundamental realities of transitional justice. Different contributors can express antithetical perspectives on the same process and offer contrary intuitions about matters as basic as how victims and perpetrators will perceive a given measure in a particular context. These debates are best resolved by primary empirical data, and cross-national analysis affords the greatest scope for rigorously establishing clear links and general patterns.

A second recommendation, therefore, is greater emphasis on comparative behavioral studies of the selection and impact of transitional justice processes. Admittedly, cross-national studies of this sort are difficult to conduct, for financial, administrative, and technical reasons. A potential solution might be greater collaboration among researchers from different countries and regions, whether by implementing studies simultaneously in multiple settings or by extending previous analyses to new settings. A good example of this approach is the West Africa Transitional Justice Project, which I initiated in 2006 to examine victims' responses to the processes undertaken in Ghana, Liberia, Nigeria, and Sierra Leone, building on past work that my colleagues and I conducted in Rwanda, South Africa, Uganda, and the former Yugoslavia. Initiatives such as the conference on which this book is based are helping build the contacts and lay the foundations for international networks that can enable and sustain more of these constructive partnerships. As a result, the next generation of research will hopefully afford better insight, based on careful theorization and rigorous comparative analysis, into the significance of transitional justice processes.

References

Ambrose, Brendalyn. 1995. *Democratization and the Protection of Human Rights in Africa: Problems and Prospects*. Westport, Conn.: Praeger.

Andrews, Molly. 2003. "Grand National Narratives and the Project of Truth Commissions: A Comparative Analysis." *Media, Culture and Society* 25 (1): 45–65.

Aspen Institute. 1989. *State Crimes: Punishment or Pardon?* Aspen, Colo.: Justice and Society Program of the Aspen Institute.

Backer, David. 1997. "Appraising the Past amid Political Transitions." Master's thesis, University of Michigan.

———. 2003. "Civil Society and Transitional Justice: Possibilities, Patterns and Prospects." *Journal of Human Rights* 2 (3): 297–313.

———. 2004. "The Human Face of Justice: Victims' Responses to the Truth and Reconciliation Commission Process in South Africa." PhD diss., University of Michigan.

Barahona De Brito, Alexandra. 1993. "Truth and Justice in the Consolidation of Democracy in Chile and Uruguay." *Comparative Politics* 46 (4): 579–93.

———. 1997. *Human Rights and Democratization in Latin America.* Oxford, UK: Oxford University Press.

Barahona de Brito, Alexandra, Carmen González Enríquez, and Paloma Aguilar, eds. 2001. *The Politics of Memory and Democratization.* Oxford, UK: Oxford University Press.

Bates, Robert, Avner Grief, Margaret Levi, Jean-Laurent Rosenthal, and Barry Weingast. 1998. *Analytic Narratives.* Princeton, N.J.: Princeton University Press.

Benedetti, Fanny. 1996. "Haiti's Truth and Justice Commission." *Human Rights Brief* 3 (3): 4–5.

Benomar, Jamal. 1993. "Justice after Transition." *Journal of Democracy* 4 (3): 3–14.

Bilbija, Ksenija, Jo Ellen Fair, Cynthia Milton, and Leigh Payne, eds. 2005. *The Art of Truth-Telling about Authoritarian Rule.* Madison: University of Wisconsin Press.

Boed, Roman. 1998. "An Evaluation of the Legality and Efficacy of Lustration as a Tool of Transitional Justice." *Columbia Journal of Transnational Law* 37 (2): 357–402.

Boraine, Alex, Janet Levy, and Ronel Scheffer, eds. 1994. *Dealing with the Past: Truth and Reconciliation in South Africa.* Cape Town: IDASA.

Borneman, John. 1997. *Settling Accounts: Violence, Justice, and Accountability in Post-Socialist Europe.* Princeton, N.J.: Princeton University Press.

Botha, Belinda. 1998. "Truth Commissions and Their Consequences for Legitimacy." PhD diss., University of Houston.

Brahm, Eric. 2005. "Patterns of Truth: Examining Truth Commission Impact in Cross-National Conflict." Paper presented at the Annual Convention of the International Studies Association, Honolulu.

Brahm, Eric, Geoff Dancy, and Hunjoon Kim. 2008. "What Is a Truth Commission and How Can We Understand It?" Paper presented at the Annual Convention of the International Studies Association, San Francisco.

Buford, Warren, and Hugo van der Merwe. 2003. "Reparations in Southern Africa." Paper presented at the Southern Africa Reconciliation Project Workshop, Johannesburg.

Calhoun, Noel. 2004. *Dilemmas of Justice in Eastern Europe's Democratic Transitions.* New York: Palgrave Macmillan.

Cardenas, Sonia. 2001. "Adaptive States: The Proliferation of National Human Rights Institutions." Working paper, Carr Center for Human Rights Policy, Harvard University.

Cassel, Douglas. 2006. "The Expanding Scope and Impact of Reparations Awarded by the Inter-American Court of Human Rights." In *Out of the Ashes: Reparations for*

Gross Violations of Human Rights, ed. Marc Bossuyt, Paul Lemmens, Koen de Feyter, and Stephan Parmentier. Antwerp: Intersentia.

Chapman, Audrey, and Patrick Ball. 2001. "The Truth of Truth Commissions: Comparative Lessons from Haiti, South Africa, and Guatemala." *Human Rights Quarterly* 23 (1): 1–43.

Cohen, Stanley. 1995. "State Crimes of Previous Regimes: Knowledge, Accountability, and the Policing of the Past." *Law and Social Inquiry* 20 (1): 7–50.

Crocker, David. 2000. "Truth Commissions, Transitional Justice, and Civil Society." In *Truth v. Justice: The Formal Efficacy of Truth Commissions—South Africa and Beyond,* ed. Robert Rotberg and Dennis Thompson. Princeton, N.J.: Princeton University Press.

Dahill-Brown, Sara, Courtney Hillebrecht, Tricia Olsen, Leigh Payne, and Andrew Reiter. 2007. "International Influences on Domestic Decisions of Transitional Justice." Paper presented at the Annual Meeting of the Midwest Political Science Association, Chicago.

David, Roman. 2003. "Lustration Laws in Action: The Motives and the Evaluation of the Lustration Policy in the Czech Republic and Poland." *Law and Social Inquiry* 28 (2): 387–439.

———. 2006a. "In Exchange for Truth: The Polish Lustrations and the South African Amnesty Process." *Politikon: South African Journal of Political Studies* 33 (1): 81–99.

———. 2006b. "From Prague to Baghdad: Lustration Systems and Their Political Effects." *Government and Opposition* 41 (3): 347–72.

David, Roman, and Susanne Choi. 2003. "Money, Truth, and Forgiveness: The Reparation of the Victims of Communism in the Czech Republic." Paper presented at the Nineteenth World Congress of the International Political Science Association, Durban.

Diamond, Larry. 1997. *Consolidating the Third Wave Democracies.* Baltimore, Md.: Johns Hopkins University Press.

———, ed. 1999. *Developing Democracy: Towards Consolidation.* Baltimore, Md.: Johns Hopkins University Press.

Diamond, Larry, and Leonardo Morlino, eds. 2005. *Assessing the Quality of Democracy.* Baltimore, Md.: Johns Hopkins University Press.

Duggan, Colleen, Claudia Paz y Paz Bailey, and Julie Guillerot. 2008. "Reparations for Sexual and Reproductive Violence: Prospects for Achieving Gender Justice in Guatemala and Peru." *International Journal of Transitional Justice* 2 (2): 192–213.

Elster, Jon. 2004. *Closing the Books: Transitional Justice in Historical Perspective.* Cambridge, UK: Cambridge University Press.

———. 2006. *Retribution and Reparation in the Transition to Democracy.* Cambridge, UK: Cambridge University Press.

Ensalaco, Mark. 1994. "Truth Commissions for Chile and El Salvador: A Report and Assessment." *Human Rights Quarterly* 16 (4): 656–75.

Espinoza Cuevas, Victor, María Luisa Ortiz Rojas, and Paz Rojas Baeza. 2002. *Truth Commissions: An Uncertain Path?* Geneva: Association for the Prevention of Torture.

Garrett, Stephen. 2000. "Models of Transitional Justice—A Comparative Analysis." Paper presented at the Annual Convention of the International Studies Association, Los Angeles.

Geertz, Clifford. 1973. *The Interpretation of Cultures.* New York: Basic Books.

Gibson, James. 2002. "Truth, Justice, and Reconciliation: Judging the Fairness of Amnesty in South Africa." *American Journal of Political Science* 46 (4): 540–56.

———. 2003. "The Legacy of Apartheid: Racial Differences in the Legitimacy of Democratic Institutions and Processes in the New South Africa." *Comparative Political Studies* 36 (7): 772–800.

———. 2004a. *Overcoming Apartheid: Can Truth Reconcile a Divided Nation?* New York: Russell Sage Foundation.

———. 2004b. "Does Truth Lead to Reconciliation? Testing the Causal Assumptions of the South African Truth and Reconciliation Process." *American Journal of Political Science* 48 (2): 201–17.

Gibson, James, and Amanda Gouws. 1999. "Truth and Reconciliation in South Africa: Attributions of Blame and the Struggle over Apartheid." *American Political Science Review* 93 (3): 501–17.

———. 2003. *Overcoming Intolerance in South Africa: Experiments in Democratic Persuasion.* Cape Town: Cambridge University Press.

Graybill, Lyn, and Kimberly Lanegran. 2004. "Truth, Justice and Reconciliation in Africa: Issues and Cases." *African Studies Quarterly* 8 (1): 1–18.

Grodsky, Brian. 2006. "Exploring Determinants of Transitional Justice: Human Rights Accountability in Post-Communist States." PhD diss., University of Michigan.

Hamber, Brandon, ed. 1998. *Past Imperfect: Dealing with the Past in Northern Ireland and Societies in Transition.* Derry, Northern Ireland, UK: INCORE.

Hayner, Priscilla. 1994. "Fifteen Truth Commissions—1974 to 1994: A Comparative Study." *Human Rights Quarterly* 16 (4): 597–655.

———. 2001. *Unspeakable Truths: Confronting State Terror and Atrocity.* New York and London: Routledge.

Herz, John, ed. 1982. *From Dictatorship to Democracy: Coping with the Legacies of Authoritarianism and Totalitarianism.* Westport, Conn.: Greenwood Press.

Hesse, Carla, and Robert Post, eds. 1999. *Human Rights in Political Transitions: Gettysburg to Bosnia.* New York: Zone Books.

Humphrey, Michael, and Estela Valverde. 2008. "Human Rights Politics and Injustice: Transitional Justice in Argentina and South Africa." *International Journal of Transitional Justice* 2 (1): 83–105.

Huntington, Samuel. 1991. *The Third Wave: Democratization in the Late Twentieth Century.* Norman, Okla.: University of Oklahoma Press.

Huyse, Luc. 1995. "Justice after Transitions: On the Choices Successor Elites Make in Dealing with the Past." *Law and Social Inquiry* 20 (1): 51–78.

IAHCR. 2008. "Jurisprudencia: Casos contenciosos," www.corteidh.or.cr/casos.cfm (accessed August 14, 2008).

Jelin, Elizabeth. 2007. "Public Memorialization in Perspective: Truth, Justice and Memory of Past Repression in the Southern Cone of South America." *International Journal of Transitional Justice* 1 (2): 138–56.

Kaye, Mike. 1997. "The Role of Truth Commissions in the Search for Justice, Reconciliation and Democratisation: The Salvadorean and Honduran Cases." *Journal of Latin American Studies* 29 (3): 693–716.

Kenney, Charles, and Dean Spears. 2005. "Truth and Consequences: Do Truth Commissions Promote Democratization?" Paper presented at the Annual Meeting of the American Political Science Association, Washington, D.C.

Kerr, Rachel, with Erin Mobekk. 2008. *Peace and Justice: Seeking Accountability After War.* Cambridge, UK: Polity Press.

Kim, Hunjoon. 2005. "Expansion of Truth Commissions: Comparative Analysis of 84 Countries between 1974 and 2002." Paper presented at the Annual Meeting of the Midwest Political Science Association, Chicago.

King, Gary, Christopher Murray, Joshua Salomon, and Ajay Tandon. 2003. "Enhancing the Validity and Cross-Cultural Comparability of Survey Research." *American Political Science Review* 97 (4): 567–83.

Kritz, Neil, ed. 1995. *Transitional Justice: How Emerging Democracies Reckon with Former Regimes.* Washington, D.C.: United States Institute of Peace Press.

Lambourne, Wendy. 2002. "Justice and Reconciliation and Post-Conflict Peacebuilding in Cambodia and Rwanda." PhD diss., University of Sydney.

Lanegran, Kimberly. 2005. "Truth Commissions, Human Rights Trials and the Politics of Memory." *Comparative Studies of South Asia, Africa and the Middle East* 25 (1): 111–21.

Levitsky, Steven, and Lucan Way. 2002. "The Rise of Competitive Authoritarianism." *Journal of Democracy* 13 (2): 51–65.

Lie, Tove, Helga Binningsbø, and Scott Gates. 2006. "Post-Conflict Justice and Sustainable Peace." Paper presented at the Annual Meeting of the American Political Science Association, Philadelphia.

Los, Maria. 1995. "Lustration and Truth Claims: Unfinished Revolutions in Central Europe." *Law and Social Inquiry* 20 (1): 117–162.

Lutz, Ellen, and Kathryn Sikkink. 2001. "The Justice Cascade: The Evolution and Impact of Foreign Human Rights Trials in Latin America." *Chicago Journal of International Law* 2 (1): 1–34.

McAdams, A. James, ed. 1997. *Transitional Justice and the Rule of Law in New Democracies.* Notre Dame, Ind.: University of Notre Dame Press.

McFaul, Michael. 2002. "The Fourth Wave of Democracy and Dictatorship: Noncooperative Transitions in the Postcommunist World." *World Politics* 54 (2): 212–44.

Mayer-Rieckh, Alexander, and Pablo de Greiff, eds. 2007. *Justice as Prevention: Vetting Public Employees in Transitional Societies.* New York: Social Science Research Council.

Minow, Martha. 1998. *Between Vengeance and Forgiveness: Facing History after Genocide and Mass Violence.* Boston: Beacon Press.

Nalepa, Monika. 2000. "Why Are Communists Penalized? Models of Coming to Terms with the Past." Unpublished manuscript, Department of Political Science, Columbia University.

———. 2003. "Punish All Guilty or Protect the Innocent? Designing Institutions of Transitional Justice." Paper presented at the Annual Meeting of the Midwest Political Science Association, Chicago.

———. 2005. "Explaining and Designing Truth Revelation Procedures." PhD diss., Columbia University.

Nowak, Manfred. 2006. "Reparation by the Human Rights Chamber for Bosnia and Herzegovina." *In Out of the Ashes: Reparations for Gross Violations of Human Rights,* ed. Marc Bossuyt, Paul Lemmens, Koen de Feyter, and Stephan Parmentier. Antwerp: Intersentia.

Olsen, Tricia, Sara Dahill-Brown, Courtney Hillebrecht, Leigh Payne, and Andrew Reiter. 2008. "Justice from the Outside In: International Organizations and Transitional Justice." Paper presented at the Annual Convention of the International Studies Association, San Francisco.

Pankhurst, Donna. 1999. "Issues of Justice and Reconciliation in Complex Political Emergencies: Reconceptualizing Justice, Reconciliation and Peace." *Third World Quarterly* 20 (1): 239–55.

Peskin, Victor. 2005a. "Trials and Tribulations: International Criminal Tribunals and the Politics of State Cooperation." PhD diss., University of California, Berkeley.

————. 2005b. "Beyond Victor's Justice? The Challenge of Prosecuting the Winners at the International Criminal Tribunals for the Former Yugoslavia and Rwanda." *Journal of Human Rights* 4 (2): 213–31.

Pion-Berlin, David. 1993. "To Prosecute or Pardon? Human Rights Decisions in the Latin American Southern Cone." *Human Rights Quarterly* 16 (1): 105–30.

Popkin, Margaret, and Nehal Bhuta. 1999. "Latin American Amnesties in Comparative Perspective: Can the Past Be Buried?" *Ethics and International Affairs* 13: 99–122.

Popkin, Margaret, and Naomi Roht-Arriaza. 1995. "Truth as Justice: Investigatory Commissions in Latin America." *Law and Social Inquiry* 20 (1): 79–116.

Posner, Eric, and Adrian Vermeule. 2004. "Transitional Justice as Ordinary Justice." *Harvard Law Review* 117 (3): 761–825.

Przeworski, Adam, and Henry Teune. 1970. *The Logic of Comparative Social Inquiry.* New York: John Wiley and Sons.

Quinn, Joanna. 2003. "The Politics of Acknowledgement: Truth Commissions in Uganda and Haiti." PhD diss., McMaster University.

Quinn, Joanna, and Mark Freeman. 2003. "Lessons Learned: Practical Lessons Gleaned from Inside the Truth Commissions of Guatemala and South Africa." *Human Rights Quarterly* 25 (4): 1117–49.

Reif, Linda. 2000. "Building Democratic Institutions: The Role of National Human Rights Institutions in Good Governance and Human Rights Protection." *Harvard Human Rights Journal* 13 (Spring): 1–69.

Roht-Arriaza, Naomi. 2005. *The Pinochet Effect: Transnational Justice in the Age of Human Rights.* Philadelphia: University of Pennsylvania Press.

Rosenberg, Tina. 1995. *The Haunted Land: Facing Europe's Ghosts after Communism.* New York: Random House.

Ross, Amy. 1999. "The Body of the Truth: Truth Commissions in Guatemala and South Africa." PhD diss., University of California, Berkeley.

Rubio-Marín, Ruth. 2007. *What Happened to the Women? Gender and Reparations for Human Rights Violations.* New York: Social Science Research Council.

Rwelamira, Medard, and Gerhard Werle. 1996. *Confronting Past Injustices: Approaches to Amnesty, Punishment, Reparation, and Restitution in South Africa and Germany.* Durban: Butterworths.

Schabas, William, and Shane Darcy, eds. 2005. *Truth Commissions and Courts: The Tension between Criminal Justice and the Search for Truth.* New York: Springer-Verlad.

Segovia, Alex. 2007. "The Reparations Proposals of the Truth Commissions in El Salvador and Haiti: A History of Non-Compliance." In *Justice as Prevention: Vetting Public Employees in Transitional Societies,* ed. Alexander Mayer-Rieckh and Pablo de Greiff. New York: Social Science Research Council.

Sieff, Michelle, and Leslie Vinjamuri Wright. 1999. "Reconciling Order and Justice? New Institutional Solutions in Post-Conflict States." *Journal of International Affairs* 52 (2): 757–79.

Sikkink, Kathryn, and Carrie Booth Walling. 2005. "Errors about Trials: The Political Reality of the Justice Cascade and Its Impact." Paper presented at the Annual Meeting of the American Political Science Association, Washington, D.C.

Skaar, Elin. 1999. "Truth Commissions, Trials, or Nothing? Policy Options in Democratic Transitions." *Third World Quarterly* 20 (6): 1109–28.

Skaar, Elin, Astrik Suhrke, and Siri Gloppen, eds. 2005. *Roads to Reconciliation.* Lanham, Md.: Rowman and Littlefield.

Smith, Kathleen. 1995a. "Decommunization after the 'Velvet Revolutions' in East Central Europe." In *Impunity and Human Rights in International Law and Practice,* ed. Naomi Roht-Arriaza. New York: Oxford University Press.

———. 1995b. "Destalinization in the Former Soviet Union." In *Impunity and Human Rights in International Law and Practice,* ed. Naomi Roht-Arriaza. New York: Oxford University Press.

Snyder, James, and Leslie Vinjamuri. 2003. "Trials and Errors: Principle and Pragmatism in Strategies of International Justice." *International Security* 28 (3): 5–44.

Sonis, Jeffrey, Hugo van der Merwe, Cyril Adonis, David Backer, and Hlaha Masitha. 2002. "Forgiveness among Victims of Political Violence: Evidence from South Africa's Truth and Reconciliation Process." Paper presented at the American Psychological Association Convention, Chicago.

Sriram, Chandra Lekha. 2004. *Confronting Past Human Rights Violations: Justice vs. Peace in Times of Transition.* London: Taylor and Francis.

Sriram, Chandra Lekha, and Amy Ross. 2007. "Geographies of Crime and Justice: Contemporary Transitional Justice and the Creation of 'Zones of Impunity.'" *International Journal of Transitional Justice* 1 (1): 45–65.

Steiner, Henry, ed. 1994. *Truth Commissions: A Comparative Assessment—Proceedings of an Interdisciplinary Discussion.* Cambridge, Mass. Human Rights Program at Harvard Law School and World Peace Foundation.

Stover, Eric, and Harvey Weinstein, eds. 2005. *My Neighbor, My Enemy: Justice and Community in the Aftermath of Mass Atrocity.* Cambridge, UK: Cambridge University Press.

Teitel, Ruti. 1999. *Transitional Justice.* New York: Oxford University Press.

Van der Merwe, Hugo. 1999. "The Truth and Reconciliation Commission and Community Reconciliation: An Analysis of Competing Strategies and Conceptualizations. PhD diss., George Mason University.

Weschler, Lawrence. 1990. *A Miracle, a Universe: Settling Accounts with Torturers.* New York: Pantheon.

Widner, Jennifer. 2008. "Constitution Writing and Conflict Resolution," http://www.princeton.edu/~pcwcr/ (accessed August 1, 2008).

Zakaria, Fareed. 1997. "The Rise of Illiberal Democracy," *Foreign Affairs* 76 (6): 22–43.

Appendix Table A2.1 Implementation of Transitional Justice Measures, 1974–2008

Country (Year(s) of Transition)	Prosecution	Lustration/ Purge	Banning	Financial	Property	Employ	Other	Truth Commission	Independent	Human Rights	Constitution	Pardon	Amnesty
Afghanistan (2002)	2005–									2002	2004		2005
Albania (1993)	1993–95	1995								1993	1998	1997	
Algeria (1999)	1999–2005 2004–							2003–05	2003–04	2001			1999 2005 2002
Angola (1994)										2005			
Argentina (1983)	1983–90 1993–96 1998–2004			1991 1994 1998–1999			1985 1991 2004	1983–84		1993	1994	1989–90	1983 1986 1987
Benin (1991)	1991									1990	1990		1989 1991
Bolivia (1982)	1986–93			2002 1995 2002				1982–84	1984–86	1997	1994		
Brazil (1985)					1991				1980–85	1995	1988		1979
Bulgaria (1989)	1991–92	1991	1992					1991		1990	1991		1990
Burkina Faso (1978, 1991)								1999		1998	1977 1991		
Burundi (1993, 2000)								2005–	1995–96		2001		2005

continued

Appendix Table A2.1 Implementation of Transitional Justice Measures, 1974–2008, *cont.*

Country (Year(s) of Transition)	Prosecution	Other Sanctions		Reparations				Investigation		Institutional Reform		Immunity	
		Lustration/Purge	Banning	Financial	Property	Employ	Other	Truth Commission	Independent	Human Rights	Constitution	Pardon	Amnesty
Cambodia (1979, 1993)	1979 2003–		1994						1994–2004	1998	1993		1994
Cameroon (1990)										1990	1996		1992
Cape Verde (1991)											1992		
Central African Republic (1991, 2008)	1986 1994 2008–							2003–		1999	1994	1993	2008
Chad (1990)	2000–							1991–92		1995	1990 1996		1994
Chile (1990)	1991–			1992– 2001–06 2003				1990–91 2004–05		2001	1989		1979
Comoros (1990, 2002)										2006	2001		
Congo-Brazzaville (1992)											1992		1999
Côte d'Ivoire (2000)									2004	2008	2000		2003 2007

Country								
Czechoslovakia (1989)	1991	1991	1991	1991				
Czech Republic (1993)						1999	1993	
Slovakia (1993)						1994	1993	
DRC (2001)	2006–	1998–2007			2002–06	2003	2006	2008
Ecuador (1996)	1997				1996–97	1998	1998	2000
El Salvador (1992)	1990–92, 1998	1992, 2002–06, 2005			1992–93	1991	1992	1991, 1993
Ethiopia (1991)	1994–				1993–97	1995	1995	
Eritrea (1993)						1999	1996	
Fiji (2001)	2001–04					2000	1991	2005
Gabon (1990)							1994, 1996	
Gambia (1996)	1990–2000				1992–94	2001	1995	1995
(East) Germany (1989)	1990–2000	1990	1992–93	1989–92				
Ghana (1979, 1992)	1975–76, 1984				2002–04	1993	1992	1992
Greece (1974)			1974		2001–06	1975	1975	
Grenada (1983)	1984							
Guatemala (1994)	1996–2003	2000, 1999–2005			1997–99	1987	1994	1986

continued

Appendix Table A2.1 Implementation of Transitional Justice Measures, 1974–2008, *cont.*

Country (Year(s) of Transition)	Prosecution	Other Sanctions		Reparations				Investigation		Institutional Reform		Immunity	
		Lustration/ Purge	Banning	Financial	Property	Employ	Other	Truth Commission	Independent	Human Rights	Constitution	Pardon	Amnesty
Guinea-Bissau (1999)	1999–2001							1998–99					2002 2008
Haiti (1991, 1994)	1995–97			1998– 2006–08	1998–		1998–	1994–96		1987	1987		1994
Honduras (1982)	1986–89 1994–97			1989 2000 2006				1993		1992	1982		1987 1991
Hungary (1989)		1994		1992	1991					1995	1989		
India (1977)	1978–80							1977		1993			
Indonesia (1999)	2000–04							1999–2000 2004–08		2000	2002		
Timor-Leste (1999)	2002–			2001				2002–05 2004–08	1999–2000		2002		
Iraq (2003)	2004–	2003–04						2000–01			2005		2008
Kenya (1992)	2003–			2002					2005–	2002	1992		2007
Lebanon (1989, 2000, 2005, 2008)	2007–							2001–02 2004–05			1990		1991

Country								
Lesotho (1999)					2000–01		2002	
Liberia (1997, 2003)	2003–				2006–	1997		2005
Madagascar (1992, 2002)	2002–04	1996–				1996 1996	1992 1995	2004
Malawi (1994)	1994 1995							
Mali (1992)	1992–93 1997–2001					1996	1992	1993 1999
Mauritania (1992, 2007)					2000–01	1998 1992	1991	1993
Mexico (2000)	2002–				1998 2004–05	2001 1990	1990 1996	1998
Mongolia (1990)								
Morocco (1999)		1999				1990	1996	1998
Mozambique (1994)						2005	1990	1992 1989–90
Namibia (1990)					1990–91	1991	1991	
Nepal (1990, 2008)		1997–2005		2001			1990	1990
Nicaragua (1990)						1995	1995	1990
Niger (1991, 1999)					1999–2002	1998	1995	1999
Nigeria (1979, 1989, 1999)					2001–02	1995 1986 1997	1999 1997 1994	1994 1995
Pakistan (1988)						1997	1994	
Panama (1991)	1991–2004	2001						
Papua New Guinea (1998)	2004–06 2007							
Paraguay (1993)	1994–2004		2006		2004–	1995	1992	1995

continued

Appendix Table A2.1 Implementation of Transitional Justice Measures, 1974–2008, *cont.*

Country (Year(s) of Transition)	Prosecution	Other Sanctions		Reparations				Investigation		Institutional Reform		Immunity	
		Lustration/ Purge	Banning	Financial	Property	Employ	Other	Truth Commission	Independent	Human Rights	Constitution	Pardon	Amnesty
Peru (1990, 2000)	2001–04			1996–2007				2001–03		1995 2001	2001		1995
Philippines (1986)	1989–90 1993			1996 2004				1986–87		1987	1987		1991
Poland (1989)	1991	1997		1996				1989–91		1989	1992		
Portugal (1974)										1978 1991	1976 1982		
Romania (1989)	1989									1991	1991		
Rwanda (1993, 1994)	1994– 1996–								1993 1999 1999–2000	1999	2003		
Sao Tome (1990)											1990		1990
Seychelles (1991)											1991 1993		
Sierra Leone (1996, 2000)	2002–							2002–04		1996			1999

Country								
South Africa (1994)	1996–	1994–	1998–2000, 2003	1995–98	1995	1994, 1996	2008	1992, 1995
South Korea (1987)	1996		1990	2000–02, 2000–	2001	1988		
Spain (1975)				1994–97	1978, 1998	1978		1977
Sri Lanka (1994)	1998			1998–2002		1978		
Sudan (1986)					1994	1998		
Suriname (1987, 1991)	1999		1993–94, 2005, 2005, 1995, 1998			1987, 1992		
	2007–							
Taiwan (1986)				1992–2006		1991–2005		
Tanzania (1992)					2000	2000		
Togo (1991)					1987	1992	1991	
Tunisia (1987)					1991	1987, 1991, 2002	1989	
Turkey (1983)		1983	1981	1986–95	1983	1982, 1995	1983	
Uganda (1986)	1995				1996	1995	2000–	
USSR (1989)						1990		
Armenia (1991)					2003	1995		

continued

Appendix Table A2.1 Implementation of Transitional Justice Measures, 1974–2008, *cont.*

Country (Year(s) of Transition)	Prosecution	Other Sanctions		Reparations				Investigation		Institutional Reform		Immunity	
		Lustration/Purge	Banning	Financial	Property	Employ	Other	Truth Commission	Independent	Human Rights	Constitution	Pardon	Amnesty
Azerbaijan (1991)										1996	1995		
Belarus (1991)											1994		
Estonia (1991)	2003							1998–		1992	1992		
Georgia (1991, 2003)			1991							1995	1992 1994		
Kazakhstan (1993)										2002	1993 1995		
Kyrgyzstan (1993, 2005)		1993								2002	1993		
Latvia (1993)	1994 2003–04	1991	1991							1995	1993 1998		
Lithuania (1990)	1998–2001	1991–92 1999		1994	1991			1998–2007		1994	1992		1991
Moldova (1994)										1994	1994		
Russia (1991)										1993	1993		
Tajikistan (1994)										1998	1994 1999		

Country						
Turkmenistan (1992)				2007	1992	1991
Ukraine (1989, 2005)				1998	1996	
Uzbekistan (1992)			1999	1995	1992	
UK/Northern Ireland (1998)	1991		1998–2005 / 1998–2002 / 1994–98 / 1985	1999	1997	
Uruguay (1984)	1985–86 / 2002	1996–2002	1985 / 2000–03		1992	1985
Yugoslavia (1989, 2000)	1993–	1996–	1996–			
Bosnia and Herzegovina (1992)	2005–		2001 / 2003–04	1994	1994	
Croatia (1991)	2003–			1992	2001	
Macedonia (1991)	2008 / 2003			1997	1990 / 2000	
Serbia and Montenegro (2003)	2004–06			2003	1991 / 2003	
Montenegro (2006)					2002	
Serbia (2006)				2003	2007	
Slovenia (1991)	2006–			1993	2006 / 1991	

Appendix Table A2.1 Implementation of Transitional Justice Measures, 1974–2008, *cont.*

Country (Year(s) of Transition)	Prosecution	Other Sanctions		Reparations				Investigation		Institutional Reform		Immunity	
		Lustration/ Purge	Banning	Financial	Property	Employ	Other	Truth Commission	Independent	Human Rights	Constitution	Pardon	Amnesty
Zambia (1991)								1993–95		1997	1991 1996		
Zimbabwe (1979)				1980	1980		1980			2007	1979		1980 1988

Key: Year(s) Domestic process

Year(s) Process with domestic and international elements

Year(s) International process

Appendix Table A2.2 Cross-National Comparative Analysis of Recent Transitional Justice Processes

Reference	Cases	Unit of Analysis	Method	Main Theme(s)
Herz 1982	Southern Europe (+ Germany, Italy, Japan)	Countries	Case studies	Policymaking Regime stability Democratic consolidation
Weschler 1990	Latin America	Societies	Discourse analysis	Accountability
Huntington 1991	New democracies	Countries Governments	Large-N analysis	Regime stability Democratic consolidation
Benomar 1993	Africa Eastern Europe Latin America	Countries	Case studies	Policymaking
Barahona de Brito 1993, 1997	Chile Uruguay	Countries	Case studies	Democratic consolidation Justice Truth
Ensalaco 1994	Chile El Salvador	Truth commissions	Institutional analysis	Policymaking/implementation
Hayner 1994	15 countries	Truth commissions	Institutional analysis	Policymaking/implementation
Pion-Berlin 1993	Argentina Chile Uruguay	Truth commissions	Institutional analysis	Policymaking/implementation
Ambrose 1995	Africa	Countries	Case studies	Democratization
Cohen 1995	Various	Individuals Societies	Discourse analysis	Information Justice Impunity Social control
Huyse 1995	Various	Countries	Case studies	Policymaking
Los 1995	Czechoslovakia Poland	Countries	Discourse analysis	Justice Lustration Truth
Popkin and Roht-Arriaza 1995	Chile El Salvador Honduras	Countries	Case studies	Accountability

continued

Appendix Table A2.2 Cross-National Comparative Analysis of Recent Transitional Justice Processes, *cont.*

Reference	Cases	Unit of Analysis	Method	Main Theme(s)
Rosenberg 1995	Eastern Europe	Individuals Communities	Interviews Discourse analysis	Victimization
Smith 1995a, b	Czechoslovakia East Germany Hungary Poland Soviet Union	Countries	Case studies	Decommunization
Benedetti 1996	El Salvador Haiti	Truth commissions	Institutional analysis	Policymaking/implementation
Rwelamira and Werle 1996	Germany South Africa	Countries	Case studies	Amnesty vs. punishment Reparations
Borneman 1997	Eastern Europe	Countries	Case studies	Decommunization
Kaye 1997	El Salvador Honduras	Truth commissions Countries	Case studies	Reconciliation Democratization
Boed 1998	Czech Republic Eastern Europe	Countries	Case studies	Policy efficacy
Botha 1998	New democracies	Countries	Large-*N* multivariate statistical analysis	Legitimacy Protest activity
Minow 1998	Rwanda South Africa Yugoslavia	Countries	Case studies	Vengeance Forgiveness
Pankhurst 1999	Africa	Countries	Case studies	Justice Reconciliation
Popkin and Bhuta 1999	Argentina Chile El Salvador Guatemala Honduras South Africa	Countries	Case studies	Accountability Amnesty Reparations Truth
Ross 1999	Guatemala South Africa	Truth commissions	Discourse analysis	Truth Memory

Study	Countries	Unit of analysis	Method	Focus
Sieff and Vinjamuri Wright 1999	Argentina, Rwanda, South Africa, Yugoslavia	Governments	Case studies	Policymaking
Skaar 1999	New democracies	Countries	Case studies, Bivariate statistical analysis	Policymaking
Teitel 1999	Various	Governments	Case studies	Policymaking/implementation
Crocker 2000	Argentina, Chile, Guatemala, South Africa	Truth commissions, Civil societies	Case studies	Policymaking/implementation, Government–civil society interface
Garrett 2000	Various	Countries	Case studies	Policymaking
Nalepa 2000, 2003, 2005	Czech Republic, Hungary, Poland	Governments, Legislatures, Individuals	Game theory, Case studies, Elite interviews	Policymaking
Chapman and Ball 2001	Guatemala, Haiti, South Africa	Truth commissions	Case studies	Truth
Hayner 2001	20+ countries	Truth commissions	Interviews, Institutional analysis	Policymaking/implementation
Lutz and Sikkink 2001	Latin American countries	Countries, Courts, Advocacy networks	Case studies	International norms, Prosecutions
Espinoza Cuevas, Ortiz Rojas, and Baeza 2002	Argentina, Chile, El Salvador, Guatemala, South Africa	Truth commissions, Individuals, Civil societies	Interviews, Institutional analysis	Policymaking/implementation, Government–civil society interface, Justice, Reparations
David 2003	Czech Republic, Poland	Countries	Case studies	Lustration
Lambourne 2002	Cambodia, Rwanda	Countries	Case studies	Reconciliation, Peacebuilding

continued

Appendix Table A2.2 Cross-National Comparative Analysis of Recent Transitional Justice Processes, *cont.*

Reference	Cases	Unit of Analysis	Method	Main Theme(s)
Andrews 2003	East Germany South Africa	Truth commissions Societies	Discourse analysis	National narratives
Backer 2003	Various	Governments Civil societies	Case studies	Policymaking/implementation Government–civil society interface
Buford and van der Merwe 2003	Malawi Mozambique Namibia South Africa Zimbabwe	Governments	Interviews Case studies	Reparations
Quinn 2003	Haiti Uganda	Countries Truth commissions	Case studies	Public acknowledgment Development of democratic institutions
Quinn and Freeman 2003	Guatemala South Africa	Truth commissions	Case studies	Policymaking/implementation
Snyder and Vinjamuri 2003	31 countries	Countries	Case studies	Political order Institutionalization of justice
Calhoun 2004	East Germany Poland Russia	Governments Societies	Case studies Discourse analysis	Policymaking
Elster 2004	Various	Governments	Case studies	Policymaking
Graybill and Lanegran 2004	Rwanda Sierra Leone South Africa	Truth commissions	Case studies	Policymaking/implementation
Posner and Vermeule 2004	26 countries	Governments	Case studies	Policymaking/implementation
Sriram 2004	Argentina El Salvador Honduras South Africa Sri Lanka	Governments	Case studies	Policymaking/implementation Accountability
Brahm 2005	170 countries	Countries	Large-*N* multivariate statistical analysis	Democracy Protection of human rights

Kenney and Spears 2005	16 countries in Latin America	Countries	Large-*N* multivariate statistical analysis	Democratization
Kim 2005	84 countries	Countries	Large-*N* multivariate statistical analysis	Adoption of truth commissions
Lanegran 2005	Cambodia Rwanda Sierra Leone South Africa Timor-Leste	Countries Truth commissions Trials Tribunals	Case studies	Policymaking/implementation Memory
Peskin 2005a, b	Rwanda Yugoslavia	Governments Tribunals	Case studies	Compliance with international law Deterrence Peacebuilding
Roht-Arriaza 2005	Argentina Chile	Individuals Courts Advocacy networks	Interviews Legal history	Criminal prosecutions
Sikkink and Walling 2005	85 countries	Countries	Large-*N* bivariate statistical analysis	Justice cascade Relationship between truth commissions and domestic and foreign prosecutions
Cassel 2006	13 Latin American countries	Legal judgments	Case studies Bivariate analysis	Court-ordered reparations
David 2006a	Poland South Africa	Countries	Case studies	Policymaking/implementation Amnesty vs. lustration
David 2006b	Albania Bulgaria Czechoslovakia Germany Hungary Iraq Poland Serbia	Lustration systems	Case studies	Policymaking/implementation Social and political impacts
Lie, Binningsbø, and Gates 2006	187 countries	Countries	Large-*N* multivariate statistical analysis	Recurrence of violent conflict

continued

Appendix Table A2.2 Cross-National Comparative Analysis of Recent Transitional Justice Processes, *cont.*

Reference	Cases	Unit of Analysis	Method	Main Theme(s)
Grodsky 2006	Croatia Poland Serbia Uzbekistan	Governments	Case studies	Policymaking/implementation
Dahill-Brown et al. 2007	79 countries	Transitional justice measures	Large-*N* multivariate statistical analysis	Policymaking/choice of measures
Jelin 2007	Argentina Chile Uruguay	Countries	Case studies	Memorialization
Rubio-Marín 2007	Guatemala Peru Rwanda Sierra Leone South Africa Timor-Leste	Countries	Case studies	Reparations Gender
Segovia 2007	El Salvador Haiti	Countries	Case studies	Policymaking/implementation Reparations
Sriram and Ross 2007	Sierra Leone DRC Uganda	Countries	Case studies	Policymaking/implementation Amnesty/impunity
Brahm, Dancy, and Kim 2008	34 countries	Truth commissions	Bivariate analysis	Institutional parameters Policy implementation
Duggan, Bailey, and Guillerot 2008	Guatemala Peru	Countries	Case studies	Reparations Sexual/reproductive violence
Humphrey and Valverde 2008	Argentina South Africa	Countries	Case studies	Relationship between victims/survivors and state

Kerr with Mobekk 2008	11 countries	Courts/tribunals Truth commissions	Case studies	Policymaking/implementation Judicial reform Rule of law Reconciliation Capacity building Engaging local population Addressing victims' needs
Olsen et al. 2008	72 countries	Transitional justice measures	Large-*N* multivariate statistical analysis	Policymaking/choice of measures

Note: This list excludes an extensive set of edited books that collectively examine aspects of transitional justice processes in multiple countries (e.g., Aspen Institute 1989; Boraine, Levy, and Scheffer 1994; Steiner 1994; Kritz 1995; McAdams 1997; Hamber 1998; Hesse and Post 1999; Barahona de Brito, González Enríquez, and Aguilar 2001; Bilbija et al. 2005; Schabas and Darcy 2005; Skaar, Suhrke, and Gloppen 2005; Stover and Weinstein 2005; Elster 2006; Mayer-Rieckh and de Greiff 2007).

3

Truth Finding in the Transitional Justice Process

Audrey R. Chapman

This chapter examines some of the issues surrounding the mandate of truth finding in the transitional justice process, with the aim of helping identify a research agenda for better understanding the factors affecting this process and its impact on post-conflict societies. Within the array of transitional justice mechanisms, the focus here is primarily on the work of truth commissions, because they have been central in efforts to document and come to terms with the past. Beginning with some reflections on the truth-finding functions of transitional justice mechanisms and their limitations, we then consider factors affecting the truth-recovery process, including differences in the mandates assigned to truth commissions, their priorities and approaches to their assignments, and their methodological orientations and approaches. Then follows a discussion of issues involving the dissemination of findings and the responses of various sectors in the society. Parts of the chapter build on previous work by the author and others (Chapman and Ball 2001; Chapman and van der Merwe 2008).

Establishing the truth about past human rights violations and patterns of violence is a central dimension of transitional justice processes. Nevertheless, truth recovery is a complex and ambiguous task affected by a wide range of factors, including conceptions of what constitutes social truth; the mandate, methodology, and resources of the body undertaking the truth finding; and social and political receptivity to the process. Also, procedural decisions made by those working within a specific transitional justice mechanism, sometimes without an awareness of the implications, often have important consequences for truth finding. It is therefore essential to examine the nature of the "truth" that transitional justice mechanisms are mandated to find, and their capabilities and limitations in doing so.

Importance of Truth Recovery in Transitional Justice Processes

Writers on transitional justice processes frequently emphasize the importance of truth telling and truth recovery, especially to victims and participants in the struggle against oppression but also to the future of the society. Janet Cherry's chapter in this volume underscores this point. The human rights and international legal communities have advocated strongly that there should be no impunity for the perpetrators of massive or gross human rights abuses. Despite the difficulty of doing so, many human rights advocates, as well as former victims, argue that international law obliges states to respond to massive and systematic violations of basic human rights by investigating, prosecuting, and punishing the perpetrators. Apart from the question of accountability, some human rights specialists argue that there is a right, especially for victims, to know the truth (Mendez 1997, 261). Documenting the past to overcome communal and official denial of the atrocities, violence, or abuses and getting official and public acknowledgment thereof are also seen as essential components of the reform process necessary to establish or strengthen the foundations of a society that respects the rule of law and protects human rights (Minow 1998, 117–22).

Another theme in the literature is that official truth-finding processes are a precondition if members of a society that has experienced collective violence and severe human rights violations are to put the past behind them and be ready for reconciliation (Huyse 2003, 26). As Archbishop Desmond Tutu states in his widely quoted foreword to the South African Truth and Reconciliation Commission's (TRC's) multivolume report, "Reconciliation is not about being cosy; it is not about pretending that things were other than they were. Reconciliation based on falsehood, on not facing up to reality, is not true reconciliation and will not last" (South African TRC 1998, 17). It is also assumed that uncovering the truth about past abuses and acknowledging the suffering of victims contribute to the restoration of their human and civil dignity and their psychological healing (South African TRC 1998, 123–34).

There is also the assumption that truth recovery can provide insight into how and why the violence and human rights abuses happened and that it can thereby help prevent their reoccurrence. The Sierra Leone Truth and Reconciliation Commission's (TRC's) report opens with this reflection: "It is only through generating such understanding that the horrors of the past can effectively be prevented from occurring again. Knowledge and understanding are the most powerful deterrents against conflict and war" (Sierra Leone TRC 2004a, Overview, para. 1).

Governments and international institutions have used a variety of mechanisms to document and account for collective and state violence and severe human rights violations. These have included commissions of inquiry, court proceedings within or outside the countries where the abuses occurred, truth commissions—some of which are also tasked with promoting reconciliation—and historical commissions. The mechanisms differ in their goals, methodologies and modes of operation, and standards of what constitutes truth. Cases brought to national courts or international tribunals addressing abuses that occurred under previous regimes use legal approaches to seek to determine the culpability of alleged perpetrators in committing specific, often narrowly defined offenses and to determine what constitutes appropriate punishment. In contrast, truth commissions undertake a much broader inquiry, to provide a narrative of the kinds of abuses that occurred during a defined historical period. In that effort, they collect thousands of testimonies, hold public hearings, and engage in investigations and other types of research. Historical commissions, as their name implies, generally address events in the past that affected specific ethnic, racial, or other groups; they are not part of political transitions and may not even deal with current issues. Also, some governments establish commissions and committees of inquiry focused on a set of past human rights violations of more limited scope, which are less independent than truth commissions (Freeman and Hayner 2003, 122–24).

Of these mechanisms, truth commissions have the mission most focused on broad truth recovery. A legal process is typically based on a far more extensive investigation of a particular case or cases, and it also uses a higher standard of proof—"beyond a reasonable doubt"—than does a truth commission, which usually relies on a preponderance of evidence to reach its conclusions. However, courts do not usually attempt to write definitive historical accounts of mass human rights violations or to reconstruct a comprehensive history of a conflict. Moreover, trials are difficult to conduct and generally ill suited to illuminate a period of history or deal with subtleties of facing a past marked by collective violence and other forms of atrocity (Minow 1998, 51, 58). In some special circumstances, an international court may seek to situate individual acts within long-term systematic policies, as the International Criminal Tribunal for the former Yugoslavia did in some of its judgments in order to deal with the probative requirements of genocide and crimes against humanity (Wilson 2005), but this is rare.

Truth commissions have a greater capacity to investigate and assess, over time intervals, what took place and why, and to recommend necessary legal and institutional reforms to avoid the recurrence of violence and human rights abuses. To that end, truth commissions have been vested with a wide range of responsibilities, some explicit and others implicit, related to truth finding. Typically, the mandate includes several of the following assignments:

- Establish an authoritative and historically accurate record of the past.
- Overcome communal and official denial of the atrocity, violence, or abuses and gain official and public acknowledgment of them.
- Identify victims of human rights violations and abuses.
- Certify whether applicants for reparations qualify as victims.
- Create a "collective memory," or common history, for a new future not determined by the past.
- Identify the architects of the past violence and exclude, shame, and diminish perpetrators for their offenses.

Truth commissions are also often tasked with other assignments, such as the following, which are not specifically related to investigating the past:

- Restore dignity to victims and promote psychological healing.
- End and prevent violence and future human rights abuses.
- Legitimate and promote the stability of the new regime.
- Promote reconciliation across social divisions.
- Educate the population about the past.
- Forge the basis for a democratic political order that respects and protects human rights.
- Recommend ways to deter future violations and atrocities.
- In the case of the South African TRC, determine the eligibility of applicants for amnesty (Chapman and Ball 2001, 15–16).

The dilemma is that many of these tasks are quite different in nature, and even some of those related to truth recovery entail very different approaches. Establishing an authoritative record of the past, for example, necessitates an extensive research effort using a variety of scientific methods. Documenting criminal action will depend on the relevant legal definitions and specific juridical investigation techniques. Attempting to write an official or common history has epistemological and methodological requirements beyond the capacity of most truth commissions. It involves going beyond merely gathering the facts, to place them in an interpretative framework that explains the antecedents, circumstances, and contexts of the violations, as well as the perspectives of the victims and the motives and perspectives of the persons responsible for authorizing and committing the abuses. Efforts to do so and to establish a version of the past that transcends subjective and contesting views may incline a truth commission to attempt to close the door prematurely on the past before all the relevant information is available or known (Bundy 2000, 13–15).

Moreover, some of the tasks assigned to truth commissions may conflict with, or at least detract from, truth finding. Restoring dignity to victims and promoting psychological healing call for attention to the subjective rather than the strictly objective dimensions of knowledge. Nation building, public education, and recommendations for reforms emphasize the public applications and accessibility of the findings, but if the investment of time and effort in public outreach impairs the quality or rigor of truth recovery, the benefits of doing so may be short-lived. Forging the basis for a democratic political order, legitimating and promoting the stability of a new regime, and promoting reconciliation across social divisions all involve the formulation and implementation of long-term public policies that truth commissions, with their short timeline and limited resources, are ill suited to undertake. Moreover, efforts to promote the legitimacy of the post-conflict political order may incline a transitional justice institution to advance political myths that obfuscate responsibility and distort the legacy of political violence (Leebaw 2008). In light of these problems, more attention needs to be given to the potential incompatibilities in these assignments and to how such incompatibilities affect the work and impact of truth commissions.

Limitations of Truth-Finding Processes

Some analysts writing on truth commissions initially portrayed the task of truth finding primarily as confirming widely held beliefs about the past. As an example, Priscilla Hayner, one of the most knowledgeable experts about truth commissions, commented in a 1994 article:

> The most straightforward reason to set up a truth commission is that of sanctioned fact finding: to establish an accurate record of a country's past, and thus help to provide a fair record of a country's history and its government's much disputed acts. . . . But "fact finding" is perhaps an inaccurate description of investigations which often end up confirming widely-held beliefs about what has happened and who is responsible. In many situations that warrant a post-mortem truth commission, the victimized populations are often clear about what abuses took place and who has carried them out. . . . Given this knowledge, the importance of truth commissions might be described more accurately as acknowledging the truth rather than shaping it. (Hayner 1994, 607)

But developing an official authoritative account of what is often a contested past, and doing so in an objective and careful manner according to standards of historical or social science research—let alone the strict legal standards of a court of law—require far more than merely confirming widely held beliefs about what has happened and who is responsible. It is a very difficult task, especially in a society in which different sectors of the population have widely differing views of what happened and why. In her 2001 book *Unspeakable Truths,* Hayner offers a quite different assessment. She observes that official truth seeking is a cumbersome and complicated affair and that the expectations for truth commissions are almost always greater than what these bodies can reasonably hope to achieve:

> Perhaps most underappreciated, still, is the sheer difficulty of undertaking these endeavors, of fairly documenting and representing a "truth"—however that is defined in different countries—in the course of a short and intensive period of investigation, when the issues under exploration often remain the most sensitive of the day and when the commission's task is to reach and fairly represent the stories of thousands upon thousands of victims. (Hayner 2001, 7)

The truth-recovery process in post-conflict and post-repression societies invariably makes two important assumptions: first, that discovering the truth about the past is desirable, and, second, that it is feasible to do so. Both these assumptions are more problematic than first appears. Social and political groups are likely to have differing views on the desirability of documenting past human rights abuses and identifying those responsible. Those who were the authors and beneficiaries of the violence inflicted by past regimes usually prefer that the past be forgotten or ignored. In contrast, victims typically welcome the establishment of a truth commission, but their views about the priorities of truth seeking usually focus on identifying the perpetrators and their motives and not on the broader social truths that truth commissions are usually assigned to uncover. Even democratically elected governments nominally committed to human rights and the rule of law may be reluctant to prosecute their predecessors vigorously, for fear that doing so may destabilize society or impede the recovery process. Also, the new leadership may be averse to having its own movement's record scrutinized.

It is also worth noting that the nature of truth is itself a complex and elusive concept, especially in a deeply divided society (Chapman and Ball 2001, 4–9). As an article written by a former staff member of the South African TRC points out, "It [truth] is so commonly used that it seems to be a transparent notion, clear to all who are involved or interested in redressing past abuses, but 'truth,' like 'justice' and 'reconciliation,' is an elusive concept that defies rigid definitions" (Parleviet 1998, 142). Postmodern thinkers have amply shown that discovering a social truth—any social truth—is difficult under the best of circumstances. And truth commissions typically function in an environment of sharply conflicting and politically freighted versions of the past. Far from being a mere marshaling of self-explanatory facts just waiting to be discovered, the writing and interpretation of history under such circumstances will inevitably be complicated and highly contested.

Not only is documenting the truth about the past an overwhelming and inherently controversial task, but many truth commissions are also supposed to go beyond describing what occurred, to seek what has been characterized as a "deeper" truth—to determine why the violence and human rights violations occurred, how such crimes were possible, what the causal links were, and what the societal and moral context of the conflict was that enabled the crimes to take place (Dimitrijević 2002, 206). The goal is a truth that goes beyond documentation, to determine responsibility and try to ensure nunca más (never again)—that is, that widespread abuses or collective violence will not be repeated. To do so requires understanding the structural sources of violations and the causal relations well enough to make recommendations on institutional reforms. All these are complex undertakings, requiring collection of the appropriate data, accompanied by analysis and interpretation using sophisticated social science methodologies. Few of the lawyers and jurists in leadership positions on most transitional justice bodies have the type of training needed to understand the rigorous methodological requirements of such an endeavor. This places a burden on the transitional justice bodies' senior staff, who, depending on their professional backgrounds and training, may be better able to design and oversee comprehensive truth-recovery processes, but they are unlikely to be able to do so without the understanding and support of the leadership.

Also, cultures vary in how they approach and value truth telling, especially in public settings. An ethnographic study of a provincial public hearing held by the Sierra Leone TRC, for example, explores the factors discouraging those testifying at the hearings from telling the truth. The author identifies a variety of reasons, some involving the special circumstances in the district where the hearing was held, and the confused relationship of the TRC with the Special Court in Sierra Leone, which led some perpetrators to assume (erroneously) that testimony to the TRC could be used for prosecutions by the Special Court (Kelsall 2005, 380–81). But the author also makes the point that public truth telling lacks deep roots in the local cultures of Sierra Leone (Kelsall 2005, 382–85). Another study of the Sierra Leone TRC makes the further point that the TRC's focus on truth telling as part of the global paradigm of redemptive memory conflicted with local techniques of forgetting as the preferred way of dealing with traumatic memories (Shaw 2007). Given the disparity between the TRC's expectation and local cultural paradigms, the blandness of the testimony of most witnesses who testified in these hearings suggests that they came more with the intention of staking a claim for reparations against the government than of telling the whole truth about what had happened (Kelsall 2005, 369–71). Despite all their admonitions to victims to express the truth, the whole truth, and nothing but the truth, the commissioners were rarely able to get beyond detached facts from victims and half-truths, evasions, and outright lies from perpetrators (Kelsall 2005, 380).

Most truth commissions rely on victims' testimony as a primary source of data, but in testifying about such experiences, victims tend to give voice to the deep subjective dimensions of their horror and not the objective knowledge and facts that transitional justice mechanisms require (Strejilevich 2006). Moreover, memory is inherently subjective and vulnerable to change over time—particularly memories related to traumatic experiences and public events. Public memories are especially likely to be influenced by a variety of interpretative factors, including community, cultural, or traditional myths and personal fantasies. "All social memory, be it documented through the oral, written or visual mediums, is both reconstructed and selective" (Field 1999, 5). Toine van Dongen of the Dutch Ministry of Foreign Affairs, who has had extensive experience in fact-finding as a member of the UN Working Group on Enforced or Involuntary Disappearances, stresses the gap between perception and reality: "I do not believe in truth, I believe in perceptions. . . . People have a certain impression of how reality is, which is their perception of reality; they call it objective reality themselves, but essentially, it always is subjective reality. Thus, for most people there is no wedge between reality and perception: perception is reality" (Parlevliet 1998, 146).

At the least, facts may be "loaded" with different meanings when considered from divergent perspectives. An event leading to fundamental abuses of human rights may be recollected and interpreted quite differently by different victims, and even by a single person when given different stimuli and specific questions—let alone by a victim and a perpetrator. A 1999 paper by Janet Cherry analyzing the work of the TRC in South Africa's Eastern Cape province identifies three different "truths" that were revealed in its amnesty hearings: the "truth" of the security police, the "truth" of the ANC, and the "truth" of the public and those involved in Congress of South African Students who were not part of any military actions. "To the (mainly black) supporters of the liberation movements and mass movements, the stories were of their heroes and martyrs—people who were presented as courageous activists, who were ruthlessly tortured and murdered by the security police. To the security police, these people were terrorist pawns of an international revolutionary communist conspiracy" (Cherry 1999).

Further complicating the situation, the source of so-called victim testimony may be not the actual victim but a relative. Many of the victims of atrocities and gross human rights abuses may have disappeared or been killed; thus, the testimony to the truth commission about the event may come from a mother, wife, sister, or brother who likely was not a direct witness to the events in question. Most testimonies at the public hearings sponsored by the South African TRC, for example, were presented by black women about the experiences of black males who were their husbands, sons, or lovers, who were victims of the security forces (Harris 1999).

Also, transitional justice mechanisms, whether judicial prosecutions or truth commissions, typically operate under serious constraints: weak legal institutions, limited resources, dependence on cooperation from officials who served the previous regime, missing data, and political environments that limit their mandates and options. The systematic suppression or destruction of incriminating evidence is a common problem. For example, the Guatemalan Commission for Historical Clarification (CEH) was unable to obtain the archives of the military and security forces, but after the publication of its report, records from a secret military archive detailing the fate of two hundred victims who were "disappeared" by the Guatemalan military—records that had been denied to the CEH—were made available to several human rights organizations. And these records are likely just a small part of the relevant data that were hidden or destroyed to protect the perpetrators and inhibit the commission's inquiry. In the case of South Africa, the apartheid regime regularly purged the archives of huge volumes of sensitive documents, particularly those dealing with security issues. On the eve of the political transition, the security establishment structures, increasingly apprehensive about certain state records passing out of their control, began an even more systematic and vigorous effort to destroy state records (South African TRC 1998, 227–29).

Given the magnitude of their task and the limitations of time and resources under which they function, truth commissions have to be very selective in what they cover and emphasize. And in this process, truth commissions frequently "shape" or socially construct the truth. This may occur consciously, or it may be inadvertent. The Guatemalan CEH, for example, focused on violations to the indigenous Maya population in the highlands during the 1980s, to the relative exclusion of examining serious violations that occurred among the Ladino (of mixed European and Native American ancestry) population in the late 1960s—most likely because of the difficulties in finding victims and documentary sources related to this earlier period. Most of the victims were killed, and few human rights organizations functioned during this period. Because truth commissions cannot investigate all potential cases or events, they frequently choose representative or significant ones—what the South African TRC referred to as "window cases." This raises the question of the criteria used in making the selection, and the basis for considering them representative or significant. Time constraints in preparing reports can also lead to superficiality and oversimplification.

The focus on gross violations of human rights that is typical of many truth commissions imposes yet another set of constraints. It often results in efforts to describe and quantify the extent of such abuses at the expense of dealing with a wider range of problems and the structural factors contributing to them. The findings of the South African TRC, for example, have been characterized as a "diminished truth" because its narrow lens reflected the experience of a tiny minority: perpetrators as state agents and victims who were political activists. According to Mahmood Mamdani, the TRC's account of torture, murder, rape, and disappearances failed to address adequately the wider range of abuses inflicted by the apartheid system, such as forced removals, which affected a much broader segment of the population (Mamdani 2000, 58–61).

Factors Affecting the Work of Truth Commissions

Mandates and Terms of Reference

Although comparative analysis tends to equate all truth commissions, these bodies vary considerably in their mandates, resources, approaches, orientation and professional backgrounds of their commissioners, and methodologies. The nature and focus of their findings about the past reflect these differences.

The mandate assigned to a specific truth commission plays a decisive role in determining its priorities and the nature of the truth it will attempt to investigate. Many truth commissions have restricted terms of reference, reflecting the political compromises that led to their creation. Typically, truth commissions emerge out of negotiated settlements in which there are no clear victors and vanquished. Often the architects of the violence and abuses, or at the very least their supporters, retain political influence and power. Those ceding their positions of power frequently attempt to impose conditions that will restrict a specific commission's powers and the kinds of issues that it will be able to investigate. Or the mandate may reflect the priorities and concerns of those drafting the mechanisms under which the commission was established—people who may deem it in the country's interest to have a short transition period.

One important consideration is the type of abuses that a specific truth commission is assigned to investigate. The scope can vary considerably. The 1983–84 Argentine National Commission on the Disappearance of Persons (CONADEP) was mandated solely to clarify the acts related to disappearances where no body was found. The terms of reference of the 1990–91 Chilean National Commission on Truth and Reconciliation were broader and included disappearances, torture resulting in death, executions by government forces, and killings by private citizens for political reasons. Like the 2002–03 Ghanaian National Reconciliation Commission, many truth commissions are mandated to document the nature and causes of serious violations and abuses of human rights, often termed "gross violations of human rights," with some latitude to define whether that also includes such abuses as torture, illegal detention, abduction, incitement, and other serious acts of violence. In some cases there are additional qualifications; for example, the terms of reference of the South African TRC specified that the human rights abuse had to be inflicted because of a political motive, and the mandate to the Ghanaian commission also tasked it with investigating and determining whether the "violations and abuses were deliberately planned and executed by the state or any public institutions, bodies, organizations, public office holders or persons purporting to have acted on behalf of the State" (Ghanaian National Reconciliation Commission 2004, vol. 1, ch. 1, para. 1.7.4).

Some human rights commissions have been tasked with assessing the antecedents, factors, and context of the violence and abuses, such as the government policies or economic inequities and power disparities that gave rise to the gross human rights abuses. This wider analysis, if done appropriately, can be more significant than findings related to particular events and specific cases, both in understanding the causes of conflict and in underpinning recommendations for reform. Even if truth commissions are mandated to undertake this broader analysis, they may not necessarily do so. For example, the South African TRC, despite its terms of reference to deal with the background and context of the gross human rights abuses, did not deal systematically and in any depth with the institutionalized racism of the apartheid system, which arguably had a far more profound and abusive impact on the population than did any other factor. As a consequence, the killings, abductions, torture, and severe ill treatment of persons were treated more as the product of decisions and actions by individuals than as the outcome of the apartheid system.

Another factor shaping truth finding is the length of the historical period that a transitional justice mechanism is assigned to cover. Despite the brutality of both Duvalier dictatorships, which governed Haiti for more than thirty years beginning in 1957, the Haitian National Commission on Truth and Justice was mandated to deal only with the human rights abuses of the Cedras military regime, which overthrew President Jean-Bertrand Aristide in September 1991 and governed through October 14, 1994. The Guatemalan CEH had responsibility for a longer and more appropriate period, approximately coinciding with the internal armed confrontation that began in 1962 and ended with the signing of the 1994 peace accords. The South African commission was assigned to investigate a span of more than thirty years, from March 1960 through the elections in May 1994—a long period to document, but certainly not the full sweep of apartheid history (Chapman and Ball 2001, 13–14).

Yet another consideration is whether a truth commission can identify perpetrators by name in making its findings or is legally barred from doing so by virtue of amnesty agreements or the terms of peace agreements. Sometimes a truth commission can use creative forms of analysis to transcend these limitations. For example, the Guatemalan Historical Clarification Commission's mandate prohibited it from naming individual perpetrators, but it compensated by examining the roles of institutions and the social structure that produced the violence—in the process making findings of even greater import. Somewhat ironically, despite or perhaps because of its limited mandate, the Guatemalan commission undertook a penetrating analysis of the official policy of racism and social exclusion and determined that the Guatemalan military had engaged in genocide against the Indian population.

Even when a truth commission has the legal authority to name names, however, it may be difficult to do so. Unraveling chains of command to identify not just the perpetrators who inflicted the violence, but also the intellectual authors, is very difficult. Moreover, legal considerations may preclude doing so. The Sierra Leone Special Court would not allow the Sierra Leone TRC to question its detainees. And on the eve of the release of the first five volumes of the South African TRC report, both former president F.W. de Klerk and the African National Congress leaders petitioned the courts for injunctions against the publication of findings about them. Nevertheless, as the Guatemalan experience shows, the inability to identify those responsible for the crimes does not necessarily undermine the effectiveness of a truth-finding mechanism's critique.

Time and Resource Constraints

Truth commissions have significant time constraints built into their mandates. Most begin with an explicit time limit, often just six to nine months, to complete all investigations and write a report. Sometimes the initial period is extended. The Haitian truth commission worked for nine months, the Ghanaian and Guatemalan commissions eighteen months, the Peru Truth and Reconciliation Commission two years, and the South African TRC two years and eight months, with an extension of two years for the Amnesty Committee to complete its work. The short official duration of truth commissions—quite inconsistent with an assignment to discover the "truth" of a disputed period of history—has obvious implications for the scope of their investigations and documentation.

Truth commissions typically have severe resource constraints, although the magnitude of this problem has varied considerably. At one end of the spectrum, for example, the Haitian Commission operated on probably a little more than $1 million, with a staff of about seventy-five people, and ran out of funds before it could publish its final report. At the other end, the South African commission received something on the order of $28 million from the government treasury and perhaps another $5 million from foreign donors, which enabled it to fund a staff of over four hundred at its peak—several times the size of most other commissions—with a separate research department (Chapman and Ball 2001, 16–17). Many other truth commissions operated on budgets in the range of $5 million to $10 million.

Conceptions and Approaches to Truth Finding

The mandates and terms of reference that shape the commissions' truth-finding roles have varied, as have the interpretations and methodologies brought to the task. In some cases, the approach of the commission's leadership to truth recovery has been explicit. In others, it has not been clearly articulated. Often a wide range of policies about a variety of matters, some substantive and others procedural, affect the capacities of the commission and the nature of its conclusions, but those making these determinations may not realize the implications at the time decisions are made. Two considerations are the relative emphasis given to the objective versus subjective dimensions of truth finding and to macro versus micro truth—that is, conclusions about the trends, patterns, and causes rather than about findings concerning particular events or the status of individual victims and perpetrators.

The South African TRC had the most self-conscious and intentional conception of truth of any truth commission to date. Its report distinguishes between four notions of truth: factual, or forensic, truth; personal, or narrative, truth; social, or "dialogue," truth; and healing and restorative truth. According to the TRC, factual, or forensic, truth is impartial evidence that tells truth at two levels: (1) about individual events, cases, and people; and (2) about the nature, causes, and extent of gross violations of human rights. Narrative truth evokes the cathartic benefits of storytelling: Victims make meaning and sense out of their experiences through narration, and under certain circumstances, storytelling contributes to psychological healing after trauma. Narrative truth was central to the work of the TRC, especially to the hearings of the Human Rights Violations Committee, to whom victims told their stories in public hearings, and the TRC model of public hearings was then adopted by several other truth commissions. Social, or "dialogue," truth refers to the process and dialogue that surrounded the committee's work: As the TRC report said, "The public was engaged through open hearing and the media" (South African TRC 1998, vol. 1, 110). The fourth kind of truth—healing and restorative truth—refers to the truth that comes from validating the experience of people. The TRC wrote, "Acknowledgement is an affirmation that a person's pain is real and worthy of attention. It is thus central to the restoration of the dignity of victims" (South African TRC 1998, vol. 1, 114).

This understanding of truth comes with several problems or caveats. The first is that this fourfold typology was derived midway through the life of the TRC process and was more a description of the process than a carefully thought-out epistemology that guided the program's development. Also, it reflects the tendency of the TRC to privilege the subjective over the objective dimensions of truth. Of these four approaches, only factual, or forensic, truth refers to the impartial and objective evidence that most truth commissions have understood to be central to their mandate. The three other forms of truthfinding frame as truths ideas that other commissions may have had but have expressed as additional goals, not as alternative approaches to truth. Moreover, the TRC's attention to objective truth focused primarily on micro truth, that is, findings about particular events or the status of individual victims and perpetrators, rather than on macro truth, or conclusions about the trends, patterns, and causes.

Tensions between the Sierra Leone TRC and the Sierra Leone Special Court may have motivated a somewhat more explicit interpretation of truth by the Sierra Leone TRC. The report of the Sierra Leone TRC explicitly states that the standard of proof employed was not the "criminal" standard of "proof beyond a reasonable doubt." Instead, the commission used a "balance of probabilities" approach, in which those claims that are shown to be probable are accepted as true. Somewhat like the South African TRC, the Sierra Leone TRC distinguishes between factual/forensic truth, personal/narrative truth, and social/popular truth. The commission states that its findings represent "a summation of the main conclusions that emerged from the process of establishing the 'factual or forensic' nature of the conflict" (Sierra Leone TRC 2004a, vol. 2, ch. 2, para. 576). It further acknowledges that these findings agree with some of the personal and social truths and disagree with others. Nevertheless, it argues that the courts are limited in their ability to reach the broader truth, because "where violations of human rights have become endemic, individual prosecutions of just a handful of alleged perpetrators are unlikely to reveal the full knowledge of the cruelty and extent of the violations" (Sierra Leone TRC 2004a, vol. 2, ch. 2, para. 577). The "child-friendly" version of the Sierra Leone TRC offers the following description of the truth-recovery process:

> Each person's story is part of the truth. . . . Each story is like a piece of a very large puzzle. Nobody can tell the truth alone. . . . Only when we collect the stories together will we begin to see the whole truth which is as vast and infinite as the night sky. If we study the truth very carefully we will come to understand each other, and we will come to understand what happened in our country. (Sierra Leone TRC 2004b, Introduction, 1)

Micro and Macro Levels of Truth Finding

Truth commissions are far better suited to pursue what can be termed "macro truth" than "micro truth" (Chapman and Ball 2001). To determine accountability, both macro truth and micro truth are essential, but the type and level of findings differ considerably. Macro truth provides a framework for understanding the structural causes of violence, leading to the identification of the broader causes and intellectual authors of the abuses. Micro truth points to the circumstances and the identification of the individuals, groups, or units of the security or armed forces that committed particular crimes.

Whatever else truth commissions are assigned to do, their mandates usually include tasks related to assessing macro truths, such as determining the magnitude of past violence and the patterns, trends, and locations of its occurrence. Typically, truth commissions are also expected to explain the causes of the violence and, sometimes, to identify the ideological or political justification used to legitimize it. For example, the Guatemalan CEH reported that two hundred thousand people were killed, 83 percent of whom were Mayan, leading the commission to conclude that the state had engaged in genocide against the Mayan community (Guatemala CEH 1998, Introduction).

While micro truths are important, especially to victims, truth commissions are not particularly good at determining the details of thousands of cases. They lack the time, staff, and resources to undertake such a massive investigative task. Moreover, when a commission does issue microtruth findings, it is vulnerable to error. Most truth commissions rely on victims' testimony as the primary source of data, and as noted above, memory is inherently subjective and likely to be influenced by a variety of interpretative factors, including community, cultural, and traditional myths and personal fantasies. In the aggregate, these inevitable discrepancies have little or no effect on the determinations of macro truth. But in the context of micro truth, the errors provide critics with a basis for attempting to discredit the entire process.

Macro truth also involves the determination of who was ultimately responsible for the patterns of human rights violations, when and why decisions were made to repress and abuse communities and groups, how the decisions were enacted, and what kinds of structural factors enabled them to happen. In societies with pervasive human rights violations, the perpetrator who pulls the trigger is not usually a participant in the policymaking that gave rise to the violence or in the decisions that resulted in the crime's commission. Specific violations are usually the outcomes of orders taken at higher levels of the government, military, or security forces. To determine ultimate responsibility, therefore, it is necessary to identify the intellectual author(s) and the chain of accountability for the abuse.

Methodologies

Truth commissions often experience tensions between two perspectives: legal arguments versus social science evaluation. Commission lawyers will establish a set of legal definitions about what constitutes a violation of a given norm of domestic law, international human rights law, or international humanitarian law. They may then seek examples, in the form of particular cases, that demonstrate the violation of the norm in question. This kind of work seeks to argue that a norm was violated, making the claim in the strongest possible terms. In contrast, social scientists, who are less well represented in truth commissions, ask how often the norm was violated, in absolute and proportional terms. Was the norm violated more frequently in some circumstances or time periods than in others? Why might the norm have been respected on occasion? And, most important, how can we find evidence to address these questions using methods that are not self-fulfilling?

Truth commissions are charged with broad objectives that require answers to the social science questions posed above. Broad structural generalizations to determine systematic patterns of abuse, causes and origins, strategies and mechanisms of the violations, or consequences and effects cannot be satisfied by a simple aggregation of cases, no matter how many, because a simple aggregation might exclude cases that tend to contradict the generalization. Instead, methods must be devised that would find evidence to confirm or—if such evidence exists—contradict the assumptions with which the commission began its work. However, truth commissions do not usually employ methods that allow them to frame, test, and potentially reject a series of hypotheses.

One way to make generalizations is to seek out all the cases and other evidence that support the claim, and if there are enough such cases and they are sufficiently dramatic, to conclude that the generalization is valid. A second method is to appoint an arbitrator, have advocates and opponents of a claim make their strongest possible arguments before the arbitrator, and then allow the arbitrator to rule on the generalization. Both these methods are derived from legal and political procedure, and in fact, they dominate decision making at truth commissions. The second method is better but is nonetheless vulnerable to a weak presentation of one of the two contending positions.

Scientific methods proceed quite differently. Beginning with a hypothesis, the scientific method seeks data with which to test the hypothesis. For example, an analysis of genocide would require a comparative measure of rates of killing among groups hypothesized to have suffered genocide and rates among otherwise similar groups that are not thought to have suffered genocide. If the killing rates were essentially the same among all groups, then this would be evidence of a very violent moment, but not of genocide. But if killing rates were much higher among the groups in which genocide is hypothesized, this finding would support the genocide hypothesis. Obviously, not all scientific methods are statistical; forensic methods in particular have been enormously useful to truth commissions. But what scientific methods all share is the possibility of finding the unexpected and refuting underlying assumptions. Legal and other methods based on unsystematically collected evidence do not have this characteristic.

Another difference between legal and social science generalization methods is the relative importance that each assigns to trends and patterns versus individual cases. As we noted earlier, many truth commissions use a "balance of probabilities" method, by which something was judged true if there was more evidence for than against. The balance of probabilities method, derived from civil litigation, works well in making judgments about individual cases, but less well in drawing generalizations from the thousands of findings obtained by this method. Thus, although the South African TRC was charged with finding "systematic patterns," its report focuses almost exclusively on cases—there is little broader, or macro, analysis. In contrast, the Guatemala commission explicitly invoked a range of social science disciplines and employed a significant number of social scientists. This may partly explain its greater relative success at establishing macro findings (Chapman and Ball 2001, 20–24).

Public versus Nonpublic Operations

Until the time of the South African TRC, it was assumed that truth commissions would collect and analyze their data away from the glare of public scrutiny, to protect their sources' privacy and confidentiality and facilitate the staff's work. The South African commission, however, decided to hold public hearings and invested much of its staff time and resources in doing so. Subsequent truth commissions have generally followed the South African model. This has important consequences for the nature of a commission's public exposure and the quality and kind of data it collects. Truthtelling procedures through public hearings are often less a means of eliciting facts or evidence than of enabling survivors to relate in their own words what happened to them and their loved ones. Public acknowledgment of these experiences is assumed to provide a sense of dignity and worth to victims who were formerly silenced, and thereby to symbolize the break with the past (Stanley 2002, 3). As a consequence, deponents are rarely cross-examined or questioned vigorously. Whereas interviewing deponents in private primarily provides factual information, public hearings generally facilitate subjective truth and, for those few people who get to give their stories, narrative truth. The presentation and collection of information are shaped by the selection of people to appear—usually a very small percentage of those who give statements—and by the time constraints of getting through a large number of deponents in a few days' time. This can result in an emphasis on process over product.

There is often a significant difference between the private, or individual, truth of those who have been victims of human rights violations or have witnessed human rights violations and the public, or social-level, truth that truth commissions are generally mandated to present. Many victims who offer testimony to truth commissions understand truth in terms of efforts to document the details of the events that they witnessed and to identify those responsible. They assume that these efforts will substantiate and validate their memories of these events. Deponents in the South African TRC's human rights violations hearings, for example, frequently emphasized their desire to meet the perpetrators of the crime in order to understand their motives and—when the deponent was not the victim—learn the details of the violation. But truth commissions, even when they have substantial investigative units, as this TRC did, do not have the time and resources to identify individual perpetrators and arrange meetings between victims and perpetrators. To what extent, then, does the inability to satisfy victims' expectations about micro truth affect the process of reconciliation?

Assessing the Impact on Society

Credibility and Acceptance of the Findings

Transitional justice mechanisms operate in a divided population with sharply differing perceptions of the past. In such a setting, it is important to assess the credibility and acceptance of the process and the findings, particularly which groups accept and which groups reject the conclusions drawn. To what extent do key groups—victims, perpetrators, architects of the violence, beneficiaries of the past regime, bystanders, and the new leadership—believe that the truth commission or courts proceeded in an unbiased, fair, and objective manner? Were the procedures consistent with the commission's terms of reference? Do most people believe that the transitional justice mechanism used appropriate methodologies and considered valid sources of evidence? To what extent were the findings contested because of the methods and approaches used?

The second set of considerations relates to the substance of a truth commission's findings. As noted above, truth commissions frequently address different types of subject matter in their reports. Some, like Chile's, focus on a narrow set of gross violations. Others, for example, the Guatemalan CEH, offer a much broader analysis of patterns of violence. Some truth commissions, such as El Salvador's, identify specific perpetrators; others do not. No research has yet assessed the implications of the inclusiveness and type of findings for reconciliation. Several important questions need further research: Did the truth commission's report offer a coherent and credible intellectual interpretation, broadly acceptable to a wide range of communities and groups, of the causes of the past violence and repression? Or did the findings lead to further conflict among various actors and groups? Did the commission identify the architects of the past violence—whether individuals, institutions, or groups—and if so, what were the implications? Does the identification of specific perpetrators lessen the tendency of former victims to stigmatize entire groups?

Developing a Common History

Frequently the task of a truth commission is to go beyond the mere recovery of facts about the past and place these within an interpretative framework. The objective is to offer a new official version of a nation's history during a specific period as the basis for a shared national identity and political culture. While based on research and analysis, the writing of such a history also involves a strong element of interpretation and social construction. Efforts to explain the past invariably involve selectivity, since some facts are given far more emphasis than others, as well as interpretation, since causes and motives are imputed. Thus, the writing of such a history can become a focus of contention. Major actors realize that at stake are the historical record and understanding of the past, as well as their own options for future roles. Therefore, yet another factor to assess is how successful a truth commission has been in going beyond documenting a set of findings on specific violations to formulate a new "collective memory" or common history—if not for all antagonists, at least for future generations.

Cultural images constitute important filters of how people relate to other groups and to the wider world. In the process of crafting a new narrative history, truth commissions sometimes try to offer a set of foundational symbols—even myths—as a way of moving beyond existing images and myths held by conflicting groups and providing a new interpretative grid for past experiences. The South African TRC, for example, projected an image of South Africa as a "rainbow nation" and made the claim that members of all communities suffered under the apartheid order. This effort at an emotional as well as a rational appeal can be one of a truth commission's most beneficial results, so it is essential to evaluate how well a truth commission has managed to impart a new view or vision that can give meaning to a troubled past and allow a people to move forward.

Fostering Acknowledgment of, and Responsibility for, Past Abuses

One of the objectives of truth recovery is to achieve open and shared acknowledgment of the injuries suffered and the losses experienced, preferably within some type of shared explanatory framework—specifically including acknowledgment by the perpetrators responsible for those injuries. Optimally, the acknowledgment should include both institutional and individual expressions of responsibility and regret. However, as Leigh Payne's chapter in this volume points out, this paradigm of acknowledgment and apology rarely occurs in transitional societies, because perpetrators are loath to accept responsibility for their crimes. Very few perpetrators confess fully, express real contrition, apologize to victims or their families, or are willing to make some form of restitution. And indeed, doing so usually runs counter to the interest of former leaders, even if they are protected from prosecution by an amnesty agreement, because any such expression might challenge their standing and potential roles in the new political order, as well as their own self-regard. So yet another question concerns what a truth commission can do to foster acknowledgment—or if no meaningful expression of responsibility and regret is forthcoming, what it can offer as a meaningful substitute for acknowledgment.

Reaching Out to, and Educating, the Population

Far more than being mere intellectual exercises or even efforts to provide a measure of abstract justice, transitional justice exercises seek to inform and educate the population of a country about the past and prepare it for a different kind of future. So yet another factor to assess is those exercises' ability to accomplish this. Here truth commissions have a notable advantage over legal tribunals and courts, particularly international legal tribunals, because they operate within the national borders of the country, their processes are generally more visible, and their coverage in local media is greater. Surveys show, for example, that the populations of the former Yugoslavia and Rwanda had little awareness of the activities of the International Criminal Tribunals in The Hague and Arusha (Des Forges and Longman 2004, 56; Longman, Pham, and Weinstein 2004, 222). Some truth commissions, most notably the South African TRC, have placed considerable emphasis on being publicly accessible. The TRC's public hearings, many of which received media attention, were motivated in part by an effort to educate the population. Nevertheless, various surveys suggest that despite these efforts, there were still misunderstandings about the TRC's work and goals. Hence, the extent to which a particular transitional justice mechanism has succeeded in reaching out to different sectors of the population and how well those sectors have understood and followed its work are other important topics requiring empirical research.

Public knowledge of transitional justice processes often depends on media coverage. The nature of that media coverage can shape popular understanding of the report's findings and recommendations. As may be expected, media sources catering to different groups tend to have divergent views of the past and of the value of the transitional justice process. Slanted media coverage, characterizing the truth commission as biased, unfair, or on a witch hunt, can influence the views held by sectors of the public. So can reporting that either sensationalizes or idealizes the process. The interaction between media and transitional justice mechanisms in particular contexts is an important subject requiring further research.

The ways in which the report is disseminated are also likely to play an important role in its impact. Many truth commissions publish detailed multivolume reports that are unsuitable for the general public. Despite its emphasis on public accessibility, the South African TRC wrote a complex and largely unreadable seven-volume report, whose purchase price was well beyond the financial means of the overwhelming majority of the population. Although there was to have been a summary report, this was never written and published. In contrast with the South African TRC, the Guatemalan CEH had a coordinated strategy for public dissemination of its findings. It printed 42,000 copies of its conclusions and recommendations, to disseminate on the day of the report's presentation and to place in public libraries; and on the following Sunday, major newspapers carried supplements with most of the summary's text. The Salvadoran commission produced a cartoon version of its findings in order to reach people with low levels of education. And the Sierra Leone TRC published a children's version of its report, with the assistance of UNICEF, and also produced a video version.

But even the best written report, with an imaginative distribution and outreach initiative, is unlikely to have a long-term impact unless it is used in later years and by future generations. One potential avenue is to incorporate sections of the report, particularly its findings, into educational curricula. For reasons that have not yet been researched, this has happened in very few countries. Transitional justice models need to accord far more attention to the reform of history education (Cole 2007).

Conclusion

This chapter underscores the complexity and elusiveness of truth recovery and interpretation in transitional justice processes. Does this mean, as Michael Ignatieff claims (South African TRC 1998, vol. 1, 111), that "All a truth commission can achieve is to reduce the number of lies that can be circulated unchallenged in public discourse"? Not so. Despite the limitations identified here, transitional justice mechanisms, particularly truth commissions, can make important contributions to truth finding. Nevertheless, their efforts need to be seen as an initial rather than a final effort to document and understand the past.

References

Bundy, Colin. 2000. "The Beast of the Past: History and the TRC." In *After the TRC: Reflections on Truth and Reconciliation in South Africa*, ed. Wilmot James and Linda van de Vijver. Athens, Ohio: University Press and Cape Town: David Philip Publishers.

Chapman, Audrey. 2007. "Perspectives on the Role of Forgiveness in the Human Rights Violation Hearings." In *Truth and Reconciliation: Did the TRC Deliver?* ed. Audrey Chapman and Hugo van der Merwe. Philadelphia: University of Pennsylvania Press.

Chapman, Audrey, and Patrick Ball. 2001. "The 'Truth' of Truth Commissions." *Human Rights Quarterly* 23 (1): 1–41.

———. 2008. "Levels of Truth: Macro-Truth and the Truth and Reconciliation Commission in South Africa." In *Truth and Reconciliation: Did the TRC Deliver?* ed. Audrey Chapman and Hugo van der Merwe. Philadelphia: University of Pennsylvania Press.

Chapman, Audrey, and Hugo van der Merwe, eds. 2008. *Truth and Reconciliation: Did the TRC Deliver?* Philadelphia: University of Pennsylvania Press.

Cherry, Janet. 1999. "No Easy Road to Truth: The TRC in the Eastern Cape." Paper presented at "The TRC: Commissioning the Past," conference held at University of the Witwatersrand, Johannesburg, June.

Cole, Elizabeth A. 2007. "Transitional Justice and the Reform of History Education." *Transitional Justice* 1 (1): 115–37.

Des Forges, Alison, and Timothy Longman. 2004. "Legal Responses to Genocide in Rwanda." In *My Neighbor, My Enemy: Justice and Community in the Aftermath of Mass Atrocity*, ed. Eric Stover and Harvey M. Weinstein, 49–68. Cambridge, UK: Cambridge University Press.

Dimitrijević, Vojin. 2002. "Fact versus Truth." In *Experiments with Truth*, ed. Okwui Enwezor, 205–12. Ostfildern-Ruit, Germany: Hatje Cantz.

Field, Sean, 1999. "Memory, the TRC and the Significance of Oral History in Post-Apartheid South Africa." Unpublished paper presented at "The TRC: Commissioning the Past," conference held at University of the Witwatersrand, Johannesburg, June.

Freeman, Mark, and Priscilla Hayner. 2003. "Truth-Telling." In *Reconciliation after Violent Conflict: A Handbook*, ed. David Bloomfield, Terese Barnes, and Luc Huyse, 122-39. Stockholm: International Institute for Democracy and Electoral Assistance.

Ghanaian National Reconciliation Commission. 2004. "National Reconciliation Commission Report," Accra, Ghana, www.ghana.gov.gh/nrc/index.php.

Guatemalan CEH. 1998. "Guatemala: Memory of Silence." Spanish, http://shr.aaas.org/guatemala/ceh/mds/spanish/toc.html; and English summary report at http://shr.aaas.org/guat/ceh/report english/toc.html (accessed May 18, 2008).

Harris, Brent. 1999. "History, the TRC and the 'Essential Truth' of Experience." Paper presented at "The TRC: Commissioning the Past," conference held at University of the Witwatersrand, Johannesburg, June.

Hayner, Priscilla. 1994. "Fifteen Truth Commissions—1974 to 1994: A Comparative Study." *Human Rights Quarterly* 16 (4).

———. 2001. *Unspeakable Truths: Confronting State Terror and Atrocity*. New York and London: Routledge.

Huyse, Luc. 2003. "The Process of Reconciliation." In *Reconciliation after Violent Conflict: A Handbook*, ed. David Bloomfield, Terese Barnes, and Luc Huyse, 19–33. Stockholm: International Institute for Democracy and Electoral Assistance.

Kelsall, Tim. 2005. "Truth, Lies, Ritual: Preliminary Reflections on the Truth and Reconciliation Commission in Sierra Leone." *Human Rights Quarterly* 27 (2): 361–91.

Leebaw, Bronwyn. 2008. "The Irreconcilable Goals of Transitional Justice." *Human Rights Quarterly* 30 (1): 95–118.

Longman, Timothy, Phoung Pham, and Harvey M. Weinstein. 2004. "Connecting Justice to Human Experience: Attitudes toward Accountability and Reconciliation in Rwanda." In *My Neighbor, My Enemy: Justice and Community in the Aftermath of Mass Atrocity*, ed. Eric Stover and Harvey M. Weinstein, 206–25. Cambridge, UK: Cambridge University Press.

Mamdani, Mahmood. 2000. "A Diminished Truth." In *After the TRC: Reflections on the Truth and Reconciliation in South Africa*, ed. Wilmot James and Linda van de Vijver. Athens, Ohio: Ohio University Press and Cape Town: David Philip Publishers.

Mendez, Juan E. 1997. "Accountability for Past Abuses." *Human Rights Quarterly* 19 (2): 255–82.

Minow, Martha. 1998. *Between Vengeance and Forgiveness: Facing History after Genocide and Mass Violence*. Boston: Beacon Press.

Parlevliet, Michelle. 1998. "Considering the Truth, Dealing with a Legacy of Gross Human Rights Violations." *Netherlands Quarterly of Human Rights* 16 (June): 141–74.

Shaw, Rosalind. (2007) "Memory Frictions: Localizing the Truth and Reconciliation Commission in Sierra Leone." *Transitional Justice* 1 (2): 183–207.

Sierra Leone TRC. 2004a. *Sierra Leone Truth and Reconciliation Commission Report*, www.trcsierraleone.org/drwebsite/publish/index.shtml (accessed May 18, 2008).

Sierra Leone TRC. 2004b. *Sierra Leone Truth and Reconciliation Commission Report*, Children's Version, www.trcsierraleone.org/children/methodology.htm (accessed May 18, 2008).

South African TRC. 1998. *Truth and Reconciliation Commission of South Africa Report*. Vol. 1. Cape Town: CTP.

Stanley, Elizabeth. 2002. "What Next? The Aftermath of Organized Truth Telling." *Race & Class* 44 (1): 1–15.

Strejilevich, Nora. 2006. "Testimony: Beyond the Language of Truth." *Human Rights Quarterly* 28 (3): 701–13.

Wilson, Richard A. 2005. "Judging History: The Historical Record of the International Criminal Tribunal for the Former Yugoslavia." *Human Rights Quarterly* 27 (3): 908–42.

4

Delivering Justice during Transition: Research Challenges

Hugo van der Merwe

How can you measure justice against all that I have
suffered? It's just a word. It means nothing.[1]

The notion of justice is extremely powerful and inspiring, capturing the notion of putting things right, of restoring balance. Too often, though, it is also illusory and elusive, especially for victims of mass atrocities. As the above quote illustrates, it may also seem impossibly remote in a world robbed of meaning by overwhelming violence. Essentially, our work in this field is to hold out the possibility of restoring this meaning and to give a sense of hope for rebuilding human relationships based on some semblance of justice.

One might assume that "transitional justice mechanisms" refers to a process addressing the demand for justice for past abuses. But this is an optimistic assumption and not always correct. Sometimes these mechanisms provide direct channels for pursuing justice, but often they do more to limit the scope of justice. Justice during transition is often mainly defined by its negation: the provision of amnesty and other methods of limiting the delivery of justice. Amnesties have been a common foundation for transitional justice processes, and transitional justice measures such as truth commissions have at times been introduced specifically to overcome this legacy of impunity.[2] Doing justice can take many forms, with the most obvious (at least to an international audience) being criminal prosecution. Other measures, such as reparations, lustration, public truth telling, and traditional reconciliation practices, also sometimes form part of a justice process.

---

1. A witness whose husband and two sons were killed in an assault on her village in the former Yugoslavia, quoted by Eric Stover (2004, 115).

2. Transitional justice literature now refers to addressing the "justice gap" (Gray 2006) or the "justice deficit" (Gibson 2002) to compensate victims for the removal of their rights resulting from amnesties or other obstacles to prosecution.

Whether transitional justice mechanisms actually deliver justice is both a philosophical and an empirical question. First, there is little agreement on what it means to do justice in a transitional context: what it is in terms of process and product. This is contested among international theorists, between political groups and their leaders during peace negotiations, and even among relatives of a deceased victim. Second, there is even less agreement on how to assess whether, and to what extent, justice has been delivered.

This chapter seeks to unpack some of the key dimensions defining justice during transition, and specifically the impact of transitional justice mechanisms. I examine how existing research, mainly from other disciplines, has shaped some of the research questions that we need to ask, and I briefly review some of the international research aimed at answering these questions. The chapter concludes with some suggestions for what kind of research may be useful in guiding transitional justice policy. The research draws largely on my experience in assessing the impact of the Truth and Reconciliation Commission (TRC) on South African society and in working with survivors to formulate their agenda for justice and reconciliation.[3]

The Limited Scope of Transitional Justice

Demands for justice during transition come from many quarters. Most immediate are the demands from survivors and the families of victims. Often their desire for justice was silenced by oppressive regimes, but during the process of transition, it inevitably comes to the fore. And it is not only the victims who demand justice—calls for justice also come from society at large and, increasingly, from the international community. While justice is acknowledged as a right and a basic human need, the appropriate ways of addressing these demands for it are still far from clear.

Nader and Sursock (1986, 230) contend, "An examination of the comparative literature certainly argues for the universality of the justice motive." After a thorough review of the anthropological literature on how non-Western societies deal with disputes, Nader and Sursock conclude that "the justice motive may be a need as basic as shelter, for example, and as such, an essential requirement for understanding the human condition." This universality of the demand for justice seems to be borne out in countries going through

---

3.   With the high international interest in the TRC, much empirical research on its impact has emerged in recent years. Evaluation of other transitional justice mechanisms, however, is sadly lacking. Fletcher and Weinstein (2002, 585) argue that "a primary weakness of writings on transitional justice is the paucity of empirical evidence to substantiate claims about how well criminal trials achieve the goals ascribed to them. There have been few studies of the effects of criminal trials on victims, bystanders, and perpetrators."

political transition after violent conflict and repression. The range of ways in which it is expressed and addressed, however, is very diverse.

Providing transitional justice means addressing injustices committed during political conflict in the past (during a time of war, collective violence, or political repression). Official transitional justice mechanisms generally are narrow in scope, focusing on particular forms of abuse, designated time frames, and specific categories of perpetrators. The field is also usually quite conservatively circumscribed by a focus on human rights abuses that are defined as criminal, either in terms of international law or according to the law of the affected state.[4] Moreover, there is generally a focus on the most severe forms of abuse, such as the South African TRC's focus on "gross human rights violations."[5]

Admittedly, this is a narrow definition that limits its objectives to considering only the abuses that were motivated by gaining or maintaining political control. This focus effectively sidelines the more common economic or social abuses that generally occur in oppressive regimes—abuses that may well be the underlying reason for conflict over political power in the first place.[6]

"Transitional justice" is thus a conservative term that generally focuses only on victims and perpetrators of physical violence. The link between the political violence and the various forms of socioeconomic or structural violence that characterize many transitional societies is seen as belonging to a broader transformation or reconciliation agenda (rather than a justice agenda). Transitional justice is thus a concept that can be criticized as superficial for addressing only the excessive use of oppressive power or the ravages of collective violence rather than the basic nature of an exploitative system. Indeed, transitional justice mechanisms have been seriously criticized as a form of ideological obfuscation of underlying social injustices—a mechanism designed to divert attention away from those who benefited (and still benefit) from the system and onto only those who were directly involved in perpetrating the worst abuses.[7]

Transitional justice is generally seen as one component of a broader reconciliation process, which also includes the search for truth, forgiveness, and healing as additional elements of the broader process by which a society

---

4.   While transitional justice mechanisms focus on abuses that are carried out with a political motive, they are generally restricted to addressing cases that can be legally defined as criminal acts under domestic law. Legal acts such as lengthy imprisonment of political opponents and forced removals of black communities, for example, were not covered directly by the South African TRC.

5.   Gross human rights violations addressed by the TRC covered only acts of killing, abduction, torture, or severe ill treatment.

6.   Rama Mani (2000) differentiates between three forms of justice in times of transition: rectificatory justice (redressing specific wrongs), legal justice (reforming the legal infrastructure), and distributive justice (aimed at transforming access to power and resources).

7.   See, for example, Wilson (2000).

moves from a divided past to a shared future (Bloomfield, Barnes, and Huyse 2003). It is within this broader reconciliation agenda that social justice is recognized as a key factor. In the next chapter, Audrey Chapman examines such issues, including "the willingness and ability of the post-conflict regime to address and reduce structural sources of injustice."[8]

Another limitation of transitional justice is that it distinguishes between criminal and political offenses. In retrospectively identifying the cases that were political in nature and distinguishing these from "regular criminal violence," transitional justice creates a convenient fiction that certain acts are motivated purely by political goals while others are entirely selfish criminal acts. Establishing a transitional justice mechanism is, by implication, a decision that certain criminal acts of the past require particular attention. Drawing these boundaries can also be an attempt to bolster the fiction of a watershed transition to a post-conflict society. Thus, the argument goes, offenses committed before the transition can be either criminal or political, whereas offenses committed after the transition are by definition criminal, since the political institutions are legitimate and, therefore, incapable of human right abuses and not subject to violent political protests.

This sometimes arbitrary distinction between political and criminal, and pre- and post-transition, violence and crime throws up serious obstacles to our ability to get at the truth underlying political dynamics of the past (their linkages to criminal activities), and the links between present criminal activities and past political dynamics. We thus oversimplify (or even romanticize) pretransition politics and fail to come to grips with the political roots and socioeconomic basis of "post-conflict" crime.[9]

Despite the dangers inherent in a limited transitional justice agenda, the narrow approach is a deeply relevant one, and its success or failure holds serious consequences for transitional societies. Arising from this distinction between political and criminal violence is the idea that political offenses merit special attention. The pressure to introduce specialized transitional justice mechanisms (rather than relying on or bolstering traditional legal mechanisms) to deal with past crimes comes from both sides of the conflict. Those responsible for past abuses apply pressure to avoid having their cases heard by the regular courts, arguing that these were unusual events in unusual circumstances, which required them to act outside the law. Those who were

---

8.   See Audrey Chapman's chapter on reconciliation in this book. Also implicit in the broader reconciliation and social reconstruction agenda is the need for a transformed—or a wholly new—legal system. While such institutional transformation may ensure that justice is better served in the future, the ability of transitional justice processes to contribute toward such a goal is covered only tangentially in this chapter.

9.   See Simpson (2004) for a more detailed analysis of the linkages between political and criminal violence in South Africa.

subjected to abuses look for special treatment of their cases largely because the legal system under the past regime was unable or unwilling to take their cases seriously (and the inherited legal systems often have similar flaws). The circumstances under which the abuses occurred, and the existing legal framework to prosecute those abuses, may also provide little evidentiary or procedural basis for pursuing justice. Added to these victim and perpetrator perspectives are broader societal demands for a more comprehensive symbolic initiative to demonstrate a break with the past by providing public moral judgments on acts of violence that occurred under the old regime.

This argument for transitional as opposed to "normal" justice reflects a political battle for redefining the morality of past acts but also presents a challenge to the legitimacy and efficacy of the inherited legal system. Given the limited scope or ability of transitional justice mechanisms to deliver justice for all past abuses, one must evaluate these mechanisms as part of a broader system of justice. Beyond merely assessing transitional justice mechanisms, there is a need to place this analysis within a broader justice during transition framework. Such a framework highlights the need to transform the system and the culture of criminal justice inherited by a transitional society into a system and culture that can make sense and provide appropriate procedures for dealing with both past and present human rights abuses.

Restorative Justice

Probably the most common debate in the literature regarding appropriate forms of justice for dealing with transitional dynamics is the distinction between retributive and restorative justice. Retributive justice is commonly understood as punishment of the perpetrator by the state, through a process of judging guilt and imposing penalties commensurate with the nature of the crime. Restorative justice is defined in a range of often competing ways by different theorists. A key tension is between definitions based on goal (e.g., repairing the harm caused by the crime)[10] and definitions based on procedure (e.g., active role for victim, consensus-based decision making).[11] The different versions are, however, in agreement that the focus should be less on the crime that was committed and more on restoring or compensating for the harm done to the victim and the society. It is also generally understood to be a more inclusive process, involving participation by both victim and perpetrator.

A range of studies shows victim satisfaction with restorative justice processes for regular criminal cases and compares these with responses to

---

10. See, for example, Walgrave (2004).

11. See, for example, Zehr (1990).

formal legal processes (Marshall 1990; Coates and Gehm 1989; Umbreit 1988; Daly 2001; Latimer, Dowden, and Muise 2001). These studies provide a range of approaches to measure impact, focusing mainly on victim satisfaction but also looking at perpetrator responses and implications for reoffending.

But how victims view these contrasting options in a transitional justice context has not been sufficiently empirically evaluated and remains the subject of intense debate. The debate is mainly being pursued at a normative level, with little consideration of the practical implications for victims or offenders or the measurement of social impact. In South Africa, for example, the TRC was defined by some as an attempt to provide a restorative justice model for dealing with past abuses:

> The tendency to equate justice with retribution must be challenged and the concept of restorative justice considered as an alternative. This means that amnesty in return for public and full disclosure (as understood within the broader context of the Commission) suggests a restorative understanding of justice, focusing on the healing of victims and perpetrators and on communal restoration. (South African TRC 1998, vol. 1, ch. 5, para. 55)

The way in which transitional justice processes attempt to co-opt the language of restorative justice should be questioned, since it often distorts the meaning of restorative justice. Restorative justice is, according to most accounts, a process through which victims are given back ownership of their dispute (in contrast to retributive justice, wherein the state appropriates the role of victim by defining injustice as an act of breaking the law). As both the South Africa and Rwanda examples show, in transitional contexts, the state often appears reluctant to hand over ownership of this valuable public commodity.

A clear framing of restorative justice procedures and outcomes as they would apply in a transitional justice context is not within the scope of this chapter. Particularly because of their linkage to reconciliation goals, restorative justice approaches will likely have much to contribute to transitional justice mechanisms. Unfortunately, however, there have been few attempts to spell out practical strategies for using restorative justice interventions, and assessing their feasibility, in addressing political violence. The necessarily public and symbolic nature of much of the transitional justice process, the complex layers of perpetrator responsibility, and the assumed voluntary nature of the process (as characterized in Western criminal justice systems) offer particular challenges to restorative justice in the transitional context.[12]

---

12. Some of the challenges presented by such approaches are being examined through research and intervention efforts being pursued by the Centre for the Study of Violence and Reconciliation (CSVR). See Ramírez-Barat and van der Merwe (2005) and Greenbaum (2006).

Procedural versus Substantive Justice

Many studies in the criminal justice sphere have highlighted the importance of procedural justice in achieving satisfaction with a justice process (Shapland 1984). Scrupulous attention to procedural justice is probably just as important, if not more so, in achieving the various players' satisfaction with transitional justice mechanisms, given that transitional justice processes are easy targets for accusations of fostering bias or of constituting witch hunts.

But procedural justice is also a very difficult target to pursue in the context of a transitional government, where the legal system is discredited, resources for administration of justice are limited, and the numbers of perpetrators may overwhelm the normal systems of justice. The choice may then be between small-scale justice intervention for selected perpetrators, which can provide very limited substantive justice (relative to the total number of perpetrators) while adhering to procedural justice guarantees, and more extensive justice intervention, which encompasses more perpetrators (and victims) while compromising procedural justice safeguards for the perpetrators. Such compromises (affecting both the victims' and the perpetrators' procedural rights) are likely to face both restorative and retributive approaches.

The language of restorative justice may be used (and abused) to address certain procedural justice needs in lieu of delivering on substantive justice. The South African TRC's emphasis on consultation, storytelling, acknowledgment, and evenhandedness was sometimes perceived as an attempt to compensate for its inability to address the more difficult demands for punishment of, and direct reparations by, the perpetrators.[13] Both substance and process are key determinants of success, and attempts to substitute one for the other should be greeted with skepticism.

The Goals of Justice

There is little agreement on the actual purpose of justice; its goals seem to be a reflection of different cultures, ideologies, or paradigms. Transitional justice mechanisms are generally presented in very idealistic terms without clearly defined goals. They draw on local cultural values,[14] make reference to international human rights norms, and hold out the ideals of a newly transformed society while trying to link these to the political realities of

---

13. See, for example, Hamber (2000) and Hamber and Wilson (1999).

14. Note, for example, the TRC's explicit reference to the requirement in the South African Constitution "that there is a need for understanding but not for vengeance, a need for reparation but not for retaliation, a need for ubuntu but not for victimization."

Table 4.1. Goals of Justice by Target

Goal	Offender	Others in the Social Environment	Victim
Behavior control	Deterrence, isolation, elimination, restitution to victim	General deterrence or threat, prevention of vengeance by others	Prevention of vengeance or social disruption
Reassertion of social values and beliefs	Change in offender's belief system vis-à-vis victim or societal rule, assertion of power over offender, shaming	Vindicating rule, (re) establishing social consensus about rule, maintaining belief in state and legal system	Reaffirmation of self-image and sense of control of victims and their faith in the efficacy of state and legal system

an unstable society and the practical concerns of victims and perpetrators. Whether the transitional justice mechanisms can live up to idealistic goals or even practical demands often becomes a bone of contention during their existence and well beyond their closure.

Justice mechanisms have different criteria for success, but much overlap exists in what they aim to achieve: a change in the way people behave and a more subtle impact on their values and ways of relating to one another and to their society. Table 4.1 disaggregates the goals of justice by their behavioral and value dimensions, as well as by their targets (offender, society, and victim). It is adapted from Vidmar and Miller (1980, 571),[15] who developed it for examining criminal justice processes, but it also has great relevance for transitional justice.

The table highlights the potential contrasts between victim-centered and environment-centered or perpetrator-centered approaches. While there is much space for contention (and complementarity) between such contrasting approaches, even if a victim-centered approach were adopted, it would not resolve certain fundamental disagreements.

Transitional justice processes often focus on the wider social environment, specifically because they occur at a time when political stability is urgently needed, and their timing presents a key opportunity to redefine social norms. In these contexts, the sentiments expressed by Hannah Arendt (1964, 261) are particularly relevant:

> The wrongdoer is brought to justice because his act has disturbed and gravely endangered the community as a whole. . . . It is the body politic itself that stands in need of being repaired, and it is the general public order that has been thrown out of gear and it must be restored. . . . It is, in other words, the law, not the plaintiff, that must prevail.

---

15. The original table developed by Vidmar and Miller does not include the column for victims and focuses more explicitly on punishment goals. This version of the table also incorporates some of the ideas developed by Nader and Combs-Schilling (1976) about the functions of justice found in the anthropological literature.

But in political transition, the distinction between law and plaintiff may be a false one. The pursuit of sociopolitical-level and individual-level justice is not necessarily contradictory. Cullinan (2001, 22) argues, "By enacting legislation allowing for the pursuit of redress, a country can show its commitment to the opposition of acts which violate fundamental human rights." How the individual victim is treated is thus often symbolic of how the country views the acts of the past and how it defines its commitment to dignity and citizens' rights. The repair of the "body politic" may thus be most effectively pursued through the empowerment of victims who have been targeted and marginalized in the past. The pursuit of individual justice for victims, however, is a difficult task that is often paid lip service with no clear understanding of what it should encompass.

Addressing Victims' Needs

In the wake of experiencing severe ill treatment, victims have a range of needs. To categorize some of these as "justice needs" may seem artificial, but substantial evidence suggests that victims feel a need to see justice being done. This experience of justice does seem to assist with other individual social and psychological "recovery" processes.

How to define whether a victim has received justice? A number of factors may feed into a sense that justice has been done. At a simplistic level is the issue of whether victims feel that perpetrators have been sufficiently punished. But a more inclusive approach could also consider the sense of vindication provided by the punishment, whether victims have a better understanding of how they came to be victimized, the restoration of a sense of control to victims, their ability to regain a sense of power relative to the perpetrator, or the reestablishment of a sense of meaning in society, which may have been destroyed by the victimization.

Recent literature on transitional justice has not significantly advanced an understanding of victims' perceptions of justice in its various forms. In developing the conceptual tools for researching victims' responses to transitional justice, we are therefore generally obliged to look at the literature from "nonpolitical" criminal justice. For example, research on the experience that victims of domestic violence have of the legal system shows that key factors include space for truth telling, acknowledgment, compassion by others, protection, accountability of the perpetrator, restitution, and vindication (Alkhateeb, Ellis, and Fortune 2001, 2003).

Addressing the Impact on Offenders

The main focus of traditional formal justice is the offenders, the main goal being that they receive appropriate sanctions for their actions. While rehabilitative outcomes are also sometimes part of the goal, the simple aim of making the punishment fit the crime is the dominant sentiment driving criminal justice processes. In contrast, the intended impact of transitional justice processes on perpetrators is not spelled out in the literature. Debate about appropriate programs to deal with the reintegration of ex-combatants is, for example, clearly separated from any discussion of dealing with perpetrators of human rights abuses. Transitional justice is not generally viewed as a program for managing a problem of reintegration, reeducation, or rehabilitation.

If transitional justice is to be a forward-looking process and not simply about correcting the justice scales of the past, it must address the role of the past perpetrators of human rights abuses in the future society. Criminal justice research mainly engages with this question as it relates to the problem of recidivism. In transitional justice, however, we assume that these perpetrators will not be given the opportunity to commit similar human rights abuses, since the political context has changed (that is, the transition has effectively been accomplished). But several analysts have raised the problem of political torturers being redeployed in the criminal justice arena, where the torture of crime suspects presents a more enduring legacy, and of ex-combatants playing a key role in criminal activities in a post-conflict society (perhaps reflecting a transition to a new form of conflict). Others (Gear 2002) have pointed out the range of social problems faced by ex-combatants (a term that encompasses human rights abusers) in reintegrating successfully into their communities and society at large. Transitional justice mechanisms could help past perpetrators avoid becoming obstacles to building a new society. Broadening the focus from perpetrators to ex-combatants is perhaps also a useful approach in reintegrating armed, militarized, and marginalized sectors of society.

Addressing the Impact on the Social Environment

Two issues arise regarding the social impact of transitional justice. First, responsibility needs to be more broadly conceived than it is in criminal justice. Second, we need to understand how effectively the transitional justice mechanism has transmitted a message of social condemnation of certain acts.

Transitional justice commonly confronts the issue of responsibility on a number of levels: personal, political, and institutional. Responsibility for systematic abuses is shared by the direct perpetrator, those who gave the orders, those who acquiesced, and those who had some responsibility to prevent the abuses. A transitional justice mechanism is thus faced with the task of broadening the reach of justice beyond the direct perpetrators, of not drawing the line too sharply between perpetrators and the "innocent" members of society. The message of social condemnation, of holding people accountable, needs to be extended beyond the conventional bounds of criminal responsibility.[16]

Transitional justice's second function in the social environment is to communicate a message condemning past human rights abuses—not just particular ones, but more generally censuring the social attitudes that fostered them—as something that cannot be tolerated in a new society that is struggling to define itself.

One has to ask: Does the public feel that justice has been done? Have public norms and values been (re)defined, and is there a clear sense that the government has committed itself to ensuring compliance with these norms or values? Public opinion about the message that has been sent out and how well the relevant actors (state security forces and other potential future offenders) have absorbed this message are key in defining transitional justice's real social impact.

While transitional justice's broader impact on the society is to redefine socially acceptable behavior and thereby guide future behavior, it does this through engaging with the past. It is thus retrospective, providing a moral sanction for past actions. This is particularly significant if the formal legal sanctions (such as prosecution, imprisonment, and civil claims) are effective only in reaching a small number of the perpetrators or beneficiaries of past violations. To understand this broader sociopolitical impact of justice, we must examine both the message's intended targets and its content. Target and substance are closely linked. For example, the message of justice is commonly interpreted as "never again." Sanctions against wrongdoers give the impression that future wrongdoers will suffer similar consequences. "Never again" as a message to a particular enemy group may mean "We will never again let you do that to us." Alternatively, the message could be targeted at the political system—"Never again will we let humans be treated in such a degrading manner." But the message might be quite narrowly interpreted and thus lose its impact as a tool for promoting a human rights culture. For example, the apparent acceptance by the South African public of police abuses against criminal suspects and illegal immigrants in the new democratic society stands in clear contrast to public condemnation of past abuses. It reveals a potential shallowness of the human rights message conveyed by the TRC and other legal institutions.

---

16. A common criticism of the TRC in South Africa was that it failed to properly hold whites (who had voted for apartheid and profited from it) accountable for their complicity and active support. Similarly, the judiciary and other legal institutions have not been held sufficiently accountable for their roles in upholding apartheid laws and institutions.

A clear justice agenda would also require a clarification of the targets in the social environment. Different strategies are likely to affect these various sectors quite differently:

- the general public;
- local communities that have been torn apart by conflict;
- institutions that were responsible for abuses or that should have prevented abuses;
- beneficiaries of the oppressive system who need to confront their complicity;
- bystanders who should have done something to stop abuses;
- the international community, where a human rights framework is being developed; and
- countries implicated in supporting an oppressive government.

This complex mix of competing messages and the range of external targets can easily leave victims as a small powerless group competing for attention. In focusing on the need to shape the social environment, there is a strong danger that the symbolism will outweigh substantive concerns. A public message of condemnation and commitment to new values is possibly more easily conveyed by a few highly publicized hearings and harsh convictions of a few scapegoats than by consistent and effective prosecution of a large number of cases. The public will remember a few high-profile convictions and forget about the large number of cases that received only scant attention.

Thus, doing justice risks becoming an exercise in managing public perceptions—treating justice as something that needs to be seen to be done (rather than actually needing to be done). For example, victims and the public in South Africa have contrasting perceptions of whether the TRC delivered justice. Victims feel that the TRC did very little in this regard, whereas the public has broadly favorable opinions, based, it seems, on false impressions of the TRC's accomplishments.[17]

Moreover, the role of international players often draws considerable skepticism from local stakeholders. Rwanda's attorney general, for example, questioned the motives behind U.S. support for the International Criminal Tribunal for Rwanda (ICTR). Comparing the level of U.S. support for the ICTR to its support for local justice initiatives, he argued, "It seems like a public

---

17. For example, surveys of victims, conducted by CSVR and Jeffrey Sonis (not yet published) and by David Backer (2004), contrast with public perceptions of the TRC's achievements, reported by Gibson (2002). Eighty-five percent of survivors questioned in the Sonis/CSVR study replied that they disagreed or disagreed strongly with the following statement: "When I think about everything that has happened since I/my family experienced the worst human rights violation, I believe everything has been put right." This contrasts with the finding that only 14.5 percent of black respondents in the general population disapproved of the TRC's performance (Gibson and MacDonald 2001).

relations effort. They did nothing to stop the genocide, so now they want to appear to be standing up for Rwandans."[18] The demands of international law, including the need to establish precedents and educate the international community, are increasingly perceived as being potentially at odds with local demands for justice processes that take into account national peace processes and local concerns for reconciliation. The role of the International Criminal Court (ICC) in Uganda, for example, has raised serious questions about the appropriate priorities of justice mechanisms and about the possibility that local and international justice mechanisms might play competing or complementary roles in addressing local and international justice goals.[19]

Empirical Research on Transitional Justice

While the conceptual literature on justice is still not well developed, the empirical literature is even sparser. However, some interesting attempts have been made—projects that both develop the research tools and begin to get practical answers to the questions raised by the theoretical literature. The following is a brief review of some of these developments in South Africa and other transitional justice contexts, with a focus on methodology rather than results.

As a starting point, we may expect studies that provide measures of transitional justice, showing conviction rates, efficiency of prosecution and reparations processes, or other relatively objective measures of justice implementation. The absence of such research in most transitional societies is in itself very telling. While there is increasing information about the numbers and types of victims that need to be addressed by justice processes, data about perpetrators are often purely speculative. The data about the numbers of perpetrators implicated in the Rwandan genocide; the numbers of suspects detained; the numbers who have been tried by local courts, gacaca courts, and the ICTR; and the conviction rates in these forums are an exception, providing a useful contextual understanding of the challenges but ultimately saying little about the delivery of justice. Reflections on the lessons from Nuremberg and analyses of the effectiveness of prosecution of Nazi perpetrators do not generally comment on the low number of trials (as a proportion of the numbers actually involved in abuses) or on the low conviction rate of those tried. Given the complex and competing meanings attached to the notion of justice, such a lack of objective measurement is not surprising. Still, this lack of objective

---

18. Interview with Gerald Gahima, quoted in Des Forges and Longman (2004).

19. Empirical studies by the Refugee Law Centre (RLC), by the International Centre for Transitional Justice (ICTJ), and by the Human Rights Centre (HRC) at the University of California at Berkeley have shed useful light on these challenges.

measurement has not prevented empirical research efforts from engaging in serious attempts to assess transitional justice's impact through more subjective measures.

Victim Studies

A number of studies have made some attempt to get a clearer picture of what victims expect to be done about past injustices and what forms of intervention provide satisfaction. The CSVR, in collaboration with the American Association for the Advancement of Science (AAAS), conducted a detailed study of the South African TRC's victim hearings to examine how and when victims talked about justice. The study drew a random stratified sample, coded the testimonies using qualitative data analysis software, and analyzed these data using both qualitative and quantitative methodologies. This analysis provided a clear picture of the justice demands that victims presented to the TRC (punishment, accountability, and so on) and how these demands varied depending on demographics and the nature of the victimization experience (van der Merwe 2008).

Jeffrey Sonis, in partnership with CSVR, conducted a survey of victims in Johannesburg, South Africa, to assess their views on issues of justice and reconciliation. To provide a quantitative measure of victims' views on whether the TRC delivered justice, Sonis developed a justice scale consisting of eight components: voice, punishment, truth, accountability, acknowledgment, financial restitution, apology, and transformation.[20] The validity of the scale has been confirmed by the survey data and provides scope to start looking at how people conceive the underlying factors that constitute justice. The survey also provides some indications of which aspects of interaction with the TRC are more effective in satisfying the need for justice.[21]

CSVR conducted a qualitative study of victims who participated in the TRC amnesty process to assess their experience of engaging with the process. It conducted twenty-four in-depth interviews with victims in three

---

20. The components of the scale were (1) voice—whether the victim had an opportunity to tell his or her side of the story; (2) punishment—whether the victim feels that the perpetrator has been sufficiently punished; (3) truth—whether the victim feels that enough has been done to uncover the truth about the event; (4) accountability—whether the perpetrator has been made to explain his or her actions; (5) acknowledgment—whether the consequences of the victimization have been acknowledged by the perpetrator and the society; (6) financial restitution—whether the victim has been sufficiently compensated by the perpetrator and the state; (7) apology—whether the perpetrator has apologized adequately; and (8) transformation—whether the institutions responsible for the victimization have been sufficiently transformed.

21. The results of the survey have not yet been published. David Backer has since conducted a similar study among victims in Cape Town, which would also provide interesting comparative results on how a mechanism's justice impact varies according to specific local conditions.

provinces[22] (and twelve with the victims' lawyers and TRC officials involved in the process) to evaluate the victims' interaction with the TRC amnesty process and assess their satisfaction with the procedures and outcome. The findings provide nuanced insights into victims' views of a particular type of transitional justice intervention and unpack their varying views about how their expectations for justice were (and were not) addressed and managed by the process. While not broadly generalizable, the results provide insights on key shortcomings of a public process struggling to find a balance between truth and justice goals (Phakathi and van der Merwe 2008).

CSVR, again in collaboration with the AAAS, conducted a series of focus groups with victims who had testified at the TRC victim hearings. The focus groups covered different race and gender compositions and delved into what the victims had gained from their involvement in the public hearings and what the drawbacks had been. While confirming the importance of public testimony as a component of justice, the results also raise important questions about the dangers that such a process poses for the victims. The fact that the study was conducted some years after the public testimony was also valuable in showing how the hearings fit into a longer-term process of addressing justice needs (involving investigations, amnesty, and reparations) and in showing that the hearings cannot be evaluated without this contextual understanding (Picker 2005).

Eric Stover interviewed eighty-seven witnesses at the International Criminal Tribunal for the former Yugoslavia (ICTY) to assess their experience of participating in the process. His research also questions the supposed therapeutic value of public testimony: "The few participants who experienced cathartic feelings immediately or soon after testifying before the ICTY found that the glow quickly faded once they returned home to their shattered villages and towns" (Stover 2004, 107). However, Stover did find that witnesses believed that the trials served a purpose for society at large and for them as individuals (2004, 118). Specifically, it provided them "with a public forum where they could discharge their 'moral duty' to 'bear witness' on behalf of their deceased family members and neighbors." It also provided an opportunity to confront the perpetrators and to "restore their confidence in the order of things."

This growing body of empirical research on survivors' views of transitional justice is becoming influential in public policy discussions. Previous claims about the benefits of, and support for, various justice options have been tested and found to be inaccurate or, at best, simplistic representations.

---

22. Victims were identified using a snowball approach, which used various entry points to identify appropriate interviewees, who then would also identify other victims to interview.

Policy debates in new transitional justice contexts (e.g., Uganda) increasingly rely on surveys and systematic studies of victims' views.

Perpetrator Studies

Alongside the research on victims' experiences of the TRC amnesty process, CSVR has also examined the experience of those who applied for amnesty. Interviews were conducted with thirty-four amnesty applicants in three provinces, both with those who received and with those who were denied amnesty (some of whom were still in jail). They were questioned about their experience with the amnesty process and their perceptions of its fairness and impact. This research provided valuable insight into the feasibility of restorative justice processes that would facilitate community reintegration, particularly among those who had victimized members of their own communities or who felt a need to explain their actions to victims in a less formal setting and to give something back to society. This kind of research illustrates that the subjective experience of perpetrators is also key in understanding how justice mechanisms can be shaped to more effectively promote the desired impact on victims, perpetrators, and the social environment.[23]

A study by the Post-Conflict Reintegration Initiative for Development and Empowerment (PRIDE 2002) sought to assess the levels of knowledge among Sierra Leone ex-combatants about the TRC and the Special Court for Sierra Leone. This study, using a survey and a series of focus groups of ex-combatants in all regions of the country, showed mixed support, largely because of mistrust about the process. The study also demonstrated, through pre- and postworkshop questionnaires and focus groups, that increased knowledge of these processes led to increased support.

More in-depth studies of perpetrators' direct engagement in transitional justice processes also provide useful insights into their motives for involvement, their use of these processes for broader political goals, and the processes' longer-term function in transforming the perpetrators' role in society.[24]

Studies on perpetrators have contributed a significant new perspective on transitional justice processes as questions are raised about reintegration, restorative justice, and ongoing violence in transitional contexts. The growing intersection between transitional justice and DDR (disarmament, demobili-

---

23. This research has fed directly into follow-up interventions, which are facilitating more informal interpersonal victim-perpetrator dialogues, with broader community involvement. See Abrahamsen and van der Merwe (2005).

24. See Leigh Payne's chapter in this book, and the study by Foster, Haupt, and de Beer (2005), which gives detailed case studies of combatants from all sides of the conflict in South Africa.

zation, and reintegration) holds much promise for a more complex research approach to these challenges.

Community-Focused Studies

Several studies have approached the meaning and impact of justice processes through the lens of the local community, examining the justice mechanism within the ongoing network of relationships and links with other social institutions. This process enables an understanding of justice processes as a component of a constantly shifting negotiation of power and identity at the local level.

In their study of three war-ravaged cities in Bosnia and Herzegovina and Croatia, Corkalo et al. (2004) ask what role justice plays in rebuilding communities. Through key informant interviews and focus groups, they explore local perspectives on the need for, and role of, justice. While they found general agreement that war crimes had been committed and that these needed to be prosecuted, there was little agreement on how prosecution should happen or whom it should target. Moreover, although they find social reconstruction to be progressing very slowly, the role of formal justice (as defined by trials) is far less significant compared with broader economic reconstruction and social justice.

Similar research conducted by van der Merwe (2001) in South Africa, using focus groups and key informant interviews in two communities interacting with the TRC, found that communities' responses to their justice needs varied greatly from one group to the next. While justice was held out as a common ideal, there was little agreement about whom it should target or what form it should take. The research also found that preferred justice options are intricately linked to issues of power, reputation, and ongoing community dynamics, which continue to shift and transform in the post-conflict environment.

Ongoing studies carried out by Penal Reform International (PRI) examine the successes and failings of the gacaca courts in post-genocide Rwanda. The project uses an action-oriented approach aimed at "gathering and analyzing data about the perceptions and behaviors of different protagonists (genocide survivors, witnesses, detainees, associations, government agents, etc.) in order to create a tool for understanding the conditions in which the gacaca process takes place" (PRI 2005). Findings showed a variety of reactions to the gacaca process, since perceptions of justice delivery differed greatly between groups. Survivors expressed feeling threatened and disillusioned by the premature release of confessed detainees, who, they felt, deserved concrete retributive punishment for the crimes committed. The research then goes on to describe how these feelings of dissatisfaction undermined the overall gacaca process as participation levels began to decrease and the general population began to lose faith in the level of justice being delivered (PRI 2005). These findings contrast with the much more positive anticipation of the gacaca courts during the planning stages of the process, as seen in Longman, Pham, and Weinstein's (2004) survey of four communes. The authors note, however, that greater exposure to trauma was linked to more negative attitudes toward gacaca courts.

The Refugee Law Project (Hovil and Quinn 2005) provides a complex understanding of the intersection between local values and needs, and the contrasting justice options debated in northern Uganda. Through interviews with a range of stakeholders, they provide a more dynamic understanding of the picture, which defies simplistic portrayals of group or individual opinions.

Community studies are important tools for locating individual perceptions within a social context. Rather than view communities as homogeneous in their values and experience or harmonious in their pre- or post-conflict context, such studies allow a more historical understanding of the shifts in relations and of the meaning of justice mechanisms in transforming relationships.

Public Impact

Evaluating the impact of justice processes on the wider social environment is a very broad goal and probably achievable only through particular research windows. The broadest and most obvious impact is the effect on public opinion. Public opinion surveys have become fairly common tools in assessing public perceptions of various justice options. In South Africa, a series of opinion polls tested public views on the TRC from before it started until after its conclusion. Theissen (2008) reviews these studies and examines the trends and influences underlying the shifts in opinion. More commonly, onetime surveys provide a snapshot of public opinion on an anticipated justice process, for example, in Uganda (Pham et al. 2005) or Afghanistan (Afghan Independent Human Rights Commission 2005) or concerning an existing justice institution, as in the former Yugoslavia (Biro et al. 2004) or Rwanda (Longman, Pham, and Weinstein 2004).

Some public opinion studies have also used creative experimental design elements to explore ways to overcome problems of impunity. Gibson (2002) provides an interesting approach to evaluating the South African public's perceptions of TRC justice. Working from the assumption that granting amnesty is inherently unfair and creates a "justice deficit," he examines how the public views the impacts of different processes in overcoming this deficit. The study used an experimental design embedded in a national survey. Respondents were given alternative versions of a scenario (where different things were done to address justice) and asked to comment on each version's fairness. This allowed Gibson to examine the extent to which voice, apology, reparations, and punishment are seen by members of the public as helping overcome the perception of impunity.

Gibson and Gouws (1999) conducted an experimental study of different group perceptions of the appropriate justice process for dealing with past abuses. The study examines biases based on racial group identification in South Africa. As in the Gibson (2002) study, respondents were given alternative scenarios (with different races assigned to the perpetrator) to assess how the relationship between the respondent's and the perpetrator's race affected their perceptions of appropriate response to violations.

Studies have also been conducted of subgroups of the population, particularly looking at perceptions among beneficiaries of apartheid (whites) in South Africa. Theissen (1996) conducted a phone interview survey of whites to assess their level of acceptance of the TRC and their attitudes toward past injustices.

These studies are all very effective in showing the divisions in society on appropriate approaches to justice. Public opinion is often deeply divided along ethnic or national lines. Even within communities, there is seldom strong consensus on what justice would entail. However, the demand for some form of accountability, even in the face of political obstacles, is consistent in different contexts.

Institutional Impact

In the effort to promote public accountability and transformation, the TRC convened sectoral hearings, which also generated closer scrutiny of institutions and their complicity in apartheid. Audrey Chapman (2008) assesses the level of accountability achieved through the various institutional hearings, through examining "whether they cumulatively offer an otherwise missing structural analysis of the manner in which the apartheid system functioned and the manner in which its goals and policies informed and shaped the patterns of abuses."

Responses to the institutional hearings of the South African TRC are examined in more detail in other studies of particular sectors. Kgalema and Gready (2000), using qualitative interviews with twenty-four magistrates in Gauteng, examine their responses to the hearings in order to assess whether the legal sector hearing had much impact on their views of the past or on the longer-term process of transformation of the magistracy. Rombouts (2002) also uses a series of key informant interviews to examine the broader involvement of the legal sector in shaping and being shaped by the hearing.

The Human Rights Center, the International Human Rights Law Clinic, and the Centre for Human Rights (2000) conducted similar research, interviewing judges and prosecutors in the former Yugoslavia about their perceptions of the ICTY. They found that the ICTY had a very limited impact, even on judicial officials, due to political hostility toward the process.

Each of the above-mentioned institutional analyses provides a distinct framework for conceiving personal and institutional accountability. They all ask critical questions (and come up with disturbing answers) about the ability of different justice mechanisms to contribute to institutional transformation—a key variable in any determining justice in both the short and the longer term. Audrey Chapman provides further conceptual clarity on issues of institutional transformation in her chapter on reconciliation in this book.

Comparative Studies

International comparative research is key in assessing the universality of the justice "instinct" and in unpacking the various cultural and local meanings and orientations that develop in the face of quite different forms and contexts of abuses. A study by the Corporation for the Promotion and Defense of People's Rights (reported on by Victor Espinoza Cuevas and María Luisa Ortiz Rojas in their chapter of this book) examines victims' views of the effectiveness of truth and justice processes. Another study, conducted by CSVR in collaboration with non-governmental organizations (NGOs) in Southern Africa (Mozambique, Namibia, Zimbabwe, and Malawi), focuses more specifically on the issue of reparations. Both studies used individual interviews and focus groups with survivors to explore local victims' and human rights advocates' perspectives on the meaning of justice and on the ability of official mechanisms to address victims' needs. Both studies provide a sense of the commonalities that transcend culture and context, while also emphasizing local peculiarities and the contextual factors that shape the meaning of justice.[25]

Given the lack of conceptual development on the issue of justice, comparative research needs to be treated with particular sensitivity at this point. Simply understanding the meaning of justice in particular contexts is the first priority. Only once certain generic conceptions are identified can effective comparative analysis begin on the impact of factors such as particular victimization experiences and the effectiveness of particular justice mechanisms. Qualitative research (both local and comparative) regarding the understanding of justice in particular contexts (popular, victim, and perpetrator perspectives) is needed in order to avoid imposing conceptual assumptions that are likely to be introduced by quantitative methodologies.

---

25. The results of this research are reported in Buford and van der Merwe (2004).

However, even given these difficulties, comparative research can turn up certain general patterns that may characterize quite different contexts. For example, specific victim responses to justice needs may occur irrespective of cultural differences, or specific problems of government and public perspectives contrasting with victim demands may occur across different continents and historical stages. Comparative research can also illustrate clear contrasts where one would expect similarities and generalizable patterns. Whether these contrasts can be explained by cultural, political, or other factors would then require more detailed structured examination. Comparative research may thus provide the hope of developing more generic international frameworks for anticipating the impacts of transitional justice processes while also giving us clear warnings of the variability in local expectations regarding impact.

Research Challenges

While the research outlined above provides some exciting advances, conceptual clarification of justice and its components requires further development and implementation of these concepts. Its use in both quantitative and qualitative studies is still underdeveloped, and contrasting studies often use terms in divergent or even contradictory ways. The growth of the restorative justice field seems only to further complicate matters as it redefines the conceptual boundaries between justice, reconciliation, and healing. Some key research dilemmas that must be addressed in guiding effective justice policymaking are set out in the sections that follow.

Symbolism versus Substance

An adequate concept of doing justice must cover both the substance and symbolism of the process. Evaluating whether justice has been done is to some extent a quantitative question of how many perpetrators, proportionally, have been called to account or how many victims' needs have been addressed. To evaluate justice as a service delivered to victims, we must ask how many have seen justice done in their particular cases. In most transitional justice contexts, the picture is very bleak, given the difficulty in identifying perpetrators, locating them, proving their guilt, and imposing some form of accountability. In South Africa, for example, the number of victims who made statements to the TRC exceeded twenty-two thousand. The overlap between this and the amnesty process (with fewer than two thousand amnesty hearings) shows up the low percentage of victims who were offered even the possibility of accountability and truth.

The public's perception of justice appears not to be directly shaped by this quantitative picture. Public impressions of the TRC were shaped by media images that have focused on the most prominent amnesty cases and on victims who got to confront their perpetrators and appeared ready to forgive and move on. The TRC thus seems to have been successful in portraying an image of justice being done, that is, we have the symbolism of accountability without the substance.

This symbolism is key in shaping social attitudes, reframing social relations among groups in society, removing a perception of impunity, rebuilding faith in the rule of law, and rebuilding institutions by promoting new values. Just the same, it is dangerous to overplay this symbolism. Not holding perpetrators to account clearly has important consequences for a new democracy. A failure to grasp fully this lack of justice (and, therefore, the failure to understand the effects of unreformed perpetrators on society) undermines attempts to understand the changing nature of violence in society, the resistance to social and institutional transformation, and the victims' continued sense of marginalization.

Mechanisms that seek to deliver justice must be able to address both symbolic and substantive concerns. Both are important policy considerations. Research should be used to assess the competing strengths and weaknesses of different approaches to see how they can be addressed simultaneously rather than as competing goals. At the same time, we need to confront the convenient myths created about justice processes—particularly where they gloss over the failure to deal with victim needs and reintegrate or rehabilitate offenders and bystanders.

Universal versus Local Meaning

Any definition of justice is likely to be challenged for being culturally specific. A specific culture's understanding of justice is deeply embedded in its understanding of human nature and the basic principles of social cooperation and control. Notwithstanding the inevitable link between cultural understanding and justice, there may be more commonality among cultures when it comes to addressing justice for large-scale political abuses. While traditional remedies for dealing with local disputes are important resources, they are often of limited use in overcoming the immense challenges facing a whole society where conflicts involve parties of different cultures.

Just as the debate continues over the cultural fit of human rights as universal principles, the various justice models that can be or have been employed need to be evaluated in terms of both whether they meet universal standards and whether they fit with local cultural practices. These are not two separate frameworks, however. Increasingly, the public, and particularly the victims, in transitional societies draw on both the traditional and the modern, on local and universal values, to make sense of their experience and advocate for better treatment.

The challenge for research is not just to measure the satisfaction with the justice process but also to understand how the sense of satisfaction is shaped and transformed by processes of transitional justice (with their national and international symbolism), by victim mobilization, and by other processes of social change.

Quantitative versus Qualitative Research

Quantitative studies are important in testing and challenging claims of success or failure in achieving justice goals. The South African TRC had many examples of success in delivering justice; it also had many failures. Thus, there is much ammunition for advocates and detractors alike to use in making generalizations about the TRC's achievements. It is only through more systematic study—relying on quantitative measures—that these can be tested and successes weighed against failures.

Quantitative methodologies also force researchers to define more clearly what they mean. In the area of justice, this is crucial as without greater clarity, we may end up talking past each other, using concepts too murky to allow a lucid examination of policy options.

However, the picture provided by quantitative methodologies is seldom more than a snapshot that simplifies the issue and provides limited understanding of its dynamic nature. This fluidity in meaning and the complex interrelationship with other concepts, particularly in their various local contexts, need to be further explored through qualitative methodologies. At the same time, these complex local dynamics need to be examined in light of the international standardization of justice remedies if we are to understand the relevance of human rights concepts and their impact on local justice processes.

The fluidity of justice also points to the need for more longitudinal analysis, through both qualitative and quantitative studies. Judgments about whether justice has been done are likely to change, not just in response to what was done to deliver justice but in reaction to other changes in the social context, such as one's attitude toward the group to which the perpetrator belongs (e.g., new fears of violence) or one's own sense of identity and belonging to a victim or perpetrator group. These changes can affect whole societies, particularly through intergenerational changes (such as German perceptions of the Nuremberg trials) or through small-group dynamics (such as victim mobilization across political lines during a truth commission).

The different results that emerge from qualitative and quantitative research are illustrated through three studies conducted at a similar point in the Uganda debate over the role of the ICC vis-à-vis national amnesty and local justice processes. The studies produced seemingly contrasting findings about the desirability and feasibility of competing justice forums (Pham et al. 2005; Hovil and Lomo 2005; Hovil and Quinn 2005). However, apparent contradictions are more reflective of the goals of the researchers and their methodological orientation.[26] Read together, the three studies provide an interesting complementary overview of the distribution of viewpoints and the complex local context within which these views derive meaning.

Conclusion

Discussions of justice during transition have been dominated by political agendas and competing claims by proponents of different transitional justice mechanisms. The search for solutions and models has also produced simplistic answers to a set of problems for which we don't yet seem to understand the question. Delivering justice usually means different things to different people. It is therefore a highly emotive debate among people speaking different conceptual languages.

The urgency of the policy questions is apparent: How do we satisfy victims' justice needs? How do we address the need to rehabilitate perpetrators? How do we signify an end to impunity? How do we build public confidence in government support for human rights? How can these things best be achieved within the constraints of a political transition?

While there have been various answers to these questions as new models are implemented and policies debated, there is little consensus about whether any of the basic questions have been sufficiently answered. Claims of success have been increasingly challenged, as new perspectives (particularly from victims) come to the fore and as researchers try to assess what has been achieved. A key phase in the research process—challenging existing claims of success and failure—is well under way. Slowly, greater conceptual clarity and clearer formulation of the research agenda are emerging. As this occurs, opportunity grows apace for research to make a strong contribution to policy formulation.

References

Abrahamsen, Theresa, and Hugo van der Merwe. 2005. "Reconciliation through Amnesty? Amnesty Applicants' Views of the South African Truth and Reconciliation Commission." Research report. Johannesburg: Centre for the Study of Violence and Reconciliation.

Afghan Independent Human Rights Commission. 2005. "A Call for Justice: Conclusion of AIHRC's National Consultation on Transitional Justice in Afghanistan." AIHRC report, Kabul.

---

26. Pham et al. use a survey to assess general public views about justice and the acceptability of various justice forums. Hovil, Lomo, and Quinn approach the same topic from a more anthropological perspective to provide a more nuanced understanding of the local challenges.

Alkhateeb, Sharifa, Sharon Ellis, and Mary M. Fortune. 2001, 2003. "Domestic Violence: The Responses of Christian and Muslim Communities." *Journal of Religion and Abuse* 2 (3): 3–24.

Arendt, Hannah. 1964. *Eichmann in Jerusalem: A Report on the Banality of Evil.* New York: Penguin.

Backer, David. 2004. "The Human Face of Justice: Victims' Responses to South Africa's Truth and Reconciliation Commission Process." PhD diss., University of Michigan, Ann Arbor, http://sitemaker.umich.edu/backer/dissertation_overview (accessed March 28, 2008).

Biro, Miklos, Dean Ajdukovic, Dinka Corkalo, Dino Djipa, Petar Milin, and Harvey M. Weinstein. 2004. "Attitudes toward Justice and Social Reconstruction in Bosnia and Herzegovina and Croatia." In *My Neighbor, My Enemy: Justice and Community in the Aftermath of Mass Atrocity*, ed. Eric Stover and Harvey M. Weinstein. Cambridge, UK: Cambridge University Press.

Bloomfield, David, Teresa Barnes, and Luc Huyse, eds. 2003. *Reconciliation after Violent Conflict: A Handbook*. Stockholm: International Institute for Democracy and Electoral Assistance.

Buford, Warren, and Hugo van der Merwe. 2004. "Reparations in Southern Africa." *Cahiers d'études Africaines* 44 (1–2).

Chapman, Audrey. 2008. "Truth Recovery through the TRC's Institutional Hearings Process." In *Truth and Reconciliation: Did the TRC Deliver?* ed. Audrey Chapman and Hugo van der Merwe. Philadelphia: University of Pennsylvania Press.

Coates, Robert, and John Gehm. 1989. "An Empirical Assessment." In *Mediation and Criminal Justice*, ed. Martin Wright and Burt Galaway. London: Sage.

Corkalo, Dinka, Dean Ajdukovic, Harvey Weinstein, Eric Stover, Dino Djipa, and Miklos Biro. 2004. "Neighbors Again? Intercommunity Relations after Ethnic Cleansing." In *My Neighbor, My Enemy: Justice and Community in the Aftermath of Mass Atrocity*, ed. Eric Stover and Harvey M. Weinstein. Cambridge, UK: Cambridge University Press.

Cullinan, Sarah. 2001. *Torture Survivors' Perceptions of Reparations: Preliminary Survey*. Surrey, UK: Redress.

Daly, Kathleen. 2001. "Conferencing in Australia and New Zealand: Variations, Research Findings and Prospects." In *Restorative Justice for Juveniles*, ed. Allison Morris and Gabrielle Maxwell. Oxford, UK: Hart.

Des Forges, Alison, and Timothy Longman. 2004. "Legal Responses to Genocide in Rwanda." In *My Neighbor, My Enemy: Justice and Community in the Aftermath of Mass Atrocity*, ed. Eric Stover and Harvey M. Weinstein. Cambridge, UK: Cambridge University Press.

Fletcher, Laurel. E., and Harvey M. Weinstein. 2002. "Violence and Social Repair: Rethinking the Contribution of Justice to Reconciliation. *Human Rights Quarterly* 24 (3): 573–639.

Foster, Don, Paul Haupt, and Maresa de Beer. 2005. *The Theatre of Violence: Narratives of Protagonists in the South African Conflict*. Pretoria: HSRC Press.

Gear, Sasha. 2002. " 'Wishing Us Away': Challenges Facing Ex-Combatants in the 'New' South Africa." *Violence and Transition Series 8*. Johannesburg: Centre for the Study of Violence and Reconciliation.

Gibson, James L. 2002. "Truth, Justice, and Reconciliation: Judging the Fairness of Amnesty in South Africa." *American Journal of Political Science* 46 (3): 540–56.

Gibson, James L., and Amanda Gouws. 1999. "Truth and Reconciliation in South Africa: Attribution of Blame and the Struggle over Apartheid." *American Political Science Review* 93 (3): 501–17.

Gibson, James L., and Helen MacDonald. 2001. "Truth—Yes, Reconciliation—Maybe: South Africans Judge the Truth and Reconciliation Process." Research report, Institute for Justice and Reconciliation, Rondebosch, South Africa.

Gray, David. 2006. "An Excuse-Centered Approach to Transitional Justice." *Fordham Law Review* 74: 2621–93.

Greenbaum, Bryant. 2006. "Evaluation of the 2005 Ex-Combatants' Dialogues: External Assessment of Centre for the CSVR Ex-Combatants Reintegration and Restorative Justice Project." Johannesburg: Centre for the Study of Violence and Reconciliation.

Hamber, Brandon. 2000. "Repairing the Irreparable: Dealing with Double-Binds of Making Reparations for Crimes of the Past." *Ethnicity and Health* 5 (3–4).

Hamber, Brandon, and Richard Wilson. 1999. "Symbolic Closure through Memory, Reparation, and Revenge in Post-Conflict Societies." Paper presented at the Traumatic Stress in South Africa Conference, hosted by the Centre for the Study of Violence and Reconciliation, in association with the African Society for Traumatic Stress Studies, Johannesburg, January 27–29.

Hovil, Lucy, and Zachary Lomo. 2005. "Whose Justice? Perceptions of Uganda's Amnesty Act 2000: The Potential for Conflict Resolution and Long-Term Reconciliation." Working Paper 15, Refugee Law Project, Kampala, Uganda.

Hovil, Lucy., and Joanna Quinn. 2005. "Peace First, Justice Later: Traditional Justice in Northern Uganda." Working Paper 17, Refugee Law Project, Kampala, Uganda.

Human Rights Center, International Human Rights Law Clinic, and Centre for Human Rights. 2000. "Justice, Accountability, and Social Reconstruction: An Interview Study of Bosnian Judges and Prosecutors." *Berkeley Journal of International Law* 18.

Kgalema, Lazarus, and Paul Gready. 2000. *Transformation of the Magistracy: Balancing Independence and Accountability in the New Democratic Order.* Johannesburg: Centre for the Study of Violence and Reconciliation.

Latimer, Jeff, Craig Dowden, and Danielle Muise. 2001. *The Effectiveness of Restorative Practices: A Meta-analysis. Research and Statistics Division Methodological Series.* Ottawa, Canada: Department of Justice.

Longman, Timothy, Phuong Pham, and Harvey M. Weinstein. 2004. "Connecting Justice to Human Experience: Attitudes toward Accountability and Reconciliation in Rwanda." In *My Neighbor, My Enemy: Justice and Community in the Aftermath of Mass Atrocity,* ed. Eric Stover and Harvey M. Weinstein. Cambridge, UK: Cambridge University Press.

Mani, Rama. 2000. "The Rule of Law or the Rule of Might? Restoring Legal Justice in the Aftermath of Conflict." In *Regeneration of War-Torn Societies,* ed. Michael Pugh. London: Macmillan.

Marshall, Tony. 1990. "Results from British Experiments in Restorative Justice." In *Criminal Justice, Restitution and Reconciliation,* ed. Burt Galaway and Joe Hudson. New York: Willow Tree Press.

Nader, Laura, and Elaine Combs-Schilling. 1976. "Restitution in Cross-Cultural Perspective." In *Restitution in Criminal Justice,* ed. Joe Hudson and Burt Galaway. Lexington, Mass.: Heath.

Nader, Laura, and Andree Sursock. 1986. "Anthropology and Justice." In *Justice: Views from the Social Sciences,* ed. Ronald L. Cohen. New York: Plenum.

PRI. 2005. "Integrated Report on Gacaca Research and Monitoring: Pilot Phase January 2002–December 2004," http://www.penalreform.org/resources/rep-ga7-2005-pilot-phase-en.pdf (accessed March 28, 2008).

Phakathi, Siswe, and Hugo van der Merwe. 2008. "The Impact of the TRC's Amnesty Process on Survivors of Human Rights Violations." In *Truth and Reconciliation: Has the TRC Delivered?* ed. Audrey Chapman and Hugo van der Merwe. Philadelphia: University of Pennsylvania Press.

Pham, Phuong, Patrick Vinck, Marieke Wierda, Eric Stover, and Adrian di Giovanni. 2005. *Forgotten Voices: A Population-Based Survey on Attitudes about Peace and Justice in Northern Uganda.* New York: International Centre for Transitional Justice (ICTJ) and Berkeley: University of California at Berkeley Human Rights Center.

Picker, Ruth. 2005. *Victims' Perspectives about the Human Rights Violations Hearings.* Johannesburg: Centre for the Study of Violence and Reconciliation.

PRIDE (in partnership with ICTJ). 2002. "Ex-Combatant Views of the Truth and Reconciliation Commission and the Special Court in Sierra Leone," http://198.170.242.9/downloads/PRIDE%20report.pdf (accessed March 28, 2008).

Ramírez-Barat, Clara, and Hugo van der Merwe. 2005. *Seeking Reconciliation and Reintegration: Assessment of a Pilot Restorative Justice Mediation Project.* Johannesburg: Centre for the Study of Violence and Reconciliation.

Rombouts, Heidi. 2002. *The Legal Profession and the TRC: A Study of a Tense Relationship.* Johannesburg: Centre for the Study of Violence and Reconciliation.

Shapland, Joanna. 1984. "Victims, the Criminal Justice System and Compensation." *British Journal of Criminology* 24 (2): 131–49.

Simpson, Graeme. 2004. " 'A Snake Gives Birth to a Snake': Politics and Crime in the Transition to Democracy in South Africa." In *Justice Gained? Crime and Crime Control in South Africa's Transition,* ed. Bill Dixon and Elrena van der Spuy. Cape Town: Cape Town University Press.

South African TRC. 1998. *Truth and Reconciliation Commission of South Africa Report.* Cape Town: CTP.

Stover, Eric. 2004. "Witnesses and the Promise of Justice in The Hague." In *My Neighbor, My Enemy: Justice and Community in the Aftermath of Mass Atrocity,* ed. Eric Stover and Harvey M. Weinstein. Cambridge, UK: Cambridge University Press.

Theissen, Gunnar. 1996. *Between Acknowledgement and Ignorance: How White South Africans Have Dealt with the Apartheid Past.* Johannesburg: Centre for the Study of Violence and Reconciliation.

———. 2008. "Object of Trust and Hatred: Public Attitudes towards the Truth and Reconciliation Commission." In *Truth and Reconciliation: Has the TRC Delivered?* ed. Audrey Chapman and Hugo van der Merwe. Philadelphia: University of Pennsylvania Press.

Umbreit, Mark S. 1988. "Mediation of Victim Offender Conflict." *Missouri Journal of Dispute Resolution* 31: 85–105.

Van der Merwe, Hugo. 2001. "Reconciliation and Justice: Challenges to the TRC's Local Intervention." In *Reconciliation, Justice and Coexistence,* ed. Mohammed Abu Nimer. Lanham, Md.: Lexington Books.

Van der Merwe, Hugo. 2008. "What Victims Say about Justice: An Analysis of the TRC Victim Hearings." In *Truth and Reconciliation: Has the TRC Delivered?* ed. Audrey

Chapman and Hugo van der Merwe. Philadelphia: University of Pennsylvania Press.

Vidmar, Neil, and Dale T. Miller. 1980. "Social Psychological Processes Underlying Attitudes toward Legal Punishment." *Law and Society* 14 (3): 565–602.

Walgrave, Lode. 2004. "Restoration in Juvenile Justice." In *Restorative Juvenile Justice, Repairing the Harm of Youth Crime,* ed. Gordon Bazemore and Lode Walgrave. Monsey, N.Y.: Criminal Justice Press.

Wilson, Richard. 2000. *The Politics of Truth and Reconciliation in South Africa.* Cambridge, UK: Cambridge University Press.

Zehr, Howard. 1990. *Changing Lenses: A New Focus for Crime and Justice.* Scottdale, Penn.: Herald.

5

Approaches to Studying Reconciliation

Audrey R. Chapman

The past decade has seen a growing interest in how societies with significant internal divisions arising from collective violence, pervasive human rights violations, and civil wars can facilitate reconciliation. Currently, however, there is little agreement on how to promote reconciliation or on how to conduct research to assess the status of the reconciliation process in deeply divided societies undergoing transitional justice processes. This chapter reviews some of the key issues and the differences in perspective on reconciliation in conflict-ridden societies, with a close look at the questions and challenges surrounding national reconciliation. After a brief characterization of deeply divided societies, the next section describes some of the complexities and contextual factors involved in understanding reconciliation in general and national reconciliation in particular. The following section considers the potential role and the limitations of transitional justice mechanisms in promoting national reconciliation, and the final section discusses potential methodologies in an effort to present a research agenda for national reconciliation.

As envisioned here, national reconciliation is a long-term process with two major dimensions. First, it requires the transformation of relationships among former antagonists. The goal is to enable them to achieve sufficient accommodation and trust to be able to live together peacefully and cooperate and collaborate with one another. Second, it involves the establishment of a new type of relationship between the citizens and the government, resting on political institutions based on the rule of law and respect for human rights and thus facilitating cooperation across group boundaries, leading to a shared commitment to a common future.

Deeply Divided Societies

The term "deeply divided societies" here refers to countries with significant internal divisions resulting from severe human rights abuses, collective violence, civil war, or persistent repression by state institutions. Many governments today confront the challenge of promoting national identity and national unity amid the multiple divisions of pluralistic societies. But the situation in deeply divided societies is different both in degree and in kind, because the traumatic legacy of conflict, violence, and repression makes the challenges of nation building far greater. Even when societies are able to end the violence and initiate a transition to a new political order, societal trauma and differing interpretations of its causes can continue to be divisive. Memories of past injustice, oppression, and violations persist, sometimes across the generations, and influence societal interactions, intergroup relationships, and attitudes toward the political system. How to deal with the past can be a particularly contentious question in such circumstances, and yet doing so is central to the development of a society in which members of contending groups can learn to live together with respect for fundamental human rights and the rule of law. Added to these problems, the transition to a new political order itself tends to generate new sources of conflicts and tensions as communities vie for political power and access to resources.

Further complicating matters, institutions in deeply divided societies tend to be fragile and weak. Mass violence, repression, and gross human rights abuses often result in the delegitimation, sometimes even the breakdown, of key societal structures. The economic and political institutions, civic groups, and networks of community and personal relationships that provide the foundations for a functioning civil society and political order can also be a casualty (Fletcher and Weinstein 2002, 576). The mutual support, cooperation, trust, and institutional effectiveness that are critical to the development of a healthy community and society—or what Robert Putnam (2001, 22) characterizes as "bridging social capital"—are in short supply. The weakness and limited capabilities of social networks and political institutions impose a fundamental dilemma. Just at the point that the new regime is confronting the major challenge of rebuilding and establishing a new political system, the social and political institutions that could serve as potential instruments of transformation must first be reformed themselves.

Differing Conceptual Approaches to the Nature of Reconciliation

Just as the impact of collective violence and gross human rights violations can lead to a variety of social and political cleavages, the term "reconciliation" envisions a process of putting relationships and societies back together again. But "reconciliation," like "truth" and "justice," is an abstract and ambiguous term that carries a wide variety of connotations and understandings, and so far, there is little consensus on what it means or on how to promote it, particularly in deeply divided societies. Various social and political groups in a transitional society may disagree on how to understand reconciliation, based on their political interests and orientations (Hamber and van der Merwe 1998). Nor is there any greater consensus among researchers and policymakers. They generally concur that political or national reconciliation is significant, complex, multidimensional, a long-term process, and difficult to achieve, but on little else. One review of the literature contrasts the frequency with which the term is used with the lack of any clear account of what it means or what it requires (Dwyer 1999). Another theorist comments, "Reconciliation is a theme with deep psychological, sociological, theological, philosophical, and profoundly human roots—and nobody really knows how to successfully achieve it" (Galtung 2001, 4).

One reason for the difficulty in understanding the requirements for reconciliation is that the term refers to a wide variety of types and levels of relationships and an equally broad array of initiatives to overcome ruptures in them. Reconciliation is used synonymously with such diverse processes as peacebuilding, mutual accommodation between former antagonists, reconfiguration of individual and group identities, healing, restorative justice, social repair, and community building. Reconciliation is also both a goal —something to achieve, and a process—a means to achieve that goal (Bloomfield, Barnes, and Huyse 2003, 12).

Reconciliation refers to relationships at different levels of intimacy and inclusiveness. Historically, reconciliation was usually treated in the context of an intimate interpersonal relationship between individuals, and dictionaries often defined reconciliation as making peace, settling a quarrel, and reestablishing friendship after an estrangement (Merriam 1981, 958). Others understand reconciliation as restoring a relationship between former antagonists, either through a one-sided initiative or in a reciprocal manner (Galtung 2001, 3; Fisher 2001, 26). Much of what is proposed about the process of reconciliation derives from studying interpersonal relationships and small-scale group interactions, sometimes under controlled circumstances, but it is questionable whether these data can be generalized to apply to broader social and political processes. The requirements for reconciliation at a national level are very different from a reconnection that raises questions about forgiveness and the restoration of a previously existing close relationship (Weinstein and Stover 2004, 18). As John Paul Lederach (2001, 184) observes, "Whether personal and interpersonal processes can be built, shaped, molded, and ritualized into programs relevant to large intergroup conflicts has yet to be minimally understood, much less harnessed toward predictable outcomes."

Reconciliation is also relevant as a form of intergroup or community encounter and healing. Some of the literature purporting to deal with national or societal reconciliation and peacebuilding generalizes from research based on relatively small-group processes, sometimes from observing the dynamics of workshops in which antagonists have participated. In such a relatively intimate context, reconciliation has been seen as members of formerly hostile communities coming to accept one another, developing mutual trust, acknowledging their shared humanity, forgiving one another, and seeing the possibility of a constructive relationship (Staub and Pearlman 2001, 196–97). Another type of community study addresses the rebuilding of relationships within and between towns, cities, or villages. Accordingly, reconciliation has been viewed as reconstructing local social networks and political relationships rather than as promoting the broad and abstract values of ethnic coexistence and tolerance (van der Merwe 2001, 96). Again, because small-group or even medium-size community dynamics are quite different from those on a national scale, the direct application of findings from either of these types of study to national processes has to be treated with caution.

On a wider political level, reconciliation has been identified with efforts to foster national unity and nation building. Typically, this model emphasizes sociopolitical institutions and processes such as representative institutions and democratic political processes, commitment to the rule of law, and respect for fundamental human rights. James Gibson's (2004) *Overcoming Apartheid* and his chapter in this volume propose that reconciliation in South Africa—and presumably, by extension, in other deeply divided societies— consists of four factors: interracial reconciliation, support for a human rights culture, political tolerance, and the extension of legitimacy to the country's institutions. Interracial reconciliation refers to the nature of the attitudes toward fellow citizens of other races—specifically, trust, rejection of stereotypes, and respect for members of other races (Gibson 2004, 117). He identifies tolerance as the commitment of people to put up with one another and to allow political adversaries the full rights of democratic citizenship (Gibson 2004, 213–14). Support for a human rights culture involves commitment to the principles (abstract and applied) of human rights, including strict application of the rule of law and commitment to legal universalism (Gibson 2004, 4). Institutional legitimacy refers to the predisposition of the population to accept political institutions and acquiesce to their policy decisions (Gibson 2004, 16–17). Together these four elements deal with reconciliation between people, reconciliation with basic constitutional principles, reconciliation among groups, and reconciliation with institutions (Gibson 2004, 291). The view of national reconciliation given later in this chapter has many of the same elements.

In addition, some work on the dynamics and requirements of reconciliation deals with the international dimension. Here, although the central issue is peacebuilding between states after a period of war or conflict, some analysts assume that it is possible to apply insights gained from such international-level research to country-level processes. One effort to develop models to obtain or restore social stability and peace through reconciliation, for example, proceeds through a case study approach drawing on and comparing international and national examples, eventually to conclude that the two contexts require different models (Long and Brecke 2000).

Adding to the linguistic and conceptual confusion, approaches to reconciliation come from a wide variety of disciplines, including theology, philosophy, social psychology, peace studies, political science, law, and community studies. Many of these disciplines have differing terminologies and methodologies, which can influence how reconciliation is conceived and shape the way it is studied. The question is whether these disciplines offer complementary approaches that can be synthesized into a richer understanding or are so inconsistent that it is a matter of picking and choosing among them.

Reconciliation originated as a religious concept, and much of the work on reconciliation comes from religious thinkers. In scripture, reconciliation is primarily a theological rather than a social concept, a term used to describe God's supreme act of reconciling humankind to God's self (Muller-Fahrenholz 1997, 4). A religious perspective, even if it distinguishes between religious and political requirements, frequently emphasizes that reconciliation between people ultimately depends on reconciliation with God (Chapman and Spong 2003). Religious treatments of reconciliation, regardless of the level or scope of the unit being addressed, often emphasize the need for the transformation of attitudes. They also tend to emphasize interpersonal relationships and frequently adopt a pastoral or therapeutic perspective. Religious models generally cast reconciliation as a bottom-up process, in which the transformation of the personal attitudes of former antagonists from hostility to mutual acceptance and respect is key. This interpretation assumes that reconciliation happens to individuals and discounts the community and structural dimensions. Many religious thinkers also associate reconciliation with forgiveness. Some—for example, Archbishop Desmond Tutu, chairman of South Africa's Truth and Reconciliation Commission (TRC)—also advocate unilateral or unconditional forgiveness on the part of victims (Tutu 1999).

Like the religious model, several other disciplines approach reconciliation as primarily entailing the transformation of the attitudes and relationships of individuals, but they do not necessarily agree on the key elements. Ethicists and philosophers often understand reconciliation as a process of developing shared values and building a moral community (Ericson 2002, 27–32). In contrast, the social-psychological approach tends to emphasize attitudinal changes. Ronald Fisher (2001, 35), for example, posits that reconciliation likely involves cognitive and emotional realignment, possibly even changing a fundamental sense of group or national identity. Some of those in the field of peace studies view reconciliation as the rebuilding of relationships after conflict; according to one theorist, reconciliation is a form of personal encounter, which addresses the sources of pain and injustice in the past while envisioning a future that enhances interdependence and a shared future (Lederach 1997, 26–27).

Differing conceptions and approaches can also reflect divergent understandings of the requirements of reconciliation in deeply divided societies. At one end of the spectrum are those who hold what might be termed a "thick" view, which assumes that reconciliation necessarily involves fundamental attitudinal changes, forgiveness of those responsible for the abuses and violence of the past, and the achievement of a deep moral consensus. Some of those putting forward this view acknowledge that these requirements are very demanding and difficult to achieve, but not all proponents do. Mark Amstutz (2005) proposes a notion of "political forgiveness" that imposes moral and political burdens on both victims and offenders, such as full disclosure and acknowledgment of the truth, and moral accountability for past wrongdoing, as well as forgiveness for past offenses, not because he thinks it is feasible to achieve but because he believes anything less will not result in reconciliation and healing. The need for forgiveness between former victims and perpetrators also figured prominently in the rhetoric of the South African TRC, particularly at its human rights violations hearings. As the title of TRC Chairman Archbishop Desmond Tutu's (1999) widely read book indicates, he argued that there can be "no future without forgiveness." However, an analysis of the transcripts of the TRC's human rights violations hearings indicates that few deponents in those hearings mentioned the subject of forgiveness or viewed the TRC process as being directly related to the topic of promoting forgiveness (Chapman 2008a).

Others offer a more minimalist view of the conditions for initiating or sustaining national reconciliation in a deeply divided society. For example, Rajeev Bhargava (2000, 45–67), who does not explicitly use the language of reconciliation, argues that transforming a "barbaric" society, one in which the basic moral rules have broken down, into a "minimally decent" society able to prevent excessive wrongdoing depends on developing a societal consensus around a core of moral rules—specifically, negative injunctions against killing, maiming, or ill-treating others and basic norms of procedural justice. He believes that achieving a minimally decent society does not require that enmity or estrangement be ended between victims and their former oppressors or among groups with inherited hostilities toward one another. Nor does he believe that members of a minimally decent society have to share a particular conception of the good life or a substantive conception of justice. Similarly, James Gibson (2004, 213–14) offers a minimalist interpretation of reconciliation, linking it with the development of tolerance rather than forgiveness. He argues that reconciliation does not require that people accept and embrace one another but only that they be willing to put up with those whom they oppose.

Another major divide in the literature is whether national reconciliation should be understood as a top-down process, which is primarily dependent on political policies or initiatives, or a bottom-up process, in which community-level dynamics and the attitudes and relationships of individuals, particularly former victims and perpetrators, are the determining factors. For example, Ronald Fisher (2001, 26) argues for a bottom-up process based on reestablishing harmony between antagonists who have inflicted harm on one another. He emphasizes the importance of genuine dialogue and conflict analysis of a mutually, interactive nature to increase understanding between members of conflicting groups in order to induce cognitive changes in thinking and orientation (Fisher 2001, 28–32). According to Fisher, reconciliation in an interpersonal or intergroup encounter is more of an emotional experience, more a matter of realigning one's cognitive and emotional world—even one's sense of group or national identity—than of a rational calculus (Fisher 2001, 34–35). But it is questionable whether one can generalize from the type of small-group interactions that Fisher has studied to the national level and whether the level of harmony he describes is either feasible or necessary.

In contrast with this position, other analysts and theorists are more inclined to stress the intercommunal and political dimensions, particularly when addressing national reconciliation. Ackerman (1994, 230) views reconciliation as a peacebuilding process among peoples with long-standing animosities, achieved through fostering ongoing and continuous political, economic, social, and cultural relationships. Louis Kriesberg (2001, 48) posits that reconciliation among communities or groups that have experienced a period of rupture, atrocity, or oppression develops out of some form of coexistence. Coexistence minimally requires accommodation between members of different communities living together, with members of each group refraining from efforts to destroy or severely harm the other. Reconciliation can also proceed beyond this minimal level to include a sense of mutual tolerance and respect and even to entail relative equality in economic position and political power.

The relevance of religious approaches to reconciliation is yet another controversial topic. Religious considerations clearly influenced the South African TRC—one of the consequences of having religious figures and clergy hold key positions: chair, deputy chair, four other commissioners, and the director of research. But this approach also generated controversy within both the

TRC and the South African population, and many religious leaders were unsure about the appropriateness of the religious involvement in the TRC process (Chapman and Spong 2003). The concluding volume of the TRC's report notes, possibly as a reflection on its own experience of conflating religion and politics, "the potentially dangerous confusion between a religious, indeed Christian understanding of reconciliation, more typically applied to interpersonal relationships, and the more limited notions of reconciliation applicable to a democratic society" (South African TRC 1998, vol. 5, 440). Religious figures have also played significant roles on several other truth commissions, including those in Sierra Leone, Ghana, and Timor-Leste, but the implications have yet to be studied.

Understanding National Reconciliation

As the term implies, national reconciliation focuses on macro social and political processes. The aim here is not to denigrate the importance of smaller-scale initiatives to promote individual and group healing and reconciliation but to point out the differences between such efforts and national reconciliation. Each level and type of reconciliation raises distinctive types of issues and typically has different requirements—some require national-level initiatives, whereas others can best be resolved through group and individual interventions. The emphasis in this chapter reflects the belief that national reconciliation provides the critical framework, or "scaffolding," in deeply divided societies undergoing political transitions, that is, in such societies, some minimal level of national reconciliation and reconstruction appears to be a condition for sustainable and meaningful relationships to take root.

Differing Conceptions

So what does national reconciliation entail in a deeply divided society? Some conceptions of national reconciliation are very broad and inclusive. For instance, *A Handbook on Reconciliation after Violent Conflict*, prepared by the International Institute for Democracy and Electoral Assistance (IIDEA) in Stockholm, envisions reconciliation in such societies as a broad process that includes the following elements: finding a way to live that permits a vision of the future; (re)building relationships; coming to terms with past acts and enemies; embracing a societywide process of deep change; acknowledging, remembering, and learning from the past; and it is a voluntary process that cannot be imposed (Bloomfield, Barnes, and Huyse 2003, 214). Louis Kriesberg, an expert in conflict resolution and peace studies, also offers a broad model of reconciliation having considerable overlap with IIDEA's work. His proposal is that societal reconciliation has four dimensions: truth, in the sense of shared understandings or recognition of varying viewpoints; justice, whether in the form of punishing wrongdoers or establishing a more equitable system of relations; remorse and forgiveness; and individual and group safety and security (Kriesberg 2001, 60).

Brandon Hamber and Gráinne Kelly (2005, 38–40) offer an interpretation that comes closer to the one proposed here. As their chapter in this volume indicates, they see reconciliation in societies emerging from conflict as a process of addressing fractured relationships in a continually changing social, interpersonal, and political context. They propose that reconciliation involves five interwoven strands: developing a shared vision of an interdependent and fair society, acknowledging and dealing with the past, building positive relationships promoting significant cultural and attitudinal change, and substantial social, economic, and political change.

The Dilemma: Distinguishing Prerequisites from Core Requirements

The dilemma is that the three approaches sketched above, particularly the models of IIDEA and Kriesberg, are so comprehensive that they come close to equating national reconciliation with transitional justice. Thus, they make it difficult to define what reconciliation is and is not and blur the boundaries between the prerequisites for reconciliation and its core components. Moreover, truth finding and acknowledgment, while important dimensions of transitional justice, may not necessarily promote reconciliation—and, in some circumstances, may even complicate accommodation between groups. In most circumstances, coming to terms with the past appears to be a prerequisite, rather than a direct component, of reconciliation. And in a few contexts (e.g., Spain), there was a consensus that it would be preferable to postpone trials or commissions that reopened the past until the country was sufficiently reconciled to withstand the tensions that would likely result (Daly and Sarkin 2007, 194–95). Nor does forgiveness appear either feasible or required for promoting national reconciliation.

Building on some aspects of the views outlined above, national reconciliation in deeply divided societies is better seen as a multidimensional and long-term process with two major dimensions. First, it involves transforming social and political relationships among former antagonists. Members of major social groups and communities need to achieve sufficient accommodation, tolerance, and trust to be able to live together peacefully and cooperate and collaborate with one another. Second, it involves establishing a new type of relationship between the citizens and the government. To that end, reconciliation requires the development of political institutions and processes that nurture and sustain a stable, decent, and equitable society based on the rule of law and respect for human rights. The evolution of a new political covenant also involves inculcating political legitimacy and trust on the part of the people and a commitment to a common future. Efforts by the government to adopt policies likely to promote reconciliation and rectify the injustices and abuses that led to the social and political breakdowns are also important.

Transforming Human Relationships

It is generally agreed that national reconciliation involves a transformation of human relationships among individuals and communities from conflict to at least some level of accommodation. Several theorists and analysts link national reconciliation primarily with eliminating or managing destructive and protracted conflicts among groups that share the same territory and have membership in a common political system (Fisher 2001, 25). In an article on the requirements of community relationships in a post-conflict situation, Louis Kriesberg (1998) characterizes reconciliation as "the processes by which parties that have experienced an oppressive relationship or a destructive conflict with each other move to attain or to restore a relationship that they believe to be minimally acceptable." At a minimum, accommodation requires former antagonists to relinquish their feelings of hate and fear or their desires for revenge and retribution. Vamik Volkan (2003, 82) hypothesizes that doing so involves a process whereby former antagonists adjust their primary community identities to eliminate their exclusionary character, previously predicated on the existence of an enemy, and thereby diminish the prejudice against, and dehumanization of, members of other groups.

This reshaping of their relationships does not require that members of different communities socialize, become friends, or engage in intimate social relationships. What is critical is that members of different groups develop sufficient mutual trust and acceptance to be able to live together and cooperate and collaborate in a variety of social and political relationships.

Survey research frequently seeks to measure intergroup relationships through questions about ethnic or racial images, groups that one has the most or least in common with, the desired social distance from various groups, attitudes toward neighborhood integration and intermarriage, incidence and types of stereotyping, and the extent and kind of social interactions that respondents have or are willing to have with persons outside their own community. Aside from difficulties in framing questions that elicit truthful and accurate data, especially in the suspicious environment of post-conflict societies, how much do these responses actually tell us? Social reconstruction is a complex and long-term process, and improvements in the ability to work together in a work, political, or institutional environment may not necessarily be present in private social encounters (Corkalo et al. 2004, 152).

Also, research conducted on the views of members of relatively stable pluralistic societies, such as the United States and the UK, indicates that as countries become more diverse, the goals of intergroup tolerance and equality frequently become more elusive (Smith 2001). In stable pluralistic societies, institutions such as schools and residential areas can become more rather than less segregated over time (Winter 2003, A14). Also, it may not be necessary to like members of other groups in order to develop a strong sense of shared national identity, affirm ties based on a common citizenship, and share a commitment to the legitimacy of political institutions. Moreover, the absence of intimate social interactions across group boundaries does not necessarily inhibit collaboration in civil society or in political institutions that cut across community boundaries.

Political Institutions: A New Relationship between Citizens and Government

The second key dimension of national reconciliation is the establishment (or reestablishment) of effective national political institutions. The process is reciprocal in that the society develops a series of capabilities and, by so doing, motivates contending groups to change their political relationships and, eventually, their attitudes toward one another. These capabilities include the ability to resolve or manage conflict, promote justice and equity, and instill the democratic and human rights values likely to sustain human dignity and decency. Accommodation and conciliation of former antagonists, as well as healing, are more likely to be the outcome rather than the foundation of a long-term process of national reconciliation. So is the emergence of a sense of national identity and shared citizenship.

Prospects for national reconciliation often rest on the ability to improve the effectiveness, legitimacy, and inclusiveness of the national political system. Weak, corrupt, or biased national institutions cannot command the legitimacy required for reform and transformation. It is important for national institutions, particularly the government and the governing political party, to set an example, embodying national reconciliation by reaching across divisions and being as inclusive as possible. This may entail formal or informal power-sharing arrangements so that the groups that have been at risk have access to at least some degree of legitimate political power.

Respect for human rights is also likely to be related to the ability of a new regime and its institutions to gain respect and legitimacy. Human rights norms embody the minimum conditions for a decent society, one that is responsive to the needs of its citizens. A human rights culture protects human dignity and offers a bulwark against abuses by the government; also, the freedoms and protections associated with a commitment to human rights may forestall the outbreak of future violence.

Informed and sensitive public policies directed at reducing tensions, correcting inequities, and generating shared goals and identities can play a major role in promoting political reconciliation. The establishment of new forms of social institutions and political parties with multicommunity bases can better enable members of diverse groups to collaborate in a variety of relationships on a national as well as a local political level. Inclusive national political institutions can provide incentives to establish cross-cutting civil society institutions, political parties, and social groups, and can gradually foster a sense of common national identity superimposed over the more parochial identities still held by community members.

The willingness and ability of the post-conflict regime to address and reduce structural sources of injustice are likely to be important dimensions of national reconciliation. Many deeply divided societies are characterized by major inequalities in wealth, resources, and access to the basic needs of life. Oppressive regimes often skew the distribution of resources to favor some groups at the expense of others. The structural inequalities in access to economic and political power contribute to the breakdown of these societies and the resultant cycles of violence. For this reason, efforts to promote greater social justice through improving the situation of the poorest and most vulnerable sectors of the population and bringing about greater equity in the distribution of social, economic, and political resources may be one of the most powerful contributors to reconciliation.

The dilemma is that many deeply divided societies have fragile political institutions that lack the capacity to formulate and implement policies to foster reconciliation and rebuilding. A study of the educational system in societies emerging from identity-based conflicts shows the potential of education in dismantling cultural stereotypes and affirming the national identity while fostering tolerance and democratic values. But at the same time, such case studies underscore the difficult policy issues and the problems of instituting an appropriate curriculum (Tawil and Harley 2004).

Limited capabilities to promote reconciliation through educational curricula or other policy initiatives are in some cases compounded by the discrediting of public authorities and institutions because of either their complicity in the violence and abuses or their ineffectiveness in preventing or ending them. In such circumstances, fundamental political reforms may well be a precondition for any real reconciliation to take place. Preferably, the political reforms will institute national political institutions that can cut across the major divides of the society and operate in accordance with the rule of law and democratic values. But in practice, very few transitional societies—least of all those that have experienced destructive conflicts—have managed to establish stable and well-functioning democratic political systems.

Contextual Factors to Consider

To assess the prospects for reconciliation, the appropriate first step is to identify major sources of societal division—social, political, ethnic, racial, religious, linguistic, and economic—gauging their intensity, the proportion of the population affected, the channels through which these sources of divisiveness are being expressed, and the forms they are likely to take in the future. By definition, deeply divided societies have significant social or political cleavages, but they differ in character, and not all these social divisions have the same implications for reconciliation.

Sources, Nature, and Scale of Past Abuses

The source of the past abuses is one relevant factor. In some cases, a previous government has been the major instigator of the conflict, whereas in others, social, political, or ethnic groups have been instrumental. The nature, scale, and intensity of past violence are yet other considerations. Societies seeking to recover from the experience of genocide or ethnic cleansing are likely to have far deeper hatreds and persistent antagonisms, affecting a larger number of people, than societies that suffered from repression and human rights violations inflicted by a government attempting to hold on to power, even if its power base was a particular ethnic or economic community. The social landscape of reconciliation raises yet another set of issues when antagonists were "intimate enemies," who committed acts of collective violence against individuals with whom they had lived and interacted for many years (Theidon 2006). On a societal level, the 1994 Rwandan genocide (600,000 to 1,000,000 deaths in 100 days) has far different implications from the conflict in Northern Ireland (around 3,000 dead in 30 years). In Rwanda, the violence directly affected a far broader spectrum of the society, left deeper communal wounds, devastated social relationships and institutions, and inflicted far more profound trauma (Bloomfield, Barnes, and Huyse 2003, 41). As might be expected, research on Rwanda found that traumatic exposure to violence and the prevalence of post-traumatic stress disorder symptoms correlate with attitudes toward reconciliation (Pham, Weinstein, and Longman 2004).

Personal Security

The extent to which the new political order can protect personal security is another factor affecting prospects for reconciliation. While the transition to peace or a new political order implies that overt conflict has ended, this does not mean that all forms of political violence, or the threat of violence, have ceased. Often the threats of political violence and intimidation can continue long after the formal resolution of the conflict or can emerge in new forms.

Societies with histories of violent conflict and weak political institutions can easily be prone to new forms of political violence and escalating levels of violent crime that weaken or undermine efforts to establish a stable political order. One of several tragic examples of the recycling of political violence in new forms is Guatemala, which has one of the highest murder rates in Latin America. Drug traffickers and gang members act with impunity because criminal elements have infiltrated the country's military, police, and justice systems (*New York Times* 2008). Continued poverty and racism and growing unemployment have fueled high levels of violent crime in South Africa, raising levels of insecurity and encouraging tougher police action rather than measures to address the causes of the violence (Mohamed 2007).

Time Elapsed since Conflict

The length of time since the cessation of overt conflict and the continuing trauma caused by the violence are another set of factors to consider. Reconciliation may be hardest to promote just as a transition is beginning, when memories of the violence are still very painful and the trauma recent—which is precisely when a truth, or truth and reconciliation, commission is most likely to function. Often, reconciliation between former antagonists or between government and governed may require some level of societal healing, rebuilding a system of governance, and achieving some sense of normality. The passage of time may enable painful memories to recede and a new generation, without direct experience of the hostilities and hence more open to new kinds of relationships, to emerge. Research on Spain, for example, has shown that the willingness of a society to recover historical memories of its civil war and address their implications for justice and reconciliation may take several generations (Davis 2005, 858–80). Studies of race relationships in South Africa indicate that ten years into the transition, younger members of society are less likely to exhibit racial stereotypes and are more likely to be open to cross-racial relationships of various kinds than are their elders, who lived longer under the apartheid regime (Hofmeyr 2005, 4–5).

Past and Present Roles

It is also important to bear in mind that groups and communities in deeply divided societies bring different perspectives to the process of reconciliation, depending on their past positions and current social strata and prospects. Views on a wide variety of matters related to reconciliation will likely depend on the roles held in the past political order—whether individuals were victims, relatives of victims, perpetrators, bystanders, or beneficiaries. In many contexts, group and community memories reinforce the position and situation of individuals; in others, they may cut across them. Adding to the complexity, one person may have assumed multiple roles and may have been both victim and perpetrator, depending on the situation. Also, the dynamics at the community level may not reflect the divisions at the national level, thus adding yet another layer with differing perspectives to consider. For these reasons, research on national reconciliation needs to be "disaggregated," that is, researchers should study representatives of each of these major groups and social roles and avoid making generalizations.

Sense of Common Nationality

In deeply divided societies as in other social landscapes, individuals and groups often have multiple sources of identity. These may overlap, mitigating the impact of each of these divisions, or they may reinforce one another. Most important, members of some transitional political systems have a sense of a common nationality that coexists with other, more particularistic forms of identity. The conventional hypothesis is that the strength of national identity correlates inversely with group attachments, but a 2000–2001 survey in South Africa found that for nearly every group, the more a respondent identified with the group, the more likely he or she was to hold a strong national identity as well (Gibson 2004, 57–58). Nevertheless, even if the development of shared national identity does not displace other forms of identity, it is likely to ameliorate some effects of the divisions. The strength and relevance of a common sense of nationality and commitment to the nation among the various communities are thus other important considerations.

Effectiveness of Post-Conflict Political Institutions

As noted above, prospects for national reconciliation also rest on the effectiveness, legitimacy, and inclusiveness of the national political system and the nature of its policies. The challenge of the post-conflict political landscape is less to remove the differences between groups and more to ensure that all groups and communities may participate fully and equally and thus come to have a stake in the new order. Some considerations are whether the structure of the political system facilitates power sharing; in a multiethnic state the dispersion of power from the center to different subnational entities through some form of federalism and devolution may facilitate expanding the reach of the state to all important political constituencies. The ability of a new national government to achieve good governance and ensure the protection of human rights is another factor. The relationship between reconciliation and economic interests is another important topic. Because material deprivation is often a source of conflict, the government must often undertake economic reforms that promote greater material or economic equality, at least to a level at which differences in the standard of living do not interfere with the opportunity for political participation. Broad-based economic reforms may be more effective in responding to the needs of larger numbers of people, but they are also more difficult to enact, more costly, and riskier in terms of the reactions of the entrenched interests they affect (Daly and Sarkin 2007, 203–38).

Transitional Justice Mechanisms' Potential Role in Promoting Reconciliation

Proponents of transitional justice processes have often assumed that transitional justice mechanisms can contribute to reconciliation. These views have generally rested on assumptions that truth recovery and legal processes ending impunity can lead to, or at least facilitate, reconciliation. The motto of the South African TRC, emblazoned on its posters, was "truth, the path to reconciliation." Banners hung in many of the town halls where the commission held public hearings proclaimed "Reconciliation through Truth." But is truth or justice necessarily the path to reconciliation? Coming to terms with the past in some way, at some point in a country's history, is likely to be indispensable for long-term reconciliation. However, at least in the short term, the process of seeking to determine responsibility for the nature and causes of violence and human rights abuses under a previous regime may complicate efforts to promote national reconciliation and may even exacerbate social divisions. Such efforts to come to terms with the past run the risk of reawakening difficult and painful memories and thereby increasing tensions. Typically, no group is satisfied with the outcome of transitional justice processes, and many come away frustrated and angry. The unwillingness of perpetrators to acknowledge their crimes, apologize, or be contrite can further alienate victims. And the amnesties that often accompany negotiated settlements as a prerequisite for going forward with some form of accounting for past abuses can also be a source of continuing controversy and lingering resentments.

Recently researchers have been more inclined to acknowledge the limitations of these institutions (Barsalou 2005). Several other factors also prevent transitional justice mechanisms from being generally well suited to promoting national reconciliation and healing. Reconciliation is a complex, long-term process. Whether in the form of tribunals and other judicial bodies or truth commissions, transitional justice mechanisms are temporary bodies with limited resources and staff. Promoting national reconciliation requires major long-term policy initiatives that are outside the purview of temporary bodies set up to facilitate and consolidate political transitions. Even if mandated to promote reconciliation, these mechanisms rarely have the time, knowledge, or means to do so. Although many truth commissions make extensive recommendations about public policy initiatives, they typically do not have the power to implement them. More often than not, their proposals, whether for institutional reforms to prevent the recurrence of violence or human rights abuses or for specific levels of reparations to victims, are disregarded. This gap between recommendations and implementation can lead to criticism and disillusionment.

Also, transitional justice mechanisms typically operate at a time when the memories of the past conflict are still painful and the wounds deep. Often the goal is to get through the process as soon as possible in order to get to the agenda of recovery and economic development. Moreover, some of these bodies have a limited capacity to reach out to, inform, or influence the population. This is particularly the case with international tribunals located outside the country, where there is little awareness of their work (Des Forges and Longman 2004, 62).

Despite these limitations, the nature of the mandate, the manner in which a transitional justice mechanism approaches its role, and how it is perceived and evaluated can have significant implications for national reconciliation. As one of the most visible symbols of a break with the past, truth commissions can play an important role in shaping attitudes toward the new political order. The priorities, procedures, methodologies, and values of such a body can be a source of public education and socialization. Working with and through truth commissions can offer former adversaries a formative cooperative experience. And in a country with sharp divisions, post-conflict trials or a truth commission may be one of the first and most important shared experiences. The following issues constitute a potential research agenda for assessing a transitional justice mechanism's impact on reconciliations.

Mandate

Several truth commissions have had mandates to promote reconciliation—some implicitly and a few explicitly. The Chilean National Commission on Truth and Reconciliation, the first such body to be nominally assigned the twin objectives of establishing truth while working toward reconciliation, framed its task as "truth for reconciliation." Its purpose was "to help the nation come to a clear overall understanding of the most serious human rights violations committed in recent years in order to aid in the reconciliation of all Chileans" (Berryman 1993). While the commission sought to consult widely with the main actors in Chile's national life—particularly with relatives of victims and with human rights organizations—regarding the objectives and methods for gathering evidence to facilitate reconciliation, it did not pursue national reconciliation as an independent goal. Many subsequent truth commissions have accepted the Chilean assumption that truth is the path to reconciliation, but the precise nature of the relationship between truth and reconciliation is likely to vary depending on procedural factors and substantive outcomes. Erin Daly and Jeremy Sarkin (2007, 109) point out that it may be important to distinguish between two approaches: whether the purpose of the truth finding is (1) simply to reveal what happened or (2) to help unify people. They propose that when the commission is simply interested in truth and presents information unvarnished, it may actually impede reconciliation. In contrast, if the commission seeks to promote reconciliation as well, it may provide more of a context and balance and thereby encourage conciliatory responses to the truth on all sides. Evaluating whether contextualizing the truth helps to promote reconciliation will require further research and evaluation.

In contrast with the Chilean approach, the South African TRC was tasked with promoting both truth and reconciliation, as independent goals. It was mandated to go beyond truth finding "to promote national unity and reconciliation in a spirit of understanding which transcends the conflict and divisions of the past" (Republic of South Africa 1995). Its public hearings and its report both highlighted the significance of forgiveness and reconciliation to the future of the nation. Reflecting the prestige of the South African commission, most truth commissions established after it have included the word "reconciliation" in their titles. Examples of these include Yugoslavia's Truth and Reconciliation Commission, the Truth and Reconciliation Commission in Sierra Leone, the Ghanaian National Reconciliation Commission, the Peruvian Truth and Reconciliation Commission, the Moroccan Equity and Reconciliation Panel, and Rwanda's National Unity and Reconciliation Commission.

But the inclusion of "reconciliation" in a title does not necessarily mean that a specific truth commission addressed reconciliation in a focused manner or identified it as an independent objective. Several—for example, the National Reconciliation Commission of Ghana—have assumed that all aspects of their activities would, almost by definition, promote the goal of reconciliation. Truth commissions often have very unclear reconciliation mandates. Many researchers have pointed out the failure of the legislation that established the South African TRC to define reconciliation, offer clear instructions on the manner in which the TRC was to pursue this goal, or establish an institutional mechanism dedicated to this complicated task (Borer 2001, 3). These deficiencies contributed to the confusion often exhibited by commissioners and staff over how to proceed. And like the South African TRC, many of the truth commissions with an interest in reconciliation have had difficulty determining how to realize this mandate.

Understanding Reconciliation

How a mechanism such as a truth commission understands reconciliation (particularly national reconciliation), its strategy for promoting reconciliation, and the level of society it focuses on are other relevant topics for research. Often, however, there may be a gap between conceptual approaches to reconciliation and their translation into activities. During its existence, the South African TRC identified four different types of reconciliation: reconciliation between political parties, reconciliation between races (blacks and whites), reconciliation at a community level, and reconciliation between victims and perpetrators. But the commissioners could not decide how, concretely, to proceed. Accounts of discussions about reconciliation by prominent members of the TRC show that there were significant disagreements, particularly between those with secular and with religious interpretations (Meiring 2000, 123–33). The multiple voices dealing with reconciliation in the final report suggest that the discord on this point was never resolved. Commenting on its own record, the TRC notes in its report, "The experiences of the Commission illustrated the particular difficulty of understanding the meaning of reconciliation at a national level" (South African TRC 1998, vol. 1, 108). As a result, the TRC tended to individualize issues of reconciliation, focusing on the relationships between former victims and perpetrators while neglecting the wider national and community dimensions (Chapman 2001, 247–69).

Similarly, the Sierra Leone Truth and Reconciliation Commission (TRC) report made several insightful comments about reconciliation: that it is a long-term process with a need to continue even beyond the present generation; that it must occur at multiple levels; that it is about relationships and how to change them; that it aims at restoring the social fabric within families, communities, and the nation; and that it needs to go beyond coexistence (Sierra Leone TRC 2004, Overview, paras. 28–30). But these insights did not give rise to a commensurate set of activities. The TRC's major initiative focused on community-level hearings that sought a superficial form of rapprochement between perpetrators and victims.

Strategies for Promoting Reconciliation

Beyond the particular transitional justice mechanism's understanding of reconciliation, the specific activities and initiatives that it undertakes are yet another important issue in that mechanism's potential role in promoting reconciliation. Without additional research, it is difficult to know which, if any, of these initiatives are effective. The following are some of the strategies that transitional justice mechanisms have sought to use:

1. **Public education.** Many transitional justice mechanisms attempt to reach out and educate the population on the need for national reconciliation—some with greater intention and more sophisticated strategies than others. Truth commission reports often men-

tion this topic. The South African TRC used public hearings as a means of public information and education, and many subsequent truth commissions have followed this model. At the hearings, Archbishop Desmond Tutu, the chair of the commission, used his role as a kind of "bully pulpit" to sermonize on the importance of forgiveness and reconciliation.

2. **Community-level initiatives.** Several transitional justice mechanisms have undertaken community-level activities. The Commission for the Reception of Truth and Reconciliation in Timor-Leste (CAVR) dealt with reconciliation at two levels: the relationship of Timor-Leste with Indonesia (the oppressor and major human rights violator), and the political divisions within communities. CAVR's community reconciliation strategy sought to reintegrate people who had become estranged from their local communities through committing politically related "less serious" harmful acts. CAVR organized community-level-facilitated hearings in which perpetrators came forward, made brief presentations in which they admitted wrongdoing, and were asked by the community to undertake "acts of reconciliation," often in the form of small financial reparations. Approximately 1,400 individuals went through the process. The research conducted by the commission indicates that deponents, victims, and the community believed that the process had made a contribution to reconciliation by providing a forum for the open exchange of information and by defusing some of the anger in communities (CAVR 2005, Part 9, paras. 118–19).

3. **Use of rituals.** Many societies have traditional cultural practices and customs that seek to bring antagonists together and heal rifts, and some transitional justice mechanisms have attempted to make use of these cultural approaches to reconciliation. The major reconciliation initiative of the Sierra Leone TRC was a ceremony held at provincial public hearings, using local cultural symbols. By participating in the ritual, which was designed by the TRC with the assistance of the local community, perpetrators were to acknowledge publicly the authority of the TRC and to express remorse, while the members of the local community obligated themselves to reconcile with the perpetrators. In at least one location, a staged ceremony of repentance and forgiveness succeeded in forging a temporary reconciliation moment through providing emotional release, but it appeared unlikely to be of long-lasting significance (Kelsall 2005, 386–95).

4. **Attitudes of perpetrators and beneficiaries.** Reconciliation requires rapprochement from all sides in a conflict and from the

post-conflict leadership representing these interests. Often in post-conflict societies, however, victims appear more open to overcoming past divisions and reconciliation than do the perpetrators and beneficiaries of the previous regimes. In a study of transitional justice in the Czech Republic, for example, about half the respondents had managed to meet with their perpetrators, but only 4.5 percent had received an apology. In addition, many victims reported that perpetrators displayed persistent negative behaviors, such as being verbally offensive, arrogant, and indifferent as well as giving excuses for their past acts (David and Yuk-ping 2005, 426). As Leigh Payne's chapter in this volume shows, there are several reasons for perpetrators' unwillingness to acknowledge responsibility or apologize to victims.

5. **Development of new symbols and images.** Cultural images constitute important filters through which people see and relate to other groups and the wider world. Truth commissions sometimes try to offer a set of foundational symbols, even myths, as a way of moving beyond existing images and myths held by conflicting groups and providing a new interpretative grid for past experiences. The South African TRC was particularly sensitive to this task, perhaps because clergy are more attuned to using symbols than are, for example, lawyers and judges. The TRC projected an image of South Africa as a "rainbow nation." Claiming that members of all communities suffered under the apartheid order, it symbolized that shared suffering by reserving a disproportionate number of places for white victims in the human rights violations hearings. Commissioners, particularly Archbishop Tutu, were inclined to memorialize victims, interpreting their suffering through the framework of sacrifice for liberation, possibly to create heroes and martyrs as well as a mythology for the new South Africa (Wilson 2001, 110). These efforts, which seek to appeal on an emotional as well as an intellectual level, may be a particularly important potential contribution of a truth commission; therefore, it is important to evaluate the extent to which a specific truth commission succeeded in providing new symbols and images that give meaning to the past while enabling people to go forward into a new future.

6. **Recommendations about future activities.** Some truth commissions make recommendations about promoting reconciliation in the post-transitional justice period. CAVR, for example, acknowledged that there was a need to undertake longer-term community initiatives to heal divisions, and to that end, it recommended the establishment of an independent institution dedicated to the task

(CAVR 2005, Part 9, paras. 173–74). The nature of such recommendations, and whether they are implemented, is another potential topic for research.

7. **Implications of other activities.** In addition to the explicit strategy and activities to promote reconciliation, other dimensions of the truth commission process also have implications for intergroup relationships. On the procedural level, was the leadership of the truth-finding body representative of the major groups in the country? Did it use scientifically valid methodologies that were perceived as appropriate, fair, and unbiased? Did it give equal access to groups and communities from all parts of the country? Did its staff treat participants in the process with dignity, sensitivity, and respect? Did its activities receive widespread media coverage, and if so, how did the media sources characterize the process? Was the report with its findings widely disseminated? In terms of the substantive outcomes, was the interpretation of the causes of the past violence and repression broadly acceptable to a wide range of communities and groups, or did the findings lead to further conflict among various actors and groups? Did the commission identify the architects of the past violence—whether in the form of individuals, institutions, or groups—and if so, what were the implications of its doing so? Did the identification of specific perpetrators lessen the tendency of former victims to stigmatize entire groups?

Yet another set of significant issues to study is the way in which the truth commission's report was received and whether its recommendations were implemented. Although the Peruvian Truth and Reconciliation Commission's truth-finding process was quite thorough and its methodologies scientifically grounded, the political leadership of the country has subsequently disparaged or ignored its analysis of the causes of the violence and the recommendations made in the report (Theidon 2006, 23–25). Very rarely have post-truth commission regimes been willing to implement in full the recommendations made, and some have disregarded them completely.

Methodological Considerations and Approaches

Carefully designed empirical research can play a major role in helping theorists and practitioners better understand the requirements of national reconciliation as well as provide tools for gauging progress and identifying problems in a given society. This chapter has offered a research agenda with the goal of more accurately assessing the impact of transitional justice mechanisms on national reconciliation. The topics or lines of inquiry suggested here reflect the multidimensional and long-term nature of the reconciliation process. Given the number of issues identified and the paucity of relevant research in many deeply divided societies, there may be a temptation to attempt macro studies seeking to provide answers to a wide range of issues. This would be a mistake. Just as there are no easy shortcuts to national reconciliation, there are no shortcuts to researching the subject. Both the reconciliation and the relevant research need to be understood as "a gradual, slow, and complex process" (Abu-Nimer, Said, and Prelis 2001, 346).

In view of the range of approaches to reconciliation, it is important to conceive clearly the notion of reconciliation being applied as the basis for the study and to break it down into researchable and measurable components. In doing this, the researcher must be sensitive to the potential contributions, as well as the limitations, of various disciplines. Because reconciliation is a process, the best way to conduct research is to have time-series data that can show the evolution of attitudes, institutional capabilities, and processes. To be an accurate measure, time-series data require careful replication of methodologies and samples. In the absence of such data, researchers should be sensitive to the time context of their research and of the findings of different studies that they use for comparison. In designing and conducting research on reconciliation in deeply divided societies, it is essential to differentiate between the specific impact of transitional justice processes and the broader effects of other societal factors.

Given the very different experiences that various communities and societal sectors will have had under the previous oppressive regime or period of conflict—and perhaps of the transitional justice process as well—research should always carefully disaggregate among these communities to focus on a specifically designated group or sector. It is particularly important to differentiate among former victims or relatives of victims, perpetrators, beneficiaries, and bystanders. The design and sample for the research should take into account the likelihood that the perspectives of various communities and individuals within those groups will differ according to their experiences and their current social status and location.

It is also important to bear in mind some of the inherent difficulties of conducting research on reconciliation. In deeply divided societies, reconciliation is a complex and sensitive topic. Asking directly about reconciliation may not elicit helpful or reliable data; there may even be little understanding of the term—indeed, many languages may not even have a precise linguistic equivalent. As the results of a 2002 national survey of adult South Africans' attitudes about reconciliation indicate, even after the TRC experience, South Africans continue to have problems understanding the term "reconciliation" and agreeing on what it means. Nearly a third of the respondents were unable to provide any definition of the word. The other two-thirds had a wide range of views identifying reconciliation with notions of forgiveness, unification, peace, racial integration, forgetting the past, and dealing with the past (Lombard 2003). Similarly, in a 2004 survey in Northern Ireland, a significant number of interviewees found it difficult to engage with the topic in a meaningful way and were vague in the details of how to achieve it. Few people could articulate a vision of what a reconciled society would look like. Views of reconciliation were influenced both by professional roles and by ideological positions of the respondents (Hamber and Kelly 2005, 41–48).

Because reconciliation is a long-term process, it would be best to undertake longitudinal studies, replicating the methodology and design, to measure changes over time. One project that does so is a series of reconciliation barometer surveys conducted by the Institute for Justice and Reconciliation (IJR) in South Africa, in collaboration with the Markinor survey firm. At the time of this writing, IJR had conducted five rounds of national surveys based on socially and racially representative samples. The first was in 2003 and the fifth in 2007. IJR used the same sampling methodologies, questionnaires, and interviewing techniques to allow for maximum comparability (IJR 2007).

Various empirical methodologies have been applied to research related to the study of national, political, and social reconciliation. Each of these methodologies has strengths and limitations.

Quantitative Surveys

Quantitative surveys measure attitudes at a particular point in time. Such surveys can be small scale and local, with limitations in generalizing the results, or larger representative surveys, based on samples drawn through scientific methodologies. Surveys based on random selection and population-based sampling have the advantage of enabling researchers to draw conclusions about the attitudes of a large and diverse population from a relatively small sample size. James Gibson's chapter in this volume describes how he conducted a survey on a national sample of nearly four thousand persons in South Africa in 2000–01 to evaluate the response to the TRC.

Qualitative Surveys

Qualitative surveys, based on a semistructured or open-ended interview questionnaire, are another option for studying national reconciliation. Brandon Hamber and Gráinne Kelly's chapter in this volume describes a study of conflict and reconciliation in Northern Ireland. To ensure that the questions were clear and rigorous and addressed the entire research theme, they piloted their semistructured instrument twice: once with a research advisory group and then with representatives of the communities. The questionnaire was then administered in three of Northern Ireland's twenty-six district council areas, which were selected to provide contrasting as well as common features, to representatives of three groups: a community relations officer, a voluntary sector member with responsibility for community relations work, and a councillor with a particular interest in peacebuilding. After the interviews were conducted, the project team extracted themes and categorized and interpreted them.

Systematic Analysis of Transcripts

Many truth commissions follow the South African model, conducting public hearings. Some also make written transcripts of the hearings available. This offers the possibility of undertaking systematic analysis of transcripts to assess what took place during the truth commission process. A study of the South African TRC by the Advancing Science, Serving Society (AAAS) Science and Human Rights Program and the Centre for the Study of Violence and Reconciliation used both quantitative and qualitative methodologies to analyze the transcripts of a stratified random sample of 429 of the 1,819 transcripts from the human rights violations hearings on the TRC Web site. The study ascertained the views of former victims on several topics, including forgiveness and reconciliation, and on the interchange between the deponents and commissioners on these topics (Chapman, 2008a, 2008b).

In-Depth Interviews

In-depth interviews can offer insight into the views of key groups on reconciliation, and their assessment of transitional justice processes. A study of religion and reconciliation in South Africa, for example, conducted in-depth interviews with thirty-three key religious figures, employing a common research instrument to explore their concepts of reconciliation, their evaluation of the TRC, and their views on the status of reconciliation in South Africa, but the findings could not be generalized from the interviewees to the larger religious community (Chapman and Spong 2003).

Anthropological Studies

Anthropological studies, including participant observation, offer yet another approach to studying reconciliation. Kimberly Theidon directed a project focusing on mental health, reparations, and the micropolitics of reconciliation for the Ayacuchan office of the Peruvian TRC. This anthropological study used participant observation and lengthy conversations with 403 members of seven communities in the area, with the goal of better understanding the local forms and logic of social relations, their transformation, and the cultural expressions of grief, anguish, and loss (Theidon 2006). In field studies conducted along with a study of intercommunity relationships in the cities of Vukovar, Croatia, and Mostar, Bosnia-Herzegovina, researchers made four-week visits every four months over a two-year period, beginning in September 2002. As participant-observers, their task was to make contacts with city residents, observe their interactions, and chronicle their way of life. Field data included perceptions of objective changes over time in areas of reconstruction, economic growth, employment, schooling, health care, culture, sporting events, religion, media, civil society, safety, politics, and everyday life (Corkalo et al. 2004, 144).

Focus Groups

Focus groups, usually involving relatively small and homogeneous groupings and a facilitator, provide another methodological option. The homogeneous composition is intended to put the participants at ease and make discussion more feasible. Focus groups are used both to field-test instruments before large-scale surveys and to collect supplementary data. The research project in the Balkans described in the previous paragraph also conducted focus groups in those cities. Altogether, the study conducted eight focus groups composed of six to eight people drawn from representatives of war victims, non-governmental organizations, young people (eighteen to thirty years old), and entrepreneurs. Each focus group was homogeneous. The focus group protocol addressed such issues as outcomes and consequences of the war; the effects of war on physical and mental health; relations among ethnic groups before, during, and after the war; war crimes; and reconciliation (Corkalo et al. 2004, 144).

The Way Forward

As we can see, the policies adopted by post-transition regimes can either foster or impede national reconciliation. Policy analysis and assessments of the impact of different types of public policies on reconciliation are key. The development of an international database of empirical research on public policy and national reconciliation, accessible to researchers with similar interests, could be an important contribution to the process of understanding the impact and effectiveness of governmental initiatives on reconciliation.

Systematic research on national reconciliation is just beginning. We do not yet have clear procedures for how to achieve reconciliation, or even for measuring and evaluating the success of efforts to that end. Only additional research in a wide range of societies will help clarify many of the issues raised in this chapter. Hopefully, future evaluations of research on reconciliation will be able to determine how reconciliation can be an ongoing self sustaining process.

References

Abu-Nimer, Mohammed, Abdul Aziz Said, and Lakshitha S. Prelis. 2001. "Conclusion: The Long Road to Reconciliation." In *Reconciliation, Justice, and Coexistence: Theory and Practice,* ed. Mohammed Abu-Nimer, 339–48. Lanham, Md.: Lexington.

Amstutz, Mark. 2005. *The Healing of Nations: The Promise and Limits of Political Forgiveness.* Lanham, Md.: Rowman and Littlefield.

Barsalou, Judy. 2005. "Trauma and Transitional Justice in Divided Societies." United States Institute of Peace *Special Report* 135, www.usip.org/pubs/specialreports/sr135.html (accessed June 18, 2008).

Berryman, Philip E., trans. 1993. "Report of the Chilean National Commission on Truth and Reconciliation." Vol. 1, No. 13. Bloomington, Ind.: Notre Dame University Press.

Bhargava, Rajeev. 2000. "Restoring Decency to Barbaric Societies. In *Truth v. Justice: The Morality of Truth Commissions,* ed. Robert I. Rotberg and Dennis Thompson, 45–67. Oxford, UK: Princeton University Press.

Bloomfield, Daniel, Teresa Barnes, and Luc Huyse. 2003. *Reconciliation after Violent Conflict: A Handbook.* Stockholm: International Institute for Democracy and Electoral Assistance.

Borer, Tristan Anne. 2001. "Reconciliation in South Africa: Defining Success." *Kroc Institute Occasional Paper* 20:OP:1.

CAVR. 2005. "Report of the Commission for the Reception of Truth and Reconciliation in Timor-Leste," www.ictj.org/downloads/PR.060130.CAVRReportonICTJsite.Eng.pdf (accessed May 26, 2008).

Chapman, Audrey. 2001. "Truth Commissions as Instruments of Forgiveness and Reconciliation." In *Forgiveness and Reconciliation: Religion, Public Policy, and Conflict Transformation,* ed. S. J. Helmick and Rodney L. Peterson, 247–68. Philadelphia and London: Templeton Foundation Press.

———. (2008a). "Perspectives on the Role of Forgiveness in the Human Rights Violations Hearings." In *Truth and Reconciliation in South Africa: Did the TRC Deliver?* ed. Audrey R. Chapman and Hugo van der Merwe, 66–92. Philadelphia: University of Pennsylvania Press.

———. 2008b. "The TRC's Approach to Promoting Reconciliation in the Human Rights Violations Hearings." In *Truth and Reconciliation in South Africa: Did the TRC Deliver?* ed. Audrey R. Chapman and Hugo van der Merwe, 45–65. Philadelphia: University of Pennsylvania Press.

Chapman, Audrey, and Bernard Spong, eds. 2003. *Religion and Reconciliation in South Africa: Voices of Religious Leaders.* Philadelphia and London: Templeton Foundation Press.

Corkalo, Dinka, Dean Ajdukovic, Harvey M. Weinstein, Eric Stover, Dino Djipa, and Miklos Biro. 2004. "Neighbors Again? Intercommunity Relations after Ethnic Cleansing." In *My Neighbor, My Enemy: Justice and Community in the Aftermath of Mass Atrocity,* ed. Eric Stover and Harvey M. Weinstein, 143–61. Cambridge, UK, and New York: Cambridge University Press.

Daly, Erin, and Jeremy Sarkin. 2007. *Reconciliation in Divided Societies: Finding Common Ground*. Philadephia: University of Pennsylvania Press.

David, Roman, and Susamme Choi Yuk-ping. 2005. "Victims on Transitional Justice: Lessons from the Reparation of Human Rights Abuses in the Czech Republic." *Human Rights Quarterly* 27, no. 2 (May): 392–435.

Davis, Madeleine. 2005. "Is Spain Recovering Its Memory? Breaking the Pacto del Olvido." *Human Rights Quarterly* 27, no. 3 (August).

Des Forges, Alison, and Timothy Longman. 2004. "Legal Responses to Genocide in Rwanda." In *My Neighbor, My Enemy: Justice and Community in the Aftermath of Mass Atrocity*, ed. Eric Stover and Harvey M. Weinstein, 49–68. Cambridge, UK, and New York: Cambridge University Press.

Dwyer, Susan. 1999. "Reconciliation for Realists." *Report from the Institute for Philosophy & Public Policy* 19 (spring-summer): 18–19.

Ericson, Maria. 2002. *Reconciliation and the Search for a Shared Moral Landscape: An Exploration Based upon a Study of Northern Ireland and South Africa*. Frankfurt: Peter Lang.

Fisher, Ronald. 2001. "Social-Psychological Processes in Interactive Conflict Analysis and Reconciliation." In *Reconciliation, Justice, and Coexistence: Theory and Practice*, ed. Mohammed Abu-Nimer, 25–46. Lanham, Md.: Lexington.

Fletcher, Laurel E., and Harvey M. Weinstein. 2002. "Violence and Social Repair: Rethinking the Contribution of Justice to Reconciliation." *Human Rights Quarterly* 24 (August): 573–639.

Galtung, John. 2001. "After Violence, Reconstruction, Reconciliation, and Resolution." In *Reconciliation, Justice, and Coexistence: Theory and Practice*, ed. Mohammed Abu-Nimer, 3–24. Lanham, Md.: Lexington.

Gibson, James L. 2004. *Overcoming Apartheid: Can Truth Reconcile a Divided Nation?* New York: Russell Sage Foundation.

Hamber, Brandon, and Gráinne Kelly. 2005. *A Place for Reconciliation? Conflict and Locality in Northern Ireland*. Belfast: Democratic Dialogue.

Hamber, Brandon, and Hugo van der Merwe. 1998. "What Is This Thing Called Reconciliation?" *Reconciliation in Review* 1 (1): 3–6. Johannesburg: Centre for the Study of Violence and Reconciliation.

Hofmeyr, Jan. 2005. "The Transition Generation: Political Orientations of Young South Africans." *SA Reconciliation Barometer* 3 (October): 4–5, www.ijr.org.za/politicalanalysis/reconcbar/newsletter3iss2 (accessed May 15, 2008).

IJR. 2007. "Reconciliation Barometer." Capetown, www.ijr.org.za/politicalanalysis/reconcbar/newsletter (accessed May 15, 2008).

Kelsall, Tim. 2005. "Truth, Lies, Ritual: Preliminary Reflections on the Truth and Reconciliation Commission in Sierra Leone." *Human Rights Quarterly* 27 (2): 361–91.

Kriesberg, Louis. 1998. "Paths to Varieties of Inter-Communal Reconciliation." Unpublished paper presented at the Seventeenth General Conference of the International Peace Research Association, Durban, June.

———. 2001. "Changing Forms of Coexistence." In *Reconciliation, Justice, and Coexistence: Theory and Practice*, ed. Mohammed Abu-Nimer, 47–64. Lanham, Md.: Lexington.

Lederach, John Paul. 1997. *Building Peace: Sustainable Reconciliation in Divided Societies*. Washington, D.C.: United States Institute of Peace Press.

————. 2001. "Five Qualities of Practice in Support of Reconciliation Processes." In *Forgiveness and Reconciliation: Religion, Public Policy, and Conflict Transformation*, ed. Raymond G. Helmick and Rodney L. Petersen. Philadelphia and London: Templeton Foundation Press.

Lombard, Karen. 2003. "Reconciliation after a Decade of Democracy: A Descriptive Analysis of South African Engagement with Reconciliation." Paper presented at the Nineteenth Annual Congress of the International Political Science Association, Durban, June.

Long, William J., and Peter Brecke. 2000. *War and Reconciliation: Reason and Emotion in Conflict Resolution*. Cambridge, Mass., and London: MIT Press.

Meiring, Piet. 2000. "The Baruti versus the Lawyers: The Role of Religion in the TRC." In *Looking Back, Reaching Forward: Reflections on the Truth and Reconciliation Commission of South Africa*, ed. Charles Villa-Vicencio and Wilhelm Verwoerd, 123–33. Cape Town: University of Cape Town Press.

Merriam Company. 1981. *Webster's New Collegiate Dictionary*. Springfield, Mass.: G. and C. Merriam Company.

Mohamed, Seera. 2007. "Unemployment and Violent Crime," www.polity.org.za/article.php?a_id=100843 (accessed May 26, 2008).

Muller-Fahrenholz, Geiko. 1997. *The Art of Forgiveness: Theological Reflections on Healing and Reconciliation*. Geneva: WCC.

New York Times. 2008. "Guatemala News," Topics.nytimes.com/topc/news/international/countriesandterritories/Guatemala/index.html (accessed July 10, 2008).

Pham, Phuong N., Harvey W. Weinstein, and Timothy Longman. 2004. "Trauma and PTSD Symptoms in Rwanda: Implications for Attitudes toward Justice and Reconciliation." *JAMA* 292, no. 5 (August 4): 602–21.

Putnam, Robert D. 2001. *Bowling Alone: The Collapse and Revival of the American Community*. New York: Simon and Schuster.

Republic of South Africa. 1995. "Promotion of National Unity and Reconciliation Act." Capetown, *Government Gazette* 361, no. 16579.

Sierra Leone TRC. 2004. *Truth Commission Report of Sierra Leone*, www. trcsierraleone. org/ (accessed July 10, 2008).

Smith, Tom. 2001. *Intergroup Relations in a Diverse America: Data from the 2000 General Survey*. Washington, D.C.: American Jewish Committee.

South African TRC. 1998. *Truth and Reconciliation Commission of South Africa Report*. Cape Town: CTP.

Staub, Ervin, and Laurie Anne Pearlman. 2001. "Healing, Reconciliation, and Forgiving after Genocide and Other Collective Violence." In *Forgiveness and Reconciliation: Religion, Public Policy, and Conflict Transformation*, ed. Raymond G. Helmick and Rodney L. Petersen. Philadelphia and London: Templeton Foundation Press.

Tawil, Sobhi, and Alexandra Harley, eds. 2004. *Education, Conflict and Social Cohesion*. Geneva: UNESCO International Bureau of Education.

Theidon, Kimberly. 2006. "Justice in Transition: The Micropolitics of Reconciliation in Postwar Peru." *Journal of Conflict Resolution* 50, no. 3 (June): 1–25.

Tutu, Desmond. 1999. *No Future without Forgiveness*. New York: Doubleday.

Van der Merwe, Hugo. 2001. "National and Community Reconciliation: Competing Agendas in South African Truth and Reconciliation Commission." In *Burying the Past: Making Peace and Doing Justice after Civil Conflict*, ed. Nigel Biggar, 85–106. Washington, D.C.: Georgetown University Press.

Volkan, Vamik D. 2003. "Large-Group Identity: Border Psychology and Related Societal Process." *Mind and Human Interaction* 13: 49–76.

Weinstein, Harvey, and Eric Stover. 2004. "Introduction: Conflict, Justice and Reclamation." In *My Neighbor, My Enemy: Justice and Community in the Aftermath of Mass Atrocity*, ed. Eric Stover and Harvey Weinstein, 1–26. Cambridge, UK: Cambridge University Press.

Wilson, Richard A. 2001. *The Politics of Truth and Reconciliation in South Africa: Legitimizing the Post-Apartheid State.* Cambridge, UK: Cambridge University Press.

Winter, Greg. 2003. "Schools Resegregate, Study Finds." *New York Times*, January 21.

6

Taking Stock of Truth and Reconciliation in South Africa

Assessing Citizen Attitudes through Surveys

James L. Gibson

In deeply divided societies throughout the world, many efforts have been made to create "reconciliation" out of "truth." The question these efforts typically address is, Does "truth" in fact contribute to "reconciliation"? To answer—or even understand—this question, both terms must be given clear conceptual and operational definitions. This chapter contends that both concepts can be measured scientifically and that one means of doing so is through a survey of ordinary people. The meanings of "truth" and "reconciliation" are explicated here, and a discussion of both the strengths and the weaknesses of using survey-based measures is presented, based primarily on the methodological approach adopted in *Overcoming Apartheid: Can Truth Reconcile a Divided Nation?* (Gibson 2004a). This chapter's most general conclusion is that the claims of truth processes can and should be treated as susceptible to rigorous scientific investigation.

Since its inception in the mid-1990s, an enormous amount has been written about South Africa's truth and reconciliation process, espousing every view imaginable. Some believe that the truth and reconciliation process did great damage to the country; others, however, see the process as successful, if only because it helped avoid a civil war. The most salutary view asserts that the process made a positive contribution to the creation of a more democratic South Africa. So, was the truth and reconciliation process successful? Answers of yes, no, maybe, and maybe not are readily found in extant writings. As Villa-Vicencio and Ngesi (2003, 292) assert, "In South Africa today, there are perhaps as many views on the [Truth and Reconciliation Commission (TRC)] as there are people."

The diversity of opinions on the operation of the truth and reconciliation process is matched by the diversity in research methodologies. Some analysts focus on the logic of the law; others assess the process using normative criteria. Empirical analysis employs methods as diverse as the collection of anecdotal material; the use of focus groups, participant observation, and other ethnographic methods; and in a limited number of cases, systematic surveys of representative samples (or subsamples) of the South African population. While it is unclear that different substantive conclusions are necessarily associated with different research methodologies—and indeed, the methods differ as well in terms of how they frame the research question—methodological eclecticism clearly characterizes analysis of the truth and reconciliation process in South Africa.

One research methodology that has been employed rather sparingly is systematic surveys of representative samples of South Africans. This no doubt reflects, in part, the substantial costs of such surveys, but another contributing factor may be a lack of awareness of the strengths and weaknesses of this approach. Thus, the purpose here is to describe and assess a major survey-based study of the success of South Africa's truth and reconciliation process. The chapter focuses on a variety of methodological issues associated with scientific research on truth and reconciliation, using a major new analysis of the work of South Africa's truth and reconciliation process (Gibson 2004a) as an example. The major questions addressed include (1) whether the TRC was successful at promulgating a "truth" that now serves as a collective memory of apartheid, (2) to what degree individual South Africans are reconciled, (3) whether "truth" in fact has made a contribution to reconciliation, and (4) if it has, why and how (through what processes). The chapter discusses how the key concepts were put into practice and provides an overview of the survey methodology. General issues of survey design are considered, with particular attention to experiments embedded in representative surveys, as well as questions about the validity and reliability of the data collected. The chapter concludes with observations about extending this type of research to other political systems confronted with pressing issues of transitional justice.

Reconciliation as an Attribute of Individuals

South Africa's truth and reconciliation process sought to change society in two important respects. First, it attempted to create a "collective memory" for the country, that is, it sought to codify and interpret the apartheid experience. This is not just a chronicle of who did what to whom; instead, it is an authoritative description and analysis of the history of the country. Was apartheid a crime against humanity? Was the criminality of apartheid due to the missteps of a few rogue individuals, or was apartheid criminal by its very ideology and institutions? These are questions for which the TRC provided unambiguous and, by its own accounting, definitive answers. My goal in this research is not to assess the historical accuracy of these claims but rather to determine the degree to which ordinary South Africans accept the truth as promulgated by the TRC—its "collective memory."

Second, the truth and reconciliation process sought to create a more reconciled South Africa, an explicit component of which was the creation of a culture of human rights that would protect against abuses by the authorities in the future. Thus, an important research question is whether the truth and reconciliation process succeeded in creating "truth" and "reconciliation" in South Africa.

To be sure, the truth and reconciliation process had other objectives as well. For instance, it was charged with identifying those who had committed gross human rights violations during the struggle over apartheid and, under some specific circumstances, with extending amnesty to these miscreants. The TRC was also involved in compiling a list of those subjected to human rights abuses and in making recommendations for compensation for these victims. Thus, one can readily ask whether the process was successful at performing a number of assigned (and assumed) functions.

The focus of this research is not particularly on participants in the truth and reconciliation process but on society at large. For instance, it is important to determine whether a collective memory has indeed been created for South Africans. To answer this question requires measuring individual-level acceptance of the TRC's collective memory through assessing the distribution of opinion within the entire society. Similarly, to ask whether a culture is supportive of human rights is first to ask whether individual South Africans—the population as a whole—attach value to those human rights. Consequently, a crucial research question addresses the impact of the process on the broader society, not just on perpetrators and victims.

It should therefore be obvious that "reconciliation" is here understood as an attribute of individual citizens. Perhaps a more conventional viewpoint treats reconciliation as a characteristic of societies or groups. For instance, the TRC's final report refers to the following types of relationships: of individuals with themselves, between victims, between survivors and perpetrators, within families, between neighbors, between communities, within different institutions, between different generations, between racial and ethnic groups, between workers and management, and, "above all, between the beneficiaries of apartheid and those who have been disadvantaged by it" (TRC 1998, vol. 5, 350–51). Although determining the degree of reconciliation (as, for example, through analyzing change in levels of reconciliation in a nation-state over time) is an interesting pursuit, a central contention of this research is that any understanding of reconciliation profits from beginning with an examination of the beliefs, values, attitudes, and behaviors of ordinary people. If reconciliation means groups getting along together, then obviously reconciliation requires that individual South Africans hold certain attitudes and act in certain ways. A polity may be more than the sum of the individuals living within its territory, but it is impossible to understand a society without first understanding individual citizens—in this case, the degree to which they are "reconciled."

What, then, does a "reconciled" South African look like? This is not the place to present a full-blown discussion of my concept of reconciliation. (For such a discussion, see Gibson 2004a.) Instead, it is reasonable simply to postulate that the construct "reconciliation" refers to at least four specific and perhaps even independent components:

1. Interracial tolerance, defined as the willingness of people of different races to trust each other, reject stereotypes about those of other races, and generally get along.
2. Political tolerance, the commitment of people to put up with each other, even those whose political ideas they thoroughly detest.
3. Legitimacy, in particular the predisposition to recognize and accept the authority of the major political institutions of the new South Africa.
4. Support for the principles (abstract and applied) of human rights, including the strict application of the rule of law and commitment to legal universalism.

This is perhaps not an exhaustive definition of reconciliation—there may be other important components to the concept—but most quarrels would surely concern themselves with the need to include additional aspects of reconciliation rather than whether these particular dimensions are central to the concept. A reconciled South African is one who respects and trusts those of other races, who is tolerant of those with different political views, who extends legitimacy and respect to the major governing institutions of South Africa's democracy, and who supports the extension of human rights to all South Africans. Thus, from this theoretical vantage point, it is necessary to investigate reconciliation between individuals, among groups, with basic constitutional principles, and with the institutions essential to the new South African democracy.

Thus, this research treats "reconciliation" as something of a meta-concept—a superordinate umbrella encompassing political and racial tolerance, support for human rights, and the extension of legitimacy to political institutions. Though this is a conceptual innovation, once reconciliation is understood in this fashion, it is a fairly simple matter to turn to established measures of the subcomponents.

Interracial Tolerance

Interracial tolerance requires that South Africans of every race accept all other South Africans as equals and treat them as equals, extending dignity and respect to them. This may mean that people come to interact with each other more (the breakdown of barriers across races) and communicate more, leading to greater understanding and perhaps acceptance, and ultimately resulting in the appreciation and exaltation of the value of racial diversity and multiculturalism (the "rainbow nation"). Thus, as an empirical matter, it is necessary to consider how ordinary people in South Africa feel about fellow citizens of other racial groups.

In this study it was necessary, therefore, to ask South Africans their views about members of other racial groups, which is a bit more complicated than first appears. In principle, it would be desirable to ask members of each major racial grouping their attitudes toward all other groups, as in asking blacks to evaluate whites, colored people (in South African usage, those of mixed racial background), and those of Asian origin. In practice, such a strategy would require dozens of individual questions, which would simply consume too much of the available interview time and would also be quite taxing on the respondents, so the Reconciliation Survey deemed it impractical. Thus, an alternative measurement scheme was necessary.

The optimal strategy for black and for white respondents was not difficult to identify: Black respondents were asked their views of whites; white respondents were asked their views of blacks. To ask those who were clearly either superordinate or subordinate under apartheid about each other makes perfect sense from the point of view of the future of interracial reconciliation in South Africa. More complicated calculations were involved in selecting the optimal group about which to ask colored and Asian respondents. Given the geographic concentration of colored people in the Western Cape and those of Asian origin in KwaZulu-Natal, it is unreasonable to query respondents from these two groups about each other. The choice then boils down to asking them about either whites or blacks.

Colored and Asian respondents were asked about their opinions of the black majority, not because there is no need for interracial reconciliation between whites and colored people or between those of Asian origin and whites. Nor do any analysts believe that white racism is confined to attitudes toward black South Africans. Instead of emphasizing historical relationships among South Africa's four main racial groupings, the Reconciliation Survey chose to focus on the contemporary relationships between each of the racial minorities (whites, colored people, and those of Asian origin) and the black majority. The TRC itself was more interested in relationships between whites and blacks, largely because it was addressing South Africa's apartheid past. As blacks move into positions of economic, social, and political power within South African society—as they surely must and will—then the question of whether there can be reconciliation between the racial minorities and the racial majority is of considerable importance. By asking about the interracial reconciliation of these groups, it is not presupposed (or even hypothesized) that levels of reconciliation will be low. Indeed, perhaps one of the least investigated issues from an empirical viewpoint is whether those who were "black" under the old system of apartheid are now sufficiently well reconciled to unite in a political coalition.

This decision to ask colored people and those of Asian origin about black South Africans was based in part on the interracial conflict manifest in the focus groups that were held. Both the colored focus group (held in Cape Town) and the Indian group (held in Durban) revealed substantial antipathy toward black South Africans. Among colored people, this conflict seemed to focus on affirmative action and other means by which black South Africans were able to gain economic advantage over colored people (e.g., the job requirement that an employee speak Xhosa).

Of course, substantial conflict exists between colored people and whites, especially over jobs (and that conflict was clearly manifest in the focus group). But since the possibility of significant interracial antipathy between colored and black people exists and is possibly exacerbated by economic competition, the survey questions explore this potentiality.

Similar remarks during the Indian focus group contributed to the decision to focus on Indian-African relations. Many of the Indian participants in the focus groups expressed a keen awareness of the history of conflict in Africa between Indians and blacks. Thus, it seemed reasonable to explore the degree of racial reconciliation between black South Africans and those of Asian origin.

In an ideal world with unlimited resources (including the resource of respondents' patience in answering our questions), all South Africans would have been asked about the three other racial groups. By asking colored and Asian respondents about black South Africans, no ideological statement is being made, nor is anything prejudged about the findings. Politically, black South Africans are dominant in South Africa (as befits a group constituting 78 percent of the population). The questions, therefore, asked the ethnic and political minorities about their relations with the African majority. In designing questions in this way, it is not presupposed that colored and Asian attitudes toward whites are harmonious and free of antipathy and ill will (and vice versa), although it is postulated that how the three racial minorities relate to the black majority is a crucial element of interracial reconciliation in South Africa.

Political Tolerance

Political tolerance is normally understood as putting up with political ideas with which one strongly disagrees. (For examples, see Sullivan, Piereson, and Marcus 1982; Gibson 1992; and Gibson and Gouws 2003.)

Thus, the measurement objective requires that people be asked about repressing ideas and groups they find objectionable. Respondents are asked to select a political group to which they strongly object (the "least-liked" group) and are then queried about restricting the dissemination of the ideas of the group (e.g., banning speeches by group members). This approach to measuring intolerance works especially well in South Africa, since tolerance is a much-discussed concept and since efforts to ban speech and ideas occur with some frequency (e.g., so-called hate speech) and are therefore familiar to ordinary people. Thus, on this component, reconciliation is easily measured, since the concept taps into a well-established research tradition.

Legitimacy of Political Institutions

Measuring reconciliation as the willingness to cede authority to the country's major political institutions relates directly to a large body of literature. (See Gibson and Caldeira 2003; and Gibson, Caldeira, and Baird 1998.) Researchers have long been concerned with measuring the legitimacy that political institutions enjoy, and a great deal of agreement exists on conceptual and operational approaches to the concept. Legitimacy is the unwillingness to accept or countenance changes in the structure of institutions that would tend to undermine their ability to function as designed. For instance, endorsing proposals to limit judicial independence (e.g., making judicial salaries dependent on the government) amounts to rejecting the role of the judiciary as a neutral forum for managing political conflicts in society. As with political tolerance, reconciliation as legitimacy is quite readily assessed with reference to extant theoretical and empirical work, so little original work on measuring this aspect of reconciliation is necessary.

Support for the Principles of Human Rights

By far the most difficult of the dimensions of reconciliation is support for the concept of human rights. This is in part because few previous studies have treated a "human rights culture" in rigorous empirical terms as an attribute of individual citizens. The measurement strategy was therefore considerably more challenging than for other aspects.

Just exactly what attitudes and values are central to human rights? One can imagine a long list of values, but surely that enumeration would include the following:

- Support for the rule of law: a preference for rule-bound governmental and individual action.
- Political tolerance: the willingness of citizens to "put up with" their political enemies.

- Rights consciousness: the willingness to assert individual rights against the dominant political, social, and economic institutions in society.
- Support for due process: the commitment to nonarbitrary, explicit, and accountable procedures governing the coercive power of the state.
- Commitment to individual freedom: a basic dedication to anything that enhances the ability of individuals to make unhindered choices.
- Loyalty to democratic institutions and processes: human rights—of both majorities and minorities—are essential to making liberal democracy function effectively.

These grand concepts provide some guidance for an empirical inquiry into attitudes toward human rights, although, of course, each requires a great deal more consideration and clarification.

In this research, primary focus is on support for the rule of law. This is useful since a cardinal foundation of human rights is the idea that authority must be subservient to law. Law certainly does not "guarantee" human rights—rights are often lost through entirely "legal" means, and legal "guarantees" may ultimately depend on political forces—but without law, citizens are dependent on the beneficence of authorities. Unless South Africa can develop a culture respectful of the rule of law, it is difficult to imagine that human rights can prosper. At least some observers of South African politics agree with this approach. Slye (2000, 170) defines a human rights culture in the South African context as "a political culture that values human dignity and the rule of law." He asserts that the creation of such a culture is one of two necessary conditions for reconciliation. (The other condition is accountability for past violations.)

Rule of law is a concept subject to various definitions and interpretations. Following extant research on attitudes toward the rule of law (e.g., Gibson and Gouws 1997), this research posits that the rule of law is a continuum bounded by universalism and particularism. Though the concept is usually applied to the state, it is equally applicable to the behavior of individual citizens. Further, though rule of law is probably necessary for democratic government, it is certainly not sufficient. The rule of law may be enlisted by both dictatorial minorities and tyrannical majorities. Finally, rule of law has meaning as an attribute of the institutions, cultures, and belief systems of ordinary citizens. Thus, one of the most important definitions of "reconciliation" is support for a human rights culture in South Africa; more specifically, human rights require that South Africans support the rule of law.

The Meaning of "Truth"

Whether one agrees with the findings or not, the central elements of the TRC's understanding of South Africa's history include these understandings:

> That apartheid was a crime against humanity and that therefore, those struggling to maintain that regime were engaged in an evil undertaking. The commission's final report asserted that "the Commission—as part of the international human rights community—affirms its judgment that apartheid, as a system of enforced racial discrimination and separation, was a crime against humanity. The recognition of apartheid as a crime against humanity remains a fundamental starting point for reconciliation in South Africa" (TRC 1998, vol. 1, 94; see also vol. 5, 222). Even the "minority position" issued with the report asserts that this section of the majority viewpoint "adequately addresses this issue," even as it tried to provide some additional context for why the South Africans acted as they did. (TRC 1998, vol. 5, 448–50)

> That both sides in the struggle over apartheid committed horrific offenses, including gross human rights violations. Indisputably, the TRC documented that agents of the apartheid state committed numerous gross human rights violations, just as it documented gross human rights violations by the African National Congress and the Inkatha Freedom Party. Desmond Tutu asserts in the Commission's Final Report, "We believe we have provided enough of the truth about our past for there to be a consensus about it. There is a consensus that atrocious things were done on all sides." (TRC 1998, vol. 1, 18)

> That apartheid was criminal both due to the actions of specific individuals (including legal and illegal actions) and because of actions of the state institutions themselves. The TRC's final report often refers to the state as the perpetrator, and the South African state is specifically indicted for gross human rights violations. (TRC 1998, vol. 5, 212)

The truth promulgated by the TRC is very much the truth of discrete events. One approach to measuring truth acceptance among ordinary South Africans would therefore be to focus on whether people are aware of specific incidents and abuses. The Reconciliation Survey chose not to take this tack, in part because it would be quite time-consuming to canvass knowledge of a wide variety of events and incidents, and in part because people most likely acquire specific information only on issues that are of some direct relevance or interest to them. Instead, the survey focused on the lessons learned from the revelations of the TRC. This is certainly what might be called an "interpretative" truth, but it might also be called "historical understandings." It seems obvious that the lessons the TRC wanted people to learn from its activities involve these broad understandings rather than acceptance of its description and explanation of any given discrete event. The details of any given incident in South Africa's apartheid past are inevitably contested. (See, for instance, Jeffery 1999, which takes the TRC to task for what the author claims are specific historical inaccuracies in the commission's findings.) The TRC sometimes refers to this as understanding the "context" of these incidents, by which it means understanding the larger social and institutional forces that allowed a specific abuse to take place. To understand context is to provide an explanation for individual actions. The TRC clearly perceived its mandate in terms of both factual truth and explanatory truth (even if this mandate may have been self-assumed rather than delegated by the law establishing the commission). That apartheid was evil, that atrocities were committed by all sides in the struggle, and that the evil of the system was an evil of institutions and not individuals are the broad understandings of the past that the TRC sought to impart. These are the lessons the TRC wanted people to learn.

Consequently, the survey respondents were asked to judge the veracity of each of these statements. On the basis of their replies, an indicator was created of the degree to which the individual participated in the TRC's truth. My goal here is not to assess the historical accuracy of these claims but rather to determine the degree to which ordinary South Africans accept the truth as promulgated by the TRC—its collective memory. When the "truth leads to reconciliation" hypothesis is considered, in every instance the hypothesis being investigated is that those South Africans who accept the truth as documented by the TRC are more likely to be reconciled. "Truth" as used in this research means the TRC's truth, nothing more.

Using Surveys to Measure Truth and Reconciliation

If one wants to know how reconciled South Africans are (and what causes some to be more reconciled than others), few appropriate research designs are available. Whenever a research objective seeks to draw conclusions about a population as a whole, conducting a representative survey is the most useful approach. (Some even argue that sampling produces more accurate results than conducting a census.) Representative surveys allow us to interview a relatively small number of people yet draw conclusions about the entire population of the country. (See, for example, Schuman and Corning 2000.) Obviously, no justification whatever exists for drawing general conclusions from samples of students, from the comments of participants in a focus group, or even from interviews with activists. If the research question is defined in terms of whether the population holds certain views, attitudes, and values, then no substitute for the representative sample exists.

Overview of the Truth and Reconciliation Survey

This study is based on a representative survey of the South African mass public, conducted in 2000-01. A total of 3,727 face-to-face interviews were completed. The average interview lasted eighty-four minutes. The overall response rate for the survey was approximately 87 percent. Nearly all the respondents were interviewed by someone of their own race. Interviews were conducted in the respondents' language of choice, with a large plurality of the interviews (44.5 percent) being done in English. The questionnaire was first prepared in English and then translated into Afrikaans, Zulu, Xhosa, North Sotho, South Sotho, Tswana, and Tsonga. The sample included representative oversamples of whites, colored people, and those of Asian origin.

Survey Methodology

The first step in designing a survey project on transitional justice is to explicitly define the population from which the sample will be drawn and about which statistical inferences will be made from the data collected. No survey ever purports to be representative of the entire population of a country. For instance, all surveys impose a minimum age on the respondents. In South Africa, where there is sometimes talk about lowering the minimum voting age to sixteen, this is an issue of some consequence. The Reconciliation Survey of 2001 defined the population as South Africans of eighteen years or older.

Other ways in which a population might be restricted include the requirement of citizenship. This is a most difficult filter, since one must establish at the beginning of an interview the respondent's citizenship status. Not only are illegal aliens unlikely to admit their status, but questions of this nature may also arouse suspicion. Moreover, the filter is quite costly to implement, because respondents are discarded when they are found not to be citizens. A citizenship requirement has never been imposed in these surveys; and therefore, the population to which the studies generalize is often described as the "residents" of South Africa.

Since sampling is based on selecting residences (before enumerating the individuals within the residences), people without a residence (e.g., homeless people) are excluded from participation in the survey. In addition, however, residents of hostels were systematically excluded from the design. Hostels are essentially dormitories (with communal toilets). There are two types of hostels in South Africa: those run by companies (including the mining companies) and those organized by political parties for itinerant workers and the poorest of the poor. It is difficult for survey researchers to get access to the former (since the hostels are located on company property), and interviewing in either would be dangerous. It is routine in South Africa for survey researchers to exclude hostel residents from their populations. The Reconciliation Survey did, however, include people living in informal housing such as squatter camps and backyard shacks. To exclude respondents living in this type of housing would be to produce a seriously unrepresentative sample.

A few places in the country are so heavily guarded that it is impossible for interviewers to gain entry. Thus, wealthy white South Africans are almost always underrepresented in surveys.

If generalizability to a larger population is desired, then survey participants must be randomly selected. Random selection is typically combined with stratification by race to allow for generalizations about each of the major racial groups in South Africa. In addition, some surveys stratify by language so that they can, for instance, draw conclusions about differences between English-speaking and Afrikaans-speaking whites. Samples in the United States are routinely adjusted through a process termed "poststratification." This is a system of weights designed to make the sample more representative of the population. Dramatically falling response rates in the United States make poststratification essential for most surveys. The Reconciliation Survey employed poststratification, but because the response rate was high in the first place, this was probably unnecessary.

Questionnaire Construction and Translation

The questionnaire in a survey encapsulates the theories to be tested. Thus, each question in a questionnaire should clearly represent a concept, and a "conceptual map" must be developed, assigning each question within the survey to a specific and unique concept.

This process is facilitated to some degree by the use of established scales. For instance, standard measures of dogmatism are drawn from Rokeach's (1960) work on measuring closed-mindedness. Existing measures should be used to the extent possible because such scales have known estimates of reliability and validity and because they allow comparison with previous survey results (see Robinson, Shaver, and Wrightsman 1999). Virtually all the concepts used in the survey are measured through multiple indicators. For instance, interracial reconciliation is represented by nine individual questions. The advantages of multiple-item indices are numerous: Reliability estimates can be calculated (e.g., internal consistency, as in Cronbach's alpha); items of low validity can be discarded without undermining entirely the measurement of the concept; and multiple indicators allow the use of sophisticated statistical techniques such as LISREL. Employing single-item indicators to produce point estimates of public opinion is one of the least useful objectives of surveys. For most purposes, a minimum of four items per scale is imposed. This is a very small number of items, with the result that many of our scales are estimated to have relatively low reliability. (Reliability is virtually always increased by using more items.) The trade-off is between measuring more concepts poorly and measuring fewer concepts more reliably. Since variance in dependent variables is always especially critical, concepts to be explained (dependent variables) should employ a larger number of indicators.

Once the survey instrument is constructed in English, the arduous process of translation occurs. Producing a valid and reliable instrument in eight different languages is demanding, to say the least. When the English version of the questionnaire is translated into the other languages by professional translators, care is taken to ensure that colloquial language is used, irrespective of ordinary rules of grammar and syntax. The translated version of the questionnaire is then translated back into English by separate translators. This process produces what is called an "output version" of the questionnaire, which must then be compared to the original "input version." This comparison process is arduous. The translator, the back-translator, members of the survey firm fluent in each of the languages, and the investigators themselves are assembled. Each question is reviewed seriatim, as a group, to determine the fidelity of the translation. Performing this task as a group is extremely useful, since the translator and back-translator will often negotiate the language to be used. Then comparisons are typically made between the words used in closely related languages (e.g., Nguni languages, such as Zulu and Xhosa). The result is that each question is perfected in each language. These sessions (dubbed "reconciliation meetings") typically last dozens of hours over several days. The questionnaire at this stage in the process typically includes about 125 percent of the questions to be used in the actual interview. This strategy is adopted so that the final instrument can discard items found to be difficult to translate, to be of low reliability or validity, or to produce little variance.

The questionnaire must then be pretested. This process begins with a handful of practice interviews, which are typically observed (through one-way mirrors) by employees of the survey firm and the investigators. One can learn a great deal from such interviews, especially regarding question order, since it is so difficult to anticipate order effects in the abstract. Debriefing the respondents in these practice interviews is extremely valuable. (For example, ambiguity in the meaning of words can be identified.)

After revising the instrument, a formal pretest is conducted. Here we typically deviate from ideal practice, which would be to conduct some thirty to fifty interviews in each of the languages. As an economy measure, we usually conduct about seventy-five pretest interviews. An important choice must be made between limiting those seventy-five interviews to a very few languages and trying to ensure representation of each of the languages. Since very little "within-language analysis" of the pretest data can be conducted, a useful practice is to try to select languages in proportion to the prevalence of the language in the South African population. Such a strategy does little to identify language-specific problems in the questionnaire but allows for at least some estimate of the overall reliability and validity of the items in the total pretest population.

The pretest data are formally analyzed using various statistical techniques. Factor analysis is useful for establishing the dimensionality of a set of items. Reliability can be assessed using Cronbach's alpha. Individual questions should be scrutinized for degenerate variance and correlations with other questions in the scale. On occasion, an entire scale may perform so poorly that it must be deleted altogether rather than repaired. Since the primary purpose of surveys is to discover and explain individual differences in attitudes, questions that fail to differentiate among respondents are rarely included (deliberately, at any rate) in surveys. This can be misleading at times, however. For instance, we routinely measure attitudes toward the rule of law and find that support for the rule of law is not especially well established in South Africa. However, there are many aspects of the rule of law that are not explored, because consensus (or even unanimity) exists (e.g., that the judiciary ought not to be subservient to the government of the day). It is always important for analysts to give a clear indication of the specific nature of the variance they are investigating.

Since the primary objective of this analysis is to reduce the long version of the instrument to a questionnaire of acceptable length, few items are constructed or reconstructed at this stage of the process. To the extent that this does take place, the translation/back-translation process must be repeated. Since there is typically little time and energy available for translation at this stage of the project, the decision is often limited to the dichotomous choice of whether to include or exclude an individual item.

Pitfalls in Survey Research on Truth and Reconciliation

One of the first obvious pitfalls of conducting surveys of this size and sophistication is that they are costly. The Truth and Reconciliation Survey cost approximately $150,000. Moreover, a huge investment of time is necessary, since it would be extremely unwise for an investigator to turn over all the details of a survey to a survey research firm. In the surveys we have conducted in South Africa, I have been intimately involved in every stage of the survey process, including sample design, questionnaire construction, and, of course, all analysis. Myriad ways exist for survey firms to reduce costs (e.g., substitution of respondents when the designated interviewee is not available), so careful monitoring of each step in the research process is essential and requires considerable knowledge of survey research theory and practice.

Several recognized threats to the quality of survey data exist and deserve some consideration. For example, a threat in all surveys is that respondents will give replies that they believe are socially appropriate or desirable or that they think will please the interviewer. This creates systematic measurement error, which is, of course, a serious threat to validity. Social desirability influences can be especially dangerous when our questions concern such sensitive issues as racial prejudice.

Surveys are fine ways of measuring attitudes, and in transitional justice research, the attitudes of ordinary citizens (for example, on support for a human rights culture) are of great interest. But a conventional criticism of survey research is that it often fails to consider actual behavior. Some standard replies to this criticism are that attitudes are propensities to behave, that attitudes have been shown to be moderately connected to actual behaviors, that we often measure behavioral intentions or hypothetical behaviors in surveys, and that we do in fact occasionally measure self-reports of actual behavior. But some still contend that concepts such as "reconciliation" must refer to the ways in which citizens act toward each other and that surveys are not very effective means of studying such action.

There is some validity to this criticism. The main difficulty with assessing behavior is that action is typically highly contextual. When citizens do not tolerate the views of other citizens, a set of circumstances—a context—is inevitably involved. Civil liberties conflicts are hard to anticipate (unlike voting behavior, such controversies do not materialize at regular intervals), making them difficult to study via survey methods.

A conventional and powerful criticism of the survey method is that often the picture that emerges from surveys is highly static. My reconciliation survey asks how reconciled South Africans were in 2001. Obviously, reconciliation is a highly dynamic attribute that waxes and wanes over time. Of course, there is no inherent limitation of the method that makes it resistant to more dynamic approaches. For instance, Gibson and Gouws (2003) report a panel study in South Africa in which they examine the factors that bring about changes in levels of political intolerance. Three-wave panel studies allow considerable precision in estimating the nature of change. Such surveys are expensive (and repeated cross-sections are therefore sometimes treated as an alternative), but survey research is no more constrained than any other approach as a methodology to conduct cross-analysis; the only issue is resources. Just as those who study subatomic particles require expensive machinery, those who seek to understand how people change in transitional societies must be provided with the resources adequate for employing appropriate and useful survey technologies.

Discussion and Concluding Comments

There is much more to survey research methodology than conducting a survey. Perhaps the most important advantage of the survey methodology is that it forces the researcher to address certain methodological issues that are pertinent to every form of research. The question of whether results can be generalized is just as appropriate for qualitative case studies as for survey research. Validity and reliability are not just desiderata for quantitative measurement; they apply with equal force to open-ended qualitative interviews and even to unstructured discussions with people. Social desirability effects are just as devastating to participant observation research as to systematic surveys. The conceptual criteria by which the quality of "data" is assessed—quantitative, qualitative, anecdotal, and so on—do not vary by the type of data. With surveys, however, researchers simply cannot avoid addressing these important questions.

Surveys nonetheless have certain limitations and cannot answer all important research questions in the study of transitional justice. One should be particularly unimpressed with conclusions drawn from traditional question-and-answer surveys (a context in which the respondent simply answers questions posed by the interviewer). Rather, surveys that are interactive with the respondent, that attempt to build context into questions, and that try to develop estimates of the amount of measurement error in the data collected seem likely to produce the most useful information. For example, persuasion experiments (Gibson and Gouws 2003, chaps. 6 and 7), the use of experimental vignettes (Gibson and Gouws 2003, chap. 5; Gibson 2004a, chap. 7), and studies of change over time (Gibson and Gouws 2003, chap. 8) all offer some degree of dynamism to survey designs.

But even surveys of this type are limited in many important ways. For instance, even despite some efforts to measure certain aspects of social networks, the survey approach is primarily egocentric and is therefore subject to the "Robinson Crusoe" critique. (Individuals exist as if they were solitary beings, living alone on an island.) Hypothetical questions, even those designed to mimic reality, can never fully capture the dynamics of real events. Surveys typically represent a single slice in time of a dynamic process. In real political disputes, citizens do not have "attitudes"; instead, they hold positions that often evolve and transform in response to a variety of factors. Are South Africans reconciled with each other? At the level of individual interactions, the answer varies almost daily. Surveys can never provide much more than indications of propensities, with actual events often contributing greatly to how the propensities get tailored to specific circumstances.

Nonetheless, by being so self-conscious about their methods, surveys hold the greatest promise for understanding attitudes such as truth acceptance and individual-level reconciliation. Indeed, the best that research can ever do is not to eliminate measurement error—such a goal is unobtainable—but rather to try to estimate the magnitude of error and anticipate its likely consequences. Few other methodologies are capable of performing this important task.

Can the methodology of this South African study of truth and reconciliation be exported to other transitional societies? Probably, although several attributes of the South African process make it particularly amenable to this sort of analysis. For one thing, where the transitional justice project is confined to elites and does not seek broad social change, the views of ordinary people may be of lesser importance; also, ordinary people may hold less well defined views. South Africa's TRC actually sought to change society, and it understood change as starting with the beliefs, values, attitudes, and behaviors of individual citizens. Consequently, the commission sought to penetrate all corners of South African society—and was extraordinarily successful in doing so.

Also, timing is important for studies of transitional justice. No effort to transform a society can succeed quickly; therefore, studies conducted at the beginning of a reconciliation process are likely to find that social change has failed. One must be quite careful to situate research within the historical context. This research was conducted a few years after the TRC ceased most of its activity; to conduct the survey earlier might not have been very useful. For example, a study on reconciliation between Arabs and Israelis at ongoing points in a peace process, when so much is subject to change, may not be particularly useful.

And third, it may be that in some transitional contexts important elites have a strong interest in ensuring that studies of reconciliation fail. South African elites were generally united in favor of reconciliation, with few voices calling for retribution instead. In cases where there is not such ideological consensus, several roadblocks to public opinion studies can be created. Several years ago, a study that simply asked questions about whether Muslims, Serbs, Croats, and Bosniaks should be tolerated in Bosnia-Herzegovina was itself judged to be incendiary by local people.

There are plenty of important unanswered empirical questions in the study of transitional justice, but none is more important than that of understanding how individual citizens learn new styles of thinking and behaving under newly constituted regimes. To the extent that reconciliation requires social change, few methodological choices exist. If analysts are to understand the people of a society, then we must talk to them, and the talk must be as rigorous and representative as possible. Surveys provide an extremely powerful tool for holding such conversations.

Acknowledgments

This research has been supported by the Law and Social Sciences Program of the National Science Foundation (SES 9906576). Any opinions, findings, and conclusions or recommendations expressed in this material are those of the author and do not necessarily reflect the views of the National Science Foundation. The project is a collaborative effort between Amanda Gouws, Department of Political Science, University of Stellenbosch (South Africa), and me. I am indebted to Charles Villa-Vicencio, Helen Macdonald, Paul Haupt, Nyameka Goniwe, Fanie du Toit, Erik Doxtader, and the staff of the Institute for Justice and Reconciliation (South Africa) for the many helpful discussions that have informed my understanding of the truth and reconciliation process in South Africa. Eric Wolfish provided valuable research assistance.

References

Gibson, J. L. 1992. "Alternative Measures of Political Tolerance: Must Tolerance be 'Least-Liked'?" *American Journal of Political Science* 36 (2): 560–77.

———. 2004a. *Overcoming Apartheid: Can Truth Reconcile a Divided Nation?* New York: Russell Sage Foundation.

———. 2004b. "Does Truth Lead to Reconciliation? Testing the Causal Assumptions of the South African Truth and Reconciliation Process." *American Journal of Political Science* 48 (2): 201–17.

Gibson, J. L., and G. A. Caldeira. 2003. "Defenders of Democracy? Legitimacy, Popular Acceptance, and the South African Constitutional Court." *Journal of Politics* 65 (1): 1–30.

Gibson, J. L., G. A. Caldeira, and V. A. Baird. 1998. "On the Legitimacy of National High Courts." *American Political Science Review* 92 (2): 343–58.

Gibson, J. L., and Amanda Gouws. 1997. "Support for the Rule of Law in the Emerging South African Democracy." *International Social Science Journal* 152 (June): 173–91.

———. 2003. *Overcoming Intolerance in South Africa: Experiments in Democratic Persuasion.* New York: Cambridge University Press.

Jeffery, Anthea. 1999. *The Truth about the Truth Commission.* Johannesburg: South African Institute of Race Relations.

Robinson, J. P., P. R. Shaver, and L. S. Wrightsman, eds. 1999. *Measures of Political Attitudes.* San Diego, Calif.: Academic Press.

Rokeach, Milton. 1960. *The Open and Closed Mind.* New York: Basic Books.

Schuman, Howard, and Amy Corning. 2000. "Collective Knowledge of Public Events: The Soviet Era from the Great Purge to Glasnost." *American Journal of Sociology* 105 (4): 913–56.

Slye, Ronald. 2000. "Justice and Amnesty." In *Looking Back, Reaching Forward: Reflections on the Truth and Reconciliation Commission of South Africa,* ed. Charles Villa-Vicencio and Wilhelm Verwoerd. Cape Town: University of Cape Town Press.

Sullivan, J. L., J. E. Piereson, and G. E. Marcus. 1982. *Political Tolerance and American Democracy.* Chicago: University of Chicago Press.

TRC. 1998. *Truth and Reconciliation Commission of South Africa Report.* Cape Town: Juta.

Villa-Vicencio, Charles, and Si'fiso Ngesi. 2003. "South Africa: Beyond the 'Miracle.'" In *Through Fire with Water: The Roots of Division and the Potential for Reconciliation in Africa,* ed. Charles Villa-Vicencio and Erik Doxtader. Claremont, South Africa: David Philip.

7

Survivor Studies

The Importance of Evaluating the Effects of Truth Commissions on Survivors of Human Rights Violations

Jeffrey Sonis

This chapter examines the importance of comprehensive survivor studies in evaluating the success of truth commissions. Through evaluating the effects of truth commissions on survivors, we can begin to understand whether the benefits of public and private survivor testimonies are as effective for the survivors themselves as they are for the overall success of the truth commission. This chapter sets out to describe some important principles needed for the successful implementation of survivor studies. To understand these principles, we must answer the following questions: (1) What should be studied, that is, what are the most important research questions to address in evaluating the effects of truth commissions on survivors of human rights violations? (2) What research designs and methods are most suitable for identifying those effects? (3) What are the important ethical principles that must be followed in carrying out research with survivors?

Most of the goals of truth commissions have a societal focus: identifying patterns of past abuses, developing socially constructed versions of truth (what happened and why), promoting reconciliation among groups of people, assessing accountability for previous human rights violations, promoting respect for the rule of law and principles of human rights, and developing recommendations for societal transformation to prevent future violations of human rights (Hayner 2001; Kritz 1997). All these goals, by their very nature, deal with the 99.9 percent of people in a country who never interact personally with a truth commission. These are frequently seen as the most important goals of a truth commission, and the goals by which it may be judged a success or a failure. When people talk about the "effect" of a truth commission, they are usually referring to the degree to which these goals are achieved.

But it is equally important to consider the truth commissions' effects on the relatively small group of survivors of gross human rights violations who interact directly with the commissions (Minow 1998, 2000). (Note: In this chapter, we use the term "survivors" to refer to people who suffered direct harm and to the family members of people who disappeared or were murdered or disabled. The term "deponent" is used to refer to survivors who either submitted a statement to a truth commission in private or testified in a public hearing, or both.)

Survivors of human rights violations are central to the overall mission of truth commissions for multiple reasons (Friedman 2000; Hamber 2001; de la Rey and Owens 1998; Ignatieff 1997). Survivors contribute to the achievement of the truth commissions' social goals described above, because their words and experiences are the raw data from which patterns of human rights violations can be identified and their causes deduced. If survivors were not willing to share their painful stories, it would be nearly impossible for a truth commission to identify what happened and why. But if the very process of generating the data used to identify patterns of abuses further harms survivors, then that truth commission can hardly be considered successful. A second important reason to consider truth commissions' effects on survivors who interact directly with them is that transformed societies have a special moral obligation to those who have suffered the worst.

Some truth commissions have recognized the centrality of survivors by including an emphasis on survivors in their explicit objectives. The South African Truth and Reconciliation Commission (TRC) stated that one of its goals was to promote national unity and reconciliation by (among other things) "restoration of human and civil dignity of victims of human rights violations through testimony and recommendations to the President concerning reparations for victims" (South African TRC, 1999). Other truth commissions have not explicitly recognized survivors in their objectives, but that does not diminish the centrality of survivors to those commissions' overall success.

What Should Be Studied?

Good questions drive good research. The two most important criteria for determining which questions to address in a study of survivors who interact with truth commissions are novelty—that is, originality—and importance. A novel research question is one that has never been asked before or that has been asked but not answered adequately. Answering the question must generate new knowledge. A study based on an unoriginal question cannot be justified, because it is unethical to ask research participants to undergo any risk, or even inconvenience, if new knowledge is not generated. Moreover, unoriginal research wastes precious time and resources.

But even if a research question has been answered adequately in one setting, the same question (or a variant of it) may still be novel when applied to different historical circumstances and a different truth commission. As an example, take the following research question: Are survivors who testify in public hearings of a truth commission more likely to feel that justice has been served than are survivors who submit statements to a statement taker? Even if a study of the South African TRC answered that question adequately, it still may be a novel question if applied to truth commissions in Ghana, Peru, or elsewhere. Whether the question is novel will depend primarily on whether the research in one setting (e.g., South Africa) is generalizable to other settings (e.g., Ghana or Peru). Generalizability, also known as "external validity," will depend on the degree to which the historical circumstances, types of human rights violations committed, and actions of a truth commission in one country are similar to those in another country.

In studies of survivors who interact with truth commissions, it is not hard to identify a novel research question, simply because the field is so new. Virtually any research question is novel right now. The key issue is not finding a novel question but identifying, from among the novel questions, the most important ones.

The second major criterion for research questions is that they be important. An important research question is one that has the potential to make a difference in people's lives. But this begs the question, important for whom? A research question may be important to (1) survivors, (2) the truth commission in a particular country, (3) the country as a whole, (4) future truth commissions, and (5) scientists who study truth commissions.

Some questions will be important for only one of these groups, while others may be important for more than one. Let's take three examples. Suppose a study is undertaken to answer the following question: To what extent was the Sierra Leone Truth and Reconciliation Commission (TRC) successful at soliciting statements from survivors in different regions of Sierra Leone? The answer to this question will undoubtedly be important to survivors in Sierra Leone and to Sierra Leone's TRC, but it may have limited significance for future truth commissions. One the other hand, a study designed to determine whether there were aspects of interaction with the TRC in Sierra Leone that predicted positive mental health outcomes among survivors is likely to be important to future truth commissions, since the answer may help those truth commissions develop and implement procedures that promote positive outcomes among survivors. Finally, a study designed to develop a new instrument to measure perceptions of justice among survivors of human rights violations who submitted statements to the TRC in Peru may be enormously important to researchers studying truth commissions, but not immediately important to any of the other groups. These types of research questions should not be denigrated, despite the lack of immediate importance for survivors or for the current TRC, because research tools that advance the field will frequently be enormously important to survivors and to other truth commissions in the future.

Several other criteria should also be used to determine which research questions to pursue. The research question should be feasible to answer, based on the resources available and the expertise of the research group, and should be answerable using ethical research methods.

One of the most important issues regarding research questions is, who decides which question is important: survivors, the truth commission, or the researchers? The traditional approach to science holds that the research questions should be identified and selected exclusively by the researcher. The participatory research paradigm holds that the research questions should be identified and selected by the research participants, in this case, the survivors (Graham and Chandler-Coutts 2000). Both extreme positions have pitfalls. There are two problems with having the researchers identify and select the questions: First, important questions may be overlooked by researchers; and second, the research questions selected by the investigators may not be perceived by the survivors or the truth commissions as relevant to their experiences. The problem with having survivors or truth commissions alone select the research questions is that they may be less likely to select questions that are not immediately applicable to their lives but are nonetheless important for moving the field forward. For instance, developing a psychometric instrument to measure perceptions of justice among survivors of human rights violations is crucial to understanding the effect of truth commissions on survivors, but survivors may not have identified that need. Also, grant-funding agencies are unlikely to fund a project that does not identify at least some research questions before the project's initiation.

In virtually all situations, the best research grows out of a collaborative approach to identifying research questions—one that involves the survivors, the truth commission, and the researchers. This can be implemented in the following way. First, the researchers should try to identify and include survivors in the research team. One way to do this is to select a community advisory board consisting of survivors (Galea et al. 2001). But this may be difficult to do in a country where many violations were committed by members of rival political parties or groups. Members of conflicting groups may be reluctant to be on an advisory board together. Even worse, if an advisory board includes survivors from only one of the groups, survivors from conflicting groups may be reluctant to participate in the research and will usually not trust the objectivity of the findings. Second, the research team should meet with members of the truth commission to solicit their input about important questions to address. In most situations, it is best not to include members of the truth commission on the advisory board. If survivors are dissatisfied with the truth commission in various ways, an advisory board consisting of both survivors and truth commission members may be too rancorous to provide effective guidance to the researchers. Moreover, if survivors who are dissatisfied with the truth commission believe, even incorrectly, that the research project is being directed by the truth commission, they may feel that the findings are a whitewash. Third, the research team should try to identify issues important to survivors and the truth commission by reviewing transcripts of public hearings and conducting open-ended interviews or focus groups with survivors and with truth commission employees who interact with survivors. Fourth, based both on the important issues identified in step 2 and on a careful review of existing literature on truth commissions, the research team should develop a list of potential research questions. Fifth, the potential research questions should be reviewed with survivors and modified according to their feedback.

Appendix 1 shows a broad set of research questions that meet the originality and importance criteria and that should be applicable to studies in a wide range of countries.

Principles of Research for Survivor Studies

Regardless of the question or the design, all survivor studies should be concerned with common core principles of research to ensure validity of inference and generalizability to groups of people who were not sampled. "Internal validity" refers to the degree to which the results obtained from a study sample reflect the truth (Rothman and Greenland 1998, 118). Truth is defined as the results that would be obtained if everyone in the target population participated in the study and if all the measures were completely accurate. The target population is the population from which the sample was drawn. Three major types of bias can compromise the internal validity of a study. The first, confounding bias, is a distortion in the results due to a mixing of the effects of one factor with the effects of some other extraneous factor (Rothman and Greenland 1998, 120). Confounding occurs when the extraneous factor is associated with both the factor of interest and the outcome, which can lead to erroneous conclusions unless confounding is controlled in the analysis. A study to determine whether testifying in a public hearing (versus submitting a statement in private) is associated with perceptions of justice illustrates the principle of confounding. If demographic characteristics, such as age or gender or income or type of victimization, are associated with testifying, and if those same characteristics are associated with perceptions of justice, the association between testifying and perceptions of justice will be distorted.

The second type, selection bias, is a distortion in the results due to a difference between people who participated in a study and those who were theoretically eligible but did not participate (the target population) (Rothman and Greenland 1998, 119). Selection bias will be present if the association between the factor of interest (e.g., testifying) and the outcome of interest (e.g., justice) is not the same for those who participated in the study (the study sample) as for those who were theoretically eligible but did not participate. Selection bias is usually generated by the methods used to select the sample. If a study uses a random-digit dial telephone survey to identify and then select survivors in a developing country, the survivors who are identified are likely to be dramatically different from the total group of all survivors in that country, since poor and rural survivors are much less likely to have telephones.

Measurement bias is a distortion in the result due to error in measurement of the variables in a study (Rothman and Greenland 1998, 125–33). Measurement bias is common in studies of survivors who interact with truth commissions, simply because there are few standardized instruments to measure the major outcomes of interest, such as perceptions of justice, desire for reconciliation, and others.

"External validity" (or "generalizability") refers to the degree to which the results of the study are applicable to other (external) populations (Rothman and Greenland 1998, 118). If the findings from a study of survivors in South Africa can be generalized to survivors in other countries, then the study has high external validity. External validity is an issue of judgment, not statistics. Selection bias, however, is different from lack of external validity In selection bias, the issue is whether the results are distorted by differences between the sample and the group being sampled (the target population), whereas for external validity, the issue is whether there are differences between the results in the sample and the results that one would expect in some external population.

Research Designs for Survivor Studies

Once the research question has been selected, the research group needs to identify the most appropriate design for answering that question. The best design for a study of survivors is the one that is most appropriate to answer the research question. This may seem obvious, but it can be forgotten by investigators in thrall to naive hierarchies of research design that hold randomized trials up as the gold standard for all research.

There are several dichotomies that drive the research design. These are described below.

Can the research question be answered with qualitative or quantitative methods?

Qualitative research is ideally suited to answering research questions that have to do with meaning, interpretation, and social processes—topics that are difficult (if not impossible) to research with standard questionnaires or surveys (Inu 1996; Malterud 2001). Also, qualitative research can be used to help generate hypotheses in areas where little is known (Malterud 2001). Quantitative research is appropriate for testing specific hypotheses, to evaluate whether one truth commission intervention (e.g., debriefing after testifying) is more effective than another, and to identify factors that predict positive or adverse outcomes among survivors. Since the field of truth commission research is so new, one effective design is to build both qualitative and quantitative elements into a research project.

Can the research question be answered with an individual or group (ecological) study design?

Many questions about survivors who interact with truth commissions are focused on processes and outcomes among individual survivors. Research to answer those questions uses an individual design, in which individual survivors are included as participants and are the unit of analysis. However, some research questions are focused on groups of people, such as entire communities or countries (Susser 1994; Greenland and Robins 1994). In South Africa during the apartheid era, the pattern of abuses varied markedly in different regions of the country and within different communities in the same region. An important question, then, is whether, given those different patterns, the South African TRC had different effects on communities in different regions. Likewise, if the goal of a study is to determine whether a truth commission process that is implemented countrywide (such as debriefing survivors after they testify in a public hearing) is effective, then the only way that question can be answered is by comparing countries where truth commissions used that process to countries where the process was not used. These questions can be answered only through aggregate, or ecological, designs in which the unit of observation and analysis is the community or country and not the individual survivor. Although ecological designs are problematic if inferences derived from measurement and analysis of variables at the community level are applied to individuals within those communities (the "ecological fallacy"), they are the only type of design that is appropriate for comparing aggregate-level effects across communities or countries (Koepsell and Weiss 2003; Susser 1994). The past fifteen years have seen much methodological work on ecological studies and multilevel studies (including measurement and analysis at both the individual and aggregate level), and readers are referred to this work for details on design, measurement, and analysis of these types of studies (Blakely and Subramanian 2006; Kawachi and Berkman 2003; Morgenstern 1995).

Can the research question be answered through analysis of data at one point in time, or does it require analysis of data at multiple points in time?

If the goal of the research is simply to identify the prevalence of a situation or outcome among survivors, then a cross-sectional study that gathers data at one point in time will be sufficient (Grimes and Schulz 2002). If the goal of the study is to determine the proportion of all survivors who submitted statements to a truth commission, then a cross-sectional study will suffice. However, if the goal of the study is to determine the effect of the truth commission on survivors, a longitudinal study, which gathers data from survivors at multiple points in time, is the best design. This is because almost all outcomes of interest are likely to change over time. For example, if the goal of the research is to determine whether survivors experience an increase in depressive symptoms after testifying in a public hearing, it would be ideal to collect data immediately after they testify, as well as six and twelve months later, since the short-term reactions of survivors may differ dramatically from the long-term reactions.

Does the research question imply a comparison?

Even when not stated outright, most research questions have an implied comparison embedded in them. If the goal of the research is to determine whether survivors who submit a statement to the truth commission develop a sense of political empowerment, the obvious question is, compared to whom? Compared to survivors who testify in public hearings? Compared to survivors who do not submit a statement? Compared to people who were not survivors of human rights violations? Accordingly, most survivor studies should include a comparison or control group of some type that will enable the researchers to draw valid conclusions.

Sampling

How to develop a sample of deponents (survivors who submit statements or testify in public hearings)

The development of an appropriate sample is the most challenging aspect of research with survivors. The first challenge is to identify and select a group of survivors who gave statements or testified in a public hearing. A random sample from the universe of deponents is the only way to avoid potential selection bias (Kelsey et al. 1996, 311–14; Kish 1965, 18–21). One approach to developing a random sample of deponents, though not usually feasible, is a random sample of the entire country. Deponents are but a fraction of all survivors in a country, and survivors of the types of gross violations explored by truth commissions are a small fraction of all people in a country. In South Africa, there were 21,296 deponents at a time that the country's population was approximately 4.5 million (South African TRC 1999; Statistics South Africa 2001). A researcher who tried to develop a sample of 100 deponents using a random sample of the population of South Africa would need to draw a sample of 190,176 people. Clearly, that approach is not feasible.

A second possible approach is to develop a sampling frame of deponents from truth commission records and then draw a random sample from that frame. A sampling frame is a list of deponents, along with contact information such as address or phone number (Kish 1965, 18–21). However, truth commissions may be reluctant or unwilling to release contact or identifying information of people who testified or submitted statements to researchers unless the deponents themselves gave prior approval. In South Africa, several research groups tried unsuccessfully to obtain a list of deponents from the TRC. The TRC was reluctant to release that information because it believed this would violate the confidentiality of deponents. Moreover, even if truth commissions are willing to release this information to researchers, research ethics committees in some countries may be unwilling to let researchers use a list that contains contact information not explicitly approved by the people on the list (Gold 1996, 130–34; Brody 1998, 51–52).

A third possible approach is to develop a sampling frame of testifiers from information in the public record. The names of people who testify in public hearings are usually included on a truth commission Web site, in a local newspaper, or on an official document of the truth commission, such as the final report. However, finding contact information can be more difficult. If a person who testifies reports his or her community of residence and has an uncommon name, it may be possible to find contact information in a phone book or through local community leaders. In a pilot study that my collaborators and I conducted as part of a larger study of South Africa's TRC, contact information could be obtained on less than 10 percent of people from the Gauteng region who testified in public hearings. *Since only 10 percent of the target population can be identified in this way, and since those who can

---

* The South African collaborator referred to in this study is the Centre for the Study of Violence and Reconciliation.

be identified probably differ substantially from those who cannot (if they have a phone, they are probably wealthier), this is unlikely to be an adequate method of developing a sampling frame of testifiers. Further, this approach cannot be used to develop a sampling frame of people who submit statements but do not testify, since their names are not part of the public record.

A fourth approach is to sample from community groups with a large number of survivors who have submitted statements or testified. In South Africa, Khulumani is a survivor support group established in 1995 by the survivors and families of the victims of the political violence that occurred during the apartheid era (Hayner 2001). Khulumani helped survivors engage with the South African TRC throughout its tenure and, as a result, developed a membership with a high proportion of people who submitted statements or testified. As part of a study of the South African TRC, my collaborators in South Africa and I created a sampling frame from the membership of Khulumani and then selected a random sample of those on the frame to create a sample of people who submitted statements to the TRC (Backer 2005). An obvious issue with this approach is that the survivors who both submit statements and are members of community groups may vary substantially from the total universe of survivors who submit statements. In South Africa, Khulumani members were more likely to be female, to be of African descent, and to report murders than was the universe of all survivors who submitted statements to the TRC; they were also less likely to report torture (Backer 2005). The demographic differences between community groups and all survivors who submit statements are not, however, an issue of internal validity but rather of external validity (generalizability) (Rothman and Greenland 1998, 133–34). As long as the sample is similar to the universe of community group members, the study will be a valid assessment of community group members who submitted statements. The degree to which the findings from community group members are generalizable to the universe of all survivors who submitted statements is an issue of judgment, and it depends on how similar the groups are. In the South African example, a study of Khulumani members is unlikely to be generalizable to all survivors who submitted statements.

A fifth approach is to use snowball sampling, a technique that has been used in other disciplines to identify hard-to-reach samples (Atkinson and Flint 2003). In snowball sampling, a deponent gives the researchers the name of another deponent, and so on. This sampling strategy takes advantage of social networks and can be quite efficient. However, it is very difficult to identify all the selection factors that play a role in the development of snowball samples, and empirical studies of snowball sampling procedures have shown substantial selection bias (Atkinson and Flint 2003).

A sixth approach is to recruit a sample through advertising in the print and broadcast media. The problem with this approach is that people who

read or hear the advertisements and people who respond to them are unlikely to be a random sample of the universe of people who submit statements or testify (Ganguli et al. 1998).

Without question, the best sampling approach is to obtain a list of deponents from the truth commission directly. As described above, this can
be difficult or impossible if it is attempted after the truth commission is in
progress or has terminated. However, if a research group works with a truth
commission from its inception, it may be able to have the truth commission
include a simple question about willingness to be contacted in the future,
such as "Research scientists are interested in finding out how you feel about
your experiences with the truth commission. Can they contact you in the
future to discuss this with you?" Contact information could be released if
the person answered affirmatively, but not otherwise. An affirmative answer
could be seen as permission to be contacted but should not be construed
as consent to participate in the study. This approach has genuine promise
for producing high-quality research that meets strict ethical guidelines for
privacy and confidentiality for potential research participants (Brody 1998,
51–52).

In many situations, snowball sampling and recruitment through
advertising may be the only options available. In that case, it is vital that
the researchers include a large number of demographic questions in the
questionnaire. If demographic data on the people who submit statements
or testify are described in the truth commission final report, it may then
be possible to determine the degree to which the sample differs from the
universe of all survivors who submitted or testified.

How to develop a sample of nondeponents (survivors who did not submit statements or testify in public hearings)

The second challenge in sample development is to identify and select a control group, that is, a group that can be compared to the sample of deponents.
People who were survivors of gross violations of human rights but did not
give a statement to the truth commission or testify in a public hearing constitute the ideal comparison group, because they were theoretically eligible
to give a statement or testify but did not. There are multiple approaches to
developing this comparison group.

A random sample of the entire population of a country may be a realistic method of identifying survivors who did not submit a statement or
testify, but only if the prevalence of gross violations of human rights is very
high. The Peruvian Truth and Reconciliation Commission (TRC) estimated
that approximately 69,000 people died or disappeared as a result of human
rights violations between 1980 and 2000 (United Nations Foundation 2003).
Peru's 1990 population was approximately 22.3 million. If we assume that

every person who was murdered or disappeared had approximately ten first-degree relatives (spouse, parent, child), then 3,194 people would need to be surveyed to identify a sample of 100 first-degree relatives of people who were murdered or disappeared. This approach is very inefficient (97 out of 100 people surveyed would not be eligible for the sample) and would be costly, but it is at least theoretically feasible. This approach might be reasonable if it is embedded in a national survey to determine attitudes toward the truth commission among the general populace.

A second approach would be to conduct a random sample of community groups that have a large number of survivors as members, such as Khulumani in South Africa. The methods, strengths, and weaknesses of this approach were described above, in the section on developing a sample of deponents.

Cluster sampling is a third approach (Ferrinho et al. 1992; Malilay, Flanders, and Brogan 1996). For this method, a research assistant who completes a face-to-face interview with a deponent follows an explicit algorithm (e.g., face the house just interviewed, then turn ninety degrees to the right, walk thirty feet, and approach the nearest house on the left) to identify a household for screening. The interviewer uses a method to randomly select an adult living in the selected household (e.g., the person with the next birthday in the calendar year) and then uses a screening questionnaire to determine whether that adult has been a victim of a gross violation of human rights. If so, that person is invited to participate in the study. My collaborators in South Africa and I conducted a pilot study to determine the feasibility of this approach in Katorus township, near Johannesburg, which had a high prevalence of human rights violations during the apartheid era. Of the fifty households that were approached using a directional algorithm and an instrument to screen for human rights violations, we identified five adults who were survivors of gross violations of human rights and who had not given a statement or testified before the South African TRC. The screening questionnaire took less than 15 minutes to complete. (See Appendix 2 for the screening questionnaire.) Since ten households would need to be approached to identify one eligible person, and since each screening interview took 15 minutes, 150 minutes (2.5 hours) would be required to identify each survivor who did not submit a statement or testify in public. While not ideal, this is certainly a feasible method to identify a sample of nondeponents when the prevalence of human rights violations in a community is high. Moreover, the statistical principles of cluster sampling have been worked out and have been used extensively to develop samples in developing countries for many different types of research (Malilay, Flanders, and Brogan 1996; Bennett et al. 1991).

"Friend control" is a fourth approach to developing a sample (Rothman and Greenland 1998, 102–3). Each deponent is asked to give the researcher the names and contact information of friends who themselves were survivors of human rights violations. One of those survivors is selected using a random method (e.g., random numbers or next birthday in the calendar year) and then invited to participate in the study. This method is different from the snowball sampling technique described above. In the snowball sampling technique, the participants constitute a chain, traceable back to one or a few participants, whereas in the friend control technique, each nondeponent is linked to only one deponent who is participating in the study. The friend control technique is efficient and feasible but can produce biased samples (Kaplan, Novikov, and Modan 1998). Nondeponents who are identified by friends may be more similar to the deponents than the universe of nondeponents would be, and nondeponents with many friends are more likely to be included than nondeponents with fewer friends. The direction and magnitude of selection bias introduced by this approach can be difficult to determine.

Radio and newspaper advertisements can also be used to recruit participants. As noted above, survivors who respond to advertisements may be different from survivors who don't. It is usually difficult to sort out the degree of selection bias introduced with this method. If possible, it is useful to include a large number of demographic variables on the survey questionnaire; that way, it will be possible to compare the characteristics of the sample to the characteristics of survivors from population-based studies of survivors, if these have been conducted by other researchers.

Measurement of Key Constructs

The key dilemma in measuring key constructs in survivor studies is the use of standard versus new questionnaire instruments. Standard instruments facilitate comparison across time and place, and they may have high reliability and high validity in some settings. (Reliability is absence of random error, and validity is the degree to which the instrument measures what it purports to measure [DeVellis 1991, 43].) However, in research with survivors who interact with truth commissions, standardized instruments may be problematic.

One problem with standardized instruments is that they are frequently developed in populations that are culturally and linguistically different from those in the countries where truth commissions have been empaneled. Instruments to measure post-traumatic stress disorder (PTSD), desire for vengeance or forgiveness, or exposure to human rights violations that were developed in one country may not be valid in a group of survivors in another. (It is important to remember that validity is not an inherent property of an instrument, but rather a property of an instrument in a particular con-

text [DeVellis 1991, 43–50; Streiner and Norman 1995, 145–46]). The Enright
Forgiveness Inventory (EFI), developed in the United States, measures beliefs,
feelings, and behavior toward a perpetrator (Subkoviak, Enright, and Wu
1995). One of the items in the behavior subsection is "be biting when talking with him/her." When this instrument was pilot tested in South Africa,
survivors did not even know what this phrase meant. In addition, multiple
items in the belief section of the English version of the EFI (e.g., "wretched,"
"horrible," "evil," and "a bad person") were translated with the same word
in Sotho, one of the languages used in South Africa.

Standard instruments also may not include important elements of key
constructs that are specific to the country being studied. The Harvard Trauma Questionnaire (HTQ) was originally developed for use with Cambodian
refugees and has been considered the best instrument to measure torture
and related trauma (Mollica et al. 1992). But many of the important abuses
that were specific to apartheid-era South Africa, such as being framed by the
police or being forced to become an informer, are not included on the HTQ.

A third problem is that a standard instrument may be measuring a construct that is related in name only and is completely different from the construct of interest. For example, among survivors, desire for justice is one of
the driving motivations in their lives. The best-known instrument to measure
perceptions of justice is the Belief in a Just World Scale (Rubin and Peplau
1975). However, this instrument was developed to understand why people
sometimes blame innocent victims for the victims' misfortunes, and the
item content is clearly not applicable to measurement of perceptions of justice among survivors of human rights violations, as shown by the following
items: "Movies in which good triumphs over evil are unrealistic"; "The political candidate who sticks up for his principles rarely gets elected"; "People
who find money in the street have often done a good deed earlier that day"
(Rubin and Peplau 1975).

New instruments developed as part of the study may have greater linguistic and cultural relevance to the survivors in the country being studied,
may include more items directly applicable to the experiences of survivors
in that country, and may measure the specific construct in question rather
than one that is similar in name but vastly different in practice. However,
new instruments have one major problem: Their validity and reliability are
uncertain. Unless a separate instrument development sample is used to generate psychometric data about the new instrument, the data used in the study
can be used to support the reliability and validity of the instrument or to
evaluate the major research questions being studied, but not both.

Inclusion of an instrument development phase at the beginning of the
study can be a partial solution to this measurement dilemma. The instrument
development phase should be used to complete the following tasks:

1. Gather qualitative data from survivors who submitted statements or testified and from survivors who didn't, using semistructured interviews with open-ended questions or focus group interviews. The purpose of this phase is to try to understand the worldview of the survivor, from his or her perspective. Appendix 3 shows a list of focus group questions that my research group used in a study of survivors who interacted with the South African TRC. The data can be used to generate new ideas about constructs that are important to measure (e.g., neighborhood cohesion in a study of the South African TRC) and components of key constructs that had not been considered previously (e.g., including "institutional transformation" as a component of justice).

2. Based on the initial research questions and the ideas generated from the qualitative data, identify the key constructs to be measured.

3. Search the research literature to identify existing instruments that measure key constructs.

4. For each of the instruments identified, review the original scientific article describing the instrument to determine whether the instrument was designed to measure something similar to what is needed for the survivor study. Also, look at the content of the items to see whether they are measuring what is needed for the survivor study.

5. If an instrument appears to be suitable, adapt the instrument in the following ways:
   - Translate the instrument if necessary, and have a separate individual back-translate it. Assess the back-translation for semantic equivalence, and revise the instrument as needed.
   - Add items if key elements are not included.
   - Pilot test the instrument with a small group of survivors. Items that are unclear, confusing, or irrelevant to survivors should be revised or eliminated.

6. If there is no instrument to measure the construct (e.g., perceptions of justice among survivors of human rights violations), develop a new instrument, using the following guidelines recommended in standard texts on scale development (DeVellis 1991, 51–90; Streiner and Norman 1995):
   - A pool of items should be generated based on themes identified from the qualitative data, which measure the construct in question. Each key domain should be measured with several items phrased differently, and some of the items should be worded in reverse format. For example, an instrument to measure perceptions of justice among survivors included two items on repa-

rations: (1) "I have received fair payment from the government for my suffering"; and (2) "The monetary compensation I have received from the government for the suffering I experienced as a result of the violation is not enough."

- The measurement scale and format should be determined. The items can be phrased as declarative statements, and respondents asked to indicate the degree of agreement or disagreement (a Likert scale), or items can be phrased as questions. Each approach has strengths and weaknesses.

- "Experts," including survivors, people who work with or advocate for them, and truth commission staff members, should review the items for completeness, relevance, and clarity, and items should be revised, deleted, or added as needed.

- The items should be administered to a development sample of survivors, if possible. Other instruments should be included as necessary to assess construct validity—the degree to which the new instrument is associated with standard instruments of other constructs in theoretically expected ways. For example, to assess the construct validity of a new instrument to measure perceptions of justice, an existing instrument on desire for vengeance could be included, since one would expect that people who believe that justice has been delivered would be less likely to desire vengeance.

- Items, and the scale as a whole, should be evaluated individually. Good items will have a large response variation and a mean score near the middle of the scale range and will show a strong correlation with the total score on the scale. Items that perform poorly should be eliminated, since they will not contribute to the validity or reliability of the scale. Internal reliability of the instrument should be assessed using Cronbach's alpha, which is a measure of the proportion of variance in scale score that can be attributed to the true score (DeVellis 1991, 25–26). Alpha can also be calculated after deleting one or more items; if alpha is unchanged when an item is deleted, the item is not contributing to the reliability of the scale and should be deleted (DeVellis 1991, 87–88).

- The construct validity of the instrument should be assessed. In general, moderate strength correlations between the new instrument and other related instruments are the best indicators of construct validity (DeVellis 1991, 48). If correlations are very high, it suggests that the two instruments may be measuring the same thing. Correlations between the new instrument and unrelated instruments should be low.

Data Analysis

There are no features unique to analyzing quantitative data from survivor studies. However, by far the most important feature of the analysis is control of confounding. Many factors are associated with whether a survivor submits a statement to a truth commission; these include the type of human rights violation experienced, expectations of the truth commission, and other types of trauma experienced. If these factors (and other demographic characteristics) are associated with any of the outcomes in the study, such as desire for vengeance, desire for reconciliation, and perception of justice, then the association between giving a statement and any of those outcomes will be biased unless confounding is controlled in the analysis. Regression modeling techniques can be used to control for confounding, but a detailed discussion of those techniques is beyond the scope of this chapter. Rothman and Greenland (1998, 359–432) provide a sophisticated yet approachable discussion of the use of regression modeling to control for confounding.

Ethics of Survivor Research

All researchers who include humans in their studies must grapple with issues pertaining to informed consent, risks and benefits to research participants, selection of research participants in accordance with the principles of justice, and respect for the welfare of research participants (Brody 1998, 31–54; Emanuel, Wendler, and Grady 2000). This includes considering that the study itself may lead to psychological distress in the participants because study questions may encourage subjects to think about the injustices they have suffered. But these issues have unique twists in research with survivors of human rights violations, due to the vulnerability and lack of trust that can be induced by trauma and to the power imbalance between the researchers and the survivors who participate in research (Eth 1992; Neugebauer 1999). The researcher must consider the ethical ramifications of every element in the design and conduct of survivor studies.

Informed Consent

There are multiple wrinkles in the informed consent process in research with survivors. The first issue is how much detail should be provided in the informed consent process and how long the informed consent document should be. The primary goal of informed consent is to provide the potential participant with the information about risks and benefits of participating in the research that a reasonable person would need in order to make an informed decision about participating. An informed consent process that is complete should give participants a good idea about the general and specific risks that participation entails. It should not leave participants guessing at the degree of potential distress that they may experience from participating (Collogan et al. 2004). In general, most research ethics committees in developed countries have taken the stance that more information is better and, accordingly, require researchers to create multipage informed consent documents that list every possible adverse effect, no matter how rare. But long and detailed consent forms may undermine the true goal of informed consent. Research participants perceive long forms as a way of protecting the researchers, not the participants (Mann 1994). Further, long and detailed forms may be reminiscent of government forms that have been used to take away survivors' rights, not protect them. Long forms, replete with complete information on virtually every risk and benefit—even those that are minimal or rare—may induce psychological distress during the consent process, even before the research ever begins. Finally, detailed consent forms may make it difficult for potential research participants, particularly if they have limited reading or writing skills, to comprehend and remember the really key information that they need in order to give informed consent (Flory and Emanuel 2004). This phenomenon may be more likely to occur in potential research participants who have significant PTSD or depression secondary to their victimization, since those disorders, when severe, can be associated with cognitive impairment (Yehuda et al. 2004).

Although informed consent is paramount, studies have shown that potential subjects frequently fail to understand the research that they have consented to participate in (Estey, Wilkin, and Dossetor 1994). It is important to mitigate any confusion stemming from the consent process and make consent forms the necessary length to ensure that the potential subject understands the research that will be undertaken. Generally, to increase comprehension and retention, researchers should condense the length of the form, revise the content of the form to make it more comprehensible and readable, improve formatting through the use of techniques like larger font size and italics, and add graphics (Flory and Emanuel 2004). Researchers should work closely with their ethics committees to develop a consent form that includes materially important information but is not so long that it confuses or scares survivors who are deciding whether to participate in the research.

The consent form's introduction should state an invitation for potential subjects to participate in research and should describe what is meant by "research." The consent process should also tell subjects why they are eligible to participate. Likewise, subjects should also be informed of the study's purpose, procedures expected to be used, potential benefits to the subject, and potential costs. They should also be informed that participation is voluntary. To help the greatest number of potential subjects understand what the study entails, the reading level of the consent form should be set somewhere from sixth to eighth grade, depending on the population being studied (Silverman et al. 2005).

Enhanced consent forms, with discussion following reading of the form, may also increase understanding when compared to merely reading the consent form (Flory and Emanuel 2004). Increased person-to-person contact may make the potential subject feel at ease by allowing the subject to ask questions and validate his or her participation in the research. According to Flory and Emanuel (2004), "Using a standard consent process and adding an extra meeting with a qualified person [such as a nurse or outside educator] are the most reliable approach to improving understanding, based on the currently available evidence." Also, removing unnecessary standardized content serves to shorten forms and may improve the subject's understanding (Flory and Emanuel 2004).

A second issue related to informed consent is assessment of the subject's competency to give informed consent to participate in research. To give informed consent, a potential research participant must be mentally competent. Gross violations of human rights can induce psychiatric disorders, such as depression, anxiety, and PTSD, in some survivors. When those disorders are severe enough, a survivor's ability to understand relevant information and make sound decisions based on that information may be compromised (Berg and Appelbaum 1999, 83–87). There are no screening instruments currently available that let research assistants quickly assess whether a potential participant is mentally competent to give consent (Berg and Appelbaum 1999, 97–98). Moreover, performance of such an assessment could be perceived by survivors as insulting and demeaning. On the other hand, it would be unethical to include in the research any of the few survivors who are not competent to decide about participating in the project (Brody 1998, 129–33). The best solution to this dilemma is to educate research assistants who recruit participants about the signs and symptoms of severe depression, anxiety, and PTSD. If the research assistant believes that a survivor may lack competence but still wants to participate in the study, a professional trained in psychological trauma should interview the survivor. (A related but different issue—referral of people identified as having psychiatric disorders—is discussed below, in the section on minimizing harms.)

Risk-Benefit Calculus

One of the most important principles of research ethics is that the risks incurred by the research participants must be outweighed by the benefits to the participants and society (Emanuel, Wendler, and Grady 2000). The most important theoretical risk to survivors who participate in research on truth commissions is psychological distress as a result of answering

questions about their victimization experience. Although the risk of induc-
ing psychological distress during the interview process is an important
concern, there is minimal evidence to suggest that significant harm will
occur and a substantial body of evidence suggesting that it will not.

Some studies that have been conducted on reactivation or exacerbation of
PTSD have shown that "stimuli directly reminiscent of the original trauma,"
such as exposing soldiers with PTSD to another combat situation, are required to reactivate or exacerbate PTSD (Solomon 1987). Even in the context
of imaginal exposure treatment for PTSD (a form of psychotherapy in which
persons with PTSD are asked to imagine their trauma in detail), only a small
minority have even a short-term increase in PTSD symptoms (Foa et al. 2002).
However, other studies have suggested that intense but nonspecific stimuli
can lead to increased symptoms of PTSD. Kinzie and colleagues (2002), for
example, reported that some Bosnian and Somali refugees had an increase in
flashbacks and nightmares after viewing televised images of the September
11 terrorist attacks. Thus, while it is unlikely that the interview process of a
research project will create stimuli strong enough to reactivate or exacerbate
PTSD symptoms, researchers still need to be aware of that possibility.

Differences between the research process and the trauma itself also
suggest that participation is unlikely to cause significant harm (Collogan
et al. 2004). The traumatic situation was one that was unpredictable and
arbitrary—in other words, an environment that could not be controlled by
the study subject. Disaster-focused research, on the other hand, occurs in a
calm environment, which is both highly predictable and controlled (Collogan et al. 2004). Thus, given the characteristics of the research environment,
study subjects are likely to feel comfortable and at ease, even though they
are asked to remember traumatic experiences.

Second, most studies of trauma survivors using either semistructured or
structured interviews have not reported significant adverse psychological
effects experienced by the subjects. The author of a large study of Cambodian
refugees noted, "Our large population-based study in Thailand using the
HTQ in the Khmer camps (N = 1,500) did not precipitate a single distraught
respondent who needed acute psychiatric care" (Mollica and Caspi-Yavin
1991). The authors of the National Vietnam Veterans' Readjustment Study
(NVVRS), the largest and most comprehensive evaluation of PTSD ever completed, reported, "NVVRS participants were followed up by phone about a
week after their interviews and asked specifically about [the study's] impact
on them, if any. During these calls, referral assistance was offered to all who
requested it. In fact, the number of interviews in which participants were
distressed was small and no reactions were severe." They conclude, "Based
on our experience in conducting a variety of epidemiological studies of PTSD,
we believe that participation in such assessments is not 'harmful' in any

meaningful sense. Although a minority of participants will experience an observable emotional reaction to the assessment (e.g., may become tearful when describing details of an exposure) and may experience some distress, that experience is not in and of itself damaging" (Schlenger et al. 1997, 154).

Third, studies that have explicitly addressed the question whether participating in research on trauma is harmful to research participants have consistently shown that about 10 to 20 percent of participants report psychological distress from participating, and a small minority—typically the patients with the greatest baseline distress—report severe distress from participating (Newman, Walker, and Gefland 1999; Carlson et al. 2003; Kassam-Adams and Newman 2002; Ruzek and Zatzick 2000; Newman and Kaloupek 2004). The participants who report distress typically indicate that the research process made them think about things that they did not want to think about. There is some evidence, though not uniform across studies, that severity of trauma exposure, advanced or young age, previous history of psychological distress, social vulnerability, and physical injury may be associated with increased risk of experiencing distress during participation in trauma-related research (Neman and Kaloupek 2004; Collogan et al. 2004). Importantly, even participants who experienced distress were unlikely to report regret about participating in the research. In one study, 48 persons (19 percent of participants) reported that the research was more upsetting to them than they had expected, but only one person regretted participating (Newman, Walker, and Gefland 1999). Similar findings have been reported by other studies (Newman and Kaloupek 2004).

While a small percentage of participants may experience distress, 25 to 80 percent of research participants feel that they have benefited in some way from participating in trauma-related research (Newman and Kaloupek 2004). Persons who have participated in trauma research have reported the following types of benefits: (1) the feeling that by advancing research, they are helping others who have suffered; (2) clarification of memories of their trauma; (3) new insights into their problems; (4) catharsis. Even though participation in a research study is completely different from disclosure in the context of a safe, ongoing therapeutic relationship with a trusted counselor, most persons who participate in trauma research report that discussing their trauma during a research interview made them feel better (Newman and Kaloupek 2004).

All these findings indicate a low likelihood that survivors participating in studies of truth commissions will experience severe or long-lasting harm. This is important because it means that the risk-benefit calculus required by most research ethics committees will usually be tipped in favor of benefit from this type of research. Some research ethics committees, while well intentioned, believe that research with survivors has a great risk of traumatizing participants. In that case, researchers should educate their ethics committees by informing them about empirical research with findings to the contrary. As D. G. Kilpatrick (2004) has put so eloquently in an editorial about trauma-focused research, "It has been stated that everyone is entitled to their own opinions, but they are not entitled to their own facts. This wise principle should apply to all of us, including to IRB members. Therefore, it is incumbent upon all of us to base our decisions about research and protection of research participants on facts—not opinions. Our opinions may tell us that this type of research is inherently risky, but the facts say otherwise."

However, the low risk of harm to participants does not mean that the risk of harm should be dismissed or that steps shouldn't be taken to minimize the distress to participants. The goal must also be to minimize potential harm by protecting the individual rights of human research subjects, such as their rights not to be subjected to additional distress if they so choose (Collogan et al. 2004). Victims of human rights violations who participate in studies on truth commissions may experience any of the following potential harms: inconvenience; strong and painful emotions such as anger, shame, and anxiety; and fear that their words will be revealed to other victims or to government authorities (Collogan et al. 2004). The principle of respect for the welfare of research participants requires that researchers take steps to minimize potential harm to them (Emanuel, Wendler, and Grady 2000). For survivor studies, these steps include the following:

- Limit the number of questions directly related to the victimization experience.
- Avoid an "interrogation" style of interviewing, in which interview questions are fired rapidly at participants.
- Use some open-ended questions to give participants a greater feeling of control.
- Give participants time to "come down" after the interview.
- Give participants breaks from the interview process that are sufficient in length and frequency.
- Ask participants at various points throughout the interview whether they are comfortable, and if they are not, make the necessary provisions to increase the comfort level or pause the interview.
- Describe the resources that are available to the participant should he or she suffer distress, psychological or otherwise, during the interview process.
- To make the subject feel comfortable, have trained interviewers of the same nationality as the subject conduct the interviews.

Existing community resources for trauma survivors should be explained to all participants, regardless of whether they experience distress. Finally, a professional with expertise in psychological trauma should be enlisted as a backup who can be contacted if the research assistant conducting the interview feels that the participant is experiencing severe distress (Boscarino et al. 2004).

Ethics of Recruitment

Research participants must be selected in a manner consistent with the principles of justice (Emanuel, Wendler, and Grady 2000). In practical terms, this means that recruitment of survivors should not be coercive. While it is reasonable and appropriate to offer monetary incentives to participants to reimburse them for their time, the amount of money that is offered should not be so large that participants choose to participate primarily for the money (Dickert and Grady 1999). In addition, while it is reasonable to build relationships with community organizations to build trust between survivors and the research team, it is important to make sure that survivors who belong to those organizations do not feel pressure from them to participate.

Methodological Lessons Learned from Survivor Studies

Although the issues discussed in this chapter are relevant to survivor studies globally, most of the recommendations are drawn from experiences with survivor studies from South Africa and focus on responses to truth commissions. The purpose of this section is to review the methodological aspects of survivor studies of transitional justice mechanisms of all types, not just truth commissions, that have been conducted in other countries to determine whether there are methodological lessons that can be learned from survivor studies worldwide.

The most striking aspect of this endeavor is that the body of empirical research on the effects of transitional justice on survivors is very small indeed. I conducted detailed searches using multiple databases (Medline, PsycINFO, Sociofile, International Bibliography of the Social Sciences, Worldwide Political Science Abstracts, and Area Studies databases such as African Studies, Bibliography of Asian Studies, and Hispanic American Serials Index) using multiple keywords (e.g., "truth commission," "transitional justice," "memorials," "restitution," "reparations," and "tribunal"), and I reviewed the bibliographies of articles that were judged to be relevant. Using that approach, I identified only a handful of articles or books that (1) focused on survivors' responses to transitional justice and (2) used empirical research processes. Most of the published works on survivor responses to transitional justice are based on theoretical explorations of what survivors might feel. This section focuses on those few empirical investigations of how they actually do feel.

Survivor Studies Identified

Priscilla Hayner's (2001) book *Unspeakable Truths: Confronting State Terror and Atrocity* is a critical analysis of truth commissions around the world. Hayner attempts to identify the processes and outcomes of truth commissions by examining the views of major stakeholders, including commissioners, non-governmental organization leaders, university faculty members, government officers, human rights workers, and others. Hayner also includes several sections devoted to survivor responses. From the list of persons interviewed, shown in Appendix 2 of the book, it appears that less than 5 percent of the nearly five hundred persons interviewed were survivors or family members who interacted directly with a truth commission. Hayner does not provide information on how survivors were sampled (i.e., identified and selected for interview), though it appears that convenience sampling was used. There is no information provided on the methods that were used to interview survivors, although based on survivors' quotations used in the book, it appears that unstructured, open-ended questions were used. Hayner's book is a masterful comparison of truth commissions around the world. However, since nonrandom sampling was used, it is uncertain whether the sample of survivors included in the book is similar to the universe of all survivors. Since only unstructured interviews were used, it is unclear whether the survivor responses reported in the book represent consistent, reliable, and valid measurements of survivor attitudes.

Eric Stover (2005) studied the "meaning of testifying" used for witnesses to the International Criminal Tribunal for the former Yugoslavia (ICTY), using in-depth open-ended interviews. His sample included eighty-seven persons who testified at one of the trials of the ICTY, involving Bosnian Muslim, Croat, and Serb victims. Stover reports that he selected "unprotected witnesses" (persons whose identities had been made public in court) from one of seven trials that were taking place in 1997. However, the book does not report (1) how many trials of the ICTY were in progress at the start of the study and how many "unprotected" witnesses had testified by 2001; (2) the methods used to select the seven trials that were the basis of the sample; (3) the methods used to select witnesses from the seven trials; and (4) the response rate among persons who were invited to participate. The survey questionnaire is included as an appendix and includes primarily open-ended questions, such as "What motivated you to testify in The Hague?" and "Could you tell me about the experience of testifying?" The method by which the qualitative data were analyzed was not reported.

Despite the methodological limitations of the sampling process noted above, Stover's book is rich in detail and provides a wealth of important information about the experience, meaning, and effect of testifying before a tribunal. It is an excellent example of the strengths of qualitative research.

Pham, Weinstein, and Longman (2004) conducted a landmark study of attitudes of Rwandans regarding three transitional justice mechanisms: the International Criminal Tribunal for Rwanda, traditional trials in the Rwandan courts, and gacaca, an adaptation of the traditional participatory community conflict resolution mechanism. Pham and colleagues used multistage stratified cluster sampling to draw a random sample from four regions in Rwanda. Though designed to be a population-based study of attitudes of all Rwandans, it is also a study of survivors, simply because of the scope of the Rwandan genocide—any random sample of Rwandans would, by default, include a large proportion of people who were survivors of the cataclysmic genocide that took place in 1994. For example, 94 percent of the study's participants reported at least one traumatic event, and 73 percent had a close family member who was killed. What is particularly notable about the Pham et al. study is that it incorporated virtually all the "best practices" recommended in this chapter:

- Random sampling techniques were used to draw a sample.
- Standardized instruments were used, when available, to measure standard constructs such as PSTD.
- Qualitative research methods, including individual interviews and focus groups, were used to identify issues important to survivors.
- New instruments were developed to measure fundamental constructs, such as reconciliation, for which no existing instruments existed.
- The study instrument was pilot tested in persons who were not included in the final sample.
- Multivariate modeling techniques were used to control for important confounding factors.

However, since Pham et al.'s study did not include or identify a subsample of survivors who interacted directly with one of the transitional justice mechanisms, it is impossible to compare responses among survivors who interacted directly with the transitional justice mechanism against responses among survivors who did not participate in transitional justice directly—one of the most important questions for survivor studies.

Biro et al. (2004) conducted two surveys of attitudes toward reconciliation and (ICTY) among residents of two towns in Croatia and one in Bosnia that were strongly affected by the 1991–95 wars in Yugoslavia. Like Pham and colleagues, Biro and colleagues used stratified cluster sampling to select a random sample from the war-torn areas. Their sample included a large number of survivors, though they were smaller proportionally than in Pham et al.'s sample. For example, 15 percent of Biro's sample (compared to 73 percent of Pham et al.'s sample) had lost a family member due to the conflict. Also like Pham and colleagues, Biro and colleagues used standard instruments to measure standard constructs and developed new instruments to measure constructs—such as reconciliation and attitudes toward the ICTY—for which no standard instruments existed. Biro et al.'s study, like Pham et al.'s, did not include a separate sample or a subsample of survivors who interacted directly with the transitional justice mechanism (the ICTY).

Sonis et al. (2008) conducted a national study in Cambodia of trauma, mental health, and attitudes toward the joint U.N.-Cambodian trials of the Khmer Rouge, before the onset of the public hearings. The study used a complex, multistage sampling process to develop a national probability sample of Cambodians from all twenty-four provinces. Though designed as a population-based study, it was also a study of survivors, due to the prevalence of exposure to trauma during the Khmer Rouge era. (Over 95 percent of persons over the age of thirty-five had experienced at least one of nine Khmer Rouge era traumas.) Sonis et al.'s study shared all the methodological strengths of Pham et al.'s study, but had several additional virtues. First, the sample was a true national probability sample rather than one from selected regions of the country, as in Pham et al.'s study. Second, data collection began before the onset of the public hearings, and a grant proposal has been submitted to the United States National Institutes of Health for three additional waves of data collection over the next three years. If funded, it will be the first national longitudinal study of the responses to any truth commission or tribunal. This is important because a longitudinal design is the only way to determine whether tribunals produce changes in attitudes over time. However, like Pham et al.'s, this study is not designed to include or identify a subsample of survivors who testify before the tribunal.

Lessons Learned

This brief review of published survivor studies reveals several important issues for survivor studies of transitional justice. First, rigorous methods can be used to develop new instruments to measure key constructs, such as reconciliation and justice. However, since there is no consensus on the definition or measurement of those constructs, each survivor study has tended to create new instruments. This makes it difficult to compare results across countries or even across different studies in the same country. The field of transitional justice studies would be enhanced if standard instruments could be developed to measure important constructs such as reconciliation and perceptions of justice among survivors.

Second, random sampling methods have been used to generate samples of survivors. Cluster sampling approaches, in particular, can be useful for generating a sample of survivors from an area with a high prevalence of previous human rights abuses. However, these approaches still do not solve the problem of generating a random sample of persons who have interacted directly with a transitional justice mechanism, such as a truth commission or criminal tribunal, to compare to survivors who have not interacted directly. None of the studies reported above was able to identify such a sample, confirming the assertion earlier in the chapter that generating a random sample of deponents is the most challenging aspect of survivor studies.

Conclusion

Research with survivors can be enormously helpful in understanding the effect of truth commissions. While the effects on survivors may or may not mirror the effects on the country as a whole, it is vital to understand the effects of truth commissions on those who report their victimization experiences to these commissions.

The specific principles described in this chapter have clear implications for the ways that survivor studies can best be implemented. Survivor studies should incorporate the perspectives of survivors and of the truth commission. Usually, the best way to do this is to form an advisory board that includes survivors and also to solicit input from truth commission members. Researchers should try to work with the truth commission from its inception, since this may be the best way to develop a sampling frame that can be used to develop a random sample of survivors.

Since answers to many of the questions about the effects of truth commissions on survivors depend on detecting changes in responses over time, researchers should, whenever possible, consider longitudinal data.

Research with survivors can and should be done in a way that protects the rights of research participants. There is now a large body of empirical research documenting the low probability that survivors who participate in trauma research will report significant distress and a high probability that they will report benefit from participating. Nonetheless, researchers should incorporate elements into the design to minimize potential distress, as described in this chapter, and build into the research protocol a mechanism for referring participants for mental health evaluation and treatment if significant distress occurs.

References

Atkinson, Rowland, and John Flint. 2003. "Accessing Hidden and Hard-to-Reach Populations: Snowball Research Strategies." www.soc.surrey.ac.uk/sru/SRU33.html.

Backer, David. 2005. "The Human Face of Justice: Victims' Responses to South Africa's Truth and Reconciliation Commission Process." (PhD diss., University of Michigan). *Dissertation Abstracts International* 65:3969A.

Bennett, S., T. Woods, W. M. Liyanage, and D. L. Smith. 1991. "A Simplified General Method for Cluster-Sample Surveys of Health in Developing Countries." *World Health Statistics Quarterly* 44 (3): 98–106.

Berg, J. W., and P. S. Appelbaum. 1999. "Subjects' Capacity to Consent to Neurobiological Research." In *Ethics in Psychiatric Research: A Resource Manual for Human Subjects' Protection*, eds. H. A. Pincus, J. A. Lieberman, and Sandy Ferris. Washington, D.C.: American Psychiatric Association.

Biro, Miklos, Dean Ajdukovic, Dinka Corkalo, Dina Djipa, Petar Milin, and Harvey Weinstein. 2004. "Attitudes toward Justice and Social Reconstruction in Bosnia and Herzegovina and Croatia." In *My Neighbor, My Enemy*, ed. Eric Stover and Harvey Weinstein. Cambridge, UK: Cambridge University Press.

Blakely, Tony, and S. V. Subramanian. 2006. "Multilevel Studies." In Methods in *Social Epidemiology*, eds. J. Michael Oakes and Jay S. Kaufman. San Francisco: Jossey-Bass.

Boscarino, Joseph A., Charles Figley, Richard Adams, Sandro Galea, Heidi Resnick, Alan R. Fleischman, Michael Bucuvalas, and Joel Gold. 2004. "Adverse Reactions Associated with Studying Persons Recently Exposed to Mass Urban Disaster." *Journal of Nervous and Mental Disease* 192 (8): 515–24.

Brody, Baruch. 1998. *The Ethics of Biomedical Research.* New York: Oxford University Press.

Carlson, Eve B., Elana Newman, Jill Walker Daniels, Judith Armstrong, David Roth, and Richard Loewenstein. 2003. "Distress in Response to and Perceived Usefulness of Trauma Research Interviews." *Journal of Trauma and Dissociation* 4 (2): 131–42.

Collogan, Lauren K., Farris Tuma, Regina Dolan-Sewell, Susan Borja, and Alan R. Fleischman. 2004. "Ethical Issues Pertaining to Research in the Aftermath of Disaster." *Journal of Traumatic Stress* 17 (5): 363–72.

de la Rey, Cheryl, and Ingrid Owens. 1998. "Perceptions of Psychosocial Healing and the Truth and Reconciliation Commission in South Africa." *Peace and Conflict: Journal of Peace Psychology* 4 (3): 257–70.

DeVellis, Robert F. 1991. *Scale Development.* Vol 26. Newbury Park, Calif.: Sage.

Dickert, Neal, and Christine Grady. 1999. "What's the Price of a Research Subject? Approaches to Payment for Research Participation." *New England Journal of Medicine* 341 (3): 198–203.

Emanuel, Ezekiel. J., David Wendler, and Christine Grady. 2000. "What Makes Clinical Research Ethical?" JAMA 283 (20): 2701–11.

Estey, Angela, Georgeann Wilkin, and John B. Dossetor. 1994. "Are Research Subjects Able to Retain the Information They Are Given during the Consent Process?" *Health Law Review* 3 (2): 37–41.

Eth, Spencer. 1992. "Ethical Challenges in the Treatment of Traumatized Refugees." *Journal of Traumatic Stress* 5 (1): 103–10.

Ferrinho, P., A. Valli, T. Groeneveld, E. Buch, and D. Coetzee. 1992. "The Effects of Cluster Sampling in an African Urban Setting." *Central African Journal of Medicine* 38 (8): 324–30.

Flory, James, and Ezekiel Emanuel. 2004. "Interventions to Improve Research Participants' Understanding in Informed Consent for Research: A Systematic Review." *JAMA* 292 (13): 1593–1601.

Foa, Edna B., Lori A. Zoellner, Norah C. Feeny. 2002. "Does Imaginal Exposure Exacerbate PTSD Symptoms?" *Journal of Consulting and Clinical Psychology* 70 (4): 1022–28.

Friedman, Merle. 2000. "The Truth and Reconciliation Commission in South Africa as an Attempt to Heal a Traumatized Society." In *International Handbook of Human Response to Trauma*, eds. Arik Y. Shalev, Rachel Yehuda, and Alexander C. McFarlane. New York: Plenum.

Galea, Sandro, Stephanie Factor, Sebastian Bonner, Mary Foley, Nicholas Freudenberg, Mary Latka, Ann G. Palermo, and David Vlahov. 2001. "Collaboration among Community Members, Local Health Service Providers, and Researchers in an Urban Research Center in Harlem, New York." *Public Health Report* 116 (6): 530–39.

Ganguli, M., M. E. Lytle, M. D. Reynolds, and H. H. Dodge. 1998. "Random versus Volunteer Selection for a Community-Based Study." *Journals of Gerontology Series A: Biological Sciences and Medical Sciences* 53 (1): M39–46.

Gold, Ellen B. 1996. "Confidentiality and Privacy Protection in Epidemiologic Research." In *Ethics and Epidemiology*, eds. Steven S. Coughlin and Tom L. Beauchamp. New York: Oxford University Press.

Graham, Kate, and Michelle Chandler-Coutts. 2000. "Community Action Research: Who Does What to Whom and Why? Lessons Learned from Local Prevention Efforts (International Experiences)." *Substance Use and Misuse* 35 (1–2): 87–110.

Greenland, Sander, and James Robins. 1994. "Invited Commentary: Ecologic Studies—Biases, Misconceptions, and Counterexamples." *American Journal of Epidemiology* 139 (8): 747–60.

Grimes, David A., and Kenneth F. Schulz. 2002. "Descriptive Studies: What They Can and Cannot Do." Lancet 359 (9301): 145–49.

Hamber, Brandon. 2001. *Does the Truth Heal? A Psychological Perspective on Political Strategies for Dealing with the Legacy of Political Violence.* Washington, D.C.: Georgetown University Press.

Hayner, Priscilla. 2001. *Unspeakable Truths: Confronting State Terror and Atrocity.* New York: Routledge.

Ignatieff, Michael. 1997. "Digging Up the Dead." *The New Yorker* 73 (34): 84–93.

Inu, Thomas 1996. "The Virtue of Qualitative and Quantitative Research." *Annals of Internal Medicine* 125 (9): 770–71.

Kaplan, Sara, Ilya Novikov, and Baruch Modan. 1998. "A Methodological Note on the Selection of Friends as Controls." *International Journal of Epidemiology* 27 (4): 727–29.

Kassam-Adams, Nancy, and Elana Newman. 2002. "The Reactions to Research Participation Questionnaires for Children and for Parents (RRPQ-C and RRPQ-P)." *General Hospital Psychiatry* 24 (5): 336–42.

Kawachi, Ichiro, and Lisa Berkman, eds. 2003. *Neighborhoods and Health.* New York: Oxford University Press.

Kelsey, Jennifer., Alice Whittemore, Alfred Evans, and W. Douglas Thompson. 1996. *Methods in Observation Epidemiology.* 2nd ed. New York: Oxford University Press.

Kilpatrick, Dean G. 2004. "The Ethics of Disaster Research: A Special Section." *Journal of Traumatic Stress* 17 (5): 361–62.

Kinzie, J. David, James K. Boehnlein, Crystal Riley, and Landy Sparr. 2002. "The Effects of September 11 on Traumatized Refugees: Reactivation of Posttraumatic Stress Disorder." *Journal of Nervous and Mental Disease* 190 (7): 437–41.

Kish, Leslie. 1965. Survey Sampling. New York: John Wiley and Sons.

Koepsell, Thomas D., and Noel S. Weiss. 2003. *Epidemiologic Methods: Studying the Occurrence of Illness.* New York: Oxford University Press: 281–308.

Kritz, Neil J., ed. 1997. *Transitional Justice. Vol. 1, General Considerations.* Washington, D.C.: United States Institute of Peace Press.

Malilay, J., W. D. Flanders, and D. Brogan. 1996. "A Modified Cluster-Sampling Method for Post-disaster Rapid Assessment of Needs." *Bulletin of the World Health Organization* 74 (4): 399–405.

Malterud, Kristi. 2001. "Qualitative Research: Standards, Challenges, and Guidelines." Lancet 358 (9280): 483–88.

Mann, Traci. 1994. "Informed Consent for Psychological Research: Do Subjects Comprehend Consent Forms and Understand Their Legal Rights?" *Psychological Science* 5 (3): 140–43.

Minow, Martha. 1998. *Between Vengeance and Forgiveness: Facing History after Genocide and Mass Violence.* Boston: Beacon Press.

———. 2000. "The Hope for Healing: What Can Truth Commissions Do?" In *Truth v. Justice: The Morality of Truth Commissions,* ed. Robert I. Rotberg and Dennis Thompson. Princeton, N. J.: Princeton University Press.

Mollica, Richard F., and Yael Caspi-Yavin. 1991. "Measuring Torture and Torture-Related Symptoms." *Psychological Assessment* 3, 581–87.

Mollica, Richard F., Yael Caspi-Yavin, Paola Bollini, Toan Truong, Svang Tor, and James Lavelle. 1992. "The Harvard Trauma Questionnaire. Validating a Cross-Cultural Instrument for Measuring Torture, Trauma, and Posttraumatic Stress Disorder in Indochinese Refugees." *Journal of Nervous and Mental Disorders* 180 (2): 111–16.

Morgenstern, Hal. 1995. "Ecologic Studies in Epidemiology: Concepts, Principles and Methods." Annual Review of Public Health 16: 61–81.

Neugebauer, Richard. 1999. "Research on Violence in Developing Countries: Benefits and Perils." *American Journal of Public Health* 89 (10): 1473–74.

Newman, Elana, and Danny G. Kaloupek. 2004. "The Risks and Benefits of Participating in Trauma-Focused Research Studies." *Journal of Traumatic Stress* 17 (5): 383–94.

Newman, Elana., Edward A. Walker, and Anne Gefland. 1999. "Assessing the Ethical Costs and Benefits of Trauma-Focused Research." *General Hospital Psychiatry* 21 (3): 187–96.

Pham, Phuong N., Harvey M. Weinstein, and Timothy Longman. 2004. "Trauma and PTSD symptoms in Rwanda: Implications for Attitudes toward Justice and Reconciliation." *JAMA* 292 (5): 602–12.

Rothman, Kenneth, and Sander Greenland. 1998. *Modern Epidemiology.* 2nd ed. Philadelphia: Lippincott-Raven.

Rubin, Zick, and Letitia A. Peplau. 1975. "Belief in a Just World and Reactions to Another's Lot: A Study of Participations in the National Draft Lottery." *Journal of Social Issues* 29 (4): 73–93.

Ruzek, Josef I., and Douglas F. Zatzick. 2000. "Ethical Considerations in Research Participation among Acutely Injured Trauma Survivors: An Empirical Investigation." *General Hospital Psychiatry* 22 (1): 27–36.

Schlenger, William, John Fairbank, B. Kathleen Jordan, and Juesta M. Caddell. 1997. "Epidemiologic Methods for Assessing Trauma and Posttraumatic Stress Disorder." In *Assessing Psychological Trauma and PTSD,* eds. John P. Wilson and Terence M. Keane. New York: Guilford Press.

Silverman, Henry J., John M. Luce, Paul N. Lanken, Alan H. Morris, Andrea L. Harabin, Cathryn F. Oldmixon, B. Taylor Thompson, and Gordon R. Bernard, for the NHLBI Acute Respiratory Distress Syndrome Clinical Trials Network (ARDSNet). 2005. "Recommendations for Informed Consent Forms for Critical Care Clinical Trials." *Critical Care Medicine* 33 (4): 867–82.

Solomon, Susan. 1987. "Reactivation of Combat-Related Posttraumatic Stress Disorder." *American Journal of Psychiatry* 144 (1): 51–55.

Sonis, Jeffrey H., James L. Gibson, Joop de Jong, Nigel P. Field, Sokhom Hean, Dorie Meerkerk, and Ivan Komproe. "PTSD and Disability in Cambodia: Associations with Desire for Revenge, Perceived Justice, and Attitudes toward the Khmer Rouge Trials." Under review, *JAMA.*

South African TRC. 1999. *Truth and Reconciliation Commission of South Africa Report.* Vol. 1. London: Macmillan.

Statistics South Africa. 2003. "Census 2001," www.statssa.gov.za/SpecialProjects/Census2001/Census2001.htm.

Stover, Eric. 2005. *The Witnesses: War Crimes and the Promise of Justice in The Hague.* Philadelphia: University of Pennsylvania Press.

Streiner, David, and Geoffrey Norman. 1995. *Health Measurement Scales: A Practical Guide to Their Development and Use.* 2nd ed. Oxford, UK: Oxford University Press.

Subkoviak, Michael J., Robert D. Enright, and Ching-Ru Wu. 1995. "Measuring Interpersonal Forgiveness in Late Adolescence and Middle Adulthood." *Journal of Adolescence* 18 (6): 641–55.

Susser, Mervyn. 1994. "The Logic in Ecological: 1. The Logic of Analysis." *American Journal of Public Health* 84 (5): 825–42.

United Nations Foundation. 2003. "Peru Truth Commission Says 69,000 Died in Maoist Insurgency." September 15. www.unwire.org/UNWire/20030902/449_7925.asp.

Yehuda, Rachel, Julia A. Golier, Sarah L. Halligan, and Phillip D. Harvey. 2004. "Learning and Memory in Holocaust Survivors with Posttraumatic Stress Disorder." *Biological Psychiatry* 55 (3): 291–95.

Appendix 1

Research Questions Applicable to Survivor Studies

1. Access to the truth commission by survivors
   a. What barriers, if any, did survivors experience in attempting to gain access to the truth commission to submit a statement?
   b. Who didn't submit a statement to the truth commission, and why? Were survivors who submitted statements to the truth commission similar to all survivors in the country?
   c. Which methods of publicizing the truth commission were most effective in reaching survivors?

2. Survivor expectations
   a. What do survivors want from truth commissions?
   b. Are there factors that predict what survivors want from truth commissions?
   c. What can truth commissions do to meet survivor expectations?

3. What characteristics of the truth commission predict satisfaction among survivors who submit statements or testify in public hearings?
   a. Process of truth commission (e.g., degree of empathy of statement taker, extent of ongoing communication with the survivor, debriefing provided to survivors after testifying in public, attention given by truth commission to perpetrators)
   b. Outcomes of truth commission (e.g., reparations, amnesty given to perpetrators, version of "truth" endorsed by commission)

4. What characteristics predict positive or negative outcomes among survivors who submit statements or testify?
   a. Demographic characteristics
   b. Characteristics of the human rights violation (e.g., violation to self or family member)
   c. Truth commission characteristics

5. What outcomes are important to survivors, the truth commission, or the country, and how can they be measured?
   a. Perception that justice has been achieved
   b. Psychological sense of community
   c. Catharsis
   d. Political empowerment
   e. "Moving on" (resolution)
   f. Forgiveness
   g. Desire for reconciliation
   h. Psychological distress
   i. Psychiatric disorder (e.g., post-traumatic stress disorder)
   j. Desire for vengeance

Appendix 2

Screening Questions to Determine Exposure to Human Rights Violation

1. At any time in your life has anyone ever attacked you with a gun, knife, or some other weapon, regardless of whether you ever reported it?
   a. Yes
   b. No (Go to Q. 3)

2. What was the relationship to you of the person(s) who did this?
   a. Husband or wife
   b. Other relative (mother, father, brother, sister, cousin, aunt, uncle)
   c. Friend
   d. Neighbor
   e. Policeman or other government official
   f. Member of rival group
   g. Unknown

3. Have you ever been in a building or vehicle that was bombed, blown up, or set on fire?
   a. Yes
   b. No (Go to Q. 5)

4. What was the relationship to you of the person(s) who committed the act?
   a. Husband or wife
   b. Other relative (mother, father, brother, sister, cousin, aunt, uncle)
   c. Friend
   d. Neighbor
   e. Policeman or other government official
   f. Member of rival group

5. Have you ever been imprisoned for political activity or suspected political activity?
   a. Yes
   b. No

6. During the time that you were in prison, were you ever
   a. Beaten with fists or other objects?
   b. Suffocated?
   c. Threatened with death?
   d. Burned?
   e. Forced to go without food or water?
   f. Denied access to medical care?
   g. Tortured?
   h. Caned?
   i. Shocked with electricity?
   j. Forced to stand or sit in one position for a long time?

Appendix 3

Focus Group Questions for Groups with South African TRC Participants

1. Tell us your name and where you live.

2. Think back to the time that you decided to give a statement to the TRC. What prompted you to give a statement to the TRC?

3. Think back to the time when you gave a statement to the TRC. What was going through your mind just before you gave the statement? What was going through your mind while you were giving the statement? What was going through your mind immediately after giving the statement?

4. What interaction did you have with the TRC after you gave a statement?

   Probes:
   a. What did you hope to get from the TRC?
   b. What did you expect to get from the TRC?

5. What did you like best about your personal interaction with the TRC?

6. If you could change one thing about the way that you were treated by the TRC, what would it be?

7. In what ways, if any, did the TRC help relieve your suffering?

8. In what ways, if any, did the TRC make your suffering worse?

9. The word "justice" regarding human rights violations can mean a number of things. What does it mean to you?

   Probes:
   a. Punishment
   b. Amnesty
   c. Reparation
   d. "Restorative" justice
   e. Unbuntu
   f. Accountability

10. There was a lot of talk about forgiveness during the time of the TRC. What does "forgiveness" mean to you?
    Probes:
    a. Are forgiveness and reconciliation the same thing? If not, how are they different?
    b. Can you have reconciliation without forgiveness?
    c. Can you have forgiveness without reconciliation?

11. What would need to happen for you to forgive the perpetrators?
    Probes:
    a. What would the perpetrators need to do for you to forgive them?
    b. What would the government need to do for you to forgive it?
    c. What effect did the TRC have on your ability to forgive?

12. In what ways did your victimization affect the way that you relate to the people in your community?
    Probes:
    a. Your attitudes to friends; to neighbors; to political activists
    b. Changes in the way that others behaved toward you
    c. Did the TRC change these relationships?

13. If you had the chance to do it over, would you give a statement to the TRC?

14. Is there an important question we've missed?

8

Confessional Performances

A Methodological Approach to Studying Perpetrators' Testimonies

Leigh A. Payne

When perpetrators confess to authoritarian state violence, not only do they read a carefully prepared script, they also act it out. They imbue their performance with political meaning through what they say, how they say it, and where and when they make their confessional performance. But perpetrators do not shape the political meaning of these confessions all on their own. Audiences also participate, employing media representations to reinforce or counter the perpetrators' intended political meaning. A performative methodology allows researchers to explore the political struggle that is generated by different audience interpretations of these confessional performances. This chapter lays out not only the contributions that such an approach makes to social science analysis but also the problems that researchers will confront in using it.

What does it mean politically when perpetrators of authoritarian state violence publicly admit to their violent pasts? This is the main question behind the research project for *Unsettling Accounts* (Payne 2008), a study of perpetrators' confessions in countries emerging from authoritarian rule, including Argentina, Brazil, Chile, and South Africa. To get at that question, the study uses a performative approach, that is, it explores not only what perpetrators say (their script) but also how and why they say it (their acting), when and where they say it (the timing and staging), and the political impact they make (the audience response).

By selecting countries that have adopted a variety of transitional justice arrangements, the project explores how and when perpetrators' confessions might contribute positively to "nunca más" memory projects—that is, projects that use collective memory to ensure that past violence is not repeated. The South African Truth and Reconciliation Commission (TRC) had to confront this issue directly by granting amnesty to apartheid-era perpetrators who made full disclosure of the political violence they had committed (as long as the violence proved proportionate to the political motive involved). For the first time in history, an institutional process encouraged perpetrators of state violence to tell their stories. Although war crimes trials such as those conducted in Nuremberg and Tokyo had provided an opportunity for charged perpetrators of violence to defend themselves, these earlier processes had come with no guarantees of amnesty. Subsequent pardons and amnesty laws granted perpetrators immunity from prosecution, and several perpetrators used these protections to confess their past violence to the media without the threat of trials. Creative legal strategies that circumvented the pardons and amnesty laws have landed some of these confessed perpetrators in jail. A similar phenomenon occurred in Chile. A truth commission process and an amnesty provision provided no institutional arrangement to extract confessions from perpetrators and protected them from prosecution. As in the Argentine case, however, some perpetrators faced trials and imprisonment, and others made confessions in the media. Blanket amnesty in Brazil shielded perpetrators from any official inquiry into their acts or their identities, and most perpetrators remained silent. Until the TRC, therefore, perpetrators' confessions played almost no official role in the transitional justice processes, although confessions about past violence were publicly made.

The TRC became a model that subsequent truth commissions have considered adopting, and yet, despite its global influence, no systematic analysis has examined the value of perpetrators' confessions to transitional justice processes. Unsettling Accounts, with the performative approach it adopts, fills this void by exploring the kinds of confessional texts that emerge from these different institutional arrangements and what those texts mean for memory politics. The project examines how confessions are shaped by the institutional processes in which they emerge and how confessions, in turn, shape the transitional justice processes. Ideally, the project will contribute to designing a blueprint for future truth commissions or other transitional justice arrangements that will overcome some of the limitations of those in the past.

Perpetrators' Confessions and Memory Politics

The theoretically thin literature on perpetrators' confessions in transitional justice settings assumes a positive relationship between perpetrators' public confessions and four key components of nunca más memory politics: truth, acknowledgment, justice, and collective memory. Because perpetrators have witnessed events that occurred in clandestine detention centers or in armed confrontations, their confessions should expose the truth about specific events—about what happened and to whom (truth). Moreover, by rupturing the authoritarian regime's code of silence, perpetrators' confessions should confirm victims' accounts of wrongdoing (acknowledgment).

Perpetrators' testimonies should also uncover details of who did what to whom and help determine when, in addition to the restorative and symbolic justice processes, to advance retributive justice for past violations of human rights (justice). Finally, perpetrators' confessions should contribute to establishing an authoritative history that repudiates past human rights violations (collective memory).

The South African TRC could be viewed as an embodiment of this ideal. By calling on perpetrators to confess, the TRC assumed that truth, acknowledgment, and collective memory had greater value than retributive justice for a nunca más memory project (although the TRC threatened with prosecution those who did not confess and those who did not receive amnesty).

The Unsettling Accounts project, in contrast, challenges the assumed positive relationship between perpetrators' confessions and transitional justice. Drawing on comparative and performative analyses, it demonstrates that perpetrators rarely provide full disclosure, even if they do confess (acting, script: truth). Moreover, full disclosure does not necessarily involve condemnation of the past but sometimes resurrects the old authoritarian regime's justifications for violence (script: acknowledgment). Rather than promoting justice, confessions without prison sentences reinforce a sense of perpetrators' impunity and their capacity to do harm again in the future (timing, staging: justice). Memory poles—that is, an enduring and conflictual divide over how the past is remembered, instead of a shared collective memory—sometimes emerge from perpetrators' confessions (audience: collective memory). (See Popkin and Roht-Arriaza 1995.)

A Performative Research Design

To analyze the script, acting, timing, staging, and audience response to perpetrators' confessions, the Unsettling Accounts project required a variety of research methods. Initially it focused only on the text, through discursive and content analysis. The first step was to accumulate written transcripts of perpetrators' confessions and analyze their content and the narrative devices they employed. From this preliminary analysis, a typology of confessions was built, producing a range of perpetrators' public accounts, which resembled confession in some form but often lacked the act of atonement generally associated with the term "confession." However, the etymology of the term "confession" revealed that even perpetrators' accounts that failed to show remorse qualified as confessions. Definitions of "confession"—related to the Latin terms "fari" ("speak") and "fibula" ("fable")—range from admission of guilt to a simple declaration (Onions 1992; Brown 1993). Perpetrators may confess, therefore, without ever admitting the truth or any wrongdoing.

Indeed, the analysis of the content of perpetrators' accounts revealed that remorse is one of the least common forms of confession. The most common way in which perpetrators confess to their past is through the language of denial or simply by remaining silent, but amnesia, revenge, fiction, sadism, and heroism are other narrative forms that perpetrators use to describe their past actions.

Although an analysis of the confessional text suggested that few remorseful confessions emerged, it could not, by itself, explain whether remorseful confessions did produce the positive relationship anticipated in the literature or whether the other types of confessions failed. Neither could discursive and content analysis alone determine what types of transitional justice arrangements might produce the kinds of confessions conducive to a positive relationship between perpetrators' confessions and nunca más memory politics. Finally, confessional texts by themselves failed to show the impact of these texts on society, or audience response to them. In other words, analysis of discourse and content hinted at challenges to the assumed relationship between perpetrators' confessions and nunca más memory politics but could not fully test the hypothesis or explain the context in which such a hypothesis could be confirmed.

The project went beyond the script, focusing on additional components of the confessional performance—acting, timing, staging, and audience—to analyze the political meaning of the confessions more fully. "Performance" in this sense does not mean a made-up or fictional theatrical event but draws instead on the root of the term as "a carrying through, actualizing, making something happen." Perpetrators' confessions, in this sense, resemble Austin's notion of "speech acts": "Performance of a text does not just 'say' something; it does something, and we need to reflect more deeply on that doing" (Palmer 1977, 20). A performative approach involves understanding the political meaning generated from the interaction of actors and acting (perpetrators), scripts (confessional text), timing (phase in the political transition), staging (institutional arrangement), and audience (public response).

Performative analysis is not new to the social sciences. From the 1950s to the 1970s, "dramaturgical analyses" explored "what performance is taking place or what meaning is being portrayed to an audience and how the elements that make up the performance contribute to that meaning" (Feldman 1995, 42). They focused on "people and groups within society who have access to resources and who use these resources to invoke and manipulate meaning" (Feldman 1995, 66). The specific characteristics of a performance—scene, act, agent, agency, and purpose—provided a set of categories for organizing observations (Burke 1952). But earlier dramaturgical analyses missed the crucial role that audiences play in social drama. Audiences provide more than the object of the performance in confessional performances—they perform themselves, challenging perpetrators' interpretation of the past and its implications for contemporary democracy and reenacting their own interpretations. Confessional performances, moreover, respond to, and are shaped by, political context, or timing—another theatrical element missing from dramaturgical analyses.[1]

Also, dramaturgical analyses focused on everyday occurrences involving social actors largely unconscious of acting or playing on a political stage (Messinger, Sampson, and Towne 1962). In contrast, perpetrators deliberately take a public stage to make their confessions. What evolves constitutes a social drama, a suspension of "normal everyday role playing, they interrupt the flow of social life and force a group to take cognizance of its own behavior in relation to its own values, even to question at times the value of those values" (Turner 1982, 92). These are surprise acts with dramatic significance for contemporary politics. They appear as historical reenactments, but ones without consensus in society. Audiences often interpret them as cautionary and morality tales with profound implications for contemporary politics. A dramatic political struggle ensues.

Victims in perpetrators' confessional performances play a key role as audiences. Certainly performative methodology could reverse that relationship, focusing on victims as the performers of testimonials and perpetrators as part of their audience. Researchers would examine the same set of theatrical elements and observe a similar social drama and struggle over the political meaning of victims' testimonies. Literary and performance scholars have begun to conduct some of this work (Becker 2000; Caruth 1995; Dorfman 1991; Patraka 1996; D. Taylor 1994).

Process-tracing techniques helped analyze the "doing" of the performance. Process tracing, defined as a means to "reconstruct actors' definitions of the situation and an attempt to develop a theory of action," involves the researcher, and not the actors themselves, in defining actors' perceptions and actions through participant observation, open-ended interviews, media archives, and published accounts (George and McKeown 1985, 35). In addition to the written confessional texts, a performative approach also involves understanding how the actors present themselves and why (acting), by using video transcripts of their confessions. It involves comparison with what they say and how they act on other confessional stages, allowing for analysis of confessional performances in interviews, trials, and television shows. It involves building chronologies of perpetrators' personal and public life as well as of the events that transpired in their countries, so that the researcher can better understand why they speak out when they do. And it involves understanding how different audiences interpret their text,

---

1.   Many thanks to Craig Calhoun for this insightful observation.

acting, timing, and staging by tracing their coverage in the media, analyzing video transcripts, exploring opinion survey analysis, and conducting interviews. For this reason, the research involved mining perpetrators' written confessions, written and video court and truth commission transcripts, television appearances, radio shows, print media interviews, public opinion polls, and books and articles written by or about the perpetrators. The research also involved personal interviews with perpetrators, survivors, lawyers, commissioners, and human rights activists. It required extensive time (over three years), travel (to South Africa, Argentina, Brazil, and Chile), and language skills (in English, Spanish, and Portuguese). Local experts assisted in analyzing and translating non-English sources in South Africa. This research revealed not only what perpetrators said but also how they appeared, when and where they appeared, and what impact they had on their audiences.

Types of Confessional Texts

Njabulo Ndebele's (1998, 27) elegant formulation of "reinventing oneself through narrative" best describes the importance of the text for perpetrators' confessional performances. This project involved careful analysis of a variety of confessional texts generated in a range of different transitional justice environments. The same type of confessions emerged, regardless of the institutional arrangement. Some types of confessional stages, however, produced a greater density of a particular type of confession, suggesting a strong relationship between staging and text. That relationship proved difficult to test, though, since perpetrators tend to include a combination of confessional narrative forms in a single performance. Audiences, however, reduce the confession to a single form. Thus, while an individual might strongly express remorse, an audience may consider the confession to be a denial since the perpetrator has forgotten, omitted, or denied events from the past. Discursive and content analysis produced the range of narrative forms used in each confessional text. It also provided hints on how the institutional arrangement and political timing influenced the nature of the confession provided. Video transcripts, media analyses, and interviews with lawyers, human rights activists, victims, and perpetrators revealed the range of audience responses to the confession.

Remorseful confessions are rare, emerging only when perpetrators believe that contrition might help them avoid prosecution or reduce their punishment, when they feel betrayed by their commanding officers and seek to distinguish their own acts from the callousness of the regime, or when they can break with their past life—for example, through religious conversion or recovery from addiction. Certain opportunities provided by transitional justice institutions—such as exchanging truth for amnesty, or plea-bargaining arrangements—may generate more remorseful confessions than do other arrangements. Audiences, however, often doubt the sincerity of remorseful confessions, particularly when they include payoffs, such as amnesty from prosecution.

Silence is the most common and powerful form of perpetrators' accounting for the past. It involves analyzing the unspoken truth about the past: the nonconfession. In some cases silence represents power: the capacity of the repressive apparatus to maintain loyalty from within and protection from the new democratic government. This power may rely on the shared value of silence or on coercion and the capacity to threaten retribution. But silence may also mask fragmentation and a lack of consensus within the repressive apparatus about the past. Silence protects the institution from evoking disagreements over the past that would weaken its internal authority and its public image.

But how to analyze a text that does not exist? Silence is rarely total. Strategic silences, or silence around certain acts or events, usually coexist with disclosure as a means of appearing to cooperate with investigations while shielding certain aspects of the past from public scrutiny. Therefore, researchers must look for what is not present as well as what is present. Victim and survivor groups assist in this regard by attempting to break silence and "out" perpetrators and their past. How perpetrators respond to their "outing" reveals much about their earlier silence. In addition, perpetrators sometimes discuss why they will not reveal any details about the past. Analyzing those justifications for remaining silent provides insights into the silence itself. To analyze silence, therefore, researchers must use content analysis to explore what is unsaid in confessional texts, conduct interviews with those who remain silent, and employ process-tracing techniques to analyze archives and probe perpetrators' responses to public "outing" of past events.

Denial, like confession, offers another unusual form of confession that perpetrators engage in. Perpetrators acknowledge that violent acts occur but deny their own personal involvement in them or any knowledge about them at the time. Denial may also involve admitting atrocities, though it blames those atrocities on mistakes, rogue forces, or deranged individuals who acted on their own. By accepting the events but denying personal or institutional responsibility for them, denial impedes, rather than advances, the nunca más project of remembering in order not to repeat. The challenge for the researcher is to distinguish between denial and silence, denial and heroism, and denial and fiction or lies.

Although denials many times constitute lies and fiction about the past, perpetrators also generate other kinds of lies. In "false confessions," perpetrators confess to acts that they did not commit. Confessions that have led innocent individuals to death row have revealed that people with limited intelligence or limited legal resources may falsely admit to a criminal act to end interrogation or to secure a lesser sentence than they might get if convicted or because they do not understand the consequences of their confession of guilt. But fictitious confessions also provide would-be perpetrators with the promise of recognition and power. Media outlets searching for perpetrators to provide sensationalist accounts of past violence often offer both fame and fortune to those willing to comply with a story. These lies often create false hopes among victims and survivors that they may find out the "truth" of what happened. But hope disappears and a deeper pain returns when they discover that these confessions involve fabrication, not truth. It is important to realize that the lies or fiction is not to be found in the text itself. Rather, researchers must trace the reactions to the confession, including cross-examination, media accounts, and public declarations by human rights activists.

Moreover, every confession may contain "lies." Eager to establish a coherent narrative about their past, perpetrators, like all of us, filter and select facts. These "vital lies" constitute the stories perpetrators tell themselves to live with their past acts, but they are only partially based on verifiable events (Goleman 1985). Researchers face the challenge of examining how perpetrators and their "handlers" lie in their performance through appearances, gestures, and text. This involves comparing performances by the same perpetrator on different stages and tracing media and archival accounts to determine the degree of continuity or disruption with earlier or later public performances.

In contrast to fictitious confessions is amnesia, in which perpetrators confess that they do not remember what happened. These perpetrators usually have partial memory of events but block out, or pretend to block out, the identities of their victims, the number of violent events they engaged in, the distinguishing features of their victims, or other specifics about the violent events. Perpetrators claim to have forgotten details of torture and killing, just as workers in any environment might forget events in a normal week of work sometime in the past. Events blur together or remain as only vague memories. Some perpetrators claim to suffer from post-traumatic stress disorder, which prevents them from remembering the violence they committed. But victims and survivors, whose lives were transformed by these forgotten "details," reject perpetrators' amnesia as willful forgetting to avoid disclosure. Researchers often cannot determine whether perpetrators' amnesia is willful or involuntary, but analysis through interviews with psychiatric experts can help determine whether sufficient medical evidence corroborates the perpetrators' claims. Tracking different confessions by the same perpetrator may reveal what types of events the perpetrator "forgets," suggesting at times a pattern of denial. Moreover, perpetrators may also "forget" events they once claimed to remember.

Heroic confessions justify and glorify past violence by using "just war" analogies to elevate perpetrators' acts from murder to patriotic and heroic sacrifice. After authoritarian rule, it may seem impractical for soldiers or police even to attempt to raise the heroic banner to explain their past violence. But it is precisely in that context that individuals are motivated to do so. Members of the security forces either believe or want themselves and others to believe that they were doing the right thing during the "dirty wars." They received rewards, accolades, and promotions for those acts of violence. They refuse to accept shame for what they did and use heroic narratives to continue to claim dignity and respect for their acts. For victims and survivors of violence, heroic confessions attempt to legitimize past violence, often resurrecting the authoritarian regime's version.

At times, heroic confessions exude depraved pleasure at having committed violence. Sadism, often masked in written confessions, is exhibited in the confessional act through physical and spoken language. These are rare yet powerful confessions that shock viewers. The media emphasize these accounts since they produce dramatic copy and fit images of depraved perpetrators. But only rare—and probably deranged—perpetrators would publicly admit to enjoying violence, despite such admissions' overrepresentation in films, novels, and cartoons.[2] In this way, media representations of sadistic perpetrators subvert the nunca más memory project by attributing the violence to deranged individuals rather than a systematic effort to silence and eliminate a sector of society.

Revenge confessions provide more to advance the transitional process through text than any other form of confession by perpetrators. Perpetrators, usually those already convicted of crimes, use their confession to indict others so that they do not pay the price of the regime's violence alone. They recount the details of events they participated in or observed, including details that extend beyond their own involvement and identify those who issued the orders, knew about the orders, or carried them out. In some cases, perpetrators make revenge confessions as a personal vendetta; in others, they feel betrayed by the security institution or particular officers in it.

Perpetrators' confessions are important documents that must be analyzed. Discursive and content analysis can reveal the patterns of confessions that emerge across contexts. But these confessional documents do not give the entire picture. Moreover, audiences rarely read them in their entirety. Instead,

---

2.   As Murray Edelman (1988, 5) eloquently states, "Only in bad novels and comic books do characters knowingly do evil and boast of it. In life, people rationalize their actions in moral terms."

they are often excerpted in newspapers or on television. And the visual representation of these confessions often has as profound an effect on their audiences as the text itself. Analyzing the acting and staging in live or mediated performances thus proves vital in researching public performances. Process tracing provides the researcher with a means of analyzing media reports and archives to deepen the analysis of the text, acting, and timing of the performance, as well as a means of analyzing how the timing and staging might shape a particular narrative text and acting style.

Actors and Acting

Perpetrators tell one story with their confessional texts, but who they are and how they present their confession shape how the public responds to them. In addition to the script, therefore, perpetrators possess "nonverbal instruments," as Lincoln (1994, 5) calls them: "the whole theatrical array of gestures, demeanors, costumes, props and stage devices through which one may impress or bamboozle an audience." Lincoln identifies what one looks for in a confessional performance: clothing, grooming, accent, body language, size or other remarkable physical traits, mood, and details added to create an image.

The list shows that perpetrators do not always have control over their performance. While they might be able to shape opinions by dressing in a particular way, they cannot easily change their physical appearance or accent. Analyzing the interaction of the audience and staging with the actor and acting requires examining the efforts taken by the perpetrators or by others involved in producing the confession to present a particular image. Erving Goffman (1959) distinguishes between "presentations of self" that are sincere, that is, believed by the perpetrators themselves, and those that are cynical, in which perpetrators (or their lawyers or the media outlet behind the confession) deliberately toy with the audience. The performative approach does not focus exclusively on whether the presentations are sincere or cynical but also on whether audiences judge them sincere (and thus believable) or cynical (and thus suspect).

Perpetrators generally attempt, through their appearance as through their text, to overcome the stigma of having committed criminal violence. Although most psychologists agree that given the right set of conditions, nearly anyone could be induced to act violently, most media and fictional portrayals transform perpetrators into psychopaths.[3] The typical shock we express at

---

3. This was not always the case. The Authoritarian Personality (TAP) study, for example, attempted to explain fascist propensities in individuals with a particular type of childhood experience, especially an excessively restrictive upbringing. This type of background produced two seemingly contradictory traits that would lead to following fascist-style leaders and committing acts of aggression. Conventionalism and submission to authority, combined with repressed

discovering that normal people, or people who look normal, could commit acts of cruelty reveals our own desire to believe that we can distinguish good from evil through appearance.

Perpetrators, consciously or unconsciously, play on that tendency and use nonverbal mechanisms to present themselves as "normal" people, even if they admit to committing violence. Lifton (1986) terms this strategy "doubling," in which perpetrators separate what they did (killing or torturing) from who they are (loving father and husband, generous and caring friend). "Born again" perpetrators and those recovering from drug and alcohol addictions carry doubling one step further by making a break with their past. They distinguish their former lives, as nonspiritual and addicted individuals, from their lives today, as new people incapable of committing those acts. A particular look, mood, facial expression, and attire project images of normality that contrast sharply with the particular acts committed by state torturers or killers.

Similarly, perpetrators often present themselves as victims, through script and acting meant to evoke sympathy for their situation. This acting technique could be called "the gray zone," linking it to Primo Levi's (1989) notion of the blurring of boundaries between perpetrators and victims in particularly violent political moments. In these cases, perpetrators project fear and powerlessness, pathos and loss, to suggest that they became the unwilling executioners of state policies over which they had no control and by which they themselves were threatened.

In sharp contrast with these images, perpetrators may also exude a sense of loyalty or duty through emotion and body language. Hannah Arendt's (1963) observation of Adolph Eichmann's trial performance, including his narrative devices and his nonverbal cues, suggested a man driven not by violent hatred but by a desire to please his superiors and do a good job. But the "banality of evil" does not explain those perpetrators who use their confessional performances to glorify the past and their role in it as self-sacrifice, heroism, and patriotic duty to defend the nation against its enemies.

Perpetrators do not invent their presentations of self; they adopt and adapt them. They act out identities drawn consciously or unconsciously from available cultural, institutional, and gender norms. They try to make their acting consistent with their confessional text, playing a role that their audience can understand. Only rarely do perpetrators take on the role of the psychopath. In some of these cases, they may actually fall into the small percentage of

---

frustration with authority, would lead to aggression against identifiable out-groups (Adorno, Frenkel-Brunswik, Levinson, and Sanford 1950). For at least one analysis based on biology, see Badinter 1995. Recent studies have shown how seemingly normal people have the capacity to commit violence. See, for example, Altemeyer 1988; Bird et al. 1994; Huggins, Haritos-Fatouros, and Zimbardo 2002; Milgram 1974; and Zimbardo, Haney, Banks, and Jaffe 1973.

infirm individuals within the authoritarian regime's repressive apparatus. At other times, their acts themselves may have affected their emotional and mental health, and in others, their performances have been manipulated by the media or others to exaggerate their mental or emotional unbalance.

Through analysis of all of a perpetrator's confessional performances—video archives, live appearances, and media coverage of confessional performances—researchers can trace the public image that the perpetrator projects. When the performances change, researchers have the opportunity to examine what factors shape or derail a perpetrator's public image. Media coverage and interviews allow researchers to further examine how audiences interpret the perpetrator's public image. For example, audiences' interpretations might be subliminally affected by the staging of the confession.

Timing

Confessions occur in a particular historical and political moment that shapes not only what perpetrators say but also how they are interpreted by their audiences. Confessions both shape and are shaped by the transitional justice processes under way.

Because of perpetrators' typical silence about the past, when they do speak, they command attention from the media and the public as well as from former perpetrators and the government. The current government and the past security apparatus usually attempt to censor these confessions—sometimes taking the drastic measure of imprisoning the perpetrators—to preserve peace and keep the book on the past permanently closed. Even when the government or security apparatus retaliates against those who break the code of silence, other perpetrators tend to come forward with their own confessions. But this "performance chaining," in which one confession produces another and another, does not generate the same kind of confessions (Fuoss 1999). At times, for example, a remorseful confession by one perpetrator may produce a heroic confession by another, who feels that the remorse denigrates the dignity of the security apparatus and all those within it. These confessions can, in turn, produce a sadistic or fictitious confession by a desperate former perpetrator who seizes on an opportunity to make money or a profession from his confessional "files," even invented ones.

The performance chain transforms the context in which the original confession occurred. An early confession may emerge when an amnesty process seems firm, but perpetrators' confessions may produce new demands from human rights groups to revisit amnesty law and new information that allows lawyers to circumvent amnesty laws and try perpetrators for their past acts.

In other words, while perpetrators may take advantage of a political moment to make their confession without fear of legal reprisals, their confession may unintentionally challenge the legal community and make retributive justice possible where it never seemed possible before. To understand the impact of timing, researchers not only must engage the event itself but also must use process-tracing techniques to analyze the political meaning of the factors leading up to and following the event. Those factors shape how perpetrators act and what they say, as well as what stages they perform on and how audiences interpret their performances. Slight changes in the timing produce strikingly different confessional performances.

Confessional Stage

Institutional stages shape confessions. The stage involves not only the physical place in which a performance takes place (e.g., trial court or truth commission) but also a space that allows for public debate over its political meaning (Patraka 1996). Perpetrators' confessions often take place originally in courtrooms or truth commissions with limited public access. What tends to be remembered from these confessional performances and has political impact, therefore, is not the live, uncut version of the confession but the "mediatized" performance, edited, extracted, and manipulated for newspaper, radio, and television audiences (Auslander 1999).

Victim and survivor groups often criticize the media for focusing almost exclusively on perpetrators while ignoring victims. Stories about those who "do" seem more appealing than stories of those who have been "done to" (Taylor 1998). But for victims and survivors, the media's clinging to perpetrators' performances tends to give the perpetrators the power to shape public opinion again.

From the perpetrators' perspective, stages often take their power away. Despite carefully preparing scripts designed to minimize their guilt or responsibility (even in remorseful confessions), the live stage—and even more effectively, the "mediatized" stage—distorts the confession, producing a very different meaning. In the performance, perpetrators lose control over their own confessions.

The distortion occurs through interaction with the institutional environment itself. Although stages could be viewed as legitimizing perpetrators, when perpetrators appear in court or even before truth commissions, they wear the stigma of guilt. Moreover, they cannot control what they are asked by commissioners, judges, or prosecuting attorneys. In some cases, they may even have to address questions from victims or survivors. Television cameras and journalists follow every twitch of the eye, every muscle movement, looking for signs. The edited version, shortened to fill a few minutes of television news or an article length in the newspaper, contains the most dramatic minutes of an otherwise long and tedious process. Tears, anger, and shame are the emotions the television and print media hope to produce for their spectators and readers. Rather than simply authorizing perpetrators' words, therefore, the media can subvert those words, transforming perpetrators into monsters or weaklings.

Performance studies, and particularly those studies interested in mediatized performances, demonstrate the power of the stage to authorize certain performances and delegitimize others. Those approaches also provide the researcher with specific elements of the staging to analyze. The use of camera close-ups on a face, for example, exaggerates human characteristics, often emphasizing an emotional response from the audience, while putting other factors in a distant, or safely analytical, category (Fair and Parks 2001). Where perpetrators sit, and with whom, leaves impressions of how alone they are or whether they have the support of their colleagues. The presence or absence of victims and survivors plays an important role in audience response to the confessional performance. In thinking about the political meaning generated by the confessional performance and its staging, the researcher has an obligation to analyze not only what is shown but also what is not shown.

Audiences

Audience response involves the single most important element of the confessional performance for political analysis. The audience, as Bruce Lincoln (1994) states, does the authorizing. How audiences respond, however, depends on perpetrators' scripts, acting, timing, and staging. When perpetrators enter the living rooms of their audiences through the television set and reimpose the old justifications for authoritarian regime violence, fear and numbing may return. But where these perpetrators can face prison sentences for their crimes, a different reaction may result. Mobilized audiences can transform even heroic confessions into an opportunity to challenge the old authoritarian order and reinforce nunca más memory politics.

Confessions are, in other words, spectatorial performances, in which spectators play a key role in understanding and remembering the past (Patraka 1996). Audiences are not passive or uncritical consumers of a particular performance, nor are they easily deceived by a perpetrator's sartorial choice, body language, or visage. While the staging of the performance and the perpetrator's text may attempt to manipulate emotions, audiences bring to the performance their own understanding of the world and the place that this performance plays in it (Boal 1996). Performances seldom radically change perceptions that already exist in society; instead, they tend to reinforce them. And while one audience may feel reassured by the confessions that deny or minimize violence, other audiences recognize those performances for what they are.

For the purposes of the nunca más memory project, audiences of victims and survivors use perpetrators' confessional performances as a way to reawaken sometimes dormant perspectives about the past. The confession provides a space to reopen a debate about the past. While many individuals would like to forget about the past and move on with their lives, the perpetrator's confession makes that impossible. The past reenters contemporary society, and mobilized human rights groups can use that political moment to advance truths, acknowledge the wrongdoing, and demand justice. The perpetrator's confession itself, therefore, can become, with the involvement of audience mobilization, a key moment in collective memory about the violent past.

Victims and survivors tend to be the most vocal audiences for perpetrators' confessions. They are not, however, the only—or even the most important—audiences in terms of transitional justice. Audiences of perpetrators, or colleagues of the perpetrators, reflect the degree to which views held by perpetrators or by victims and survivors form a collective memory or remain fragmented or dangerously polarized. Reactions from within the new democratic government also constitute important indicators of the possibility of justice—restorative or retributive—or a continuation of the policy of impunity.

Analyzing audience responses involves multiple research methods. Newspapers tend to report the attitudes toward perpetrators held by opinion leaders in the human rights community, in victim or survivor groups, in the government, and in the old repressive apparatus. Public statements by these leaders provide a sense of how they have responded and the degree to which consensus or polarization about the past has occurred. Interviews with leaders not only verify the views reported in the press but also provide the opportunity to test attitudes over time. Have intervening events changed the perspectives that were once firmly held? Open-ended interviews often reveal more subtlety than the emotions expressed in news reports, since leaders can explain a particular emotion or a change in their attitudes over time. In some instances, public opinion polls can take the pulse of the population. When repeated at different historical intervals, these surveys can reflect stable and changing views within the population on issues of transitional justice.

The Challenges of a Performative Approach

A performative approach challenges the researcher by its complexity. This project, rather than being limited to merely finding and reading perpetrators' confessions—itself no small feat, given both the scarcity of confessions and the language skills required for analysis—involved a broad range of tasks. These included finding news sources that reported on the confessional event itself, and responses to it, over a decade or more; finding and watching videotaped performances by perpetrators; searching for surveys of audience responses and public opinions about transitional justice processes;

and interviewing a variety of audiences, including victims and survivors, fellow perpetrators, commanders, former and current government officials, lawyers for victims and perpetrators, human rights activists, and professionals in the therapeutic community.

To avoid an idiosyncratic finding based on a single-case study of confessions in one country and one institutional context, this project tested the hypothetical relationship between perpetrators' confessions and transitional justice through comparative analysis. Countries that had experienced a similar kind of violent past but had adopted a range of different institutional mechanisms for settling accounts with the past formed the basis of case selection. The project required lengthy field research trips to Africa and Latin America and involved several languages. It was a challenge to keep an insider's feel for the specific country context while also maintaining a strong comparative orientation. The project's success relied on research collaborators in each country—individuals who participated by answering endless questions and, more important, providing the research with local and nuanced context—often ignored in books or articles—that shed light on the particular and peculiar aspects of the confessional performances.[4] The project also required substantial research funding from the University of Wisconsin at Madison, the Social Science Research Council, and the MacArthur Foundation.

The greatest challenge of this project, however, involved the personal connections with victims and perpetrators. Perpetrators posed the initial problem of contact information. Those in jail proved easy to find but posed logistical difficulties in terms of gaining access, especially to maximum-security prisons. Some had left their previous jobs without leaving forwarding addresses. Several of these had found ways to disappear from sight, ending contact with former lawyers, therapists, and colleagues. They did not want to be found by researchers, journalists, or, perhaps, vindictive victims and survivors. Most of the confessed perpetrators lived in a precarious legal and social world that could turn against them at any time (if indeed it had not already done so). They perceived no gain from an interview while anticipating potential harm.

Establishing the interviews with perpetrators is by no means the final hurdle. Perpetrators who initially agree to talk sometimes have a change of heart, often at their lawyers' behest. Moreover, interviews with perpetra-

---

4. In South Africa, Madeleine Fullard proved an invaluable collaborator in this regard. Nicky Rousseau, Janet Cherry, and Deborah Quinn also provided the critical guidance I needed at different stages. In Argentina, I drew on the generous assistance at CELS and Memoria Abierta. In Chile, I benefited from working with the Vicaría de Solidaridad archives and researchers, particularly Carmen Garretón. In Brazil, the staff at Grupo Tortura Nunca Mais provided invaluable insights.

tors often occur in frightening places such as maximum-security prisons or remote rural regions of the country. Also, in interviews, perpetrators often possess a disarming charm that troubles researchers. For example, Carol Cohn (1987, 690), writing about nuclear defense industry advocates, refers to them as "men unusually endowed with charm, humor, intelligence, concern, and decency." Journalist Tina Rosenberg (1991, 18) wrote about her encounters with killers in Latin America, "I did not want to think that many of the violent are 'people like us': so civilized, so educated, so cultured." Perpetrators' "art of seduction" can have a detrimental effect on research if scholars fail to recognize it.

Perpetrators' seduction is not necessarily sexual but rather their conscious or unconscious capacity to draw the researcher into their world (Robben 1995). Through careful selection of words and body movements, they make themselves, their views, and their past understandable and even palatable. They convince their listener to view events from their perspective—not through a transparent process of debate or argumentation but through tiny gestures of huge significance. Discussing art or opera, sharing pictures of their children or grandchildren, introducing the researcher to their families, serving coffee or a meal, inviting the researcher back to visit, even phoning for a friendly chat—all these minor intimacies form part of a process of seduction that attempts to manipulate researchers and their judgment of the perpetrators themselves, their views, and their past actions (Robben 1995). By creating a friendship, they protect themselves from harm.

As a researcher, one takes in all these efforts. Good research involves understanding the context in which certain actions make sense to the individuals involved and understanding how they explain that coherence to outsiders. By liking the perpetrators, the researcher begins to share a perspective with them; it makes sense. But warmth closes critical distance. Just as researchers who work with victims of violence find it difficult to challenge their informants' views, so, too, some researchers of perpetrators tend to produce a sanitized version of the perpetrators' past.[5]

The performative approach provides that critical distance. Unlike in other interview situations, the researcher is not the confessor, there to hear the perpetrator's confessions and analyze them. Instead, the researcher forms part of the audience, critically analyzing the impact of the perpetrator's seduction through public confessional acts. In this way, the performative approach provided new insights into social scientists as audiences of stories, susceptible to seduction through script, acting, timing, and staging.

---

5. Pumla Gobodo-Madikizela (2003) has struggled with this issue in her book *A Human Being Died That Night: A South African Story of Forgiveness.*

By adopting the performative approach, researchers also avoid being seducers themselves. Seduction does not move in one direction only; just as informants seduce researchers, researchers also seduce informants. Because researchers want interviews or responses to surveys, they tend to use body language and speech to build trust with particular informants. Many informants wrongly believe that researchers share a common perspective on politics with them. Although researchers do not necessarily lie about their political views, they also do not correct informants who interpret encouraging nods and smiles as agreement. Thus, researchers, too, develop the tiny gestures that constitute the art of seduction, albeit with different goals. They do so to convince violent people to talk to them and disclose information that they were not willing to disclose to others.

Any researcher with the stomach for it can develop this art of seduction. Few do; most scholars avoid studying perpetrators of violence. And those who do this kind of work rarely continue for long. Employing a performative approach, however, allows researchers to study violent individuals without requiring the kind of intimacy demanded by other approaches. Instead of searching for one interpretation of perpetrators, the performative study of audiences forces researchers to find multiple interpretations and situate their own interpretations within that range.

The challenges of interviewing perpetrators, while great, do not compare to the anguish of interviewing victims. Contacts within the human rights community, relatively easy to develop, produce introductions to victims and survivors. Those with a public profile do not mind meeting researchers to discuss their past. They may even find such encounters advantageous to their political goals. Researchers studying perpetrators' confessions do not require victims or survivors to retell their stories of torture or loss, since that can usually be culled from human rights reports. But victims and survivors often feel compelled to tell their stories. The stories become an identity, like a name or a résumé, which they share with outsiders. When victims and survivors expose their vulnerability, these stories create an uncomfortable intimacy between researcher and informant, threatening to retraumatize the informant and provoking an emotional response from the researcher. In these intimate moments, researchers tend to develop an emotional bond with, and a sense of responsibility toward, victims and survivors. As with perpetrators, victims and survivors may tell intimate stories to protect themselves from harm, hoping that if researchers understand their past, they will respect as legitimate whatever response occurs, no matter how violent or how passive. Because of what victims have been through, researchers may have a harder time creating a critical distance from them than from perpetrators of past violence.

These encounters are not unique to a performative approach. In varying degrees, they confront all researchers working with human subjects. They involve ethical and personal challenges and call on researchers to become more self-critical—to consider their role as researchers in the project, how that affects their interpretation of findings (whether qualitative or quantitative), and how they will write about those findings.

A final challenge, and perhaps the most serious one for future research projects like this one, results from changes within the field of political science. Because of a tendency toward narrowing the methodological creativity in the field, young scholars may find it increasingly difficult to adapt research methods to fit research questions and may feel compelled to find research questions that allow them to use the latest methodological tools. For young scholars daring to employ interpretative methods, a performative approach may provide the kind of rigor that will allow them to test important political phenomena with legitimate research tools in comparative case studies, content and discourse analysis, process tracing, and interview techniques. Performative approaches might be adapted to the analysis of public political events, from political leaders' pronouncements on international security and insecurity (e.g., Iraq) to protests against globalization and the world economy (e.g., Seattle). While the performative approach may not satisfy those interested in more mathematical formulations of political phenomena, it is nonetheless useful because it employs tools for testing hypotheses about important political questions in contemporary life.

References

Adorno, Theodor W., Else Frenkel-Brunswik, Daniel J. Levinson, and R. Nevitt Sanford, eds. 1950. *The Authoritarian Personality.* New York: Harper.

Altemeyer, Bob. 1988. *Enemies of Freedom: Understanding Right-Wing Authoritarianism.* San Francisco: Jossey-Bass.

Arendt, Hannah. 1963. *Eichmann in Jerusalem: A Report on the Banality of Evil.* New York: Penguin.

Auslander, Philip. 1999. *Liveness: Performance in a Mediatized Culture.* London: Routledge.

Badinter, Elisabeth. 1995. *XY: On Masculine Identity.* Trans. Lydia Davis. New York: Columbia University Press.

Becker, Carol. 2000. "Memory and Monstrosity." *Performance Research* 5 (3): 60–73.

Bird, Karen, John L. Sullivan, Patricia G. Avery, Kristina Thalhammer, and Sandra Wood. 1994. "Not Just Lip-Synching Anymore: Education and Tolerance Revisited." *Review of Education, Pedagogy, and Cultural Studies* 16 (3–4): 373–86.

Boal, Augusto. 1996. "The Theatre as Discourse." In *The Twentieth-Century Performance Reader,* ed. Michael Huxley and Noel Witts. New York: Routledge.

Brown, Lesley, ed. 1993. *The New Shorter Oxford English Dictionary.* Oxford, UK: Clarendon Press.

Burke, Kenneth. 1952. *A Grammar of Motives.* New York: Prentice-Hall.

Caruth, Cathy, ed. 1995. *Trauma: Explorations in Memory.* Baltimore: Johns Hopkins University Press.

Cohn, Carol. 1987. "Sex and Death in the Rational World of Defense Intellectuals." *Signs: Journal of Women in Culture and Society* 12 (4): 690.

Dorfman, Ariel. 1991. *Some Write to the Future.* Durham, N.C.: Duke University Press.

Edelman, Murray. 1988. *Constructing the Political Spectacle.* Chicago and London: University of Chicago Press.

Fair, Jo Ellen, and Lisa Parks. 2001. "Africa on Camera: Television News Coverage and Aerial Imaging of Rwandan Refugees." *Africa Today* 48 (2): 34–57.

Feldman, Martha S. 1995. *Strategies for Interpreting Qualitative Data. Qualitative Research Methods Series* 33. Thousand Oaks, Calif.: Sage.

Fuoss, Kirk. 1999. "Lynching Performances, Theatres of Violence." *Text and Performance Quarterly* 19 (1): 1–37.

George, Alexander L., and Timothy J. McKeown. 1985. "Case Studies and Theories of Organizational Decision Making." In *Advances in Information Processing in Organizations,* ed. Robert F. Coulam and Richard A. Smith, 21–58. Vol. 2. Santa Barbara, Calif.: JAI Press.

Gobodo-Madikizela, Pumla. 2003. *A Human Being Died That Night: A South African Story of Forgiveness.* Boston: Houghton Mifflin.

Goffman, Erving. 1959. *The Presentation of Self in Everyday Life.* New York: Anchor.

Goleman, Daniel. 1985. *Vital Lies, Simple Truths: On the Psychology of Self-Deception.* New York: Simon and Schuster.

Huggins, Martha K., Mika Haritos-Fatouros, and Philip G. Zimbardo. 2002. *Violence Workers: Police Torturers and Murderers Reconstruct Brazilian Atrocities.* Berkeley: University of California Press.

Levi, Primo. 1989. *The Drowned and the Saved.* Trans. Raymond Rosenthal. New York: Vintage International.

Lifton, Robert Jay. 1986. *The Nazi Doctors: Medical Killing and the Psychology of Genocide.* New York: Basic Books.

Lincoln, Bruce. 1994. *Authority: Construction and Corrosion.* Chicago: University of Chicago Press.

Messinger, Sheldon L., Harold Sampson, and Robert D. Towne. 1962. "Life as Theater: Some Notes on the Dramaturgical Approach to Social Reality." *Sociometry* 25 (1): 98–110.

Milgram, Stanley. 1974. *Obedience to Authority: An Experimental View.* New York: Harper and Row.

Ndebele, Njabulo. 1998. "Memory, Metaphor, and the Triumph of Narrative." In *Negotiating the Past: The Making of Memory in South Africa,* ed. Sarah Nuttall and Carli Coetzee. Cape Town: Oxford University Press.

Onions, C. T., ed. 1992. *Oxford Dictionary of English Etymology.* Oxford, UK: Clarendon Press.

Palmer, Richard. 1977. "Toward a Postmodern Hermeneutics of Performance." In *Performance in Postmodern Culture,* ed. Michel Benamou and Charles Caramello. Madison, Wis.: Coda Press.

Patraka, Vivian M. 1996. "Spectacles of Suffering: Performing Presence, Absence, and Historical Memory at U.S. Holocaust Museums." In *Performance and Cultural Politics,* ed. Elin Diamond. London and New York: Routledge.

Payne, Leigh A. 2008. *Unsettling Accounts: Neither Truth nor Reconciliation in Confessions of State Violence.* Durham, N.C., and London: Duke University Press.

Popkin, Margaret, and Naomi Roht-Arriaza. 1995. "Truth as Justice: Investigatory Commissions in Latin America." *Law and Social Inquiry* 20 (1): 79–116.

Robben, Antonius C. G. M. 1995. "The Politics of Truth and Emotion among Victims and Perpetrators of Violence." In *Fieldwork under Fire: Contemporary Studies of Violence and Survival,* ed. Carolyn Nordstrom and Antonius C. G. M. Robben. Berkeley: University of California Press.

Rosenberg, Tina. 1991. *Children of Cain: Violence and the Violent in Latin America.* New York: William Morrow.

Taylor, Diana. 1994. "Performing Gender: Las Madres de la Plaza de Mayo." In *Negotiating Performance: Gender, Sexuality, and Theatricality in Latin America,* ed. Diana Taylor and Juan Villegas. Durham, N.C., and London: Duke University Press.

Taylor, Jane. 1998. *Ubu and the Truth Commission.* Cape Town: University of Cape Town Press.

Turner, Victor. 1982. *From Ritual to Theatre: The Human Seriousness of Play.* New York: Performing Arts Journal.

Zimbardo, Philip G., Craig Haney, W. Curtis Banks, and David Jaffe. 1973. "The Mind Is a Formidable Jailer: A Pirandellian Prison." *New York Times* magazine, April 8.

9

Truth and Transitional Justice in South Africa

Janet Cherry

This chapter attempts to clarify what is meant by "truth" in the context of transitional justice and explores some ideas on how to assess whether particular processes have provided truth. It focuses on the experience of the South African Truth and Reconciliation Commission (TRC), on which the author served as a staff member. The first part deals with some conceptual issues as seen through the TRC prism. The second part reflects on how other researchers do research on transitional justice mechanisms. The third section discusses research on the extent to which various transitional justice mechanisms have found "the truth."

Truth in the Context of Transitional Justice: Some Conceptual Issues

To begin with, perhaps we should ask the question, Is there a perceived need, in a particular context, for a truth-seeking process, for truth telling, for revealing what has been hidden? In the case of the South African TRC and many of the Latin American transitional justice mechanisms, there is no doubt that the public desire for truth was strong, particularly in certain unresolved cases of disappearances. In South Africa's Eastern Cape province, for example, there were many unexplained disappearances in the 1980s. The public desire for truth finding resulted in the TRC's public hearing venue in Port Elizabeth being packed with youths, who nearly broke into a riot when former security police brought an interdict preventing the TRC from hearing the case around the disappearance of Siphiwo Mtimkulu.

The story surrounding Mtimkulu's disappearance illustrates many of the truth-finding dilemmas of the South African TRC. Mtimkulu, a student activist from Port Elizabeth, was severely tortured and poisoned with thallium while in police custody in 1982. On his release, having been diagnosed with thallium poisoning, which he was lucky to survive, he brought interdicts against the minister of law and order for both torture and poisoning. Shortly after bringing the interdicts, he disappeared. From 1982 until 1997 the security police denied involvement in his disappearance. At the beginning of the TRC process, the security police brought interdicts to prevent the TRC from hearing evidence about the disappearance at its human rights violations hearings in East London and Port Elizabeth: hence the extreme anger expressed by members of the community. However, a chain of events during the investigative and amnesty processes of the TRC led a group of Port Elizabeth security policemen to apply for amnesty for a number of disappearances and murders, including that of Mtimkulu. Finally, it seemed that the TRC process would expose the truth. Even so, while the security police revealed during the amnesty hearings how they had abducted and killed Mtimkulu, they continued to deny their responsibility for his torture and poisoning, claiming that his underground activities were the motive for their decision to "eliminate" him. Thus, while the amnesty process revealed the manner of his death and the identities of those responsible, the motive for his disappearance remained unclear. The perpetrators were all granted amnesty on the grounds that (1) they had applied for amnesty for his abduction and murder, (2) they had made full disclosure of these acts, and (3) their motives for the acts were accepted as "political."

Because there was no acknowledgment of the torture and poisoning, Mtimkulu's family found it difficult to accept the word of the security policemen who applied for amnesty. In one dramatic outcome of the TRC process, one of the security policemen responsible, Col. Gideon Nieuwoudt, met with Mtimkulu's family to reconcile with them. But because he continued to deny the torture and poisoning of their son, they could not accept his apology, and Mtimkulu's son responded to the situation with an explosion of anger that left the former torturer with a fractured skull.

Such a desire for the truth to be revealed is not always present, however. Especially in localized conflicts, where people in a close-knit community have had to learn to live together again, the truth may be seen as divisive and threatening. Thus, there may be resistance to a process that attempts, many years after painful events have occurred, to unravel the details, take skeletons out of closets, and assign blame.

Second, is there real willingness and readiness, especially on the part of perpetrators of human rights violations, to speak the truth? Is the political moment there—the context in which various parties to the conflict are willing and able to speak out or can be coerced to speak out? Whether that context exists depends, of course, on the nature and outcome of the transition and on what happened to the perpetrators from the old regime.

In Belfast in 2001, I understood why the main protagonists in the conflict were not ready to speak out openly: The moment for them to do so was not yet "there." That is also why, in the Eastern Cape, those who killed Siphiwo Mtimkulu were not prepared to make a full disclosure of the truth—and why, therefore, Mtimkulu's relatives were unable to offer forgiveness. It also provides insight into why one of them felt compelled to smash a vase over the head of the security policeman who came to ask for forgiveness, fracturing his skull and making him, in turn, a victim. The emotional intensity of such cases made the South African TRC a fascinating experience, but for those of us who had lived through some of the events under scrutiny, it was much more: a profound experience of hope and then despair as the truth was almost revealed, only to be snatched from our grasp.

The answers to these key questions—whether there is a hunger for the truth and whether there is a willingness to tell the truth—will determine the broad parameters for what sort of truth can emerge in a particular context. Also, it is important to recognize that although all "truth commissions" have, at least by definition, the objective of finding the truth, this is not the case with all transitional justice mechanisms. Other mechanisms, such as war tribunals, may result in certain truths coming to light, but this is not their primary objective; mechanisms that have as their primary objective either the pursuit of justice or the granting of amnesty often have an ambiguous relationship with the search for truth.

Another important question is, What kind of truth is being sought? In its 1998 report, the South African TRC (1998, vol. 1, 110) outlined the four notions of truth used in its work: factual, or forensic, truth; personal, or narrative, truth; social, or "dialogue," truth; and healing and restorative truth. Anthea Jeffery (1999, 11) has rejected outright the TRC's use of the three "nonfactual" notions of truth. She criticizes the TRC for using these other notions of truth to "buttress its conclusions" and justify its "fudging" of its inability to find the real truth, because "it did not have sufficient 'factual' truth at its disposal at the time it wrote its report." Thus, categorizing the truth into four discrete types may not be the most useful approach. Yet, most analysts of truth commissions have, in one way or another, distinguished between "factual" truth, that is, truth based on empirically sound research, and explanatory truth. The consensus seems to be that while factual truth may be more or less flawed in particular processes, it is an essential part of the work of any truth and reconciliation process. (The debate surrounding whether databases are useful in generating empirically verifiable statistics about trends and causality is another matter, dealt with below.) Explanatory truth, on the other hand, is seen as an elusive form of truth, even for the best-resourced transitional justice mechanism.

Chapman and Ball have argued that while analysts of truth commissions may portray truth as "a single objective reality waiting to be discovered or found," in reality, "the documentation and interpretation of truth is more complex and ambiguous than many analysts and proponents of truth commissions assume," and in some cases it may require that the commission refute popular understandings through conducting "deep research" (Chapman and Ball 2001, 4). They are undoubtedly correct in this assumption. The methodological problems experienced by researchers for the TRC testify to the complexity and ambiguity of documenting and interpreting the truth.

Perhaps the most frustrating—and sometimes heartbreaking—aspect of working for the commission was the inability to complete research and investigation into a number of areas. Deborah Posel, a social historian, notes that there were high expectations that the commission would "find the truth" and explain in detail what had happened in particular communities: "People saw the TRC as an opportunity to piece together a comprehensive and detailed account of turbulent and divisive episodes in their histories, to clarify exactly who had been responsible for past traumas, how and why these had been inflicted, and to dispel any lingering doubts about who had or had not been an informer" (Posel 2002, 151). However, she argues, these expectations were not met, because the TRC, in the interests of nation building, was pulled in the direction of finding a "consensual truth" rather than a complex and divisive truth: "If the idea of individual interpersonal and communal catharsis validated the impulse towards completeness, the version of reconciliation as a national rupture with a divisive past pulled in a different direction" (Posel 2002, 151). She went on to criticize the TRC report's four notions of truth as a "very wobbly, poorly constructed conceptual grid" (Posel 2002, 155).

Cherry (1999, 2000) points up the need to develop complex, detailed particular histories. These papers explore some of the ambiguities and unresolved discrepancies of particular cases to come before the TRC. Although I am broadly in agreement with Posel, her assumption that "people" wanted the TRC to uncover the "real truth" of the past is not necessarily valid. Although in instances such as the disappearance of Siphiwo Mtimkulu this was undoubtedly the case, in many other cases the local communities preferred to hold on to their own myths about what happened rather than have possibly unpleasant truths revealed—particularly those truths relating to collaboration and divisions within communities. And, of course, different people have different expectations of truth-finding processes. The expectations of victims of human rights violations are not necessarily the same as the expectations of the communities where they live, nor are they likely to be the same as those of academic observers or historians.

Lars Buur (2001, 2002 69), in an interesting critique based on his observation of the "invisible everyday practices" of the TRC, comes to a similar conclusion. Contrasting the notions of "global truth" and "local truth," he argues that truth commissions have mainly focused on the former. He adds that the "material for the new national history was . . . cleaned of ambiguities" through the complex and contested process of statement taking, data capturing and analysis, and corroboration. He gives an illuminating example of how "lowly" TRC officials (in contrast with those empowered to make decisions, such as commissioners and committee members) influenced whether a statement was deemed a "gross human rights violation" rather than being dismissed as "out of mandate" (Buur 2001, 164–67). According to Buur, the TRC worked within a framework of a "scientific positivistic ideal," which was bound to create clear categories for quantitative analysis within the database. Although such "bureaucratically constructed truth necessitates . . . unequivocal categories so that entitlements in the form of reparation can be distributed," there is a countervailing tendency toward ambiguity and instability, which, Buur argues, had to be "contained, regulated, and neutralized" by the commission (Buur 2001, 172).

Thus, historians, sociologists, anthropologists, and even some political scientists within the TRC research department felt compelled to research particular cases or contexts in greater depth, not only to record the past but to make sense of it, to offer to those victim communities not just a recapitulation of their own words of suffering but an explanation of why and how such terrible events came about. In this effort, they were often left frustrated. In certain cases researchers did begin such detailed analytical writing, but very little of it ended up in the final report, which was constructed as a rather bland narrative illustrated by selected "window cases." The window cases often contained the best and most revealing details, although, as Posel notes, they were selected to represent and illustrate the TRC's general themes or findings rather than its ambiguities and complexities.

Finally, it should be reiterated that even in situations where the commission succeeds in "finding the truth," this new truth may not be accepted by the local community to which it refers. A further example serves to illustrate the disparity that Buur points out between the local context and the need to create a "global narrative," as well as Chapman's point about the need for deep research that challenges accepted truths. In some circumstances, communities may cling to "truths" about events that happened, even if the transitional justice process exposes those "truths" as myths. Such was the case in Langa, a black residential area in the Eastern Cape, where, in 1997, the TRC held a hearing into the Langa massacre of March 21, 1985. On that day, police had opened fire on a crowd of mourners marching to a funeral, killing twenty people. At the TRC hearing, some of the witnesses repeated the claim that a baby had been killed by the police on that day. Despite extensive calls for someone to "own" the dead baby, no one came forward to the TRC, and it seemed probable, on analysis of other evidence, that the dead baby seen in the mortuary had died of natural causes before the shooting. The TRC commissioners came to the conclusion that there was no evidence that a baby had been killed in this incident. Despite this establishment of a "global truth" in this matter, the local mythology of the "killed" baby will remain in the public consciousness of that community.

Ignatieff (1999, 171) argues that at the very least, truth consists of "factual truth and moral truth, of narratives that tell what happened and narratives that attempt to explain why it happened and who is responsible." He further argues that the Latin American truth commissions have been more or less successful in establishing the first—the factual—truth. However, when it comes to the generation of a "moral narrative—explaining the genesis of evil regimes and apportioning moral responsibility for the deeds committed under those governments"—the Latin American commissions were "infinitely less successful." This is similar to the criticisms by Posel and others of the South African TRC: that it failed to provide an explanation of events, that it was methodologically weak when it came to issues of historical causality. These methodological weaknesses are undoubtedly linked to the way that truth commissions conduct research, which is explored further below. Yet, despite the validity of such criticisms, these weaknesses do not undermine the overall project of such truth commissions. While weak on causality and specificity, if such commissions succeed in "narrowing the range of permissible lies" (Ignatieff, cited in Hayner 2001, 25), making future denial impossible, this alone is important enough to motivate and justify truth-finding processes.

After this cursory look at the conceptual clarification of truth in transitional justice mechanisms, the next concern is how the truth is derived—in other words, methodological issues. In research methodology, there are two distinct questions to explore: First, which research methods are effective in finding the truth? Second, which research methods are useful in evaluating how effective transitional justice processes were in getting at the truth?

Truth-Seeking Processes in Transitional Justice Mechanisms

The tensions within the South African TRC around the methodologies employed in finding "the truth" reflect a broader debate surrounding methodological eclecticism and a seemingly irresolvable tension between empirical truth and interpretative, explanatory, or moral truth. In the TRC this was reflected in the tension, on one hand, between historians, social scientists, and lawyers and, on the other, between social historians and those social scientists whose more empirical approach emphasized the construction of an accurate database.[1]

---

1.   Other members of the South African TRC Research Department and I have argued elsewhere about the methodological and organizational difficulties of finding "the truth" through the South African TRC process and the partial nature of the truth that emerged in specific cases. (See Cherry, Daniel, and Fullard 2002.)

The South African TRC's report, as one outcome of the TRC process, reflects this tension between the "historical analysis" approach and the empirical, or case study, approach. This tension is observed and developed by both Deborah Posel (2002) and Andre du Toit (1999). Both have argued that because the report was built around "window cases" and human rights violations (HRV) findings, its very structure led to the omission of analysis. This reflected a tension between the methodologies of historian and lawyer. It can be argued that this resulted in neither approach being followed through to its logical conclusion. The lawyers, or those social scientists who would adopt a more positivist methodology, argue that the TRC did not "test the evidence" sufficiently, and did not make findings on the basis of sufficient evidence, and did not do sufficient empirical research or make adequate use of existing statistics. On the other hand, the historians argue that the complexity and specificity of particular acts and the texture of particular contexts and moral debates were lost through the imperative of "making findings" that had to be quasi-legal.

Posel (2002, 160) notes that the rich local histories (many of which were researched but not incorporated into the final report, relegated instead to the archives) were "marginalized by the energy and effort which went into the quantitative research exercise." Many who worked on the TRC feel that this is true; whereas only a handful of researchers (with academic background and research experience) battled to do substantial qualitative research, the commission employed legions of data capturers, data analysts, and statement corroborators. The database was then meant to generate substantial quantitative and qualitative analysis, but the process was so flawed that it ultimately could not be used to full effect.

In reflecting on this very real tension between qualitative and quantitative agendas, it is worth noting that the TRC research team consisted primarily of individuals from academic backgrounds, usually in history, sociology, politics, or philosophy. Coming from such disciplines, they were inclined more toward the historical analysis approach rather than the quasi-legal or psychological "case study" approach. These two approaches were usually complementary, and the research department generally had a very good internal working relationship, with considerable interdisciplinary teamwork and the building of partnerships on certain topics or themes. However, the researchers were generally not social workers or lawyers. Their not being social workers meant that the researchers had almost no involvement in the recommendations on reparations or in the work of that particular subcommittee of the commission. And by not being lawyers, the researchers were concerned more with "telling history from below" than with building watertight legal cases, whether for victims or for perpetrators.

As du Toit (1999) noted, there was a shift within the TRC from "a narratively framed victim-oriented conception of the TRC process to a perpetrator-focused quasi-legal approach." Much of the research unit's work was done within the former conceptual framework: detailed background research for HRV hearings, historical research on the themes identified, and so on. However, by the time the final report was written, the emphasis had shifted to the latter conception. What became important were the findings that the commissioners had to make; in fact, the whole report was restructured to reflect this changed conception. Partly because of this changing emphasis and partly because of editorial constraints (a certain number of volumes and pages had been agreed on in advance), much of the continuity and analytical coherence of the research work was lost.

The relationship of the research unit to the legal aspect of the commission was complicated. On one hand, it was the investigation unit's job to corroborate each HRV statement and, where necessary, conduct further investigations. The researchers were simply to use the information in the database, analyzing it to identify trends and patterns in human rights violations. They could then incorporate such analysis in writing up the regional profiles and the sections of the report dealing with the various categories of human rights violations. But in practice, things were not so simple. Members of the research team were sometimes drawn into investigating particular cases or types of case, in some instances even doing basic corroboration work when the capacity did not exist in the regional offices. At other times the investigation unit did not share information fully with the research unit members—conducting investigations but not feeding the results to the relevant person in the research unit. Moreover, as illustrated below in the discussion of the database, there were extensive problems with the quality of the statements taken, with the way they were captured and corroborated, and, therefore, with the use of the database for analysis. Meanwhile, the HRV Committee had to make quasi-legal findings on each of the twenty thousand statements received.

Jeffery is substantially correct in much of her criticism of the TRC over this process. There was not a rigorous process of "testing the evidence," and the level of corroboration—even "low-level corroboration"—was indeed too low. However, the TRC did make clear that it was basing its findings on the "balance of probability" rather than beyond reasonable doubt—after all, in the case of HRV statements, it was merely finding in favor (or not) of an alleged victim rather than, as in a criminal court, proving (or failing to prove) the guilt of an alleged perpetrator of a crime. Thus, the burden on the commission to prove every statement absolutely true was less than Jeffery supposes.

The debate over the methodologies of history overlaps to a great extent with the debate over the methodology of constructing "truth" about the past, as distinct from the forensic truth sought in a court of law. Most historians have no means of establishing forensic truth; they cannot cross-examine witnesses of events or perpetrators of actions. Yet through drawing on a multiplicity of sources—including a number of oral testimonies from participants or witnesses if the history being created is in living memory—together with other archival and secondary sources, historians can corroborate information to construct, with a high degree of certainty and accuracy, what actually happened. Without going into detail on debates on the methodology of history, the point can be made that commissions such as the South African TRC do use precisely this somewhat eclectic "historians' methodology"—multiple sources of different kinds—in constructing of the truth. Such a methodology goes beyond both the forensic evidence in which a court of law relies and the positivist truth of particular social science methodologies.

Indeed, at least potentially, some transitional justice mechanisms can go further methodologically than historians, social scientists, or lawyers, since they have the means to draw on the methodologies of each of the three. Enriched both by the oral testimony of perpetrators, victims, and other witnesses and by the usual documentary, archival, and media sources (as well as by whatever statistical information can be generated from a powerful database on human rights violations), truth commissions have a methodological advantage—if they use it well.

But it is not easy to find the balance between forensic and narrative truth, between qualitative and quantitative research, between the global and the local, between the factual and the explanatory. Thus, whereas Posel criticizes the TRC for not being historical enough, Jeffery criticizes it for not being empirical enough.

Buur (2000) has argued that many truth-finding transitional justice processes are based in an essentially modern and liberal notion of truth as something that is empirically verifiable. Moreover, he argues, most academic analysts of transitional justice mechanisms are themselves uncritical of this notion of empirical truth. Critics of such commissions focus on the visible or legible outcomes and ignore the process by which such commissions generate "truth." In so doing, they treat as unproblematic the power relations inherent in such processes. Buur notes that since the 1999 Witwatersrand History Workshop conference, such processes have received more attention, and he emphasizes that this not only is an "outsider" view of such processes but is now retrospective. While this is probably true, it is surely a reflection of the dynamic nature of social scientific inquiry: how social reality generates intellectual reflection, which feeds back into such processes of constructing history and truth and generates further reflection. Thus, Buur is all too aware of the self-reflective nature of the intellectuals who worked within transitional justice processes. As noted above, those who made up the South African TRC's research department were from different disciplines within the social sciences and humanities—historians, philosophers, theologians, sociologists, anthropologists—yet all were fully aware of the interface between theory and practice, that is, of the methodologies being employed, even though they did not have full control over these.

Finding "bigger strategic truths" about what happened—constructing "explanatory truth" and exploring issues of causality—is what proved extremely difficult for the TRC. Clearly, some people hoped that the TRC would come up with definitive answers on questions such as who was responsible for the political violence of the early 1990s and whether there was a strategically directed "third force" behind the Inkatha Freedom Party (IFP). But it could not, and perhaps we simply have to accept that there is no hidden "answer," such as a conspiracy waiting to be revealed, and that such wars or conflicts are inherently "messy." All the most empirically thorough political scientists in the world would not be able to unravel the chain of cause and effect, the deliberately vague commands at the top, the local dynamics at the grassroots, and the interactions between them. And as often happens in such complex and protracted sequences of human rights violations, there is not likely to be consensus about either the details of what happened or who was ultimately responsible.

Of course, the "global truth" that emerges from such processes depends not only on the willingness of perpetrators and the resolve of victim communities to speak out. This "global truth" is overdetermined by the political agendas of the protagonists in the transition process, the imperative of national reconciliation, and the aim of political stability after the transition is over. So while the perpetrator "foot soldiers" have been held to account by the amnesty process, their political masters are in many cases still sharing power in government, and truths deemed to be too divisive or uncomfortable may be sanitized or even discredited in the interests of national unity.

Evaluating the Effectiveness of Transitional Justice Processes in Finding the Truth

In addition to the aforementioned analyses, from both within and without, of the South African TRC, academics such as Priscilla Hayner have conducted comparative analyses of various truth commissions. This chapter does not attempt to look at "outsider" assessments of the methods used in transitional justice mechanisms that are forensically based—war crimes tribunals or other court proceedings that rely on the more traditional methods of evidence gathering for a court of law, wherein the accused must be proven guilty beyond reasonable doubt. The question that arises is, In trying to compare various transitional justice mechanisms and assess their effectiveness in finding the truth, how does one measure this effectiveness?

The researcher can adopt Jeffery's approach and construct an argument on the basis of comparative statistical data (for example, by asking how many people were killed by the IFP and the African National Congress [ANC] respectively)[2]; how many such cases went uninvestigated by the TRC; what percentage of those who disappeared or did not return from exile were accounted for by the TRC). Good databases are invaluable in generating such statistics and enabling comparison between different transitional justice mechanisms. Of course, the "outsider" must rely on the integrity and comprehensiveness of the particular transitional justice mechanism's databases or else look to the creation of independent international databases for corroboration.

Alternatively, the researcher can adopt a method of evaluation that looks at particular actions or cases of human rights violations and assesses how effectively the transitional justice mechanism ascertained the truth in that particular case. The assumption here is that each case is complex and that empirical generalizations are not very useful in establishing truth. On a case-by-case basis, we can argue whether one or another transitional justice mechanism is more or less effective in establishing the truth. In the South African case, it has been argued that the "amnesty conditional upon full disclosure" mechanism was more effective in obtaining truth than a court of law would have been. In many of the more prominent cases that were unresolved before going to the TRC, this is clearly a valid argument: Cases such as the disappearance of Siphiwo Mtimkulu would simply not have been resolved through a court of law, as there was no forensic evidence with which to bring a case against the perpetrators. Even if criminal charges had been brought, as in the cases of Magnus Malan, Winnie Mandela, or Wouter Basson,[3] it was in the interests of those charged to deny as much as possible, since the onus was on the criminal justice process to find sufficient evidence against them to sustain a conviction—something it was unable to do in these cases. It was only through the amnesty process that the perpetrators were offered an incentive to come forward and disclose the truth. Thus, it can be argued that the "amnesty conditional upon disclosure" model was conducive to establishing the truth. This is the position taken by the TRC in its 1998 report: Despite the incompleteness of the evidence in many cases, "as many commentators have noted, trials would probably have contributed far less

---

2. Many thousands of those who died in political violence in South Africa were killed not by the state security forces but in the conflict between these two parties/movements.

3. High-profile criminal trials of former minister of defense Malan and military doctor Basson were unsuccessful. While former president Nelson Mandela's wife, Winnie Madikizela Mandela, was implicated by the TRC in the murders of at least seven people, she was convicted only on a charge of kidnapping and retained her position of political influence. She agreed to testify at a special hearing of the TRC but declined to apply for amnesty and denied her involvement in any of the murders.

than did the amnesty process towards revealing the truth about what had happened to many victims and their loved ones" (South African TRC 1998, vol. 1, 121).

One of the problems with this model of finding truth through amnesty applications is that not only is the truth, as told by perpetrators of human rights violations, usually a partial and mediated truth, but it is limited by who decided to apply for amnesty. In the case of the South African TRC, many thousands of perpetrators —notably, members of the police involved in "public order policing" and members of the South African Defence Force— did not apply for amnesty. Moreover, there were relatively few amnesty applications regarding human rights violations in the crucial period of escalating violence of 1990–1994. Thus, no analysis of amnesty applications can claim to provide a comprehensive "truth" about the perpetration of human rights violations.[4]

Comparative studies of different mechanisms, such as Hayner's definitive study, can usefully assess the extent to which each type of mechanism allows the truth to emerge. But these studies should also consider those societies where such mechanisms have not been put into place. For example, in Namibia, where seven hundred missing South West Africa People's Organization (SWAPO) detainees are still unaccounted for, the ruling SWAPO has adopted a position of what John Saul (2000, 3) terms "reconciliation through studied silence." And in Uganda, a report on human rights violations by the regimes of Obote and Museveni (between 1966 and 1999) was locked away and remained inaccessible to the public until a civil society forum published it on a Web site in January 2005. To date it has not been officially released.

Of course, where the victims or perpetrators are still alive and accessible, one of the most fruitful methods of research is to work with individuals from either group through interviews, focus groups, or other "live" methods of research. After an amnesty process, for example, the researcher can scrutinize the testimony of the perpetrators and, if possible, go back to the perpetrators themselves to corroborate evidence or explore motives. While the transitional justice mechanism is in process, the extent to which the truth is revealed by perpetrators depends, of course, on the incentives or disincentives that exist for them to reveal the truth; as explained above, even where amnesty was conditional on a full disclosure (as in the South African TRC process), the perpetrators or amnesty applicants were selective in what they chose to reveal about particular incidents. Even where the facts revealed were consistent, the motives of perpetrators were often unclear or deliberately misrepresented. Now, if the amnesty decision can be appealed—for

---

4. See criticisms of the South African TRC process by Adrian Guelke (2000) and Piers Pigou (2002).

example, in a case where amnesty was denied on the grounds of lack of full disclosure—then the perpetrators are likely to continue to obscure the truth until the legal channels have been explored. On the other hand, if the legal process is definitely over, such in-depth personal research with perpetrators may be more fruitful in revealing the truth than the commission has been, since there is no longer a legal threat influencing what they can say. Leigh Payne's (1999, 2000) research on the confessions of torturers and collaborators, using "comparative historical, discursive, performative, collaborative and interview methods" (Payne 2001, 8), is one example of how this exploration of perpetrators' motives can be taken further in the search for the truth arising from transitional justice mechanisms.

There is perhaps an even more compelling need for similar research to be done with victims after the transitional justice mechanism has completed its work. As we know from the South African experience, victims of human rights violations often feel let down, even abused, by the transitional justice mechanism that was meant to help them reach closure or even reconcile with their perpetrators. The psychological and emotional impact of truth commissions will not be explored here. It is an important area of study, but the concern here is specifically how victims relate to the "truth" aspect of such processes—victims' responses to the TRC's "truth" about particular matters vary widely, an issue examined in Sonis's chapter in this volume. This variation is not primarily a function of race, gender, age, or political identity but rather of the complexity and acceptability of the truth that was revealed.

For example, where people disappeared in exile—and there were hundreds of such cases—the TRC in many cases could not ascertain what happened to them. They were declared victims, but the families gained no further information or clarity about their fate or the whereabouts of their remains. In such cases, where closure remains impossible because of lack of information, the monetary compensation for families of victims is cold comfort. Where the truth was contested, the families of the victims were often unable to reach a clear understanding of what happened to their loved ones, and even where they would rather believe one version over another, it was often hard for them to accept that truth. In other cases, the truth was obviously being denied, as in the case of Siphiwo Mtimkulu, where the TRC accepted the forensic truth about Mtimkulu's abduction and killing, as told by the perpetrators, and granted them amnesty. However, their motives, which were linked to the earlier torture and poisoning of Mtimkulu, were not clarified and contributed to the extreme anger experienced by the family. The truth, it seemed, was about to be revealed, and then that part of the truth that had meaning for the families of the victims was denied.

Clearly, there is room for research with victims and perpetrators after the transitional justice mechanism has completed its work, though whether this will lead to a greater clarification of the truth probably depends on the particular circumstances.

In assessing the impact of transitional justice mechanisms at a community or society level, a range of research methods can be used. In individual cases, the South African TRC arrived at a more or less factually accurate "truth"; in community-based conflicts, however, it was far more difficult to reach even a minimal consensus about what happened, let alone about who was to blame. In the case of conflict in a small localized area between the ANC's self-defense units and the IFP's self-protection units, for example, the community may not have the same need to know or explore the messy truth of what happened and why. It is not interested in causality and fact in the same way that the family of a disappeared person such as Mtimkulu wishes to know what happened and why. As Guelke (2000) and others have argued, the difficulties of ascertaining the truth in such localized conflicts constitute one of the reasons why the TRC has been judged to have failed in its attempt to make sense of the extreme political violence of the transitional period of the early 1990s. There is little doubt that methodologies that involve working with groups within such communities can be effective in bringing about healing and reconciliation—and, in the process, may reveal some hidden truths or some explanation for what happened. However, it is advisable to tread with extreme caution in trying to dig up the truth in communities where people would prefer to leave well enough alone.

Researchers can also use quantitative methods to assess the effectiveness of such transitional justice mechanisms as public opinion surveys. Such methods are not particularly effective in discovering whether the particular mechanism has attained its objectives in uncovering or presenting the truth. They may, however, offer an accurate reflection of whether the society, or particular interest groups or identities within the society, accepts the "new truth" that has been brought forward by the transitional justice mechanism— in itself a potentially useful exercise.

Finally, what of the results of such processes in disseminating the final "truth" to the society and achieving consensus about "what really happened"? A thought-provoking question is, To what extent did the TRC process lead to the creation of a consensus about a new history of South Africa? At one level, the uncovering of even partial truths about past wrongs means that such wrongs will be harder to deny in the future. This is captured in Michael Ignatieff's (1999, 173) oft-quoted cynical statement that "all that a truth commission can achieve is to reduce the number of lies that circulate unchallenged." But the importance of this role of transitional justice mechanisms should not be underestimated. At another level, the researcher can try to measure consensus about "the truth" in a particular society through using the methodologies of social science. Thus, James Gibson (in this volume) argues that rigorous survey methods can be used to test empirically what people believe about their past, to ascertain whether a truth commission has been successful in creating a "collective memory."

Conclusion

Ultimately, all our methodologies can enable us to find or know only part of the truth, and only imperfectly. Whether we use them singly or in eclectic combination, the best we can hope for is an approximation of the truth. And the methodologies used in assessing the extent to which the truth has been found are likewise imperfect. But this does not diminish the importance of the search for the truth—both for those involved in transitional justice mechanisms and for those outside the mechanisms, who must play the important role of evaluating them.

References

Buur, Lars. 2000. "Institutionalising Truth: Victims, Perpetrators and Professionals in the Everyday Work of the South African Truth and Reconciliation Commission." PhD diss., Aarhus University, Denmark.

———. 2001. "Processes of Nation-State Formation: The South African Truth and Reconciliation Commission and the Practices Constituting the Modern Nation-State." In *States of Imagination*, ed. Thomas Blom Hansen and Finn Stepputat. Durham, N.C.: Duke University Press.

———. 2002. "Monumental Historical Memory: Managing Truth in the Everyday Work of the South African TRC." In *Commissioning the Past: Understanding South Africa's Truth and Reconciliation Commission*, ed. Deborah Posel and Graeme Simpson. Johannesburg: Witwatersrand University Press.

Chapman, Audrey, and Patrick Ball. 2001. "The Truth of Truth Commissions: Comparative Lessons from South Africa, Haiti and Guatemala." *Human Rights Quarterly* 23 (1): 1–43.

Cherry, Janet. 1999. "No Easy Road to Truth: The TRC in the Eastern Cape." Paper presented at "The TRC: Commissioning the Past" conference held at University of the Witwatersrand, Johannesburg, June.

———. 2000. "Historical Truth: Something to Fight For." In *Looking Back, Reaching Forward: Reflections on the Truth and Reconciliation Commission of South Africa*, ed. Charles Villa-Vicencio and Wilhelm Verwoerd. Cape Town: University of Cape Town Press.

Cherry, Janet, John Daniel, and Madeleine Fullard. 2002. "Researching the Truth: A View from Inside the Truth and Reconciliation Commission." In *Commissioning the Past: Understanding South Africa's Truth and Reconciliation Commission*, ed. Deborah Posel and Graeme Simpson. Johannesburg: Witwatersrand University Press.

Du Toit, Andre. 1999. "The Product and the Process: On the Impact of the TRC Report." Paper presented at "The TRC: Commissioning the Past" conference held at University of the Witwatersrand, Johannesburg, June 11–14.

Guelke, Adrian. 2000. "Interpretations of Political Violence during South Africa's Transition." *Politikon* 27 (2).

Hayner, Priscilla. 2001. *Unspeakable Truths: Confronting State Terror and Atrocity.* New York and London: Routledge.

Ignatieff, Michael. 1999. *The Warrior's Honour: Ethnic War and the Modern Conscience.* London: Vintage.

Jeffery, Anthea. 1999. *The Truth about the Truth Commission.* Johannesburg: South African Institute of Race Relations.

Payne, Leigh. 2003. "Perpetrators' Confessions: Truth, Reconciliation and Justice in Argentina." In *What Justice? Whose Justice? Fighting for Fairness in Latin America,* ed. Susan Eckstein and Timothy Wickham-Crowley. Berkeley and Los Angeles: University of California Press.

————. 2000. "Collaborators and the Politics of Memory in Chile." *Human Rights Review* 2 (3).

————. 2001. "Unsettling Accounts: Reconciling Violence in Post-authoritarian Societies." Proposal to John D. and Catherine T. MacArthur Foundation.

Pigou, Piers. 2002. "False Promises and Wasted Opportunities? Inside South Africa's Truth and Reconciliation Commission." In *Commissioning the Past: Understanding South Africa's Truth and Reconciliation Commission,* ed. Deborah Posel and Graeme Simpson. Johannesburg: Witwatersrand University Press.

Posel, Deborah. 2002. "The TRC Report: What Kind of History? What Kind of Truth?" In *Commissioning the Past: Understanding South Africa's Truth and Reconciliation Commission,* ed. Deborah Posel and Graeme Simpson. Johannesburg: Witwatersrand University Press.

Saul, John. 2000. "Lubango and After: 'Forgotten History' as Politics in Contemporary Namibia." Draft paper for presentation to "Public History, Forgotten History" workshop, University of Namibia, Windhoek, August 22–25.

South African TRC. 1998. *Truth and Reconciliation Commission of South Africa Report.* Vol. 1. Cape Town: Juta.

10

Too Deep, Too Threatening

Understandings of Reconciliation in Northern Ireland

Brandon Hamber and Gráinne Kelly

This chapter summarizes some of the key results of a study, conducted in 2003, that aimed to examine the understanding and implementation of reconciliation, politically and at the grassroots level, in different areas of Northern Ireland.[1] The research examined the roles played by the community and voluntary sector, as the non-governmental sector is known locally, in facilitating community reconciliation and their engagement with local government structures. The study explored a range of issues, including views and opinions on reconciliation; relevant policies, practices, and structures; relationships between and within sectors; and who should ultimately be held responsible for facilitating reconciliation. This chapter will begin by exploring the history of the concept of reconciliation in Northern Ireland, specifically the historical use of the term, how it has been used in relation to funding, and, finally, how it has been used by politicians and civil society. Following this, the methodology of the study is outlined, including definitions of reconciliation according to research participants. The chapter finishes by exploring the study's findings and outlining some key conclusions and their relevance in the current Northern Ireland context.

Introduction

In January 2003, the authors embarked on a research project on "community reconciliation" in Northern Ireland.[2] They were motivated in part by the absence of any agreed-on definition of the term "reconciliation" in the

---

1. This chapter is in large part an abridged version of a larger research report. (See Hamber and Kelly 2005).

2. This research, done under the auspices of Democratic Dialogue, was titled "Community Reconciliation: Realising Opportunities, Meeting Challenges and Ensuring New Innovation into the Future." It was funded by the EU Programme for Peace and Reconciliation under Measure 2.1 (Reconciliation for Sustainable Peace), administered by the CRC.

region, despite its increasingly common usage. The research examined the roles that the community and voluntary sector play in facilitating community reconciliation, its relationship to district councils, and the degree to which local authorities create an atmosphere conducive to such work. The objective was to help create effective partnerships and mutual understanding between sectors, clarify what "reconciliation" means, and help make that practice more sustainable.

We chose three local authorities as case studies: Armagh City and District Council, Omagh District Council, and Ballymena Borough Council. A semi-structured interview process formed the main part of the research. Three researchers conducted the interviews with fifty-eight individuals from the councils, political parties, and the community and voluntary sector. Issues explored included views and opinions on reconciliation; how reconciliation related to the interviewee's work and voluntary activities; relevant policies, practices, and structures; relationships between and within sectors; and who was deemed to hold ultimate responsibility for building reconciliation. Themes from the interviews were extracted, categorized, and interpreted by the project team within the context of the international and domestic literature on reconciliation.

This chapter summarizes some of the key results of the study. First, however, we explore some of the background to how the concept of reconciliation has been used in Northern Ireland, both in the past and now. Specifically, we outline the historical use of the term, then how it has been used in the funding for peace and reconciliation work, and, finally, how it has been used by politicians and civil society. Then follows an outline of the study's methodology, including a definition of "reconciliation" that was presented to participants in the research. The findings of the study are then discussed, and some key conclusions extracted.

Understanding "Reconciliation" in Northern Ireland

History of the Term

On the isle of Ireland, language has always been fraught with controversy. It has been used as an indicator of perceived political or religious affiliations. For example, Catholics speak of the city of Derry, whereas some Protestants call it Londonderry; republicans and nationalists might refer to the "North of Ireland," whereas some unionists may call it "the Province." Such differentiations of names and terms have resulted in an escalation of tensions and a breakdown of already fragile relationships. The language of peacemaking has not escaped the minefield of contested terminology—in which the connotations of certain words and phrases within different communities, and their popularity and appropriateness, wax and wane over time.

The search for an agreed-on or acceptable language is important in resolving any conflict. Phrases such as "community relations," "reconciliation," "peacebuilding," and, more recently, "good relations," or "community cohesion" have all been used to describe attempts to address the divisions in and around Northern Ireland. It is often difficult to track such terms' entry into the lexicon or to be sure about distinctions that others may make between them. Is there something inherently different between self-styled community relations and reconciliation projects? For the purposes of this chapter, it is not necessary to rehearse the history of the conflict in and about Northern Ireland. Suffice it to say that over a thirty-year period, the conflict has resulted in over 3,600 deaths and at least tenfold the number of injuries—this in a population of about 1.5 million people. There has been an overall death rate of 2.25 per 1,000 population (Morrissey and Smyth 2002). This is higher than Argentina's (0.32 per 1,000) and about the same as South Africa's, but substantially lower than El Salvador's (20.25 per 1,000) or Cambodia's (237.02 per 1,000) during each country's period of worst political upheaval (Morrissey and Smyth 2002). The proportion of political deaths per capita in Northern Ireland is therefore fairly high, although it is spread across a longer span of time than in other political conflicts. Also, Northern Ireland has not had as severe structural forms of violence as, for example, South Africa.

But Northern Ireland remains a deeply divided society, with mixed-marriage rates of only 5 to 12 percent (Lloyd and Robinson 2008), 94 percent of Protestant children attending de facto Protestant schools and 92 percent of Catholic children attending Catholic schools (Hayes, McAllister, and Dowds 2006), and 92.5 percent of public housing being divided along religious lines (O'Hara 2004). Space does not permit a more detailed analysis, but suffice it to say that the concept of reconciliation in Northern Ireland needs to be understood within a context of a long legacy of violence and deep social division.

The 1970s were marked by violence and intercommunal unrest in Northern Ireland. In reaction, complementary initiatives were established to sustain strained relationships, mend fractured ones, and build anew across the sectarian divide. These efforts set in motion a British government response, with the establishment of the Community Relations Commission, modeled on the UK body set up to address racism. But the commission made little impact on the worsening relationships and, oddly, was disbanded at the behest of the short-lived power-sharing executive of 1974. While some community and faith-based initiatives were maintained in the face of intensifying violence and segregation, community relations policy initiatives fell dormant for over a decade (Hughes and Carmichael 1998).

By the mid-1980s, unfolding political events, including the Enniskillen bomb in 1987 (which killed eleven people and injured dozens), prompted non-governmental organizations and bodies such as the Standing Advisory Commission on Human Rights to renew pressure on the government to address community relations in policy terms. In 1987, the Central Community Relations Unit was established. Its objective was to formulate, improve, and review government policies on community relations, and it was directly answerable to the head of the Northern Ireland Civil Service. Policies on equality, cross-community contact, and support of "cultural traditions" followed. In 1989, a community relations program was introduced, funded by the UK government and implemented through local authorities. This was based on a commitment to "bring the two sides of Northern Ireland's community towards greater understanding" and predicated on the notion that contact would help improve relationships and build greater tolerance (Central Community Relations Unit 1992). A version of the District Council Community Relations Programme continues to this day, and Community Relations Officers (CROs) are employed in each district council to administer it.

In 1990, the Community Relations Council (CRC)[3] was formed as an independent company and registered charity to promote better community relations between the two main "traditions." The council engages in administration of funding programmers, advice and information, awareness raising and advocacy, and policy development. It now plays an enhanced role in building community relations as well as being involved in the Shared Future policy framework discussed below. While more generalized community development and cultural diversity work were supported by both government sources and independent funding bodies during the 1990s, initiatives such as the district council programs and projects funded by the CRC were largely based on the contact hypothesis, which focused more specifically on the development of relationships between the Catholic and Protestant communities (Allport 1954; Hewstone and Brown 1986; Pettigrew 1998), which has dominated community relations for the past two decades. Critics have argued that much of the work in supporting greater cross-community engagement in Northern Ireland was quite superficial in that it tended to focus on what communities had in common rather than raising issues of contention that exist between them. They have accused the government of promoting an assimilationist agenda that applied little more than "sticking plaster" to the conflict (Hughes and Donnelly 2002). Republicans have continually criticized the field more broadly, claiming that it misses the root causes of the conflict—that is, British occupation (Coiste na n-Iarchimí 2003).

---

3. See www.community-relations.org.uk/.

Since the peace process and the Belfast (Good Friday) Agreement, reached in 1998, community relations efforts have developed to address an equality agenda and promote cultural and political pluralism. Other policy initiatives over the years, including needs-based housing allocation, fair employment legislation, "targeting social need," and (modestly) supporting integrated education, have all helped improve the social and economic context. But public attitude surveys indicate that optimism about relations between Catholic and Protestant communities remains low—though this has lately improved—while residential segregation is pervasive and schooling continues to be sharply divided.[4]

The emergence of strong advocates for victims and former combatants of the conflict has changed the dynamics of the reconciliation debate in recent years (Hamber, Kulle, and Wilson 2001; Hamber and Wilson 2003). A range of steps has been taken to address the needs of victims. A Victims Liaison Unit[5] was set up in the Northern Ireland Office (NIO) in June 1998, and, following devolution, a Victims Unit in the Office of the First Minister and Deputy First Minister (OFMDFM) in July 2000. In 2008, a four-person Commission for Victims and Survivors was set up. To date, the NIO and the OFMDFM claim to have spent (or allocated) over £20 million (US$39 million) on victims-related projects. From the EU, £5.8 million (US$11.5 million) was made available for 2002–04, although spending continued into 2006. Most of these developments have been oriented toward community groups, mainly self-help and counseling organizations. An initial £3 million (US$5.8 million) government core funding scheme was set up, and a further £3 million (US$5.8 million) allocated in 2003–05, for these groups, generally referred to as "victims' groups." A further extension went into effect in 2005, administered by the Northern Ireland CRC.

A range of other policy-oriented initiatives has also taken place. These have been wrapped up in a victims' strategy (Victims Unit 2002), promulgated in 2001 and subject to revision during a consultation in 2005. But official responses to the conflict have been criticized as slow and limited. Until 1998 and the Belfast Agreement, there was a "policy silence" regarding victims in health, social services, education, and other arenas (Hamilton, Thomson, and Smyth 2002). This was acknowledged by the NIO minister, Des Browne, in 2003. Reflecting on three decades of conflict, he told the *Irish Echo* that "in all that time there were no policies in relation to victims" (Holland 2003).

---

4.   See various longitudinal results from the Northern Ireland Life and Times Survey, published at www.ark.ac.uk/nilt/.

5.   This office was closed in January 2005.

Victim support services began in earnest only after the release of politically motivated prisoners as part of the agreement. This left many victims' groups feeling, at least initially, that support for them was merely a sop for justice denied. Over the years, this led to a polarization (in most but not all areas) between ex-prisoner initiatives and work with victims. Divisions also emerged within victims' groups over definitions of legitimate victimhood. It has become common for some groups to refer to themselves as "real" or "innocent" victims (Morrissey and Smyth 2002). Individuals from different sides have alleged that there is a hierarchy of victimhood, claiming that their specific victimization is given lower official priority than certain others. There have also been claims that ex-prisoners have received more attention than victims, though ex-prisoners' groups have argued that funding for them has decreased as the counterposition between victims' and ex-prisoners' organizations has sharpened.

In recent years, at least at the individual level and in some circles, there has been growing participation in processes and dialogues aimed at narrowing this gap. Contacts between ex-prisoners' and victims' groups have been growing. Victims' organizations, too, have started to articulate their needs in a manner that fits the tone of international debates on reconciliation. It has been routinely found that victims tend not to divorce truth, justice, the labeling of responsibility for violations, compensation, and official acknowledgment from healing and reconciliation (Hamber, Kulle, and Wilson 2001; Hamber and Wilson 2003). Earlier government initiatives, such as the victims' strategy, have tended to focus on service delivery and victim support, and therein lies the challenge: Setting up sufficient support services for all victims of political violence seems doable, but integrating their other needs—some of which, such as the right to justice, have perhaps been overridden in the name of peace—is infinitely more complex. But reconciliation is far larger than a focus on victims and offenders alone. As noted above, the terminology surrounding reconciliation in Northern Ireland is very fluid, with no clear distinctions made among various concepts in play.

Although literature focusing on reconciliation as a concept in Northern Ireland has been published over many years, much of it was generated by faith-based groups and firmly rooted in theological teachings. Michael Hurley (1994) collated the proceedings of a seminar into a collection, *Reconciliation in Religion and Society.* The contributions explored the concept of reconciliation, described as being "vague and ill-defined." The book places reconciliation within a Christian framework, addressing it from the perspectives of history, justice, ecumenism, ecology, politics, and gender.

An action research project by the Irish School of Ecumenics investigated sectarianism and the role of Christian religion in conflict and reconciliation. Its authors, Clegg and Liechty (2001, 43), see reconciliation as "the cornerstone of our understanding of the main goal and dynamics of moving beyond sectarianism." They reflect that the concept is "criticised from at least two main angles: some politically-orientated critics see reconciliation as a weak-minded, establishmentarian alternative to the real task of justice and structural change, while its conservative religious critics condemn reconciliation as a matter of crying peace where there is no peace." As for others, their own understanding is based on the interlocking dynamics of forgiveness, repentance, truth, and justice, "understood in part as religiously-rooted virtues, but also as basic dynamics of human interaction, including public life and therefore politics" (Clegg and Liechty 2001, 44).

The Faith and Politics Group's *A Time to Heal: Perspectives on Reconciliation* was based on nearly two decades of reflection by clergy and laypersons on the meaning of reconciliation in Northern Ireland. Yet, while they grapple with the meaning of reconciliation, they admit, "It remains hard . . . to give the word meaning and practical content . . . reconciliation as a word has been shamelessly misused, to slide away from issues of injustice and rightful disturbance. It has been used to quieten people down and lead them away from their situation" (Faith and Politics Group 2002, 5). Though significant emphasis is on the Christian vision of reconciliation, the concept of "social reconciliation" is explored. This is seen as dealing with the past, grieving, storytelling, forgiveness, acknowledgment, restitution, punishment, justice, and trust.

The faith-based contribution by David Stevens (2004) of the Corrymeela Community[6] poses the question "What can the Christian faith bring to the human search for reconciliation?" and offers some theological perspectives and reflections on biblical texts. Several other publications have focused on Christian perspectives on reconciliation in Northern Ireland, though a detailed exploration is beyond the scope of this chapter. (See for example, Love 1995; Monaghan and Boyle 1998; Morrow 2003; Thomson 1998; Wells 1999.)

There are, however, some notable departures from the theologically based literature on reconciliation in Northern Ireland. Norman Porter (2003, 12) argues for the importance of reconciliation as a moral and political ideal, which "makes demands on how we live and think as social, political, and cultural beings." Reconciliation, he believes, "entails embracing and engaging others who are different from us in a spirit of openness and with a view to expanding our horizons, healing our divisions and articulating common purposes. . . . If taken seriously, it disturbs prejudice, disrupts practices and queries priorities" (Porter 2003, 8).

There have also been some practical attempts to look at the issue. Area Development Management/Combat Poverty Agency (ADM/CPA, now

---

6. See www.corrymeela.org/.

Border Action) undertook a consultation that engendered the following definition of reconciliation: "Reconciliation is the term for the process whereby past trauma, injury and suffering is acknowledged and healing/restorative action is pursued; relationship breakdown is addressed and new sustainable relationships created; and where the culture and structures which gave rise to conflict and estrangement are transformed with a view to creating an equitable and interdependent community" (ADM/CPA 2003, 27). They also produced a helpful matrix (ADM/CPA n.d.) that divides projects into different stages along a continuum toward reconciliation. The matrix describes the depth of reconciliation (y-axis) as increasing from (1) contact, awareness, and understanding to (2) joint projects, to (3) raising conflictual issues, and, finally, to (4) changing culture and structure. It also highlights types of reconciliation work (x-axis) as (1) healing, (2) building relationships, and (3) reconstruction. Various forms of practical reconciliation activity can be slotted into the matrix. For example, the report (ADM/CPA n.d.) argues that reconciliation practice might minimally or initially include reciprocal visits, ecumenical services, joint commemorative events, documentary and cultural affirmation, and declaration of desire or intention to cease hostilities/estrangement. (This would be located at the intersection of "contact, awareness, and understanding," in terms of reconciliation depth; and "healing," in terms of type of work.) Deeper reconciliation practice might include liberating structures; innovative social technology; trade unions and law reform; civil society; use of technology to deepen democracy and social partnership ownership and participation; and equity, diversity, interdependence, and proofing/monitoring of social structures and institutions. (This would be located at the intersection of "changing culture and structure," in terms of reconciliation depth, and "reconstruction," in terms of type of work.)

Healing through Remembering, a cross-community project that undertook an extensive public consultation on ways to deal with the past, also refers to reconciliation in its report (Healing through Remembering 2002). It notes that although strategies to deal with the past can be divisive, they are integral to reconciliation. But creating unrealistic expectations of closure or reconciliation, without dealing with issues such as anger or the need for truth, is undesirable. In this sense, the report is much closer to some international perspectives that see reconciliation as linked to a range of strategies. "Healing through remembering" refers to public acknowledgment, potential truth-recovery mechanisms, a day of reflection, a living memorial museum, commemorations shared by communities, and storytelling—all essential yet challenging tasks in societies coming out of conflict (Healing through Remembering 2002).

Thus, what we see over the years in Northern Ireland is a shift and development of the concept of reconciliation. The following quotation summarizes some of the major shifts in the reconciliation debate in Northern Ireland from the late 1990s:

> Until the ceasefires of 1994, community relations work necessarily concentrated on groups outside formal politics, often small and consisting of committed pioneers, and on policy initiatives intended to facilitate long-term structural change. Following the ceasefires, reconciliation ceased to be the Cinderella of public policy and became the dominant theme of party political, government and international interest. Funding for economic and social initiatives aimed at reconciliation was offered by the European Commission. The British Government sought a peace dividend and the Clinton administration backed up its direct political involvement with support for economic investment and social change especially targeted at women and community development. A much larger reconciliation industry then emerged with substantial international backing. (Eyben, Wilson, and Morrow 2000, 11)

Reconciliation and Funding

Much of the thinking about peace and reconciliation, certainly in the past decade, has become synonymous with the European Union (EU) Special Support Program for Peace and Reconciliation in Northern Ireland and the Border Counties of Ireland,[7] which has come to dominate the scene. This program has had several phases, known as PEACE I and PEACE II (with the latter now extended as "PEACE II +" or the "PEACE II extension"), and, more recently, PEACE III. These are unique EU-funded programs, covering the six counties of Northern Ireland and the six counties of the republic nearest the border (Cavan, Donegal, Leitrim, Louth, Monaghan, and Sligo). PEACE I, introduced by the European Commission in 1995, supported more than 13,000 projects in Northern Ireland, focusing on job creation, social inclusion, urban and rural regeneration, and cross-border cooperation. Approximately €536 million (US$847 million) was made available. Money was distributed through central government, twenty-six district partnership boards (based on district council boundaries), and intermediary funding bodies and provided significant economic and social investment in Northern Ireland and the border counties.

---

7. This chapter largely focuses on EU funding, which makes up the majority of funding. However, aside from the EU, substantial funding lines are offered by the London and Dublin governments. Other major philanthropic organizations and funding bodies that have also supported reconciliation work on the island include the Northern Ireland Fund for Reconciliation, the International Fund for Ireland (IFI), and Atlantic Philanthropies (which has a "human rights and reconciliation" strand). The United States provides economic assistance through the IFI. The fund promotes economic and social advancement and encourages contact, dialogue, and reconciliation. It supports economic development both north and south in Ireland, with priority given to new investments that create jobs and reconstruct disadvantaged areas.

Although many successes were recorded at the community level, debates rage about the program's effectiveness in peacebuilding and reconciliation and, specifically, about its ability to address the causes of the conflict and to confront core issues arising from it. There was, some argued, "insufficient embedding of concepts of peace and reconciliation in many measures of the programme" (Harvey 2003, 12). Reflecting on PEACE I, Harvey wrote, "Although an understanding of issues of peace and reconciliation undoubtedly deepened during the PEACE I Programme, this was not the same as the achievement of consensus within Northern Ireland on the nature of the conflict and the nature of the 'solution.' . . . Although PEACE I had done much to normalize cross-community (and cross-border) work, there was not full agreement on a model of cross-community and single-identity work. Any successor program had to operate in an environment in which the most basic issues of the troubles remained unresolved" (Harvey 2003, 22).

A midterm review of the program found, among a range of issues, that groups had considerable difficulty measuring impacts on reconciliation and were given little guidance on how to do so (Coopers and Lybrand 1997). In the same year, the three Northern Ireland members of the European Parliament, who had strongly lobbied the European Commission in support of such a program, submitted their own midterm review (Paisley, Hume, and Nicholson 1997). While praising the program overall, they similarly highlighted its complexity and the problems of defining, and thus assessing, reconciliation. In *Taking Risks for Peace,* also published that year, the Northern Ireland Voluntary Trust (NIVT),[8] one of the intermediary funding bodies for the PEACE Program, highlighted the different interpretations of the program (NIVT 1997b), which included investment in community capacity, tackling social exclusion, and a focus on conflict resolution. It expressed concerns about how peace and reconciliation were being defined in the broader political and constitutional context (NIVT 1997b). In a later publication, the NIVT proposed that the focus on bottom-up development and community activities be maintained, with priority given to social inclusion. But it suggested, "Greater efforts must be made to discuss and refine what is meant by and involved in the process of peace and reconciliation and to adopt effective and imaginative ways of monitoring the impact of the program in supporting this process" (NIVT 1997a, 10). Following an extensive review—internal to the European Commission and, more publicly, involving the many intermediary functioning bodies (IFBs)—a new five-year PEACE Program was belatedly introduced in 2000. Approximately €500 million (US$790 million) was allocated, of which €400 million (US$632 million) was to be spent in Northern

---

8. Now known as the Community Foundation for Northern Ireland. See www.community-foundationni.org.

Ireland (the remainder in the border counties of the Republic of Ireland), supplemented by government contributions. By the end of the program, about €667 million (US$1,054 million) had been spent.

After laborious consultations, briefings, and draft documents, involving government departments, political parties, and IFBs as well as the voluntary, farming, and business sectors on both sides of the border, the commission finally adopted a new program in March 2001. The five priority areas (in order of greatest to least expenditure) were to be economic renewal; social integration, inclusion, and reconciliation; locally based regeneration and development strategies; an outward- and forward-looking region; and cross-border cooperation. In addition, three distinctiveness criteria were introduced, which each supported project had to meet in order to qualify. These were (1) addressing the legacy of the conflict, (2) taking the opportunities arising from the peace, and (3) promoting reconciliation. This program, PEACE II, has been managed by the Special EU Programmes Body (SEUPB)[9] and resulted in the expenditure of €835 million (US$1,319 million) on some 5,000 projects—larger than initial allocations. It specifically aims to encourage "progress towards a peaceful and stable society and to promote reconciliation." The SEUPB says that its research suggests that the program has been largely successful.

In a press release at the end of 2004, the body noted, "Headline figures from the research show that 96% of participants in the PEACE II Programme are more likely to have at least some friends within another community compared to 86% of the total Northern Ireland population. In terms of trust, 80% of PEACE II participants feel that members of the other community can be trusted regardless of community background, compared to just 56% of the total Northern Ireland population. Evidence also suggests that PEACE II Programme participants cross the border more often than the rest of the population at 88% compared to just 61% of the total NI population."[10]

An extension to the PEACE II Programme was agreed on, following the European Commission's recommendation in October 2004. The SEUPB also completed a consultation on the potential extension. In the SEUPB's consultation, the need to define reconciliation was again stressed. The PEACE II Programme was extended to 2006–07, with an additional €160 million (US$253 million) allocated. Plans are now under way to roll out a PEACE III Program, worth around €333 million (US$526 million), which will be allocated for a further five-year period.

In total, and projecting into the PEACE III allocation, between 1995 and 2013, €1.995 billion (US$3.152 billion) will have been spent on peace and reconciliation initiatives. As a result, the language of reconciliation has been

---

9.   See www.seupb.org.

10. Quoted from www.seupb.org/news_diff.htm.

embraced (though perhaps only superficially in some cases) by grant-giving bodies and community groups alike. However, the usage and understanding of the term are not shared. Harvey (2003) has noted that a clear definition of "reconciliation" was still not readily available from the EU (until 2005, discussed below) and that in that absence, each body tasked with administering the funding defined the term—and, therefore, what activities could be viewed as contributing to reconciliation—differently. The lack of conceptual clarity on reconciliation was one of the main reasons that the authors decided to carry out the research forming the basis of this chapter.

Reconciliation, Politics, and Civil Society

As part of the research presented in this chapter, we explored, through an audit of documents and debates, how the term "reconciliation" was or was not used in certain political and civil society contexts in Northern Ireland. The most relevant recent development has been the government-led consultation assessing organizations' and individuals' views on policies to address community relations. Published in January 2003, "A Shared Future: A Consultation Paper on Improving Relations in Northern Ireland"[11] received more than five hundred formal responses from political parties, voluntary organizations, statutory agencies, churches, businesses, district councils, strategy partnerships, and other entities. We examined a sample of responses (including all those from political parties and the main community and voluntary organizations working on relevant issues) to identify words or phrases used to discuss improving relations in Northern Ireland.

The document itself tended to use the phrases "community relations" and "good relations" interchangeably, without providing any definition or explanation. In the responses analyzed, "community relations" was the most common reference, with "good relations" a close second. "Reconciliation" was seldom used, and on the few occasions where it was, it tended to appear with "peace"—undoubtedly an influence of the EU PEACE Program. Interestingly, some respondents criticized "A Shared Future" for failing to define such terms, saying that a shared understanding of their meanings was necessary. The response submitted by the CRC began in this vein. Yet, despite its own name (Community Relations Council), it proceeded to privilege the term "reconciliation" over "community relations" for the most part, without explanation.

The final policy document, "A Shared Future: Policy and Strategic Framework for Good Relations in Northern Ireland,"[12] was published by the tasked

---

11. Available at www.asharedfuture_ni.gov.uk.

12. Available at www.asharedfuture ni.gov.uk/finalgrs.pdf.

Community Relations Unit[13] in March 2005. In his foreword, then Northern Ireland secretary Paul Murphy wrote: "The essence of reconciliation is about moving away from relationships that are built on mistrust and defense to relationships rooted in mutual recognition and trust. Where relationships have been shaped by threat and fear over a long period we must make changes. We must make those changes through policy and law to address that threat and fear. In my view the absence of trust will set back both economic and social development; we will fail to realise the talents of our more diverse society" (Community Relations Unit 2005, 3). The report did refer to criticisms of the lack of clarity in terminology and attempted to address them thus: 'Community relations' refers specifically to division between the Protestant and Catholic communities in Northern Ireland. 'Good relations' refers to Section 75(2) of the Northern Ireland Act 1998 which includes persons of different religious belief, political opinion or racial group" (Community Relations Unit 2005, 63). But the document continued to use both terms throughout, with no clear observance of these distinctions. Interestingly, the term "reconciliation" all but disappeared from the body of the text, and when it appeared, it referred directly to victims/survivors of the conflict. This might be seen as reflecting the document's politically exigent character. "Community relations" can be (mis)represented in superficial and nonthreatening terms, betokening a view of the Northern Ireland conflict rooted in individual ignorance and prejudice. Equally, "good relations" can be articulated as a routine procedure to be followed by public authorities as part of the equality agenda embracing principally section 75(1) of the Northern Ireland Act. "Reconciliation" can simultaneously appear more challenging and less predictable. This was a major theme of our wider research findings, which are discussed later in this chapter.

We also undertook an analysis of the 1998 Belfast Agreement.[14] Interestingly, the text of the agreement[15] makes scant reference to reconciliation. It appears twice in the prefatory "Declaration of Support." This affirms, "The tragedies of the past have left a deep and profoundly regrettable legacy of suffering. We must never forget those who have died or been injured, and their families. But we can best honour them through a fresh start, in which we firmly dedicate ourselves to the achievement of reconciliation, tolerance, and mutual trust, and to the protection and vindication of human rights for all" (Northern Ireland Office 1998, 1–2). Later it reads, "We must acknowledge the substantial differences between our continuing, and equally legitimate, political aspirations. However, we will endeavour to strive in every practical

---

13. The Community Relations Unit is a subunit of the OFMDFM.

14. Agreement Reached in Multi-Party Negotiations, 10 April 1998 (hereafter Belfast Agreement).

15. Available at www.nio.gov.uk/agreement.pdf.

way towards reconciliation and rapprochement within our framework of democratic and agreed arrangement." No definition of "reconciliation" in this context is provided, and the term seems to be used as a loose qualifier for setting aside past animosities and working together in a new dispensation. In the body of the agreement, however, it is used more specifically: The importance of addressing the needs of victims is acknowledged in building reconciliation, as is the funding of work in this arena. The section titled "Rights, Safeguards and Equality of Opportunity" has two subheadings: "Human Rights" and "Economic, Social and Cultural Rights." "Reconciliation and Victims of Violence" is awarded its own section within the "Human Rights" element. It concludes:

> The participants believe that it is essential to acknowledge and address the suffering of the victims of violence as a necessary element of reconciliation. . . . The participants recognize and value the work being done by many organizations to develop reconciliation and mutual understanding and respect between and within communities and traditions, in Northern Ireland and between North and South, and they see such work as having a vital role in consolidating peace and political agreement. Accordingly, they pledge their continuing support for such organizations and will positively examine the case for enhanced financial assistance for the work of reconciliation. An essential aspect of the reconciliation process is the promotion of a culture of tolerance at every level of society, including initiatives to facilitate and encourage integrated education and mixed housing. (Northern Ireland Office 1998, 18)

Clearly, therefore, while reconciliation as a concept is present in the public/official domain, it is painted with broad brushstrokes. To see whether it was used any more specifically, we used the Official Record (Hansard) to analyze debates in the Northern Ireland Assembly as it met between November 1999 and October 2002. Excluding common references to the EU Peace and Reconciliation Program, "reconciliation" was referred to during assembly debates. There was, however, a discernible difference between the parties, with Social Democratic and Labour Party (SDLP) members referring to the term seventy-five times, the Democratic Unionist Party and Women's Coalition eighteen times each, Alliance Party members thirteen, the Sinn Féin ten, and the United Kingdom Unionist Party eight. This cursory analysis suggests that the SDLP, a moderate nationalist party, has more fully integrated "reconciliation" into its official language, while others did not favor it or tended toward a more à la carte use of related terms. Thus, we can see that "reconciliation" is used sparingly at the policy and political levels and remains largely undefined. We have not carried out a more recent analysis of current parliamentary discussions, but they would be unlikely to differ substantially. Although the term "reconciliation" may have been used more frequently by some politicians in the buildup to and reestablishment of devolution in March 2007, it is still used sparingly. Much confusion remains between concepts such as "community relations" and "reconciliation," and at times they are used interchangeably, without any real sense of why one is chosen over another or of any nuances that such usage might imply.

Reconciliation is a concept that has a long history within the Northern Ireland context. As in the international debate, it has clearly moved from the sole province of the religious into mainstream policymaking. But its meaning remains vague and lacking in practical definition. Despite the extensive EU PEACE Program and more recent attempts to try to define it, there is little sign that the confusion over terminology is clearing up, particularly with the admixture of more recent terms such as "good relations" and "community cohesion." Much work remains to be done in conceptual clarification—and, more important, in assessing the impact on practice and on how the success of reconciliation initiatives is to be measured. The research presented in the remainder of this chapter is a contribution to that effort.

Methodology

From the outset it was clear that to investigate the conceptual and practical aspects of reconciliation at local levels, we would need to focus on discrete areas. Given that one of the objectives was to explore how politics at a local level constrains or promotes community-based reconciliation, a focus on district council areas seemed appropriate. We chose three local authorities as case studies. To provide external direction, a research advisory group was set up, which met every two months or so.[16] The group provided vital support, offering valuable strategic direction, suggestions for contacts, and guidance on methodology.

Out of Northern Ireland's twenty-six district council areas,[17] three were chosen to provide contrasting as well as common features. Using the 2001 census, the choice was limited to those with catchment populations of 30,000 to 60,000. This avoided areas that were very large (and therefore a little unmanageable in terms of getting a true sense of the scope of work undertaken) or quite small (and therefore arguably less active). The second consideration was geographic spread across Northern Ireland. We chose to focus on areas outside the large urban centers because these have received less research attention. The third, and arguably most important, criterion was that the areas chosen should have different demographics. Again based

---

16. The reference group comprised Sue Williams, Dominic Bryan, Ruth Moore, and Libby Keys. We acknowledge and thank them for their contribution.

17. Northern Ireland is now being restructured with seven "supercouncils," with a maximum of fifty councillors each, following the Review of Public Administration, but at the time of this research, twenty-six councils still existed.

on census figures, we chose one with a mainly Catholic population, one that was predominantly Protestant, and one that was more evenly balanced. A short list of eight areas was whittled down to three on the basis of exploration of previous research within each area, levels of voluntary activity, conversations with funders, and discussions with community relations officers and other key informants. The three district council areas chosen offered a broad geographic spread, a range of religious composition and intercommunal tension, and differing community and voluntary sector activity.

A semistructured interview questionnaire formed the main part of the research. The questionnaire was piloted twice before data collection to ensure that the questions were clear and rigorous and addressed all the research themes. The first pilot was with the research advisory group, which provided valuable feedback. The second was with exemplars of the three main strands of interviewees: two CROs from councils outside the three chosen areas, a community and voluntary sector member with responsibility for community relations work, and a local public authority representative with particular interest in peacebuilding.

In setting up the actual research interviews, our first points of contact were the CRO and the chief executive of the council within each area. Initial meetings were set up to explain the project and answer any queries, and each of the three councils agreed that it would cooperate with the researchers. A list of potential interviewees was drawn up, in consultation with the CROs and on the basis of the background data previously collated on the areas, to include a range of key stakeholders. Letters were sent to all potential interviewees, explaining the background, aims, and objectives of the research, followed up by phone calls. Interviews were conducted in the three areas, with extensive notes being taken or with the discussion being recorded, depending on the wishes of the interviewee. Three researchers[18] were involved in conducting the interviews, and fifty-eight individuals were interviewed in total. These included at least one representative from each political party represented in the council concerned (along with some independents); the CRO employed by the council; the chief executive and other relevant policy personnel; the Local Strategy Partnership manager and members (who have responsibility for the distribution of EU PEACE funding); and employees and board members of voluntary organizations engaged in what could be considered reconciliation work, including victims' groups, ex-prisoners' groups,

---

18. We are indebted to Gareth Higgins and Tony MacAulay, who conducted the field research in Armagh and Ballymena, respectively. Gráinne Kelly conducted the research in Omagh.

community development organizations, networking or umbrella groups, youth groups, and local organizations supporting ethnic minorities.

Issues explored included views and opinions on reconciliation; how reconciliation related to one's work and voluntary activities; relevant policies, practices, and structures; and relationships between and within sectors, and who was deemed to hold ultimate responsibility for building reconciliation.[19] The research generated rich data on the understanding and application of reconciliation in Northern Ireland. Although it explored specifics in the relationships between councils and community groups, it also provided a broader picture of local views. On completing all interviews, each researcher compiled a report on the case study area, based on the themes identified. The data from the interviews formed the basis of much of the analysis. This was supplemented by discussions between the researchers and the advisory group to identify cross-cutting themes, commonalities, and differences. Given the semistructured nature of the interviews, themes were easily extracted, categorized, and interpreted by the project team.

Defining "Reconciliation"

To stimulate discussion and try to frame the reconciliation debate in Northern Ireland, we presented, as part of the overall questionnaire, a working definition of "reconciliation," applicable to societies emerging from conflict. In developing the definition, we explored a number of definitions from the existing literature, including dictionaries, handbooks, academic journals, and books by practitioners. We acknowledge the specific contributions of a number of texts in that effort. (See especially ADM/CPA 2003; Assefa 2001; Bloomfield, Barnes, and Huyse 2003; Hamber 2002; Hamber and van der Merwe 1998; Lederach 1997; Porter 2003; Rigby 2001; van der Merwe 1999; and Van der Merwe 2000.)

The result is the working definition below, which is, by its nature, incomplete. We were comfortable with this imperfection, which we view as a useful, perhaps provocative, tool to stimulate further discussion rather than as a definitive statement that must be defended.[20]

We see reconciliation starting from the premise that building peace relationships requires attention. Reconciliation is the process of addressing conflictual and fractured relationships, and this includes a range of activities. It is a voluntary act that cannot be imposed (Bloomfield, Barnes, and

---

19. The questionnaires used, and summaries of the case study areas, are available in Hamber and Kelly 2005.

20. Although this text defines the term in full, we presented the respondents with only a summary version, which included an opening paragraph and the five subheadings listed.

Huyse 2003). A reconciliation process generally involves five interwoven and related strands:

1. **Developing a shared vision of an interdependent and fair society.** Developing a vision of a shared future requires the involvement of the whole society, at all levels. Although individuals may have different opinions or political beliefs, the articulation of a common vision of an interdependent, just, equitable, open, and diverse society is a critical part of any reconciliation process.

2. **Acknowledging and dealing with the past.** The truth of the past, with all its pain, suffering, and losses, must be acknowledged and mechanisms implemented, providing for justice, healing, restitution or reparation, and restoration (including apologies, if needed, and steps aimed at redress). To build reconciliation, individuals and institutions need to acknowledge their own role in the conflicts of the past, accepting and learning from it in a constructive way to ensure nonrepetition.

3. **Building positive relationships.** Following violent conflict, relationships need to be built or renewed, addressing issues of trust, prejudice, and intolerance in the process. This results in accepting both commonalities and differences and embracing and engaging with those who are different from us.

4. **Significant cultural and attitudinal change.** Changes in how people relate to one another are also key. The culture of suspicion, fear, mistrust, and violence is broken down, and opportunities and space open up in which people can hear and be heard. A culture of respect for human rights and human differences is developed, creating a context for each citizen to become an active participant in society and feel a sense of belonging.

5. **Substantial social, economic, and political change.** The social, economic, and political structures that gave rise to conflict and estrangement are identified, reconstructed or addressed, and transformed. This strand can also be thought of as being about ensuring equality or attaining equity between groups.

Although we did not explore these formally in the research interviews, two additional points are important in understanding our working definition. First, a reconciliation process always contains paradoxes, tensions, even contradictions. It is neither neat nor easy and at times can seem incongruous. Lederach (1997) notes that aspects can stand in tension with one another—for example, the articulation of a long-term interdependent future on one hand and the need for justice on the other.

The strands of our working definition can themselves create tensions in the same vein: Reconciliation requires dealing with the past but, at the same time, participating in developing a shared vision. Reconciliation looks both backward and forward. For example, fostering economic change may require a change in resource allocations within a country (say, resources moving from the wealthy to the poor), but at the same time, reconciliation requires building relationships between such groups.

Also, we cannot escape the fact that reconciliation is a morally loaded concept and that different people bring their own ideological biases. An individual's understanding of reconciliation is generally informed by his or her basic beliefs about the world. Different ideologies of reconciliation can be identified (Hamber and van der Merwe 1998; van der Merwe 1999). Thus, we need to be aware that individuals will interpret differently the dimensions of reconciliation. Trying to reconcile different ideological positions—for example, on what attitudes need to change—is precisely what the reconciliation endeavor is about.

Reconciliation is the process of addressing these five strands. It is not solely about the outcome of doing so (say, a mended relationship), because the social, interpersonal, and political context is continually changing. This process is, by definition, complex and incomplete, and paradoxes and ambivalences will persist. Reconciliation is thus by nature conflictual and dynamic. Therefore, reconciliation involves the process of addressing the five strands we have outlined, but it is simultaneously about trying to deal with the complex paradoxes and tensions between them. Reconciliation can best be measured not as an outcome but as the capacity to manage the paradoxes and tensions inherent in the process.

Findings

In terms of how individuals defined reconciliation, we found that interviewees were open to a discussion and were willing, in general terms, to explore how reconciliation related to them and fitted with their work. Although challenging ideas were aired, most interviewees were fairly vague on the details of what reconciliation might entail or how it might be pursued. From their responses, the following themes emerged on what reconciliation is primarily about:

- addressing relationships between former enemies and those estranged by conflict;
- engaging in confidence- and trust-building measures;
- rehumanizing and getting to know the "other";
- recognizing that harm has been done to another;

- showing remorse over that harm;
- providing explanations of why it happened;
- finding ways to heal old wounds; and
- seeking means of accommodation, partnership, and respect for difference, and recognizing mutual dependence.

Local public representatives and council staff generally saw reconciliation as one of many issues they faced in their daily work, but not as a priority in the midst of helping people claim their statutory rights. This suggests a legalistic understanding of dealing with past conflicts rather than a relationship-driven focus. It also suggests that they do not see attainment of rights as a component of reconciliation. In community and voluntary organizations, reconciliation tended to be seen in terms of building and mending relationships. Some representatives saw it as a priority, even when their work was not explicitly labeled as such.

There was a distinct lack of clarity among interviewees on what, specifically, reconciliation meant. Most tended to view this lack of clarity as an obstacle to intercommunal processes and policies to address the legacy of the conflict. The lack of clarity was also something of a paradox, since some interviewees were involved in work funded under the reconciliation banner. This does not mean that they did not have their own understanding of the term, but a shared understanding was not at all evident. Few could articulate a vision of what a reconciled society would look like. Several respondents seemed to hold the view that it would be more tolerant, with less segregation and greater social ease and freedom from fear. Most were fairly pessimistic about achieving this in the short term. The respondents appeared to have difficulty relating reconciliation, as a concept, to their practice. It was not a term they used in their daily work or felt particularly comfortable in using to describe what they did. Of those directly engaged in self-described peacebuilding activities, most appeared more comfortable with terms such as "community relations," "good relations," or "community cohesion." No interviewee advocated replacing these with "reconciliation," although many seemed comfortable using them interchangeably. "Reconciliation" seemed to imply a much deeper process, for which some felt that the communities they worked with were unprepared. This was one reason why they did not use the term.

Views of reconciliation were influenced by ideological stance. Some interviewees, mostly clergy and unionist politicians, made theological references. For others, however, reconciliation as a concept stimulated a negative or cynical reaction, dismissed as being theological and therefore not relevant. Little reference was made to forgiveness, often highlighted in theological literature as an important element, though it did not feature highly as a prerequisite of reconciliation, even for those from a religious background. With a few exceptions, the interviewees spoke about reconciliation in the abstract, making no reference to any changes required of themselves.

Funding from the EU PEACE Program heavily influenced perceptions. Reconciliation as a concept was largely viewed through the prism of this program—despite that few were clear on what an EU definition of the word might be. Most interviewees felt that the funding bodies provided little direction in this regard. One respondent, when asked "What is reconciliation?" said, "It's what you have to put down on a form to get the money. It is funder-speak, and it doesn't mean much to people." Few respondents made reference to reconciliation as anything other than a "two traditions" (Catholic and Protestant) issue. A more holistic understanding of the need to address relationships across society or between governments—including in areas little affected by the conflict—did not come across strongly. The absence of ethnic minorities in reconciliation initiatives also needs to be addressed.

Response to the working definition was overwhelmingly positive and brought the discussion to a different level. Several respondents were surprised by the definition's complexity. Interviewees saw reconciliation as a very abstract concept and were pleasantly surprised to see it broken down into component parts. Some questioned whether prior processes (such as confidence building) needed to happen before they could take on the issues proposed. Significantly, few interviewees spent any time commenting on or contradicting the assertion about a shared vision, which may suggest either that they fundamentally agreed with this need or that they did not view it as a priority worthy of discussion.

By a large margin, acknowledging the past was the aspect that respondents emphasized most; indeed, many felt that it must be the first step in any reconciliation process. Few interviewees, however, specified what this might involve. While most respondents definitely saw value in dealing with the past, they did not know how to deal with it effectively.

Most made some reference to the importance of building positive relationships, but this did not generate much in-depth discussion—perhaps because it was seen as self-evident. The responses on "cultural and attitudinal change" were particularly interesting because they reflected an understanding of this concept that differed from the one we intended. While some interviewees agreed that significant cultural change was important, others were uncertain about its meaning. Some perceived the statement as implying that for reconciliation to take place, people would have to change their "cultural traditions." This appeared to be particularly true of those from a Protestant background, with the inference that "culture" was intrinsic to "community" and not something that should be changed.

On socioeconomic and political change, the vast majority of respondents felt that this already enjoyed disproportionate emphasis by the EU Peace and Reconciliation Program, to the detriment of building relationships and addressing the legacy of the past.

When analyzing roles, relationships, and responsibilities for building reconciliation, we found that relationships within and between sectors had a significant impact on reconciliation. Although individual relationships were often described in encouraging terms, tensions were clearly apparent, particularly between voluntary organizations and local authorities. In all three case studies, a common thread of negativity appeared in discussions with voluntary-sector interviewees about their respective councils. To some degree, they seemed to view the council as little more than a potential funding avenue and not as a major player in reconciliation. However, this sense of lack of cooperation and joint initiative seemed to apply only to the councils as institutions and not to their staffs. Most voluntary-sector interviewees were positive about the support offered by council officials. It was obvious from our discussions that officials were often limited by the decisions of elected representatives, hampering the type and depth of work they could do. Interviewees generally perceived relationships between elected representatives as poor, and some felt that strained relationships and public disagreements had a negative impact on community relations. For example, certain councillors appeared willing to lend private support to projects but would not do so publicly, for fear of losing votes within their communal catchment areas.

There were diverse views on whether further responsibility for reconciliation should be devolved to local authorities—as later envisaged under the Shared Future policy framework, published in March 2005. Perhaps not surprisingly, council staff and councillors were generally enthusiastic about this possibility, envisioning local authorities taking the lead in much of this work, while remaining cautious of being given added responsibility without adequate planning. But respondents in the voluntary sector were generally hesitant, particularly if further funding streams were to be administered by the council. A clear picture emerged of reconciliation commonly being "politicized" within councils, that is, being treated in a partisan fashion.

We still found nervousness about promoting reconciliation—more evidence that the process is not adequately supported or understood at the political level. Especially in community organizations, we found that local politicians were blamed at times for continuing to play sectarian and polarizing politics—undermining attempts to build relationships, change attitudes, or assist in finding a common vision. A common view was that ways need to be found to stop rewarding segregation, politically and geographically.

The research found that the term "reconciliation" was not used a great deal on the ground. This reflects the limited effort, to date, to define—or at least discuss how to use—the concept, thus leaving a range of assumed meanings attached to it.

Also, reconciliation is seen as a deep and sometimes threatening process. Respondents chose at times not to use the term in their daily work, because they feared that it would scare people off. This concern may have arisen because of the perceived religious overtones of the word or because "reconciliation" was understood somehow as "coming together" in some process of social and political transformation. Thus, the respondents, with a few exceptions, seemed instinctively to understand that "reconciliation" went deeper than the more general "coexistence." Some would argue that coexistence has always been the dominant model for the majority in Northern Ireland (including the middle class, which, for the most part, was not as severely affected by the conflict as the working class) and that this has led to separate development of the Catholic and Protestant communities and, therefore, to perpetual division.

Our research suggests some readiness among the interviewees to engage in breaking down myopic understandings of the determinants of the conflict (for example, meeting across divides in some cases), but the interviewees' reaction to the term "reconciliation" also implies that much groundwork remains to be done in local communities to create conditions conducive to a deeper process of reconciliation. This also requires robust political support, both locally and generally. We found that voluntary groups are more involved in thinking about reconciliation than are district councillors or local politicians and that the voluntary sector is more philosophically and practically involved with reconciliation. Councillors are largely not engaging with the topic, and at times we had to struggle to get them interested. Most seemed locked into divisive local politics, which our community group respondents saw as undermining their reconciliation efforts. Our research suggests that considerably more vigor is needed: Reconciliation, a difficult and complex process, needs to be championed at the highest levels, and the challenges it presents must be confronted directly. The research revealed serious doubts about the ability of locally elected politicians to forward a reconciliation agenda in a nonsectarian and effective manner. Reconciliation issues have become political footballs in the council chamber, with one party grasping at issues (such as equality or the distribution of funding) in opposition to, or to the exclusion of, other parties. The research underlines a long-held criticism that some council officials or elected representatives do not take community relations seriously and that CROs often feel sidelined, with their work deemed of low priority. Most of the CROs we spoke to would argue for devolving further responsibility for reconciliation to district councils only if there was unequivocal broader support, resources were adequate, and there was significant change in how councils—and councillors—operate. The Shared Future policy framework and the review of public administration in Northern Ireland[21] set out new challenges for local government. They also offer new opportunities for councils and councillors, in partnership with practitioners within the community, to foster reconciliation.

But it is interesting to note that implementation of the Shared Future document seems to have been rolled back since the reestablishment of devolution in March 2007. The focus of local politicians seems to have turned to the economy and high-level political cooperation. Politicians have done little to acknowledge publicly, or try to address directly, the glaring divides that still permeate the society.

Conclusions

It is the specifics of not only how we define "reconciliation" that matter but also how we explain and use the concept. Even if an agreed-on definition is difficult to achieve in a society in or emerging from conflict, the onus is on us all to explain what we mean by such terms. Only through robust dialogue can we achieve a more reflective peacebuilding practice. It would be fair to say that in our research, all the respondents felt they knew something about reconciliation and viewed it as a goal to aspire to. For the most part, they appeared to value the opportunity to think about what reconciliation means, but few had a clearly defined understanding. Thus, our research confirms Norman Porter's assertion that "it is probably true to say that a majority of Northern citizens declare themselves in favor of reconciliation. The problem is that what is understood by it is often too vague or too weakly held to withstand the assaults of its detractors" (Porter 2003, 25). This lack of conceptual clarity is not confined to those we interviewed. At least at the time of our research, there was a lack of strategic thinking within statutory bodies, funding groups, and the voluntary sector about the concept of reconciliation. A practical definition, used by all in the peacebuilding field including funders, is not yet shared across the board in the Northern Ireland context.

The purpose of this research was not to come up with such a definition but to explore how people were working with the term and the different resonances it had. However, we did find that the model we posed provided some framework for the people we interviewed, by allowing them to break down

---

21. Following the 1998 Belfast Agreement and the subsequent establishment of the institutions of the devolved government, a review was made of all other aspects of public administration in Northern Ireland. Several consultation documents and processes are under way. For more details, see www.rpani.gov.uk/index.htm.

the concept of reconciliation and consider different aspects of the process. Dealing with the past was identified by many respondents as the next major component of the reconciliation agenda concerning the conflict in and about Northern Ireland, and much work remains in unpacking what this means.[22] That said, in areas where little peacebuilding work has been done, it would be a mistake to jump prematurely into this debate. As many interviewees have pointed out to us, grassroots relationship building and basic dialogue need to come first.

More broadly speaking, different societies might also have different reconciliation priorities at different times. In the South African context, for example, the reconciliation agenda has often been criticized for focusing too much on relationships and ignoring the socioeconomic context (Hamber 2002; van der Merwe 1999; Chapman and van der Merwe 2007). It appears that the opposite is true in Northern Ireland. This common criticism also perhaps reinforces the finding that in the Northern Ireland context, reconciliation is understood largely through the prism of the EU and that the term has become synonymous with the PEACE Programme, which historically has had a strong socioeconomic focus. The criticisms that our research and the other evaluations (e.g., Harvey 2003) raised about the PEACE Programme—that reconciliation needs to be more of a priority—reinforce the view that the program itself has been too focused on the notion of building "peace and reconciliation through prosperity," without thoroughly exploring how attitudinal change and relationship building will happen as a result. This has been recognized by the SEUPB, and its plans for the PEACE II extension and for PEACE III include a more rigorous focus on reconciliation. In fact, following the presentation of the initial findings of the research discussed in this chapter (Kelly and Hamber 2004, 2005), the SEUPB adopted the working definition of "reconciliation" that we presented here as the basis for its approach to reconciliation in the PEACE II extension funding program.[23] All groups applying for funding had to argue how their project met at least three of the strands of our working definition. Although this missed the subtlety of what we were trying to convey about all the strands operating with reference to one another in a dynamic way and about the need to work with the tensions between them, it was nonetheless a significant advance. The PEACE III Program will also build on our definition, although now the definition has been broken down even further by the SEUPB. The new program incorporates the key strands of the definition of "reconciliation" into the overall objectives of the program, thus assuming that

---

22. The Healing through Remembering project, which specifically focused on how Northern Ireland can deal with the past, is the most concerted such attempt by civil society. (See www. healingthroughremembering.org.)

23. See SEUPB 2005b.

projects promoting cross-community relations, shared spaces, and under-standing will contribute collectively to reconciliation in a wider sense (SEUPB 2007). It remains to be seen whether this approach, which deviates from our more holistic and dynamic understanding, will be practically helpful.

Although we were encouraged by some of the findings that reconciliation is a concept that people are attracted to and interested in putting into prac-tice, at the same time we recognize that implementing changes in relation-ships in a deeply divided society is a tremendously complex task. For some of our interviewees, reconciliation is part of their work, although few use the term to describe it. This is partly because, as mentioned above, reconcili-ation is seen as a challenging concept. Overall, there seems to be anxiety in Northern Ireland that genuine reconciliation will mean some compromise, or at least the rehumanization of old enemies. Reconciliation implies a mud-dying of the waters and fundamental change in perceptions of the "other." This was a particularly interesting finding of the research, suggesting that reconciliation is viewed as a "hard" concept and process rather than as the "soft" one that it often proves to be.

Although it is difficult to draw direct causal links between reconciliation initiatives and wider social stability, there is little doubt that Northern Ire-land is now a less violent place than it was. For example, the death rate fell dramatically after the 1994 cease-fires, only to peak again in 1998–99, with forty-four deaths that year attributed to the security situation; in 2003–04, there were seven (SEUPB 2005a). Attitudinal surveys have also found that participants in PEACE II Programs are much more likely than the popula-tion to have neighbors from the other community, to have contact with the other community at work and at community meetings and events, and to have friends from the other community (SEUPB 2004).[24] But as we mentioned earlier, residential, educational, and social segregation remains.

There is arguably a political investment in the segregation (politicians' power bases are consolidated along sectarian lines), and it is a situation that most people living in Northern Ireland either are resigned to or feel more comfortable and secure with. This might account for the anxiety of many interviewees about what reconciliation means practically and their fears that it might lead to "coming together"—a concept that makes local communities and politicians feel threatened. However, at the same time and despite such fears, the interviewees also recognized that more was needed than nonvio-lent segregation or peaceful coexistence. This suggests that reconciliation work needs to be conscious, progressive, interventionist, and directed. Also,

---

24. This research does raise important questions, however: For example, is there a selection bias, that is, are those who choose to engage in peace and reconciliation programs more pre-disposed to make contact with the "other" than is the general population?

genuine reconciliation cannot be expected to flow from investment or a peace agreement alone. This reality calls for a transformative social agenda and concentrated efforts to address relationships in deeply divided societies—a minimalist approach to reconciliation is simply not enough.

References

ADM/CPA. 2003. *Reconciliation Report: Southern Border Counties in Ireland.* Monaghan, Republic of Ireland: ADM/CPA Programme for Peace and Reconciliation.

———. n.d. "Peace-Building in the Border Counties: Implementing Reconciliation: Intention and Practice." Monaghan, Republic of Ireland: ADM/CPA.

Allport, Gordon W. 1954. *The Nature of Prejudice.* Reading, UK: Addison-Wesley.

Assefa, Hizkias. 2001. "Reconciliation." In *Peacebuilding: A Field Guide,* ed. Luc Reychler and Thania Paffenholz, 336–42. Boulder, Colo.: Lynne Rienner.

Bloomfield, David, Teresa Barnes, and Luc Huyse, eds. 2003. *Reconciliation after Violent Conflict: A Handbook.* Stockholm: International Institute for Democracy and Electoral Assistance.

Central Community Relations Unit. 1992. *Evaluation of the District Council Community Relations Programme.* Belfast: CCRU.

Chapman, Audrey R., and Hugo van der Merwe, eds. 2007. *Truth and Reconciliation in South Africa: Did the TRC Deliver?* Philadelphia: University of Pennsylvania Press.

Clegg, Cecelia, and Joseph Liechty. 2001. *Moving beyond Sectarianism Project: Religion, Conflict and Reconciliation in Northern Ireland.* Dublin: Columba Press.

Coiste na n-Iarchimí. 2003. (*Processes of Nation Building Report*). *Responses to Government Consultations on Community Relations and Resettlement of Ex-Prisoners* Belfast: Coiste na n-Iarchimí.

Community Relations Unit. 2005. *A Shared Future: Policy and Strategic Framework for Good Relations in Northern Ireland.* Belfast: Community Relations Unit, OFMDFM.

Coopers and Lybrand. 1997. *Mid-Term Evaluation of the Programme for Peace and Reconciliation.* Draft report. Belfast: Department of Finance and Personnel.

Eyben, Karin, Derick A. Wilson, and Duncan J. Morrow. 2000. *Reconciliation and Social Inclusion in Rural Areas.* Cookstown, Northern Ireland: Rural Community Network.

Faith and Politics Group. 2002. *A Time to Heal: Perspectives on Reconciliation.* Belfast: Faith and Politics Group.

Hamber, Brandon. 2002. "'Ere Their Story Die': Truth, Justice and Reconciliation in South Africa." *Race and Class* 44 (1): 61–79.

Hamber, Brandon, and Gráinne Kelly. 2005. *A Place for Reconciliation? Conflict and Locality in Northern Ireland.* Belfast: Democratic Dialogue.

Hamber, Brandon, Dorte Kulle, and Robin Wilson. 2001. *Future Policies for the Past.* Belfast: Democratic Dialogue.

Hamber, Brandon, and Hugo van der Merwe. 1998. "What Is This Thing Called Reconciliation?" *Reconciliation in Review* 1 (1): 3–6.

Hamber, Brandon, and Robin Wilson. 2003. *Recognition and Reckoning: The Way Ahead on Victims Issues* (Report 15). Belfast: Democratic Dialogue.

Hamilton, Jennifer, Kirsten Thomson, and Marie Smyth. 2002. *Reviewing REAL Provision: An Evaluation of Provision and Support for People Affected by the Northern Ireland Troubles.* Belfast: Northern Ireland Voluntary Trust.

Harvey, Brian. 2003. *Review of the Peace II Programme.* York, UK: Joseph Rowntree Charitable Trust.

Hayes, Bernadette, Ian McAllister, and Lizanne Dowds. 2006. "In Search of the Middle Ground: Integrated Education and Northern Ireland Politics." *ARK Research Update* 42 (January).

Healing through Remembering. 2002. Report of the Healing through Remembering Project. Belfast.

Hewstone, Miles, and Rupert Brown. 1986. "Contact Is Not Enough: An Intergroup Perspective on the Contact Hypothesis." In *Contact and Conflict in Intergroup Encounters,* ed. Miles Hewstone and Rupert Brown, 3–44. Oxford, UK: Basil Blackwell.

Holland, Jack. 2003. "NIO's Browne Giving Voice to Victims." *Irish Echo Online,* February 12-18, www.irishecho.com/search/searchstory.cfm?id=12713&issueid=294 (accessed June 15, 2008).

Hughes, Joanne, and Paul Carmichael. 1998. "Community Relations in Northern Ireland: Attitudes to Contact and Integration." In *Social Attitudes in Northern Ireland: The 7th Report,* ed. Gillian Robinson, Deirdre Heenan, Ann Marie Gray, and Kate Thompson, 1–19. Aldershot, UK: Ashgate.

Hughes, Joanne, and Cathlin Donnelly. 2002. "Ten Years of Social Attitudes to Community Relations in Northern Ireland." In *Social Attitudes in Northern Ireland: The 8th Report,* ed. Ann Marie Gray, Katrina Lloyd, Paula Devine, Gillian Robinson, and Deirdre Heenan, 39-55. London: Pluto Press.

Hurley, Michael, ed. 1994. *Reconciliation in Religion and Society.* Belfast: Institute of Irish Studies.

Kelly, Gráinne, and Brandon Hamber. 2004. "Coherent, Contested or Confused? Views on Reconciliation in Northern Ireland." Paper presented at "Reconciliation: Rhetoric or Relevance?" Roundtable discussion on concepts and practices of reconciliation, Belfast, June 9.

———. 2005. *Reconciliation: Rhetoric or Relevance?* Belfast: Democratic Dialogue.

Lederach, John Paul. 1997. *Building Peace: Sustainable Reconciliation in Divided Societies.* Washington, D.C.: United States Institute of Peace Press.

Lloyd, Katrina, and Gillian Robinson. 2008. "Intimate Mixing: Bridging the Gap? Catholic-Protestant Relationships in Northern Ireland." *ARK Research Update* 54 (April).

Love, Mervyn T. 1995. *Peace Building through Reconciliation in Northern Ireland.* Aldershot, UK: Avebury Press.

Monaghan, Paddy, and Eugene Boyle. 1998. *Adventures in Reconciliation: Twenty-Nine Catholic Testimonies.* Surrey, UK: Eagle.

Morrissey, Mike, and Marie Smyth. 2002. *Northern Ireland after the Good Friday Agreement: Victims, Grievance and Blame.* London: Pluto Press.

Morrow, John. 2003. *On the Road of Reconciliation: A Brief Memoir.* Dublin: Columba Press.

NIVT. 1997a. *Building Peace, Piece by Piece.* Belfast: NIVT.

———. 1997b. *Taking Risks for Peace: A Midterm Review by an Intermediary Funding Body of the EU Peace Process.* Belfast: NIVT.

Northern Ireland Office. 1998. *The Agreement: Text of the Agreement Reached in the Multi-Party Negotiations on Northern Ireland* (10 April 1998) (Cmnd. 3883) [Good Friday Agreement/Belfast Agreement]. Belfast: HMSO.

O'Hara, Mary. 2004. "Self-Imposed Apartheid." *The Guardian*, April 14, www.guardian.co.uk/society/2004/apr/14/northernireland.societyhousing (accessed June 15, 2008).

Paisley, Ian, John Hume, and Jim Nicholson. 1997. "Special Support Programme for Peace and Reconciliation in Northern Ireland and the Border Counties of Ireland Revisited." Unpublished report for Jacques Santer, President of the European Commission, October 1.

Pettigrew, Thomas F. 1998. "Intergroup Contact: Theory, Research and New Perspectives." *Annual Review of Psychology* 49 (February): 65–85.

Porter, Norman. 2003. *The Elusive Quest: Reconciliation in Northern Ireland.* Belfast: Blackstaff Press.

Rigby, Andrew. 2001. *Justice and Reconciliation: After the Violence.* London: Lynne Rienner.

SEUPB. 2004. *The EU Programme for Peace and Reconciliation in Northern Ireland and the Border Region of Ireland 2000-2006: Attitudinal Survey.* NISRA report for the Distinctiveness Working Group, PEACE II Monitoring Committee. Belfast: SEUPB.

———. 2005a. *Annual Implementation Report 2004.* Belfast: SEUPB.

———. 2005b. *PEACE II Extension: A Guide to Applying for Funding.* Belfast: SEUPB, www.seupb.org/documents/PEACE%20II%20Extension/peaceextendsumm.pdf (accessed July 3, 2008).

———. 2007. *PEACE III EU Programme for Peace and Reconciliation 2007–2013 Northern Ireland and the Border Region of Ireland Operational Programme.* Belfast: Special EU Programmes Body.

Stevens, David. 2004. *The Land of Unlikeness: Explorations into Reconciliation.* Dublin: Columba Press.

Thomson, Alwyn, ed. 1998. *Future with Hope: Biblical Framework for Peace and Reconciliation in Northern Ireland, with Study Guide.* Belfast: Pathways Series, ECONI.

van der Merwe, Hugo. 1999. *The Truth and Reconciliation Commission and Community Reconciliation: An Analysis of Competing Strategies and Conceptualizations.* Unpublished PhD diss., George Mason University.

———. 2000. "National and Community Reconciliation: Competing Agendas in the South African Truth and Reconciliation Commission." In *Burying the Past: Making Peace and Doing Justice after Civil Conflict,* ed. Nigel Biggar. Washington, D.C.: Georgetown University Press.

Victims Unit. 2002. *Reshape, Rebuild, Achieve: Delivering Practical Help and Services to the Victims of the Conflict in Northern Ireland.* Belfast: OFMDFM, Victims Unit.

Wells, Ronald. 1999. *People behind the Peace: Community and Reconciliation in Northern Ireland.* Grand Rapids, Mich.: Eerdmans.

11

Local Histories: A Methodology for Understanding

Community Perspectives on Transitional Justice

Matilde González

This chapter discusses the potential interpretations offered by historical studies of the armed conflict in Guatemala and the subsequent transition period, from the perspective of the town or community. Also discussed are ideas on approach and methodology that influenced the research and enabled the author to delve into the experiences of conflict and violence in the K'iche community. The chapter explores the failings of the existing research on Guatemala's violent history, including the ways in which that research ignores both the regional complexities of the conflict and the territorial inequalities underlying the different grounds for the conflict and for prolonged militarization throughout Guatemala. This study underscores the importance of understanding how the conflict was experienced and understood among the people of the different affected areas and the need to identify the deep transformations that the conflict engendered at the local level in daily life and in local organizations and structures.

Researchers on the conflict in Guatemala typically focus on human rights violations that occurred during the first five years of the 1980s and the subsequent massive displacement of people. Although this approach helps us understand the human suffering that occurred, it loses sight of the interpretation of the violence inherent in a system of domination, and it blurs the analysis of the functioning of the local and national powers during the war and the subsequent transition period. Such studies emphasize the outbreak of violence but often neglect to interpret the process that generated it. The current understanding of Guatemala is one of exclusion, arbitrariness, and violence that are portrayed as "normal," "current," and "unavoidable." It is not mere coincidence that research into the nature and history of violence there has only just begun, and for those who take the task seriously, there are risks. The subject of historical memory continues to be a sensitive issue for important power blocs, which prefer silence. The barrage of threats and intimidation against human rights organizations and activists, forensic anthropologists, mental health associations, and researchers who have taken up the challenge of studying contemporary history is an all too frightening reality in Guatemala today.

Within this context, the report of the Interdiocesan Recovery of Historical Memory Project (REMHI), titled *Guatemala: Nunca Más* (Office of Human Rights of the Archbishop of Guatemala 1998), and the report of the Commission for Historical Clarification (CEH), titled *Guatemala: Memoria del silencio* (CEH 1999), are vitally important points of departure. Both reports document the map and logic of the conflict in Guatemala, and both emphasize the authoritarian character of the Guatemalan state and put forward valuable recommendations to foster peace and build a democratic culture. For example, the recommendations in the CEH report translate into a series of indispensable measures to establish the foundations of a democratic state based on the rule of law. Among the measures proposed are those aimed at preserving the memory of victims, providing reparations for victims, fostering a culture of mutual respect and observance of human rights, strengthening the democratic process, and promoting national peace and reconciliation.

But now, almost a decade after publication of the truth commission reports, many of the recommendations have not yet been implemented by the state. At this stage in the transition process, there is continued concern about impunity and the lack of criminal prosecution. This lack of progress results partly from the continued presence, in important positions in the central, departmental, and local governments, of military personnel who were responsible for human rights violations during the conflict[1] and also from the weakness and general dysfunction of the justice system. At this stage in the process, the popularization and broadened use of terms such as "peace," "democratization," and "national reconciliation" are of concern, because these concepts contrast dramatically with the entrenchment of authoritarian concepts and practices in the exercise of power.

The Work to Be Done

The current transition discourse on the Guatemala conflict and the ensuing transition is based on an uncritical and uncreative research agenda. It is a research agenda that deals with "the present at present," focusing only on immediate and short-term issues and deeming everything that took place

---

1. Recent research reveals that high-ranking army officials (who were responsible for the killings and innumerable violations of human rights) occupy important positions within the government and are part of the clandestine structures of organized crime in Guatemala. On November 12, 2002, a report published in *El Periódico* (2–4) listed thirty-eight persons who were implicated.

during the thirty-six years of armed conflict to be a closed chapter and no longer relevant. It is an agenda that tolerates the absurdity of the silence in the official discourse about the past and does not take into account the work to be done. It is an agenda that seeks to study the post-conflict situation without understanding the dynamics of the conflict in local communities.

While the report of the CEH is a fundamental reference for historical research into Guatemala's past, the commission's mandate and methodology did not allow it to deal with the complexity of the conflict as seen in local and regional histories. The commission's emphasis on cataloging and documenting cases leads to a blurring of the territorial inequalities underlying the different causes for the conflict and for the prolonged militarization of Guatemala. This is one of the reasons why the report's recommendations emphasize the importance of further research and analysis of the conflict. We still need to understand how the conflict was experienced and understood among the people of the affected regions and towns. We still need to identify the deep transformations that the conflict provoked at the local level in daily life and in local organizations and structures. We still do not know, or we know very little, about the impact on local politics, the changes in the way individuals understand and experience the most intimate relationships, and the changes in knowledge and power that the conflict provoked. In other words, we still need to examine the depth and seriousness of the wounds that still have not healed and the sufferings that still persist. We need to know the condition of each part of the societal body that was injured, as well as the different processes of recovery. Only in this way can the impact (or lack of impact) of official transitional justice processes be understood in their local context.

Studying a Post-Conflict Society from a Town Perspective

From 1995 to 2001, I worked on the reconstruction of the history of a K'iche town (San Bartolomé Jocotenango)[2] that was seriously affected by conflict and militarization.[3] One purpose of the research was to understand the complexity of the conflict from a local perspective in order to provide a fuller historical interpretation. This was done by examining the multiple perspectives of causality and consequence—the diverse

---

2.   This municipality is part of a more extensive social and historical territory, situated at the southwest and southeast of the northern part of Quiché, between the hill Sacapulas, the mountain Los Achiotes, and the hill Chuacus, including the municipalities of Sacapulas, San Andrés Sajcabajá, San Pedro Jocopilas, Santa Rosa Chujuyub, and San Bartolomé Jocotenango (in Quiché) and Santa Lucía la Reforma (in Totonicapán).

3.   This research was the basis of two publications by the Asociación para el Avance de las Ciencias Sociales en Guatemala (Association for the Advancement of Social Sciences in Guatemala, or AVANCSO). See González and AVANCSO 2002a, 2002b.

scenarios, actors, relationships, and interests of the local-national power that played a role in the origin and outbreak of the conflict and the manner in which these powers repositioned themselves after the war. The project aimed to understand the distances and contrasts between the discourses of conflict and "peace" at a national level and the interpretations built at the community level as a result of the local people's experience and culture.

Another purpose of the research was to record the different expressions and mechanisms of political participation by ordinary people during the emergence and outbreak of the conflict. This was done to underscore the community's participation in the history of the nation, to document its procedures, allegations, claims and petitions, and alliances and conflicts. Finally, the research sought to retrace the reasons for acts of individual and collective resistance and the ways in which these were organized. During the conflict, individuals and groups in this community chose different options for political participation. While some accommodated and collaborated with the system of domination, many others played an active role in the resistance. From their local perspective and their particular way of understanding the world, people not only knew their history but also took decisions and actions to change it.

The motivation for this study was to approach local history in a way that would account for the complexity and diversity of cultures in Guatemala. The goal was to reveal even the smallest mechanisms through which macro social policies are implemented and to identify their impact and, thus, the different local and regional responses.

Approach and Methodology

The methodology that guided the research for this chapter was based on three precepts: (1) research at the local level, with the town or community as a privileged space for the interpretation of social change; (2) oral history as both a method and a source for societal research; and (3) the ethics of researching populations affected by war.

Research at the Local Level

The local community is an opportune space for the interpretation of social change.[4] In the case of Guatemala, we think of local history studies as a starting point for understanding the complexity of armed conflict and the

---

4. Many of the reflections in this section are drawn from the readings and discussions held by the author and other staff members of the Local History Division of AVANCSO.

ensuing transition.[5] By conducting research at the local level, we can observe with some precision the disparity between, on one hand, the national proposals and discourse that refer to the "strengthening of democracy" and, on the other, the concrete forms that exist for the exercise and deployment of power.

Community, or local history, studies enable us to understand the challenges of a country trapped in old conflicts that manifest themselves at a local-regional level. Community studies do not try to identify and catalog these micro aspects with the sole purpose of seeing how specific, varied, or different they are; instead, the analysis is aimed at revealing the way in which this variation and this specificity affect the manner in which the society functions. Therefore, one of the methodological premises of local history studies is that one cannot understand local events and factors in isolation from the complex relationships on a regional, national, and global scale. Thus, a serious study of the history of conflict from the standpoint of the community (or the region) requires deep knowledge of the economic, social, and political dynamics that have defined and continue to define contemporary history. (See Báez and Ponce 1988.)

Local history studies emphasize the internal movements of the individuals in the community, paying close attention to the complex dynamics among social subjects at different times during the outbreak of conflict and during the transition. This is based on the premise that the beginning of conflicts and contestation is accompanied by the continuous formation of new points of equilibrium, which are constantly prone to new breakdowns or ruptures (Levi 1990). This view is critical of models, built by historians and anthropologists, that explain social change of the "small" and "fragile" rural communities as if they were purely the result of external causes. Observing what is going on in these communities from a distance limits the ability to understand the movements of daily politics and runs the risk of lapsing into simplifications of reality by reflecting in a mechanistic way on the relations between individuals and rules, between decisions and actions.

In Guatemala, for example, these "views from a distance" have contributed to the denial or the invisibility of the Mayan people's agency and the relegation of these people to the category of "submissive victims" of the system. As a group becomes "victims," researchers tend to deemphasize the group's capacity to take action and make independent choices. In fact, there is

---

5.   Given that until very recently, most studies of Guatemalan communities or towns were developed from the field of cultural anthropology, a methodological proposal that might guide studies of contemporary history from the local perspective does not yet exist. It is for this reason that we draw on the discussions by the Italian microhistorians. Although the scope of microhistorical presentation is not limited to the community, its contribution is of vital importance to the critical recovery of local and regional history.

a tendency among researchers to encourage respondents to discuss the suffering caused by a certain abuse, but not the fury, the challenge, or the resistance that came with that suffering. Grossman (1999) writes that the most serious aspect of this simplification is that compassion for the victim replaces acknowledgment of, and respect for, the struggle. What is emphasized is suffering instead of political participation and resistance. This tendency reinforces and reflects an authoritarian vision of history in which the action of the majorities becomes a background against which a few "famous" individuals are placed in the limelight as the agents of history (Grossman 1999).

In contrast, studying conflict from the perspective of the community reveals that popular groups or sectors have varied and changing processes of social breakdown, rupture, and division; they cannot be portrayed through the idyllic imagery of a unified society devoid of conflict. Thus, while analyzing the long-term activities of one person (or group), we notice that the subject chooses among different political participation options, depending on the social context; there are times when the individual accommodates and collaborates with the system of domination, whereas in other situations, the same person may play an active role in the resistance. Unlike the romantic perspective that shows harmonious and cooperative relations within "the community," a local perspective analyzes the power relations, recording the link that exists between the exercise of power and violence. Community studies focus attention on the power networks that concentrate the power within the local space (local elites) and on the power blocs (economic, political, social, and cultural) that exist at the national level. In other words, a local history perspective examines the articulations established within the community, and from there outward. This articulation is expressed and repeated simultaneously at various local levels (that is, at the level of the region, town, suburb, canton, and so on).

To augment this approach, a microhistorical study must multiply the variables and the complexity of the analysis.[6] This approach, according to Bertrand (1997), is part of acknowledging the diversity of contexts and of social experiences through which the actors carry out their actions.[7] According to this approach, the contexts are seen not only as a simple, stable framework but as spaces from which the multiple experiences of a set of social actors are developed. Attention is drawn to the movement of the actors within a social group. This entails perceiving the social group as a living being, in which changes occur and where decisions are taken that do not follow a normative,

---

6. The complexity of the analysis necessarily supposes a reduction of the scale of observation to a modest level.

7. Identifying this capacity of the actors enables the historian to understand the ways and the limits of the group being studied.

predetermined course and cannot be imposed according to a single context, be it political, economic, social, or cultural.

In a transitional justice context, a local history or community studies approach allows for the complexity of the actor's behavior and takes into account the actor's ability to adapt to changing political, economic, social, or cultural realities. Community studies encompass the tensions at play among the processes of co-option, collaboration, and resistance. In particular, community studies focus on the reconstruction of the social networks (Bertrand 1997). During stages of "political transition" such as the one currently under way in Guatemala, examining the reconstruction of social networks at the local level may contribute to a more nuanced and complete understanding of periods often identified simply as "democratization" and "national reconciliation." Studying the political life, social relations, economic rules, and psychological reactions of a "town that is not important," such as San Bartolomé Jocotenango, enables us to analyze things that happen when "apparently" nothing is happening. It uncovers what happened there during the conflict and what is still happening in this "time of peace," and it points to multiple questions for what may be happening in the rest of the country.

Oral Sources

One of the peculiarities of studies of local history or microhistory is the need to look for other sources besides written documentation. This is because, in dealing with geographic spaces or social groups that are "not so important," we must confront the difficulty presented by the scarcity of written documentation. In the case of San Bartolomé, besides the insufficiency of the written record,[8] the aim of the study and the periodic research made it necessary to document the spoken word: the memory and the discourse of those who were protagonists of the events to be studied. There was a need to use oral history as a method of research.[9]

This methodology enabled us to record the different points of view of the inhabitants about the events they experienced in their recent history. During the study, we worked on the reconstruction of the history of the lives of

---

8.   It is important to point out that the documentation of the municipal archives of San Bartolomé Jocotenango is scarce because the building housing the archives was set on fire in 1983. We depended mainly on the registries of the Archivo General de Centroamérica (General Archive of Central America, or AGCA) and the archives of the Instituto de Transformación Agraria (Institute of Agrarian Transformation, or INTA), which are insufficient to orient the understanding of the problem (armed conflict) and the period studied (1880–1996). It was precisely during this period that official documentation was denied, the press was censored, and most of the information about the opposition was clandestine.

9.   Paul Thompson (1988) says that oral history as a method of research involves the established procedure of building new sources for social and historical research, based on oral testimony and systematically gathered for specific research with explicit methodological and theoretical problems and points of departure.

women and men, old and young, people who had to uproot themselves from their communities, and those who remained in the community. We carried out in-depth interviews with persons who had occupied positions of authority during that period: mayors; military commissioners; commanders of the Civil Self-Defense Patrols (PACs); teachers; old people who knew the history of the town; and representatives of the confraternities, the Catholic Church, the evangelical churches, and other groups. We also interviewed people who, at some point, had links with the history of San Bartolomé, including priests, nuns, guerrilla leaders, representatives of non-governmental organizations (NGOs), doctors, public officials, and others. The diversity of interpretations and points of view enabled us to observe the complexity of the recent history of San Bartolomé and, at the same time, compare points of view.

The life stories were recorded by means of open interviews, conducted according to an agenda agreed on by an interviewer and interviewee, which enabled us to capture the facts and events that were relevant in their lives. All the sessions were tape-recorded. We handled the taped interviews in the following manner: 1) We transcribed them word for word; (2) we read and corrected each informant's transcript; (3) we included the interviewee's contributions, corrections, and additions; (4) we classified the information contained in each story through the use of a purpose-designed instrument; and (5) we prepared cards and systematized them according to periods and units of analysis. Further, using a stand-alone copy of the word-for-word transcript, we prepared a literary construction of the stories to make them accessible to readers not involved in the research. This construction work targeted the structure of the language and the content, thereby eliminating repetition and placing the stories in chronological order according to subject.

Oral sources are valuable not only because they make up for the lack of documentation but also because they enable us to penetrate other levels of interpretation of the events, which do not appear in written history and often contradict currently accepted interpretations. Oral history is a set of perceptions including reality and imagination, symbolism, feelings, human passions—in other words, the subjective aspects, which are much more significant than the simple recollection of facts. Memory, testimonies, and oral tradition are necessary sources for extending the evidence and are irreplaceable in contexts where oral culture is the main means of production and transmission of knowledge. Ponce (1998) writes that the history of a life rescues not only the historical facts themselves but also the way in which they were perceived by the subjects of history. It is in this divergence that we find the real and the imaginary, the symbolic, the feelings—the subjective aspects that are more significant than a simple account of the facts. Portelli (1988) points out that subjectivity is as much a matter of history as are tangible facts; what the informant believes to have happened is a historical fact, as valid as what really happened.

Oral history is the point of view of "ordinary" people (Thompson 1988). This type of methodology gives a voice to those who are not privileged, who are rejected and marginalized, allowing them to bear witness to their own history and thereby providing us with a more accurate reconstruction of the past while challenging the established order. These sources enable the researcher to capture "history in process," to understand the "microsociology" of power and the interpersonal relationships that tell us the "why" of human decisions and actions. They help us gather many of the "little facts" that do not leave written records and that thus give color and texture to the historical graphics made from written documents.

Local and regional history must make use of its own sources, both in the process of discovery and in its integration and construction. Traditionally, historians use written records, which are generally produced by individuals linked to the dominant culture. This means that the ideas, thoughts, beliefs, and hopes of subordinate groups almost always arrive (if they arrive at all) through filters of "deforming" intermediaries.[10] Thompson (1988) differs with this view, arguing that oral history comes from the people and returns history to them in their own words. While offering a past and giving life to the individual's own history, it also helps find a future of self-definition. As an antidote against the simplifying generalizations of history, life stories gained through oral history methodologies show a range of experiences of the different groups and social classes that make up a society.

The Combination of Sources

Although oral history enables us to approach almost anyone, this does not mean that the process of research attached less importance to the investigation and analysis of written sources. On the contrary, the variety and wealth of sources, written, oral, and visual—including archival photos as well as paintings, drawings, and maps, through which the interviewees depicted points in their history—were what enabled us to penetrate the people's social and historical complexity. Indeed, the dialogue between written and oral sources was indispensable. Together, these various sources offer different perspectives, giving a clearer, more nuanced picture of a given period, event, or process and allowing the construction of a more complete, rich, and dynamic tale.

In our research, we retraced state policies by means of documents that were archived or otherwise on file: laws, appeals, applications, or protests by

---

10. Carlo Ginzburg (1997, preface) argues that talk of "deforming" filters and intermediaries is relative—the fact that a source is not "objective" does not mean that it is unusable.

which the residents of the municipality were trying to modify government policies. We were also able to capture the activities of the state (approvals, silences, and negations) in response to the actions by the people of San Bartolomé. In these documents appear the details of the social actors: full name and surname, place of birth, age, and even the number and registration of their documents. If the issue was land, we included details on adjacent properties, extensions, type and quality of agricultural production, former and current owners, prices, litigations, expropriations, and so on. Archived sources contributed vitally important details by locating the events in time and space. Taken together with the oral histories, this information helped provide a fuller understanding of the people's lives.

Ethics and the Process of Research

> *Although the old survivors were walking books, I could not page them anymore. They were people.* —Ewart Evans

Although the methodology of oral histories has been well developed, little has been written about what happens to those players active in the preparation of the oral account that is, what happens to the interviewee and the interviewer? How is this relationship constructed and lived?

The question of the relationship between interviewee and interviewer becomes more important when we enter the world of ideas, meanings, experiences, and intimacies of people who have been affected by war. We encounter their fear, persecution, displacement, and separation from the community and from their relations, their world, and their culture. Our primary concern was to make the process of historical research a means of psychological and social reparations. We sought ways to make the process of recounting events into a means whereby the participants could reshape their sense of their history and the role they played in it. In other words, participants were able to see themselves as actors who, when confronted with a range of options, made conscious decisions. We strove always to find ways to have the research process contribute to the restoration of relationships among living persons or between the living and the dead—the latter class of relationship being of vital importance within the K'iche culture.

The current field and practice of oral history did not provide us with easy ethical guidelines. As a result, it was necessary to take into account the approach and methodological experience of social psychology, or community mental health work, developed in the Central American region, and from it we adopted some of the criteria used during the individual interviews and collective exercises of reconstruction of the local history. These ethical criteria are explained below.

To Build Trust. One of the explicit objectives of the Guatemalan government's anti-insurgency policy was to undermine trust among the people within a community in order to inhibit their social cohesion and ensure that they would keep silent about the violence they witnessed. Also, during the war, polarization divided the people into "good people" and "bad people," "friends" and "enemies," according to the side they placed themselves on. These dynamics converted the lack of trust into a mechanism of extreme importance for one's actual physical survival.

In this environment of separation, fear, suspicion, and prolonged silences, it took time to build a relationship of trust before conducting any interviews with the men and women of San Bartolomé. This two-way relationship of trust had to be based on an understanding of who each of us was and what each expected from the others. Thus, it was important to discuss jointly the objectives, approach, and methodology of the research and what we would do with the information obtained. Finally, we explained the basic expectations and undertakings of this work. This process of building trust was slow and gradual.

The process of building trust was different for men and women. Although, in most cases, the men were prepared to tell their life stories from the beginning, it was only after they made the process their own that they transcended the formal discourse, broke their initial silence, and adopted a more critical perspective on their own intervention and the intervention of other actors in their town. In marked contrast to this, throughout our first year of conducting research in the field, the women used to say, "I don't know anything; the one who knows well, who remembers, is the man." Only later, as they heard the transcribed stories of the men of their families (husbands and fathers), trust grew and many of them stated, "It's all right; we'll talk," or "We'll tell what happened in our lives," or "We'll talk, but not here." In order to talk about the intimate details of their lives, many women needed to leave their immediate family surroundings; they needed to be in a neutral space where they could freely express their version—sometimes divergent—of the life they shared with one of the interviewed men. Most of their narrative was made in K'iche and translated by people they trusted.

After listening for one year to the stories of the men about their "harmonious" life and family relationships, it was very revealing to listen to the women, who talked not only about the political violence applied by others but also about the violence within the family space. It is for this reason that building trust with the women was much slower than with the men— because it was necessary to build trust between the parties as well as confidence within the individual women themselves, that is, to make them feel that their life and involvement were important and that they had the right to break with the official versions given by the men and express their own version. The interviewed women always started by saying, "I have nothing important to tell you." When we had concluded the process, we would read the testimony back to them and present them with a written copy of their history. They were stunned and said, "All those letters are what I told you; all that is my life."

The depth and quality of the stories depend on trust, which, as we have seen, requires time—time to achieve mutual knowledge and understanding, time to talk, and time to listen. In the case of the people of San Bartolomé, those who were more silent were the ones who most needed to talk, and the things that were kept silent were the things that had to be named and reinterpreted. It was only after a long time that people started to break the silence on their most stigmatized and painful experiences.

Another lesson was to understand that the life stories, the personal accounts, depend on time. A life story is a living thing; it is always a work in process, to the extent that the teller reviews the image of her or his own past as it progresses (Portelli 1993). When the fieldwork for this study was formally concluded, several men and women of San Bartolomé approached us again to complete their history, that is, to talk about more difficult or painful situations that they had to confront during the war. The more revealing stories—and also the most frightening—about the way in which the people of San Bartolomé lived and understood the war were gathered at a time when many needed to relate what they had not shared earlier. It was from this moment onward that several informants began to speak in the first person and acknowledged their acts, drew the faces, and named the people involved. It was at that moment that they explained in depth and detail the dynamics of the conflict in their town and went into the language and symbolic interpretation of the violent events. It was then that some women started to talk about the abuses and situations of sexual slavery that were imposed on them by the army and the PACs.[11] Perhaps a critical component to the increase in willingness to talk about these abuses was that our fieldwork coincided with the signing of the peace agreements and the formal dissolution of the PACs.

To Talk and to Listen. As social researchers, we are often in a hurry to have people talk to us and give answers about the things we are interested in researching. We want them to talk about the things that are important

---

11.   In March 1982, the Guatemalan army and the PACs carried out operations in each village of the municipality and forced the women found in their houses to come down to the center of town. They locked them in the church and parish convent, where the women were systematically raped and forced to prepare food for the whole army station for a period of six or seven months. This is a story known by the whole town, but nobody talks about it, because many of the men who were responsible or were accomplices or observers of those events are also the husbands, fathers, or other relatives of those women. Many of those women continue to live with the men responsible for the rapes.

to us. In our haste, we sometimes force things, spoiling the opportunity to establish a relaxed communication that would enable the subject to talk about the things that preoccupy him or her, the things that the subject considers important. Many times we inhibit their natural ways of structuring and expressing their ideas or memories; we interrupt their evocation of the past and the freedom of their memory.

When we use interviews or work sessions to reconstruct a life history, especially one that has been affected by extreme violence, it is indispensable to leave academic anxieties aside and open a space for the subject's emotional outpouring, thus enabling the subject to share those feelings that have been denied or hidden many times. It is essential to provide a safe space that will allow the subject to talk quietly about what happened and what is happening now and about how he or she understands and experiences the things that have happened. It means listening seriously to what the subject has to say. It means being interested and paying attention, listening, and deciphering each word, phrase, gesture, look, and means of expression that the interlocutor is communicating. It is necessary to establish a real link through which the current can flow, to open a sincere and fraternal dialogue through which human growth will be possible.

In countries such as Guatemala, where the language of violence and inequality prevails, many women and men live with prolonged silence and are waiting to be heard. They are not to be forced—yet again—through often impertinent interrogations about the experiences of their lives, as if, on top of everything else they have suffered, they should now be obliged to subordinate their own serenity and dignity to the requirements of those who are investigating them.

Mental Health Exercises

Although my methodology heeded the latest historiographic trends, I also made use of several techniques and exercises developed by social psychology. Two of the exercises were the critical reading of the path in life of each participant in the individual realm, and the workshops known as "Reconstructing Our History" in the collective realm. The objective of these exercises was for the participants to reappraise and critically interpret their agency as belligerents in their own history.

Critical Reading

In reconstructing the histories of life, we divided the working sessions into two parts. In the first part, people were expected to talk about and tell their life story without interruption. An agenda was prepared, and the informant organized the points that he or she wished to deal with into a narrative. In this part, the informants regularly needed to give a full, although general, account of their lives from childhood until the moment when they could say, "Now I have told you everything," or "That is my life," or "That's the way it was." During this narration, there was an emotional unburdening of some painful experiences that had not been confronted before, but there were also successful experiences that enabled subjects to overcome limiting situations and move forward with their lives.

In the approaches and practices of the mental health field, it is considered important to help a person not only express and acknowledge experiences but also find a meaning for them. It is only by making sense of those experiences and feelings that a person learns to confront them, overcoming the helplessness caused by so much loss and damage (Beristain and Riera 1992). It is for this reason that after the subjects' initial unburdening, we worked on preparing a second part to the collection of local histories: a critical reading of those experiences with each informant. Critical reading is a process that allows the informants to place the events in a larger context, to relate the personal experiences within the local and national dynamics in which they happened, and to revaluate the mechanisms, relationships, feelings, and abilities that enabled them to continue living despite their experiences. We tried to give value to the path they had taken and to allow them to learn from the steps they had taken—in other words, to value their ability to resist so much destruction and their ability to carry on, not as victims but as protagonists of their own vital projects.

Collective Exercises

Generally speaking, repression is carried out against people as members of a collective entity. However, people must confront these situations with their individual resources. In this manner, repression tries to produce an abyss between the individual and his or her society (Martín-Baró 1990). Therefore, in order to give meaning to the experiences, it is necessary to share those individual experiences with others who lived through the same or similar experiences. It is necessary to reestablish trust, "to open the heart and to say the words," to reestablish relationships, to re-create affection within the affected community.

With this in mind, we organized local history reconstruction workshops that were conceived as a space where the people of San Bartolomé—those who had been displaced as well as those who had not—would be able to meet again and where they could (1) share their experiences and feelings about the past, (2) make a critical reading of the personal and group experiences, (3) reconstruct a vision of the past and their common history, (4) reevaluate their participation, and (5) give shape to the fragments of history that each group or family had to live through as a result of the displacement. In other words, the workshops were understood as a space where the people, as a social collective entity, would resolve the puzzle of their local history, recovering in this way their individual and collective memories.

Below are some of the thematic lines of inquiry and reflection that we worked with in these workshops:

- what history is and what it is useful for
- the actors, spaces, and periods of history
- the history lived by "the ancestors," or the history of the past
- the history that we are now living through
- time and life changes
- San Bartolomé and its inhabitants today
- the remaking of our history and identity

These contents were developed through group discussion and plenary sessions, using creative techniques taken from community mental health sources and practices. We gave special importance to developing the creativity of the participants so that they could express their feelings, conflicts, and ideas by means of drawings, paintings, role playing, songs, and games. We also placed special emphasis on recompiling the traditions, customs, beliefs, stories, and legends belonging to the popular culture of the place, which many of the displaced people had ceased to practice or recount. These compilations were carried out by work teams who organized a cultural night, when all those attending represented and reenacted significant aspects of their history (theatrical representations of stories and legends, ballads that narrated important battles that the people fought to defend their lives, traditional dances, jokes, and poetry). This activity strengthened the unity and dignity of the group and was important to their rediscovering their roots.

A compilation of legends and stories has been published in an illustrated edition of the selected life stories (González and AVANCSO 2002a, 2002b). The compiled stories also became valuable sources for a better understanding of history, relationships, and life and death within the municipality. With these chronicles, oral tradition, myths, legends, stories, testimonies, and music, researchers must now look at the "facts" and data in a different manner to fully understand the dimensions of social practices and focus on the history of people who have been denied a history.[12]

Conclusions

Oral tradition can be the means to a fuller understanding of history. It is a dynamic discourse in constant interaction with the most contemporary

---

12. See Ponce 1998.

reality and is thus an expression of history. According to Philippe Joutard (1999), making history with oral tradition is one of the most promising sources for the years to come. The memory, words, and oral tradition of the people of San Bartolomé now present us with multiple questions about the official "truths" of the history of this country. They present us with the need to listen and to include the historical and graphical discourse of those multiple voices, perspectives, and visions of history that we often forget or prefer to ignore.

One of the main lessons of this study is that the research process is as important as—or perhaps more important than—the publication of its results, because of the participation of men and women who have remained silent for many years. These are people who, during the first stage of the fieldwork, would say, "Here, meaning was lost; time was changed," or "I can say what was seen by my eyes," or "My heart hurts when I remember." However, after several years of our coming and going and conducting research, a relationship of trust developed. This trust enabled us to work with people of all ages and social groups (the old, women, men, youths, boys, girls), with people who continued to live inside the municipality and with people who had been displaced and had gone to the capital city, to the south coast, and to Solola.

Over time, the participation of each of these people was constant, courageous, and resolute. Despite the intimidations and the state of surveillance in which they lived, the need to break the silence prevailed. To remember out loud, to name the events, became one of the most important ways to recover the senses, a way to recover their identity and the identities of their dead. While remembering, most of the people we interviewed would express reflections such as "We have to remember what happened in order to know how time changed, how life changed," or "We have to remember the things that we lived through in order to clarify the truth," or "We have to remember history in order to know, in order not to forget our roots and thus to allow new seeds to sprout." To tell a story saves the teller from oblivion, because the story builds the identity of the teller and the legacy that he or she will leave for the future. In the midst of adversity and terror, the tellers' voices are the ones that enabled the reconstruction of the contemporary history of San Bartolomé and, at the same time, the history of many other people affected by times of darkness and death. In this case, as in many others in which human dignity was violated, collective remembrance is one of the many ways to acknowledge that the events did happen, that they were unjust, and that they must not happen again.

References

Báez Landa, Mariano, and Patricia Ponce Jiménez. 1988. *Relatos de vida: historia, etnografía y novela.* Mexico City: CHRISTUS.

Beristain, Carlos, and Francesc Riera. 1992. *Salud Mental, La Comunidad como Apoyo.* San Salvador: UCA.

Bertrand, Michel. 1997. "En busca de una identidad social: Redes familiares y elite colonial en tiempos de crisis." Conference held during the summer term, Universidad Complutense de Madrid, Spain.

CEH. 1999. *Guatemala: Memoria del silencio.* Guatemala City: CEH.

Ginzburg, Carlo. 1997. *El queso y los gusanos.* Barcelona: Península.

González, Matilda, and Asociación para el Avance de las Ciencias Sociales en Guatemala (AVANCSO). 2002a. *Stories of Life and Oral Tradition in San Bartolomé Jocotenango.* Guatemala City: AVANCSO.

———. 2002b. "Time Was Changed: Conflict and Power in K'iche' Territory." *Cuaderno de Investigación* no. 17. Guatemala City: AVANCSO.

Grossman, Jonathan. 1999. "Violencia y silencio: Reescribir el futuro. Silenciar la experiencia, la resistencia y la esperanza de la clase trabajadora." *Historia, Antropología y Fuentes Orales* 21: 131–148. Barcelona: Universitat de Barcelona.

Joutard, Philippe. 1999. "Nuevas polémicas sobre historia oral. Algunos retos que se le plantean a la historia oral del siglo XXI." *Historia, Antropología y Fuentes Orales* 21: 149–62. Barcelona: Universitat de Barcelona.

Levi, Giovanni. 1990. *La herencia inmaterial. La historia de un exorcista piamontés del siglo XVII.* Madrid: Nerea.

Martín-Baró, Ignacio. 1990. *Psicología social de la guerra.* San Salvador: UCA Editores.

Office of Human Rights of the Archbishop of Guatemala (ODHAG). 1998. *Guatemala: Nunca Más. Informe Proyecto Interdiocesano de Recuperación de la Memoria Histórica (Interdiocesan Recovery of Historical Memory Project [REMHI]).* Ciudad de Guatemala.

Ponce Jiménez, Martha, 1998. "Historias de vida cotidiana. Novelando la subjetividad." In *Proceedings.* Vol. 2. Tenth International Oral History Conference, Rio de Janeiro, 868–74.

Portelli, Alessandro. 1988. *Peculiaridades de la historia oral.* Mexico City: CHRISTUS.

———. 1993. "El tiempo de mi vida: las funciones del tiempo en la historia oral." In *Historia Oral*, comp. Jorge Aceves. Mexico City: Instituto Mora and Universidad Autónoma Metropolitana (UAM).

Thompson, Paul. 1988. *La Voz del Pasado, la Historia Oral.* Valencia, Spain: Ediciones Alfons el Magnanim.

12

Practical Considerations in Comparative Research

Approaching Problems from the Bottom and from Within

Victor Espinoza Cuevas and María Luisa Ortiz Rojas

T his chapter explores some of the advantages and challenges of using comparative and qualitative research to examine the impacts of truth and reconciliation commissions (TRCs) in five countries: Argentina, Chile, El Salvador, Guatemala, and South Africa. The research project examines the perceptions of those who experienced human rights violations and those working in the field of human rights, focusing specifically on those most affected by the violence. The aim is to examine the affected populations' views of truth commissions and the reparation processes that these commissions generated (or failed to generate). The chapter provides an overview of how the research process was conceived and implemented, with a focus on the practical challenges of conducting a multicountry comparative study relying on interviews, focus groups, and other qualitative research methods.

Truth Commissions: Transitional Justice Mechanisms

Truth commissions have become one of the most important mechanisms of transitional justice in responding to the unavoidable ethical, political, and legal imperatives of governments confronting the effects of serious, massive, systematic violations of human rights. In the wake of authoritarian and dictatorial regimes and governments that have perpetrated crimes against humanity, newly elected democratic governments that wish to restore the rule of law establish these commissions to begin a process of compensation to victims and their families in keeping with international law, restore the standards of conduct broken by state terrorism in the course of armed conflict, and establish solid, credible bases for a new democratic order.

Newly elected governments often vest truth commissions with lofty goals. For example, the report of the National Commission on the Disappeared states, "One of the most important tasks facing resurgent democracy in Argentina was tackling the problem of the disappeared and determining the fate of the victims. The first indispensable reparation demanded by society after fundamental institutions had been restored was to ascertain the truth of what had happened, to 'face up' to the immediate past and let the country judge" (Comisión Nacional sobre la Desaparición de Personas 1984, 43). Likewise, Guatemala's Comisión para el Esclarecimiento Histórico, or Commission for Historical Clarification, declares, "Truth, justice, reparation and forgiveness are the pillars for the consolidation of national peace and reconciliation" (Comisión para el Esclarecimiento Histórico 1999, 62). The Supreme Decree establishing the Chilean National Commission on Truth and Reconciliation (1993, 11) states, "The moral conscience of the nation requires the clarification of the truth . . . because on the basis of the truth it will be possible to satisfy the elementary requirements of justice and create the indispensable conditions to reach an effective national reconciliation." In other words, the new governments appear to be in the initial stages of a process that aims, ultimately, to usher in a democratic system and reestablish the rule of law, with full respect for fundamental rights and freedoms, through a full examination of the past. Although these aims are clearly legitimate, many people view truth commissions as bringing less positive consequences, precisely because of the political controversies and debates that they unleash by examining what is often a contested past.

Truth commissions and other transitional justice mechanisms operate in politically fraught contexts with conflicts and tensions between the outgoing authoritarian players and the incoming democratic protagonists. Commissions also have to contend with a multitude of overlapping political, legal, and moral requirements and expectations. Given the complex issues facing these bodies, it was important to explore the different evaluations of the processes initiated by the truth commissions and their impact on society. In particular, given the central importance accorded to human rights in each truth commission, it is important to determine how the often lofty aims and goals of truth commissions have actually been implemented in a variety of different settings. To do this, a study was designed to measure the scope and relevance of the truth commission process, determine which of a particular commission's recommendations were actually implemented as public policy, and establish the extent to which the community was involved in this process. The general hypothesis was this: To the degree that the causes that generated the conditions of armed conflict and the violations of human rights—normally identified by the commissions in their final reports—still exist, it will be proportionally difficult to consolidate a democratic system.

Indeed, a key finding of the research is that the causal relationship between a truth commission and the political, juridical, and cultural conditions that reflect improved democracy is not simple. Often in countries that have instituted a truth commission, the power structures remain largely unchanged, leaving the perpetrators of the crimes protected by state institutions or other groups that retain real power in the society. Despite this reality, many in leadership and democracy movements continue to uncritically champion truth commissions as genuine democratic processes that lead to the resolution of human rights violations. Moreover, issues that remain unresolved after the formal truth commission process can easily be dismissed by the state, which often argues that now, with the truth commission process completed, it is time for the nation to move beyond the past. In the course of this research, victim advocacy groups and those active in the defense of human rights shared a strong view that the truth commission process does not adequately address the past or provide the means to restore democracy to a country shattered by widespread human rights abuses. This opinion of the efficacy of truth commissions is reflected in the following statement by one of the interviewees:

> When we talk about reparation, justice, truth, and reconciliation, we are talking about the radical transformation of a situation, the structures and the system of values that made the crimes possible. If not, how much time will have to pass until the same violence strikes again for people that did not acknowledge nor radically confront their past of violence and crime with political will? (Espinoza Cuevas, Ortiz Rojas, and Rojas Baeza 2003, 97)

The Study: Main Lines of Analysis and Reflection

The study, titled "Truth Commissions: An Uncertain Path? A Comparative Study of the Truth Commissions in Argentina, Chile, El Salvador, Guatemala, and South Africa as seen by the Victims and Human Rights Organizations," used a consultative methodology. The main sources were the experiences, reflections, opinions, and analysis given by the victims themselves, by members of human rights organizations and victims' groups, and by prominent individuals linked to the defense and well-being of the affected people. Bibliographic and documentary resources were also consulted as a necessary element of the research.

The study examined three key elements affecting the creation and functioning of each commission. First, we measured the levels of consultation with, and participation of, the victims and the various social actors, because these individuals were key to the development of the processes. In this important orientation, the research project differed markedly from many of the existing comparative research studies, which concentrate more on the objectives, procedures, scope, and outcomes of commissions and the policies they implement. The research started with the observation that the discourse around truth commissions has generally been quite removed from those people most affected by serious violations of human rights. It is for this reason that this research starts from a different perspective, which can perhaps best be described as being "from the bottom and from within." This approach allowed the researchers to learn how the victims themselves, as well as the collective bodies linked to the defense of human rights, perceive the commissions and the reparation processes that resulted (or failed to result) from them.

Therefore, the research focused on those individuals and organizations that played an essential role but were very seldom consulted about the transitional justice processes: the victims and survivors of human rights abuses, the advocacy organizations, and the human rights activists. In the course of the research, we were continually moved by these groups' interest in reflecting honestly on the significance and results of the truth commission process and in using the lessons learned from this reflection to create future transitional justice policies.

Second, the study examined the degree to which international standards and the doctrine of human rights were incorporated, in terms of a theoretical framework and concepts, within the multiple aspects of the commissions and their reports. Third, the study examined how effectively recommendations, especially reparation measures, were implemented. A careful examination of these three elements sheds the clearest light on the social, political, legal, and cultural impact of the commissions and on the processes that they set in motion. Finally, it struck us that these determining elements of our analysis were leading us to a central question, posed by a woman we interviewed: "What type of society is being built, and what type of society do they want to build?"

The first step of the research was to do a comparative analysis of the commissions, especially the following elements: the specific contexts and manner in which the various transitional justice policies were defined; the scope of their respective mandates; the legal frameworks that authorized them; and issues such as legitimacy and social participation, procedures, and integrity of the recommendations. The study then focused specifically on reparation, since the commissions were responsible for recommending a series of initiatives to their respective governments to remedy the suffering inflicted on the victims and to establish the conditions necessary to keep such events from recurring. This is a key function enabling the state to demonstrate its concern about the victims and its adherence to international rules, principles, and obligations. The concept was laid out and researched in categories that are included or implied in the term "reparation": truth, justice, reconciliation, prevention, and promotion.

Next, it was important to compare the recommendations made by the respective commissions with those actually implemented by the states and to enrich this comparison by gathering the opinions of the interviewees regarding reparation policy and the implementation of the recommendations. The study included a section that analyzed the truth commissions' significance and meaning for the mental health of the individual victims and the surviving families who have experienced social trauma as a result of wars, genocide, apartheid policies, and dictatorships. This section was included to give some space to the often silenced voices of the victims, because they are the ones who best express the experiences, thoughts, emotions, and passions resulting from the establishment, implementation, and outcomes of the TRCs. Not only are their voices touching, but they also constitute, in the closest and most meaningful way, the main testimony to the real sense of satisfaction and of frustration that people feel over the policies implemented to counteract the injustices they have suffered.

The study concludes with a set of proposals for consideration by future commissions and civil society. The proposals are based on the reflections of the interviewees, with the goal of correcting some of the truth commissions' shortcomings and implementing new measures to improve their processes.

Countries Studied

The five case study countries were chosen for two reasons. First, the history of violence in Argentina, Chile, El Salvador, Guatemala, and South Africa created a strong bond of international solidarity with the victims. Thus, the creation of the commissions had important international repercussions and also led to many expectations about the effectiveness and the appropriateness of using truth commissions, both domestically and internationally. If we look beyond their particularities, the commissions in all five countries have many paradigmatic implications. The commissions in Guatemala and El Salvador were created in the context of a peace process and backed by special missions of the United Nations; the commissions in Argentina and Chile were created by decrees at the beginning of the process of democratic transition; the commission in South Africa also had a constitutional basis, but it was endowed with an open, public procedure that made it very different from the four others. By selecting these five countries, the study can address all the current forms of truth commissions to date and can lay the foundation for comparative research.

The second reason for the selective focus was that the other three Latin American countries experienced challenges similar to those in Chile, and we had established contacts with organizations and persons active in human rights and related fields in each of those countries. And yet, we could not ignore South Africa, because of the relevance that its commission had for human rights work the world over and also because of its links with the Chilean Commission. However, including South Africa was difficult because of our relative lack of established contacts there compared with the other countries. The language barrier was an additional challenge.

Steps of the Research

The first step was to establish a cooperative network with human rights organizations and friends within and across the countries studied, both to firm up contacts and to facilitate access for interviews. In South Africa and Guatemala, this cooperation was fundamental, because the human rights organizations in those countries participated in conducting the interviews.

Through consultation, interview instruments were developed and applied. Given that the study was qualitative, open-ended interviews were prepared to assess the experiences of victims, victim groups or victim families, human rights organizations, prominent human rights activists, and commissioners. Guided by the principle that a well-developed case can demonstrate the reality of an entire community, the interviewers collected background and qualitative information that would enable an understanding of the relationships and processes and provide a context for individual experiences.

Every effort was made to interview the widest possible spectrum of victims and members of human rights organizations. Inspired by Cherif Bassiouni, the UN independent expert on the right to reparation, who pointed out that "the victim must be the point of departure for the preparation of coherent guidelines on the right of reparation" (United Nations Commission on Human Rights 1999), the researchers gave priority to the experience of victims. This was a difficult task because, given the magnitude of the violence and human rights violations that took place in these countries, several of the interviewees, human rights activists, and members of human rights organizations were familiar or linked with arrested, disappeared, or executed persons or themselves had suffered serious violations.

We conducted eighty-two interviews, involving a total of 102 persons, without differentiation by gender or other considerations. Of this total, sixty had experienced some type of human rights violation. Most interviews were with individuals, but a few group interviews (in El Salvador and Guatemala) were conducted to save time and resources. In all cases, we tried to gather individual opinions in private. Except in the case of South Africa, the vast majority of the interviews were in situ, which enabled us to learn more about the real situation within each country.

Data were also obtained from other sources and then validated directly through the individuals interviewed. In this manner, it was possible to evaluate the data within the overall truth commission process. The priority was to interview the victims first and the human rights activists later, in order to compare the views of the latter with those of the people more directly affected by the commissions' work and processes.

The research guidelines had to be adapted to the specific needs of the persons interviewed. For example, respondents, particularly victims, needed adequate time and space to communicate their experiences, feelings, and thoughts fully. After listening to a respondent, the interviewer could then steer the conversation to key points that required more in-depth focus. One serious issue was the problem of false expectations raised by the presence of researchers, mainly in relatives of victims in places where the commissions had apparently achieved little results. As interviewers, we had to be constantly aware of this pressure, accept it, and do our best to clarify in some detail the purpose of our work.

After the interviews, information provided by the interviewees was collated and classified to systematize the contents and analyze points of convergence and divergence as well as details on the significance, valuation, and context of the answers. The main problem during this process was in handling the vast amount of information collected. Qualitative research is characterized by a great deal of information—expressed and collected in words, not figures—originating from several sources: observations, in-depth interviews, open-ended questions in questionnaires, research and documentation, and so on. Thus, it becomes necessary to reduce the information to manageable formats, grouping segments of similar information in categories such as "reparation," "truth," "justice," "reconciliation," "prevention," and "promotion," saving for a later stage the process of determining connections and links to the data obtained from the interviews.

A second problem was that the statements and testimony of the interviewees tended to be lengthy and did not separate easily into clear research categories, particularly when people were discussing concerns and issues that had overlapping political, legal, and moral aspects. This created difficulties in classifying and analyzing the data and also made it more difficult to get at the precise facts and figures on the commissions. This may have to do with most of the interviewees being human rights activists, who tend to be preoccupied with their ongoing activities and not with recording and updating background information. Therefore, we often had to compare the background information from the interviews with bibliographic sources.

An additional difficulty was that most of the persons interviewed framed the questions in their capacity as human rights activists; thus, they tended to place ethical considerations over political-legal ones, that is, being human rights activists, the respondents tended to be more demanding and critical of truth commissions on topics related to truth and justice. It was hard for them to put themselves in the position of government officials and see the compromises inherent in the process, and their work reflects this bias.

The final step in the methodology was to prepare a first draft of the study and make it available to some of the interviewees in each of the five countries for their comments and observations. Their comments were then incorporated into the final version. As part of an additional step in the review exercise, the draft text was sent to several other persons who had originally provided feedback to us.

Conclusions: What Did This Methodology Achieve?

This comparative case study methodology enabled an examination of how the five truth commissions created government policies and processes for reparation. It also demonstrated how the policies of restitution, compensation, and rehabilitation were related to the suffering inflicted on victims and to the guarantees that violations would not reoccur, in accordance with international law. Using this methodology allowed us to understand the multiple dimensions and complexities of the processes in which the respective commissions evolved; the study's comparative design pointed up the commissions' common and distinct traits, their positive and negative aspects, and the similarities and differences between countries. It was possible to see how truth commissions with similar intentions resolved (or failed to resolve) problems that were more or less similar despite the different national contexts. For example, each commission had to grapple with identifying those responsible for human rights violations, getting access to information, selecting which violations to investigate, and seeking justice, among other issues—although each emerged with different processes and outcomes.

In this study, the critical perceptions of the individual victims, particularly the intended beneficiaries of reparation programs, were used to gauge the impacts of the commissions. Another measure of the impact of a truth commission was the implementation (or lack of implementation) of laws related to human rights and reparation, and the public debate and discussion that these initiatives provoked. The ensuing impact assessment was conducted through bibliographic study, consultation with official sources, reading of reports, and so on. However, the direct interviews with victims and human rights organizations were instrumental in enabling a comparison of the official discourse on truth and justice with the ways that the reparation policies were actually implemented (if they were implemented at all) and with the meaning that these policies had for victims and human rights activists.

The atmosphere of general frustration permeating the interviewees' responses reflects the deep similarities in the interpretations of the commissions' significance. The processes of democratic transition, the victims' legitimate hopes of receiving reparation for the pain and suffering caused by the crimes, and the official promises produced expectations that, in every case and for every person, far exceeded the commissions' abilities. On the other hand, detailed knowledge about frustrated expectations helps us determine the key factors to consider in improving transitional justice mechanisms.

This methodology of interviewing major stakeholders resulted in a finding that although victims acknowledge positive aspects of truth commissions, there are also many unfavorable assessments of truth commissions as instruments of transitional justice policy. This finding is important because it speaks to the gap between, on one hand, the commissions' reported performance and ability to positively affect society and, on the other, the initial criteria that underpinned their establishment and their ongoing legitimation.

What are the key research issues?

This study is based on the belief that any research must determine the impact and the real importance of truth commissions in the communities that have been on the front line of serious social and political problems and rapid social change. It is important to see how research can make these issues compatible with the needs and expectations of the victims. From a human rights perspective, is it possible in practice to fulfill the rights related to reparation and the functions of the commissions as presented by international human rights standards and instruments? It is crucially important not to evaluate the commissions per se but rather as part of a process that is essentially political. Therefore, what are the key research issues in addressing such a complex subject?

In every case, the key research issues involve knowledge and analysis of general data (at the macro level), as well as concrete and specific data (at the micro level). Based on this principle, some interview questions were general (e.g., about the concrete political, social, and cultural impact of the commissions or about the implementation of the recommendations in the community), whereas others were very specific to particular situations (e.g., "Have you told your neighbors about your experience?" or "How does telling your experience to your neighbors affect your relationship with them? Does it make it easier or more difficult?").

What are the advantages and challenges of using qualitative and comparative research methodologies?

Qualitative research methodologies were used in this study because this seemed the most appropriate way both to understand the relations and processes and to show the social reality of a whole community through the use of case studies that can be well developed and researched. The major difficulty, however, lies in creating indicators for so many different aspects of research. In this study, indicators were needed to measure such aspects as the implementation of reparation rights for individual and collective victims, the restitution of the truth, the democratization of the society, the restoration of institutional activities, and the generation of new forms of citizenship. The need for such indicators becomes even more complex when researching comparative experiences that deal with widely divergent realities. We confronted this difficulty by focusing our measures on the lines of analysis that we established: level and degree of (a) participation, (b) implementation of the reparation, (c) implementation of the recommendations, and (d) incorporation of international standards. Reparation was further sorted into truth, justice, reconciliation, prevention, and promotion. Even so, during the course of the study, we had to refer to an important and extensive range of other dimensions that could not be integrated and contained within the above classification scheme.

Despite these painstaking efforts at classification, this study is only an approximation of the subject and could not clearly determine what the commissions have achieved directly. A South African woman whom we interviewed put it aptly. There is, she said, "the erroneous assumption . . . of connecting, for example, truth and justice or truth commissions and democracy. . . . Truth, national unity, and reconciliation are long processes, and there is no evidence that these processes are linked—and even less that the TRCs can achieve them."

Another issue facing the research is the need to consider different cultural and social realities, because these relate not only to how the truth commission processes were carried out but also to the expectations of the victims and to the scope of the truth commission. It is fundamentally important to respect the diversity and cultural identities of different social groups by incorporating methodological designs that include knowledge of the language, the history of the country, and the specific history of social and economic exclusion and social and political domination suffered by the people in the study. These aspects presented an important challenge for the research. Some questions and statements made by the interviewers were not clearly understood by the victims in rural areas and remote towns. In fact, when translated, the questions asked in South Africa had to be modified according to the local perspective. To avoid this obstacle, pre-research trials need to be developed beforehand, in consultation with people closely linked to the local communities, to test the viability of the research tools.

What are some of the practical and strategic challenges facing such studies? What are the most appropriate methodologies for specific

issues such as functioning, staff, the need for specialized knowledge, and access to information? How can such studies be most effectively pursued (e.g., through international partnership/coordination of several organizations, coordination of different studies, data sharing)?

Cooperation is a vitally important element. It optimizes use of the scarce resources generally available for these studies and fosters improved access to information. Given the orientation and focus of the research on discussing practical issues and on helping societies, it is important to avoid an undue focus on knowledge that is too specialized or theoretical, too far removed from reality and concrete problems and from the specific experiences of the victims and the perpetrators. For example, in cases of financial compensation or of exhumations, it is very difficult to make a categorical judgment, because these issues reflect different values held by different people and communities. There are diverse opinions about appropriate solutions across the many contexts and realities, and these must be considered in the research.

Regarding access to information, many studies on transitional justice and human rights are often not readily accessible to poor countries. The most dramatic cases were in Guatemala and El Salvador, and this is also likely the case in other contexts, such as Sierra Leone and East Timor. In these countries, human rights activists interested in reflecting on their own processes simply do not have access to research on transitional justice issues, stymied by language barriers or financial constraints, or both. Therefore, research must be made more broadly available and distributed at least within the circles of world human rights organizations. The hope here is to establish a dialogue with those who have already carried out this type of research.

It is also important to conduct studies together with local researchers from countries that have lived through these processes of transition. This seldom happens, since research resources in rich countries are usually more easily accessible. However, collaborative research within transitional countries not only would serve to better inform research by bringing those who have a keen understanding of the context into the research design but also would provide much-needed capacity building in research skills to human rights activists within the country.

What are the ethical issues that must be considered in undertaking this type of research?

The most important consideration is that, beyond the assumptions and hypotheses, a researcher faithfully reproduces the spirit of what has been said by those consulted and incorporates the differences and the diversity of problems faced by each community. In this sense, the research must be legitimated by incorporating the various social, political, and sectarian visions of society that it has encountered in the course of its work. This is very difficult to achieve, however, because of the prejudices of the sectors that perpetrated and protected the violation of human rights and that are thus unwilling to cooperate.

Above all, this kind of research must take the side of those who suffered. Researchers cannot be neutral when working with human rights and the struggle against impunity. The research carried out by the Corporation for the Promotion and Defense of People's Rights (CODEPU) has always tried to reconstruct events together with the main actors, their families, and the witnesses. The victims say, "I wanted to talk. I had so many things to say, but nobody wanted to listen. Some said, 'You suffered so much; don't talk about it anymore.' But they didn't say it to protect me. They were only protecting themselves. So I didn't talk anymore." The researcher, though, is duty bound to let them talk and to listen closely to their voices and their stories.

References

Chilean National Commission on Truth and Reconciliation. 1993. *Report of the Chilean National Commission on Truth and Reconciliation.* Trans. Phillip E. Berryman, in cooperation with the Center for Civil and Human Rights, Notre Dame Law School. London: Notre Dame Press.

Comisión Nacional sobre la Desaparición de Personas. 1984. *Nunca Más: Report of the Argentine National Commission on the Disappeared.* New York: Farrar, Straus and Giroux.

Comisión para el Esclarecimiento Histórico. 1999. "Guatemala: Memoria del Silencio." *Conclusions and Recommendations.* Vol. 5.

Espinoza Cuevas, Víctor, María Luisa Ortiz Rojas, and Paz Rojas Baeza. 2003. *Comisiones de verdad: ¿un camino incierto? Estudio comparativo de comisiones de verdad en Argentina, Chile, El Salvador, Guatemala y Sudáfrica desde las víctimas y las organizaciones de derechos humanos.* Santiago, Chile: LOM Ediciones.

United Nations Commission on Human Rights. 1999. "Report of the Independent Expert on the Right to Restitution, Compensation and Rehabilitation for Victims of Grave Violations of Human Rights and Fundamental Freedoms."

13

Critical Challenges for the Development of the Transitional Justice Research Field

Victoria Baxter

Conducting useful empirical research, particularly in a context of political transition involving complex and sensitive issues, is not an easy endeavor. The young field of transitional justice research does not provide much guidance for new or even established researchers. The relatively recent emergence of transitional justice as a separate field of study means there is a lack of established networks of expertise. For example, there is no professional association of transitional justice researchers, and only recently has there been a journal dedicated to publishing scholarly articles on the subject. And although several conferences and workshops on transitional justice have been organized by civil society organizations and universities, many of these conferences have been dominated by the same pool of mostly Western researchers. Taken together, these factors impede effective communication between researchers coming from different disciplines, geographic locations, and skill levels.

This book has tried to provide some assistance by helping clarify conceptual challenges and exploring appropriate research methodologies. But even with clearly defined concepts and perfectly suitable methodologies, other challenges to research on transitional justice remain. Previous chapters in this book have described some of these: concerns about how research is done and how it should be disseminated and used to guide policy. Here I suggest a few key challenges that need to be addressed by individual researchers and by the field as a whole as we seek to develop a more effective, coherent, and responsive body of knowledge.

Developing Baseline Data for Measuring Impact

One of the goals of research on transitional justice processes is to understand their impact on different sectors of society: former victims, perpetrators, beneficiaries, and political institutions. Doing so requires collecting baseline data so that changes can be measured over time, and that can be problematic. Transitional justice processes are mostly short term and usually involve very short lead-up periods or preparation. Political transitions are often times of considerable confusion, with an uneven influx of resources and expertise, presenting a less than ideal situation for researchers to initiate projects to collect data. In transitions, there is a palpable sense of urgency for those involved in the process and for the donors providing resources. Therefore, collecting baseline data often falls far down on a list of priorities (if it makes the list at all). This presents a challenge for researchers who have to argue the merits of funneling limited resources into collecting data throughout the process. This may not be the most glamorous aspect of a transitional justice policy, but it becomes a vitally important resource later, when questions about impact arise.

Making Timely, Policy-Relevant Research Available

In many contexts, policymakers have only a small window of opportunity to implement a transitional justice process and therefore do not have the time to conduct a nuanced examination of the whole range of transitional justice policy options. Moreover, even if they were inclined to do so, policy-relevant research to help guide their decisions is rarely available. Even if the research has been conducted, the results are usually not shared with policymakers in easily accessible, policy-oriented formats that they can digest and use. One priority, therefore, is for researchers to find creative ways to package the research findings so that policymakers can quickly understand the relevance of those findings.

Otherwise, the resulting policy choice is likely to reflect popular appeal or conventional "wisdom" rather than a deliberative or consultative policy decision. For example, the use of a truth commission is often a foregone conclusion among policymakers, even though no one has thoroughly examined the specific needs of the particular context or the various available options. Nor is there even sufficient awareness of the range of different types of truth commission mechanisms. This phenomenon is due in part to the visibility and influence of staffers involved in previous processes. Neil Kritz points out in his chapter that there is a recognized pool of people who have worked on the South African Truth and Reconciliation Commission and with the international criminal tribunals. These individuals tend to be mobile and work in other transitional justice contexts and have therefore become influential in the development of transitional justice policy in a variety of countries. Brandon Hamber points out that in the case of South Africa, much of this cross-context lesson drawing is somewhat ironic, because ten years ago, South Africa was portrayed as a unique case in terms of the complexity of local conflict dynamics, and yet it is now often cited as an international success story for truth commissions, with applications to many other contexts.

To counter the trend of wholesale adoption of truth commission mechanisms from other countries, more research is needed documenting the real impacts of the various strategies employed by these mechanisms. Empirical studies evaluating the successes and limitations of specific aspects and procedures of various commissions would add a more refined set of perspectives. It would offer policymakers data on the relative merits of specific transitional justice policy interventions, from which to make more informed policy decisions.

Of course, the existence of more research does not, by itself, translate into policy implementation. One way that research can be leveraged is to make it more readily available to civil society groups so that non-governmental organizations (NGOs) and activist communities can use research findings, including data based on their own local research, in their advocacy strategies. Collaboration between researchers and advocacy groups can be as simple as ensuring that research findings are available to local communities. Often, academic researchers publish their studies in journals and in other forums that are simply inaccessible to local communities. Victor Espinoza Cuevas and María Luisa Ortiz Rojas found that in the course of their study in five countries, language barriers or financial constraints prevented many human rights advocates and civil society groups from having access to current and past research. This means that many groups around the world are unable to use existing research findings to inform their advocacy.

There are ways for research to make its way to local advocacy communities. One immediate option would be for researchers to make their findings available directly to advocacy communities. A researcher can easily send a copy of his or her thesis or book manuscript to the local community, with an executive summary written for a nontechnical audience and translated into the local language. This guarantees that something of value is returned to the community that participated in the study; however, it does not necessarily mean that other communities will have access or will gain from this experience. Researchers can explicitly evaluate the policy implications of their research and share these insights with civil society actors for their planning of advocacy campaigns and future strategies. This latter process requires more support and effort, but it would also go much further in seeing that research is not done simply for the sake of research or to advance the careers of Western academics but can have policy results that may improve the lives of those overcoming legacies of violence and abuse.

Building on Previous Studies Rather Than Reinventing the Wheel

There is currently very little systematic or regular sharing of data and survey design among transitional justice researchers. As a result, researchers do not have access to baseline data to use in developing longitudinal studies. In many cases, researchers do not have the resources to conduct their own panel research designs and can only sample opinions at one point in time. However, if the original questionnaire and information about the sample are made available to other researchers, follow-up studies using the same questions and sampling from a similar population could measure the change in attitudes along various points in time.

Various authors in this volume also reflect on attempts to engage with complex conceptual challenges such as justice, truth, and reconciliation. Very little debate is happening among researchers on how to bring more concrete meaning to these terms, and it appears that the development of research tools is often replicated needlessly. An international data and research tool archive could facilitate more cumulative research and provide much needed insight into the changing and contrasting perceptions and opinions about transitional justice policies.

Housing research studies, reflections on the policy implications of research, and methodological tools in a coordinated research clearinghouse or archive could therefore create new types of research opportunities. This would also alleviate the problem many researchers currently have of "reinventing the wheel" with their research designs and methodologies. Archival data from several countries would also facilitate comparative studies.

Coordinating communication among researchers would have another benefit. A common theme in this book is the need for creative, multimethodological, and interdisciplinary research designs. Many of the questions being asked about the impact of transitional justice seem to fall outside the scope of conventional research strategies, forcing researchers to become more innovative in how they approach problems. Janet Cherry's chapter highlights the need for a multimethod approach for truth commissions to recover the "truth." She argues that each of the single-method approaches for determining the truth suffers from some weakness, whereas using a multilevel, multimethodological approach creates a greater likelihood of approximating the truth than does using a single method alone.

Similarly, coordinating multiple research studies would offer a richer and more insightful approach to understanding the efficacy and impacts of transitional justice mechanisms. Leigh Payne makes this point in her chapter. She employed a performative research design to understand how confessions by perpetrators affect the understanding of the past and the legacy of impunity. In the course of her research, she discovered that simple content analysis was not sufficient to understand the implications of confessions on society, because this research method was not sufficiently dynamic to be able to fully analyze the nature of a confession. Using an innovative and eclectic research approach, she was able to examine the role of confessions "beyond the script." She argues that such methodologically eclectic approaches may provide the most appropriate means for examining a variety of transitional justice issues.

Through Western Eyes?

Another challenge for research in this area is the current dominance of academics from the developed world. Their experience and access to grants have resulted in their being able to set the agenda regarding what should be studied and how the studies should be conducted. This raises the question of whether the research reflects the needs of those in the transitional society.

There is an inherent power dynamic in research. Researchers need to be reflective about whether the very research they propose to conduct may influence choices and outcomes. The very nature of framing a question as "Truth commission or no truth commission?" may inadvertently convey the sense that these are the only two options available.

A more robust version of collaboration between researchers and civil society groups would be to use a participatory research design. This would allow local community advocates a voice in the overall design and implementation of the research, thereby creating studies that are responsive to the needs of the community and that build the research capacity of local organizations. Participatory approaches engage those sectors of society most affected by human rights violations and their aftermath, as well as those with the most to gain or lose by the use of a particular transitional justice mechanism. The addition of these views into the research design process will have the effect of broadening the current discourse about transitional justice and ensuring that research is responsive to the society's needs.

Participatory research is also particularly salient in a human rights context. (See, for example, Columbia University Center for the Study of Human Rights 2002.) Participation and empowerment are fundamental components of human rights work, which, by definition, involves confronting power structures at the local, national, and international level and transforming these structures to be more responsible, democratic, and inclusive. A key principle is that the process is as important as the outcome. A research process that is inclusive, democratic, and participatory reinforces the concept of human dignity, a core concept for human rights work. Participatory research must always guard against becoming too biased in any one direction; carefully considering several points of view when designing research processes can result in a more informed and useful study.

The transition to democracy can have a profound impact on the identity and organization of human rights groups as they try to rearticulate their mandates and strategies (Shifter 2000, 327). Civil society organizations in a post-transition context often move their focus away from documenting the abuses of a repressive regime (the "name and shame" model) to assisting a new democratic government and its policies that, at least nominally, purport to uphold the promotion and protection of human rights. Research on transitional justice mechanisms that unpacks the intended impacts and evaluates the actual outcomes of policies can be helpful to civil society groups seeking to understand where their efforts would be best invested. Current lessons about transitional justice are that the formal mechanism rarely resolves all the society's truth, justice, and reconciliation issues. Research that identifies the ways in which the truth commission failed to achieve its intended goals can provide valuable information to advocacy groups seeking to pinpoint where there is need for more accountability by government institutions, for more direct services to victims, and for a more coordinated effort to push the government into fulfilling its obligations.

When research is conducted by outside individuals and organizations, research capacity is generally not built into the communities undergoing the transitional justice process. Enhanced research capacity would allow civil society groups to better monitor the mechanisms and to evaluate their impact themselves, long after other researchers have returned to their home countries or gone on to research other contexts. Collaborative research models and the systematic transfer of skills would ensure that well-designed research on transitional justice mechanisms continues at the local level.

Doing Research Justly

One constant challenge for transitional justice researchers is to consider carefully the ethical dimensions of their studies. Ethical issues abound in this field of study. Researchers often interact with survivors of human rights abuses and widespread violence. The perspective of survivors of human rights abuses is a key dimension in understanding how transitional justice mechanisms function and how they affect various sectors in society. Working with people who have survived human rights violations or systematic violence requires special consideration by the researcher. The first issue is how to conduct the research in a way that does not further traumatize the subject. Jeffrey Sonis provides an overview of some of the benefits and limitations of the traditionally understood principles of informed consent in research designs with traumatized persons. He suggests that researchers be trained in understanding the nuances of consent in a research setting and in gauging the competency of individuals to grant consent. Sonis's research also highlights a series of recent follow-up studies with traumatized individuals who were specifically asked about the impact of the study in causing further anxiety and distress. In these studies, the majority of the respondents reported that participating in the research process did not cause further trauma. While this finding does not remove the need to fully consider the risks of such studies, Sonis suggests that carefully designed studies may create a significant net benefit for participants.

Matilde González presents an interesting view of the ethical obligations of researchers. In her study of a K'iche community in Guatemala, she included the step of bringing the findings back to the research participants and the community as part of an ethically consistent way of interacting with research participants. She describes the process of slowly building trust with the members of a community to gain their participation in a local history research project. Over many months, as trust grew between the researcher and the community, individuals were more likely to come forth with information about the violence that had occurred in their community. The final element in this trust, however, is to see that something of value is given back to the community. After taking the testimonies of individuals, González typed up the transcript and presented a finished manuscript to each respondent. She describes the reactions of individual men and women who, over the course of the research, often proclaimed that they had "nothing to say" about many subjects but were stunned to see a bound copy of their long testimony. While this aspect of the research process may have little direct impact on the research itself, it was a tremendously important gesture to honor those who participated and shared many personal details and painful memories and to ensure that the research findings remained within the community.

One of the ethical challenges for researchers, especially in this area, is how to balance demands between remaining a neutral analyst and getting more involved in advocacy initiatives. Víctor Espinoza Cuevas and María Luisa Ortiz Rojas raise the issue of what should be the appropriate role of research and the researcher. They argue that researchers "cannot be neutral when we work with human rights and the struggle against impunity." In this case, the researchers conducted their study under the auspices of an NGO working on behalf of human rights victims, and the organization's mission provided some direction to the researchers about their responsibilities and roles. But the authors raise an interesting question about whether any research should necessarily take the side of the human rights community and promote human rights issues.

In some cases, the researcher's ethical stance will be shaped by the position and the institution supporting the research. Activist communities operating under a mission of promoting human rights and ending impunity will gear their research orientations and implementation to those goals. Researchers coming from a more strictly academic background may have to reach their own balance between remaining apart and becoming more active. Discussions about balancing obligations and interests would provide some ideas for fleshing out the issues among researchers and may suggest ideas and options for engaging with local communities. An international research network could provide the appropriate forum for a dialogue on this issue.

Looking Forward

The genesis of this volume was a 2002 conference co-organized by the AAAS Science and Human Rights Program and the Centre for the Study of Violence and Reconciliation. As participants in the conference reflected on the challenges of conducting empirical research on transitional justice issues, they discussed the basic ingredients of a future project. The participants wanted to find ways to improve communication among researchers, particularly across regions and in a South-to-South context, in order to facilitate future collaborative research projects and build the research capacity of individuals and research institutions within societies undergoing political transitions. The goal was to establish a network able to provide mutual support and assistance to researchers, policymakers, and activists.

At a minimum, a network of this type would be able to create a "map of the field," charting the current research on these topics. This would eliminate the need for researchers to "reinvent the wheel" when starting new research projects. Using such a resource, researchers could get a sense of what types of study have already been done and what is currently happening in the field. New research could then build on the research findings and methods of others. This would facilitate the development of more coordinated and targeted research projects.

This resource could also provide a means for disseminating specific tools and resources to help future empirical research. For example, researchers around the world would benefit greatly from a comprehensive bibliography with categories of research, a database of available data sources (e.g., transcripts and testimonies, statistical reports of violations covered in each commission report), and a database of researchers and "experts" in the particular methodologies.[1]

---

1. The TJ Research Network Web site is now available at www.transitionaljustice.org.za/.

The second role of a network would be to build research capacity on specific research skills and methods. This could be accomplished by organizing capacity-building workshops that would provide opportunities for human rights advocates and researchers to share information about specific methods and sharpen research skills. An international network dedicated to supporting research on transitional justice issues could ensure more systematic and intensive transfer of skills. Researchers could meet with experts from related fields, such as legal scholars, criminal justice experts, and conflict resolution scholars, among others, to discuss the application of various methods, theoretical frameworks, and research designs. The goal of these exchanges would be to develop methodological "best practices" by having researchers interact and reflect on their choice of method.

The workshops would also provide spaces for individuals to reflect on the roles and responsibilities of researchers and discuss ideas for conducting research studies that are ethical and empowering for participants. These discussions could serve as the basis for position papers or guidelines for research conduct that would be made widely available to other researchers who may be dealing with the same or similar sets of concerns.

We hope that this volume provides an impetus to spark debate and encourage communication among researchers in this field, and perhaps it will also contribute to the establishment of a network of transitional justice researchers. Hopefully, this is the beginning of a dialogue and exchange that will slowly grow into a more coordinated and sustained process of building capacity in the field. In turn, such an evolution of the field will produce research that can more effectively direct efforts to deal with the legacy of abuses faced in so many countries throughout the world.

References

Columbia University Center for the Study of Human Rights Program. 2002. *Capacity Building by Human Rights Organizations: Challenges and Strategies.* New York: Columbia University Center for the Study of Human Rights.

Shifter, Michael. 2000. "Weathering the Storm: NGOs Adapting to Major Political Transitions." In *Many Roads to Justice: The Law-Related Work of Ford Foundation Grantees around the World*, ed. Mary McClymont and Stephen Golub, 327–37. New York: Ford Foundation, www.fordfound.org/pdfs/impact/many_roads.pdf (accessed June 17, 2008).

Index

About the Editors

Victoria Baxter is the deputy director of Communications and Public Affairs at the United Nations Foundation. From 2000–2006, she was a Senior Program Associate at the Science and Human Rights Program of the American Association for the Advancement of Science where she directed an advocacy program on behalf of persecuted scientists and managed a series of transitional justice projects. She cowrote the USIP Special Report, "The Urge to Remember: The Role of Memorials in Social Reconstruction and Transitional Justice."

Audrey R. Chapman is the Healey Professor of Medical Humanities and Ethics in the Department of Community Medicine at the University of Connecticut Health Center. Previously, she served as the director of the Science and Human Rights Program at the American Association for the Advancement of Science (AAAS) and as the Senior Associate for Ethics for the AAAS Program of Dialogue on Science, Ethics, and Religion. She received a Ph.D. in public law and government from Columbia University and graduate degrees in theology and ethics from New York Theological Seminary and Union Theological Seminary. She has worked on a wide range of ethical and human rights issues related to human rights, transitional justice, health, and genetic developments. She is the author, coauthor, or editor of sixteen books and numerous articles and reports. Her most recent publication is *Truth and Reconciliation in South Africa: Did the TRC Deliver* (with Hugo van der Merwe).

Hugo van der Merwe is the transitional justice programme manager at the Centre for the Study of Violence and Reconciliation in Cape Town South Africa. He is co-editor in chief of the International Journal of Transitional Justice. He received a PhD in conflict analysis and resolution from George Mason University and a BSc from the University of Cape Town with majors in statistics and sociology. He has developed and managed numerous research projects evaluating the work and impact of the TRC and examining reconciliation programs in South Africa. He has also been engaged in ongoing intervention, advocacy, and capacity-building projects related to ex-combatant reintegration, restorative justice, and victims' rights. His other edited volumes include *Truth and Reconciliation in South Africa: Did the TRC Deliver?* (with Audrey Chapman) and *Conflict Resolution Theory and Practice: Towards Integration and Application* (with Dennis Sandole).

Board of Directors

J. Robinson West (Chair), Chairman, PFC Energy, Washington, D.C.

George E. Moose (Vice Chairman), Adjunct Professor of Practice, The George Washington University

Anne H. Cahn, Former Scholar in Residence, American University

Chester A. Crocker, James R. Schlesinger Professor of Strategic Studies, School of Foreign Service, Georgetown University

Ikram U. Khan, President, Quality Care Consultants, LLC

Kerry Kennedy, Human Rights Activist

Stephen D. Krasner, Graham H. Stuart Professor of International Relations, Stanford University

Kathleen Martinez, Executive Director, World Institute on Disability

Jeremy A. Rabkin, Professor, George Mason School of Law

Ron Silver, Founder and President, The Creative Coalition

Judy Van Rest, Executive Vice President, International Republican Institute

Nancy Zirkin, Executive Vice President, Leadership Conference on Civil Rights

Members ex officio

Robert M. Gates, Department of Defense

David J. Kramer, Assistant Secretary of the Bureau of Democracy, Human Rights, and Labor, Department of State

Richard H. Solomon, President, United States Institute of Peace (nonvoting)

Frances C. Wilson, Lieutenant General, U.S. Marine Corps, President, National Defense University

United States
Institute of Peace Press

Since 1991, the United States Institute of Peace Press has published over 125 books on the prevention, management, and peaceful resolution of international conflicts—among them such venerable titles as Raymond Cohen's *Negotiating Across Cultures; Herding Cats* and *Leashing the Dogs of War* by Chester A. Crocker, Fen Osler Hampson, and Pamela Aall; and William I. Zartman's *Peacemaking and International Conflict.* All our books arise from research and fieldwork sponsored by the Institute's many programs. In keeping with the best traditions of scholarly publishing, each volume undergoes both thorough internal review and blind peer review by external subject experts to ensure that the research, scholarship, and conclusions are balanced, relevant, and sound. As the Institute prepares to move to its new headquarters on the National Mall in Washington, D.C., the Press is committed to extending the reach of the Institute's work by continuing to publish significant and sustainable works for practitioners, scholars, diplomats, and students.

Valerie Norville
Director

Assessing the Impact of Transitional Justice

Text: Palatino

Display text: Optima

Cover Design: Design Literate, Inc. and Katharine Moore

Interior Design and Page Makeup: Katharine Moore

Developmental Editor: Michael Carr

Proofreader: Maine Proofreading Services

Indexer: Potomac Indexing